THUS SAYS THE LORD

THUS SAYS THE LORD

The Message of the Prophets

JAMES M. WARD

Abingdon Press
Nashville

THUS SAYS THE LORD:
THE MESSAGE OF THE PROPHETS

This book is printed on recycled acid-free paper.

Library of Congress Cataloging-in-Publication Data

Ward, James Merrill. 1928–
Thus says the Lord: the message of the Prophets/James M. Ward.
p. cm.
Includes bibliographical references.
ISBN 0-687-41902-6 (alk. paper)
1. Bible. O.T. Prophets—Criticism, interpretation, etc.
2. Bible. O.T. Prophets—Theology. I. Title.
BS1505.2.W3715 1991
224'.06—dc20 90-28590

99 00 01 02 03—10 9 8

MANUFACTURED IN THE UNITED STATES OF AMERICA

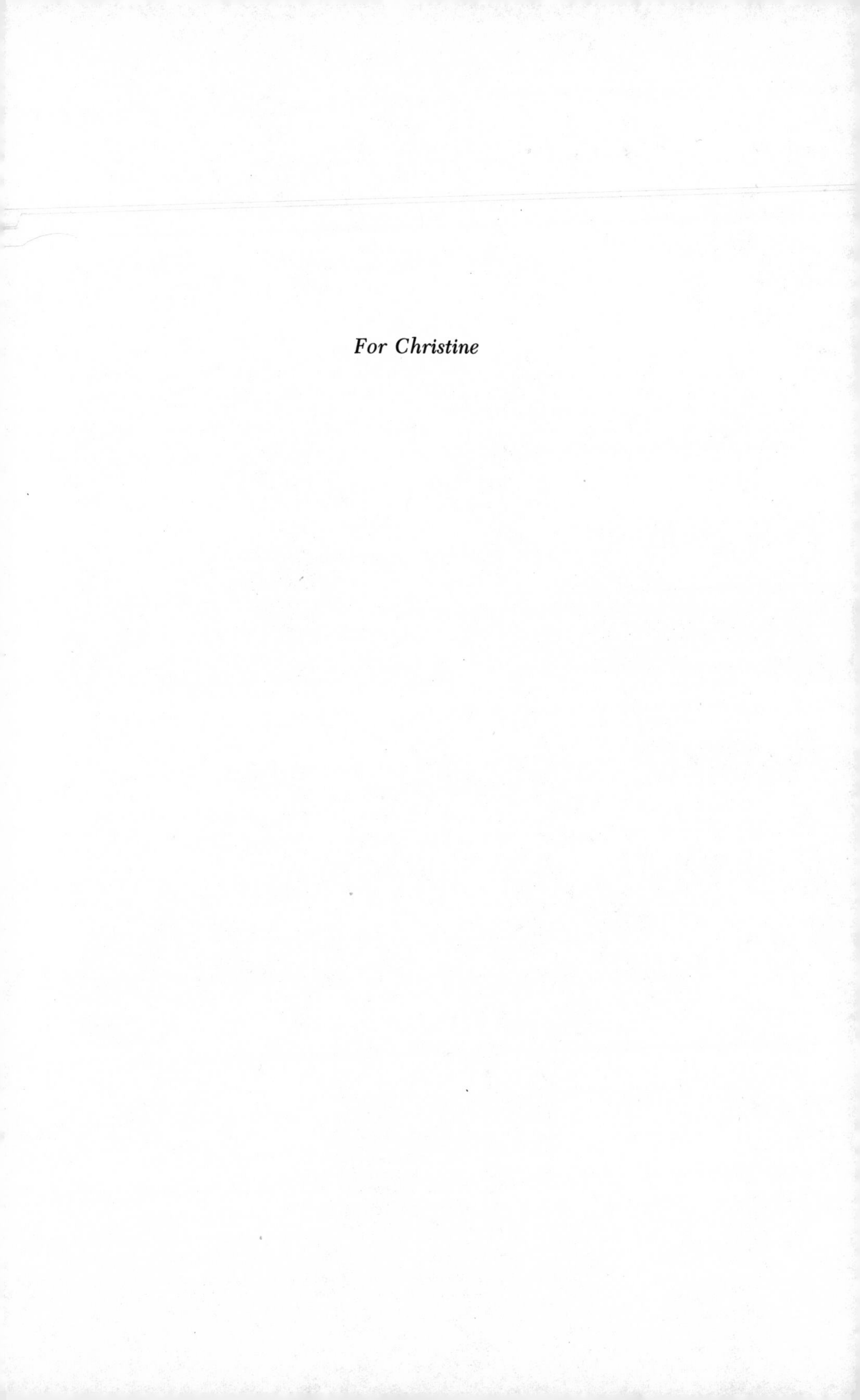

For Christine

Contents

Abbreviations

ANET	*Ancient Near Eastern Texts*, ed. James B. Pritchard. Princeton, N.J.: University Press, 1969
BDB	*Hebrew and English Lexicon of the Old Testament*, ed. Francis Brown, S. R. Driver, and C. A. Briggs. Oxford: Clarendon Press, 1952
BETL	Bibliotheca ephemeridum theologicarum lovaniensium
BJRL	*Bulletin of the John Rylands Library*
BZAW	Beihefte zur Zeitschrift für die alttestamentliche Wissenschaft
CBAT	The Complete Bible, An American Translation
CBQ	*Catholic Biblical Quarterly*
IDB(S)	*The Interpreter's Dictionary of the Bible (Supplementary Vol.)*
JB	The Jerusalem Bible
JBL	*Journal of Biblical Literature*
JMW	Author's Own Version
JPS	The Holy Scriptures. Jewish Publication Society, 1917
JSOT(Sup)	*Journal for the Study of the Old Testament* (Supplement)
KJV	King James Version
LXX	The Septuagint (Greek Bible)
MT	The Masoretic (Hebrew) Text
NAB	The New American Bible
NEB	The New English Bible

NIV	New International Version
NJB	The New Jerusalem Bible
NJV	(New Jewish Version) *Tanakh:* A New Translation of the Holy Scriptures. Jewish Publication Society, 1985
NRSV	The New Revised Standard Version
REB	The Revised English Bible
RSV	The Revised Standard Version
SBLDS	Society of Biblical Literature Dissertation Series
TDOT	*Theological Dictionary of the Old Testament*
VT	*Vetus Testamentum*
VT(Sup)	*Vetus Testamentum* (Supplement)

CHAPTER ONE

Introduction

The message of the prophets was the word of life for Israel. Grounded in faith in God, it defined the conditions of authentic existence in a world created and ordered by God. Although many of the prophets' oracles were sharply critical of Israelite belief and behavior, the purpose of their proclamation was redemptive.

> For as the rain and snow come down from heaven,
> and do not return there until they have watered the earth,
> making it bring forth and sprout,
> giving seed to the sower and bread to the eater,
> so shall my word be that goes out from my mouth;
> it shall not return to me empty,
> but it shall accomplish that which I purpose,
> and succeed in the thing for which I sent it. (Isa 55:10-11)

This affirmation from Second Isaiah defines the ultimate motive and goal of all biblical prophecy.

The message of the prophets, first and last, was a message for Israel. It originated in and for the people of YHWH.[1] Everything they did presupposed their participation in this community. They were formed by it, and they were representative of it. Thus the prophets were the voice of Israel, in dialogue with God.

This intimate connection between the prophets and the community of Israel is reflected not only in their words, but also in the development of the prophetic literature. The prophetic corpus, and many of the individual books within it, are products of a long process of transmission, expansion, and redaction. This was a communal process, for the preservation of the prophets' oracles, and their interpretation and expansion through a series of stages, were expressive of the community's faith, experience, and aspirations. Recognition of the communal dimension of the literary process has important implications for our interpretation of the prophets' mission and message.

We should look for the redactors' creative contributions to the message, contributions determined in part by their social and historical settings; we should not look simply for neutral transmission of inherited texts. With regard to the prophets' mission, we should not judge its success merely on the evidence of explicit statements in the text; we should judge it also on the evidence implicit in the preservation and redaction of the text. Thus, although at first the prophets appeared to fail in their mission, being ignored and vilified, in the end they did not fail. Not only was their witness affirmed—it was a primary factor in the continuing existence and vitality of Israel as a historic community.

The experience of Israel, reflected in the prophetic books, was historically conditioned. Although there was continuity in its life and institutions, there was also change. The principal change reflected in the prophetic corpus was the termination of the kingdoms of Israel and Judah, which led not only to the geographic displacement of part of the community, but also to its radical reshaping, politically and cultically. A definition of "Israel" during the preexilic, monarchical era was different from its definition during the exilic and postexilic eras. The changing character of the community of Israel is visible to some extent in the prophetic literature, but not entirely. Since the language used to speak to and about the community is similar throughout (except, of course, for allusions to the monarchy, which faded out), a picture of the changing constitution of the community must be drawn partly from nonprophetic sources and partly from inference. Unfortunately, however, the other extant sources are relatively few, and they give only fragmentary information about Israel's social structure and institutions. It is not until the Roman period that a substantial picture of the Jewish community emerges from those sources. Our knowledge of the community during the time of the later prophets is quite limited. We are sure it differed in many respects from the preexilic community, but we cannot describe in detail many features of its life and social structure.

This problem of defining Israel, as it is presupposed in the prophetic writings, arises partly from the paucity of the sources and partly from the nature of prophetic discourse. Much of that discourse is second-person address. In direct dialogue of this sort, the speaker does not need to identify the hearers explicitly, since their identity is understood by everyone involved. But when the speech is recorded and transmitted to others, the identity of the intended audience may become obscure. Furthermore, the audience may change during the process of redaction.

Another reason the community presupposed or addressed in the prophetic writings is sometimes difficult for us to define, is that the distinction between the real and ideal Israel is usually not made, or is made indistinctly. An example of this ambiguity can be seen in the case of the servant of YHWH in Isaiah 40–55. At times the servant appears to be the empirical Israel; at other times, a representative of Israel, or a symbol of the true, or ideal, Israel. Similar ambiguities are common. Nevertheless, despite the recurring difficulty in defining precisely the subject of the prophets' address, it is fundamental in interpreting the prophetic witness to recognize its communal setting and purpose. That prophetic witness originated in and for the community of Israel, and it was the community that preserved it. Contemporary interpretation of the prophetic message must take into account the dynamic process of interaction between the prophets and the community, as this interaction affected the various stages in the development of the prophetic writings.

The dialogue between the prophets and Israel, explicit in the words of the prophets themselves, and implicit both in the social conditioning of the prophets' thought and in the canonical process of the growth of prophetic literature, is one of the most important unifying elements in the prophetic message. This dialogue is presented as a dialogue between YHWH, the God of Israel, and Israel, the people of YHWH. Therefore, it is YHWH and Israel who are the constants in the dialogue, from book to book. However, the understanding of YHWH's relation to the people is not static, but dynamic, reflecting the changing circumstances of the people's life, and the differences in insight and conviction on the part of the writers. These differences become evident in any rigorous critical study of the prophets, and they demand consideration in interpreting their message. Nevertheless, there is substantial continuity in the prophetic understanding of YHWH's relation to Israel and the world; indeed, the continuity overall is much greater than the discontinuity from writing to writing. Through the diversity of historical situation and perspective, the underlying unity of the prophetic witness of faith in God persists, and in the end, this should be evident to the patient student of these writings. This witness of faith in God is another major unifying element in the prophetic message.

Interpretation of the message of the prophets involves consideration of both its historical setting and its canonical form. Both must be studied, whether the order of treatment of the writings is chronological or canonical. Advantanges and disadvantages exist in both alternatives. A chronological treatment makes it possible to tell a single story of the prophets in dialogue with Israel, and thus has great dramatic appeal. However, this requires numerous dislocations of the material from its canonical arrangement, as well as a fair amount of uncertainty regarding the date of some books and sections of books. Alternatively, a canonical order of treatment has the advantage of maintaining the biblical units, the books themselves, as the units of interpretation, but it has the disadvantage of requiring continual shifting of historical focus.

I have chosen a modified canonical order for this book. I will treat Isaiah, Jeremiah, Ezekiel, and the book of the Twelve Prophets in canonical order; but within this basic scheme, I will treat the major components of the books of Isaiah, Jeremiah, and the Twelve in chronological order, insofar as their order is known. In this way, we will gain some of the advantage of a linear treatment of the development of the prophetic message through time, and also be able to deal more readily, especially in the case of Isaiah, with aspects of the final redaction of the books.[2]

It is not necessary to read the book straight through in order to make sense of it. Individual chapters may be studied by themselves. However, the later chapters do presuppose the earlier ones, in the sense that some major themes of the prophetic witness are mentioned only briefly, having been discussed most fully in their earlier appearances. Given the limitations of space, this procedure seemed most economical. Accordingly, I recommend that the later chapters, especially those on the twelve prophets, be read only after the earlier chapters, at least those on Isaiah.

The first chapter will place the message in its historical and theological context. In the last chapter, after completing the exposition of the message of the individual books of the prophets, I will summarize the prophets' witness of faith in God, which is the heart of their proclamation.

The books of the prophets occupy approximately three hundred pages in a typical modern version of the Bible. Every page is significant, each one presenting numerous opportunities and problems for interpretation, and a thorough treatment of the message of the prophets would therefore need to be many times the length of this book. Since it was necessary to be highly selective, I have tried to review most of the major themes of the prophetic books, but I could not treat every relevant passage, and some minor themes have had to be omitted.

However, the purpose of this book is not to provide a comprehensive commentary on the prophetic writings, but to help students of the Bible become more deeply engaged in first-hand interpretation of the message of the prophets, and in the ongoing dialogue concerning the meaning and truth of this message for the contemporary community of faith. The present treatment of the prophetic message presupposes fairly basic knowledge of the Bible and the history of Israel. It is intended for those who wish to go beyond an introductory reading of the prophetic books, to reflect on the meaning and significance of the prophetic message in the prophets' time, and in their own.

The discussion focuses on the themes of the prophetic witness, not on the literary development of the writings. Questions of disputed authorship, such as the redaction of Isaiah 1–39, will be discussed only briefly, to indicate the judgments on which my interpretation is based. I will not attempt to marshall all the linguistic or redaction-critical evidence in support of those judgments; in most instances, they represent the majority view of critical scholars, and I frequently refer to commentaries or other standard reference works in this connection. When specific works are not cited, readers may refer to the introductions and commentaries listed in the bibliographies at the end of each chapter, where works recommended for further study are also included.

NOTES

1. See the discussion of the name of God in the next chapter.

2. The Hebrew canon contains the Former Prophets (Joshua, Judges, 1 and 2 Samuel, 1 and 2 Kings), and the Latter Prophets (Isaiah, Jeremiah, Ezekiel, and the book of the Twelve Prophets). Only the second of these two groups will be treated here.

CHAPTER TWO

The Context of the Prophetic Message

The form of the prophets' message is the word of God to Israel, and its substance is God's righteous judgment and gracious redemption. This is evident throughout the prophetic books. What is not always evident, however, are the purpose of the message and the underlying theological assumptions. Beginning to read one of the prophets is like overhearing a conversation that has been going on for some time in another room. One understands the words but is not sure what the conversation is about or who the speakers and listeners are. In order to understand the message of the prophets, it helps to place them in their historical and theological context.

THE HISTORICAL AND SOCIAL CONTEXT

The historical context of the prophetic message is the history of the people of Israel, from the last decades of the northern kingdom (ca. 750–722 BCE), through the Babylonian exile of the kingdom of Judah (598–538) and the restoration of the Jerusalem cultic community (ca. 520–500), to the reform of Ezra (ca. 400). Part of this history is covered in the books of Kings, Chronicles, Ezra, and Nehemiah, and the story told in these books provides useful background for the study of the Latter Prophets. First and Second Samuel also are useful, for although they treat an earlier period, they tell us much about the role of the prophet in Israel's history.[1]

The prophecy of Amos and Hosea is set in the northern kingdom of Israel during its final decades (ca. 750–720 BCE). Amos prophesied early in that period during the reign of Jeroboam II (ca. 785–745). The account of Jeroboam's reign in 2 Kings 14:23-29 is brief, telling only that he recovered certain lost territories for Israel. Biblical historians infer from this that Jeroboam's reign was one of political stability and strength. In the absence of evidence to the contrary, this is an acceptable, though tentative, conclusion. In any event, nothing in the book of Amos suggests otherwise. Hosea prophesied later, in a time of political disruption and, for Israel, of political dissolution. He seems to have witnessed the Syro-Israelite invasion of Judah and its aftermath (735–732, cf. Hos 5:8-15) and perhaps the last chaotic decade of the kingdom (732–722), which ended with its absorption into the Assyrian Empire.

Micah and Isaiah were contemporaries; they both prophesied in the kingdom of Judah in the last third of the eighth century. Their oracles are found in Micah 1–3 and portions of Isaiah 1–39 (First Isaiah). Isaiah 7–8, the most specific commentary on political events in Isaiah's oracles, treats the Syro-Israelite invasion of Judah from Judah's side. There is also commentary on events in the period 711–701 (see 20:1-6; 22:1-14), though the fullest treatment of the climactic event of that period, the Assyrian siege of Jerusalem in 701, is in a later, non-Isaianic section of the book (36–39). Although both Isaiah and Micah prophesied the fall of the Judean kingdom, this event did not occur during their lifetime. Judah was dominated by Assyria as a vassal state for nearly a century and was finally absorbed into a larger empire, the Neo-Babylonian. The final decades of the Judean kingdom were the setting of the oracles of Jeremiah, Zephaniah, and Habakkuk, as well as some revisions of the books of Micah, Isaiah, and Hosea. Roughly contemporary with these other writings was the book of Nahum, which celebrates the fall of the city of Nineveh (612 BCE) and the end of Assyrian domination, an important factor in preexilic prophecy.

The story of Israel told in the books of Kings ends with the destruction of the kingdom of Judah (587) and its immediate aftermath (except for the brief postscript in 2 Kings 25:27-30). There is no comparable biblical story of Israel in subsequent centuries. Therefore, our knowledge of the historical situation of the later prophetic writings is more fragmentary than that of the earlier ones. The Babylonian exile (587–538 BCE) was the general setting of the prose portions of the books of Jeremiah and Ezekiel, and of Isaiah 40–55. The various phases of the Judean restoration (from 520 until 400 or later) formed the setting of Isaiah 56–66 (and portions of 1–39), Joel, Obadiah, Jonah, Haggai, Zechariah, and Malachi.

It is not possible to date all the prophetic writings precisely, since few contain clear historical allusions, and many have undergone expansion and redaction. However, this outline of the chronology of the writings can serve as an approximate indication of their historical context. This question will be discussed further in connection with particular writings.

THE SOCIAL ROLE OF THE PROPHETS

In addition to the question of the general historical setting of the prophetic writings, the question of the institutional or social setting of prophetic proclamation in Israel is important for an understanding of the purpose and significance of prophecy. In the past, this question was usually framed to ask whether the prophets were cultic officials, but in recent years it has been broadened to include other possible dimensions of the "social location" of prophecy.[2] The answer of the majority of scholars to the question about whether the works of the Latter Prophets were written in connection with a cultic office is a clear no. These writings exhibit intimate knowledge of ritual worship in Israel, and therefore surely reflect the experience of participation in those rituals; however, most lack any definite indication that the writers themselves functioned as leaders in the cult.

Yet, we must admit that the Bible tells us relatively little about the verbal content of Israelite ritual, and therefore relatively little about what leadership in worship involved. The Torah prescribes many rituals and the offerings to be made in them; it is all but silent about what was, or was supposed to be, said in these rituals, including those that took place during the great, week-long pilgrimage festivals. We have some idea from the book of Psalms, but what we learn there is too limited to answer the question concerning the possible cultic background of most of the prophetic writings.[3] The doxologies in the book of Amos (4:13; 5:8-9; 9:5-6) and the complaints in the book of Jeremiah (11:18–12:6; 15:10-21; 17:14-18; 18:18-23; 20:7-18) are among the texts in the Latter Prophets that show formal affinity with known ritual texts. This affinity implies knowledge of the ritual tradition on the part of the writers, but not necessarily that they held a leadership role in worship. I will discuss these texts later, in the appropriate places, as well as other texts for which the question is relevant.

With regard to the possibility that any of the writers of the Latter Prophets held a noncultic prophetic "office," there is too little evidence on which to base a judgment. There is no compelling evidence, for example, that any of them functioned as Nathan did in the court of David and Solomon, or as the four hundred prophets did in the court of Ahab. Yet at least Isaiah and Jeremiah were clearly recognized as prophets whose prophesying was not merely a once-for-all occurrence, but an activity repeated over a considerable period of time. I consider this to be sufficient evidence of a prophetic "office," in the general sociological sense of an institutionalized social role, even though it was not professional in the sense that the prophets derived their livelihood from it.

Whether the prophets' role was central or peripheral in Israelite society is one of the questions being discussed by scholars today.[4] By "central," I mean that a prophet belonged to the dominant segment of society and therefore had a voice in public affairs; "peripheral" means he was outside that segment. On the assumption that prophets ordinarily share the viewpoint of the groups they belong to, scholars tend to infer that central prophets in Israel performed acts of "social maintenance" for the dominant segment of society; peripheral prophets, who represented outsiders, were critical of the status quo. The questions involved in this analysis are difficult to answer, because of the paucity of relevant information. The Bible says nothing at all about the social role and status of many of the prophets with whom we are concerned. The exceptions are Amos, Isaiah, and Ezekiel, about whom there are bits of information, and Jeremiah, about whom there is quite a lot. I will comment on them only briefly here, since I will deal with the question of their places in Israelite society in the individual chapters.

Amos was an outsider to the royal establishment of the northern kingdom of Israel, where he prophesied, apparently briefly (Amos 7:10-17). His place as prophet, if any, in the society of Judah is unknown. Isaiah appears as consultant to King Hezekiah in the story told in Isaiah 36–39, but this is an imaginative construction from a later time. Whether he actually enjoyed the confidence of kings is doubtful, when one considers that it was necessary for him to accost Ahaz in a public place in order to speak his mind on the Syro-Israelite invasion (Isa 7:3). Jeremiah, until he became a political traitor in their eyes for counseling capitulation to the Babylonians, was supported by certain members of the ruling class, notably the family of Shaphan, King Josiah's secretary of state (e.g., Jer chapters 26, 36, 38). Then he was treated like an outsider by the royal and cultic officials, threatened with death, and pilloried. Ezekiel was consulted by certain elders of the people—not members of the established Israelite society, but a group of exiles in Babylon (Ezek 14:1-5; 20:l-4).

Thus we have a fragmentary picture of prophets who addressed the dominant segment of society but did not have a regular voice in the determination of its affairs. They were not so peripheral that the dominant group took no notice of them, but they were not so central that they were regarded as members of the group. In the end, the most important thing about them was that a substantial number of their oracles was preserved, to provide the nucleus of a great prophetic literary corpus. In my judgment, these oracles were not preserved primarily because they provided "social maintenance" for this or that segment of Israelite society, though on a certain level they did, but because those who preserved them believed the witness of faith in God that they contained was true—not inerrant, especially with regard to their interpretation of particular events—but true in its fundamental understanding of the nature and purpose of God.

THE PURPOSE OF PROPHECY

What was the purpose of prophecy? This is a complex question, and it must be answered for each of the prophetic writings individually. That task is difficult because the purpose is often unstated, and made more difficult by the fact that many of the writings have undergone redaction, with different but similarly unstated intentions. In our culture, the closest literary parallel to a prophetic proclamation is the sermon delivered in church or synagogue, so one is tempted to infer similar purposes for the prophetic proclamation. There may have been some similarities, but the social setting was different, and so was the office of the speaker. The modern pastor is preacher and priest, as well as prophet, but the ancient prophet was neither priest nor pastor.

The purposes of the prophets varied, depending upon the circumstances and particular interests and disposition of the prophet. The preexilic prophets criticized both the leaders and the people of Israel for cultic idolatry, social injustice, and other abuses, both personal and institutional. And in prophesying the ruin of the kingdoms of Israel and Judah as a punishment from God, they appealed, directly and indirectly, to traditional norms of understanding and behavior. At times, they seem to have hoped that their words would stir their audience to repentance and reformation. Yet overall, their oracles express no such hope, but rather the certainty of national ruin, inward and outward. This message has been transmitted by the collectors and editors of these oracles, and it seems likely that they selected for transmission to later generations those oracles which correctly prophesied the fall of the two kingdoms, omitting those that failed to do so, however edifying they may have seemed in other respects. Thus the Bible probably does not contain a fully representative sample of preexilic oracles.

What, then, was the purpose of the transmitters? They must have wanted to say more to the remnant of the fallen kingdoms than, "They told you so!" though there may have been a measure of that. Beyond this, their primary motives seem to have been redemptive and constructive, since all the preexilic collections of doom oracles have been supplemented by words of promise. The collections were meant for exilic and postexilic generations of Jews: to help them understand the ruin of the kingdoms in theological terms, and thus to accept it; to guide and support their faith in God in their own lives. In their canonical form, the prophetic books are pedagogical and doxological. They teach the ways of God with Israel and the peoples, and they testify to God's greatness and goodness and sovereign righteousness. Sometimes they deal with specific social issues—the return of the exiles from Babylon to Judea (Isa 40–55), or the rebuilding of the temple of Jerusalem (Haggai), or the admission of certain persons to the temple (Isa 56:3-8). More often, however, they deal with perennial issues of faith. This is exactly what we would expect of books produced over a long period of time, by and for a religious community that continued over many generations. Some prophetic words specific to a single situation have been kept, but by and large, those that have been preserved are those that address recurring human failures, needs, and aspirations.

PROPHETS AND KINGS

Close associations existed between prophets and kings in Israel, and biblical accounts of the kings provide information about the prophets. The prophet Nathan was an influential member of the court of King David, and from that time on, prophets figured regularly in royal affairs: as advisors—Ahab's four hundred prophets (1 Kings 22:6); as king makers—Elisha, of Jehu (2 Kings 9:1-13); as critics—Micaiah, of Ahab (1 Kings 22:8-28). It is as critics of kings that the prophets are best known, through the stories in Samuel and Kings, and also through the prophetic writings themselves, from Amos in the eighth century (e.g., Amos 7:9, 11) to Jeremiah in the sixth (e.g., Jer 22).

The institution of prophecy is sometimes thought to have been a reflex of the monarchy, emerging and disappearing simultaneously.[5] The association, however, though close, was not that close. Prophecy continued to flourish after the exile, quite independent of the monarchy and with no real expectation of its restoration. In Haggai (2:20-23) and Zechariah (3:8) there are hints at the possibility of a royal role for Zerubbabel in postexilic Judea, but other than that, the exilic and postexilic prophetic literature largely ignores the question of an Israelite monarchy. The writers assumed or endorsed other forms of political order in Israel's world—in particular, rule by the kings of Persia. The association between the prophets and the kings of Israel did not come about because prophecy was a royal institution, but because the prophetic vocation consisted primarily of addressing the leadership of the people of Israel, and for four hundred years, that leadership happened to be royal.

Addressing the kings of Israel usually meant confronting them, for in the eyes of the prophets, the purposes of the kings and their minions were generally inimical to the integrity of the people and contrary to the will of God. As a result, much of the preexilic prophetic literature is sharply critical, negative, and judgmental. Criticism exists in the later prophetic writings as well, but it is more clearly part of a constructive message than it is in the preexilic writings. All the explicitly constructive words in Amos and Micah, for example, are redactional.

The basis of the prophets' criticism of the kings and the other leaders of Israel was a set of convictions concerning the nature of true community and the proper service of God. In other words, their presuppositions were ethical and theological. At times, it may appear that they were merely political reactionaries, branding what they did not like as idolatrous and apostate. Thus for example, Amos and Micah have sometimes been interpreted as peasant antiurbanite antiroyalists. Such a construction is always possible when social criticism is part of a religious message; whether the interpreter construes the criticism as ethically valid or merely political depends upon the viewpoint of the interpreter. Reading the prophets is a partly subjective endeavor. My own view of the prophets' social criticism is that it was based on ethical principles and deeply religious in its source and goal. It was not primarily political but theological, rooted in faith in God's righteousness and motivated by commitment to the service of God.

Interpreters of the prophets today generally treat them as presupposing the teaching of the Torah and defending the covenantal faith and institutions described there. This approach is acceptable in principle, though it must be qualified. There is considerable congruence between the theological viewpoint of the prophets and that of the narrative strands of the Torah. There is also congruence with the Decalogue, and to a some extent with the book of Deuteronomy. However, tension exists between the message of some prophets and certain basic assumptions of the priestly legislation, and even Deuteronomy. So the Torah can serve as an index of the traditions presupposed and affirmed by the prophets, but not simply in its canonical form. The Torah in this form is a postexilic work, and the majority of the prophetic writings do not presuppose it in this form. Therefore it must be used critically as a basis for interpreting the prophets' message. It is safe to say that the basic understanding of God and Israel exhibited in the narrative traditions of the Torah, and even the story itself, in its general configuration, is presupposed by the prophetic writers. However, it is not methodologically sound to assume that the prophets were acquainted with all the major parts of this story, as we know them from the completed Bible. Which specific traditions were known and assumed by the prophets as the basis of their proclamations is a question that must be answered for each individually, through a careful analysis of their words.

THE THEOLOGICAL CONTEXT

The prophets addressed a community of believers, and they took for granted that their audience shared their basic understanding of God and the religious traditions of Israel. This understanding was not problematic for the prophets, at least not until the Judean exile called into question the relation between God and Israel, and therefore Israel's understanding of God. What was problematic was Israel's behavior in the light of this understanding. The pages of the prophetic books are filled with penetrating assessments of Israel's behavior and passionate appeals for reform. Some of the prophets' basic convictions are simply presupposed, yet the cogency and effectiveness of their message depended upon the truth of those convictions. It was those that gave validity and urgency to their message and provided the theological context for their proclamation.

The foundation of the prophetic witness was belief in one God and in the unity of all created things in the power and purpose of God. This dual conviction, reflected in the Hebrew Bible generally, was distinctive in the ancient world, and it produced a distinctive vision of a righteous humanity. Among the Latter Prophets it is articulated most fully in Second Isaiah (40–55), but it is presupposed in the oracles of Amos and the other preexilic prophets.

The date of the emergence of Israelite monotheism and the contribution of the prophets to this development have been much discussed. During the first half of the twentieth century, critical scholars generally credited the eighth-century prophets with the creative insight that produced monotheism and regarded the Pentateuch as having been dependent upon the prophets. Since that time the scholarly consensus has changed: The formative traditions incorporated in the

Pentateuch are now generally thought to be earlier than the prophets, and the prophets are viewed as dependent upon these and other traditions for their basic theological understanding. This judgment provides a satisfactory premise for the present study, since we are not concerned with the prior history of the ideas contained in the prophetic books, but with the message of the books themselves. The main thing to acknowledge here is that the idea of the oneness of God governs the message of the Latter Prophets in their extant form.

In the face of the multiplicity of forces and occurrences in the inner and outer environment of human beings, the prophetic writers, among others, acknowledged one God as the source and end of all things. This faith was in stark contrast to the otherwise universal polytheism of the ancient world. Furthermore, much of the anthropomorphism in the common characterization of the gods was rejected in the prophetic witness. The gods were born, mated, fought, and died, and were subject to moral and intellectual weaknesses similar to those of human beings. None of this was true of the one God, according to the prophetic witness, and yet God was intimately related to the creation. The creatures were known by God and sustained by God day by day. Human beings, in turn, could know God sufficiently to trust God's creative purpose and to shape their lives in accordance with God's will. All things depended upon God, and God was wholly trustworthy, righteous, and compassionate.

There is no metaphysical dualism in the thought of the prophets. All things are viewed as dependent upon God for their existence, and nothing is viewed as inherently evil. Evil, in prophetic thought, is the result of human sin committed in freedom. The superior mental capacity of human beings, in comparison to that of other creatures, obviously was recognized by the prophetic writers, but they did not place a higher value on the mental aspects of human experience than on its physical aspects. The dualism of mind and matter, with its negative valuation of matter, entered Christian thought from Neoplatonism and other sources, and is foreign to the witness of the prophets and the Hebrew Bible generally. In biblical thought, the tangible aspects of creation, including the human body, are as good and as God given as the intangible. Even our rather sharp distinction between "nature" and "history" is uncharacteristic of biblical thought. Natural events and relationships are as much a part of life as are the historical, or social, events, and the two are perceived in the Bible as inseparable. Furthermore, that which is distinctively human in creation is not held up as intrinsically better than the nonhuman.

This sense of the ultimate unity of human and nonhuman creation sometimes led the prophetic writers to infer too great a proximate unity. Specifically, they interpreted some purely physical events, such as droughts and plagues of locusts, as divine punishment for human sin. This notion, expressed as a rigid doctrine in the speeches of Job's friends (though repudiated by the poet of the book of Job), appears sometimes in the prophetic books, though in less rigid form. While it is wrong with regard to the causal relation between human virtue and the processes of nature, and with regard to the relation between divine grace and justice, it is based upon recognition of the ultimate unity of all created things in God.

The prophets viewed everything in relation to God. What was "religious" or "spiritual" was not some particular aspect of life, but life itself. All human beings are dependent upon God for existence, and all of life is completely God-related. Of course, special times, places, persons, and resources can be designated for the ritual worship of God, but none of these is thereby more "godly" in its connections than are other times, places, persons, and resources. In the prophetic view, the failure to understand this unity of life and its total relatedness to God was a source of all sorts of ungodliness in Israel.

THE NAME OF GOD

The prophets usually call God *Yahweh*. This name occurs nearly three times as often in the Hebrew Bible generally as the term *'elohim* (in English, "God"), and in the Latter Prophets the ratio is even higher, rising to twelve-to-one in Ezekiel. *Yahweh* is a distinctive Israelite name, in contrast to *'elohim*, which is a common Hebrew word with cognates in the other Semitic languages. The origin of the name *Yahweh* is unknown. It might have been tribal or local, although in the Bible it does not have this significance. There it is synonymous with *'elohim*, and both designate the one true God. The writer of Genesis 4:26 declared Enosh, son of Seth and grandson of Adam, the first to use the name. This tradition is commonly assigned to the Yahwist or "J" stratum of the Pentateuch, in which the name *Yahweh* is used throughout the story of humankind. Theologically, this is an important tradition, for it makes explicit the conviction that the one worshiped in Israel as Yahweh is none other than the God with whom all people are ultimately involved.

Another tradition incorporated in the Pentateuch associates the initial use of the name *Yahweh* with the Sinaitic revelation and the exodus deliverance (Exod 3:1-15, Elohistic stratum; 6:2-9, Priestly stratum). However, the writers in both these accounts are careful to make clear that the one named with this new name is not a new God. The new name simply marks a new understanding of God on Israel's part, and a corresponding new understanding of themselves as the people of God. From this point in the biblical story, the name *Yahweh* is the characteristic designation of God. Whatever the early history of the name, in the biblical witness itself, it is inextricably linked to the story of salvation.

In Jewish practice, the name *Yahweh* is not to be spoken. This avoidance is reflected in the medieval Masoretic Text of the Hebrew Bible, where the consonantal name *yhwh* is not vocalized so that it can be pronounced, but the vowels of the title *'adonay*, "Lord", which is to be pronounced instead, are substituted. Avoidance of the spoken name is understandable as an expression of reverence for the holy God, though the biblical writers clearly show deep reverence, even while employing the proper name *Yahweh*. Its frequent use by no means diminishes the biblical reverence, but conveys a keen sense of relatedness to God and of participation in the process of salvation, which is linked closely with this name. In the remainder of this book, I will use the consonantal form of the name when referring to YHWH, except in quotations from those English Bibles which substitute the name *Lord*.[6]

THE LIVING GOD

To the prophets, YHWH was not merely an idea or the remote source of the created world, but the living God, a sustaining, judging, saving presence. They were deeply aware of the nearness of God and of God's personal claim upon them. The experience of intimate encounter with God was the foundation of their mission and the presupposition of their message. When they spoke about God, they meant a living, personal God who could be known and trusted, and to whom the appropriate response was total personal commitment. This personal relationship with the living God was the basic datum of prophetic experience as well as the basis of their proclamation.

Prophetic thought about God, like that of the Bible generally, is thoroughly anthropomorphic, in the sense that God is imagined as a living person. In prophetic discourse, God comes and goes, feels various emotions, thinks, wills, speaks, and even experiences changes of mind. The range of metaphors and similes used in speaking about God is wide. Sometimes these are merely figures of speech. However, the basic metaphor in prophetic thought about God is no mere figure of speech. God is clearly understood as a living person, dynamically related to the life of the world. This is the fundamental premise of all prophetic statements about God.

There was no neuter gender in the ancient Hebrew language, and ordinarily the masculine gender was used in language about God in the Hebrew Bible. Furthermore, many more masculine metaphors than feminine were used. Nevertheless, God is not male in the biblical witness, but transcends sexuality. This does not mean that God never was imagined as male in Israel, for the people's religious ideas often were incongruent with prophetic standards. In the biblical witness itself, however—that is, the witness actually expressed in the biblical writings—God has no sexuality. Thus the anthropomorphism of the Bible is severely limited. It is better to call it anthropopathism, for none of the physical characteristics of human beings is predicated of God. In biblical thought, YHWH is not merely a divine male.

The prophetic witness presupposes that God is vitally engaged with the world. Human life is lived entirely in relationship with God. No aspect of life falls outside the scope of this relationship, which endures as long as life itself. In other words, the relationship is both comprehensive and enduring. It does not preclude free human action; on the contrary, it demands it, for without such action, individual and corporate human life would end quickly. Human beings are not puppets, but are constituted as free, responsible creatures, with great scope for both creative and destructive action. However, they are dependent upon God for the very conditions of their existence, as are all other creatures. Moreover, the relationship of people to God is intimate, in the sense that it involves the interior aspects of life—of mind and heart—as well as the external. All in all, then, it is comprehensive, intimate, dependent, free, and enduring.

The single metaphor that best conveys all the essential characteristics of the divine/human relationship—intimacy, comprehensiveness, freedom, dependency, duration—is the metaphor of the parent. It is used a number of times by the prophets, most notably in Hosea 11, but probably was not used more often because it was employed, and abused, in idolatrous popular cults. The metaphor is that of father in Malachi (1:6; 2:10), but is both mother and father in Isaiah 45:10. Hosea used the marriage metaphor as the basis of his message in chapters 1–3, and this, as it was understood in Israel, where wives were fully dependent upon their husbands, came close to the parental metaphor in its completeness as a theological metaphor, although it is widely regarded as unacceptable today because of its sexist connotations. Many other metaphors are used to suggest more limited aspects of God's relation to people, and of acts of God within this relationship, although no other but the parental is so comprehensive a symbol of the relationship. It seems quite natural, therefore, that the parental metaphor would eventually emerge in biblical usage—that is, in the New Testament—as the central theological metaphor.

GOD AND ISRAEL

The universal divine/human relationship was not the explicit focus of the prophets' message, even though it was the logical presupposition of their thought. The focus of their message was the relationship between God and Israel. I have mentioned the tradition concerning the revelation of Israel's—and the prophets'—name for God, but I have not yet identified Israel. The prophets continually refer to Israel as the subject of their message, though they sometimes refer to particular segments or members of the Israelite community, and often they address their audience without specifying who it is.

Israel was a changing people politically, but it was always a religious community: the people of YHWH. The biblical story, from Genesis to Ezra, first depicts Israel as a man (Jacob/Israel); then, in succession, as a family, twelve tribes descended from that family, a mixed multitude of slaves, a group of fugitives camping in the wilderness, a conquering horde of immigrants, a settled population of farmer/herders, a monarchy, a divided kingdom, the dispersed remnants of the kingdom; and finally, as a religious community centered in Jerusalem. Through these changes, accompanied by changes in government, cultic organization, and population, a religious tradition developed and eventually became the primary basis of continuity for the community. Whatever other factors had determined the identity of Israel in its earlier phases—kinship, language, propinquity, or conquest—in the end, it was the religious tradition that determined it. If earlier generations had created this tradition as a theological interpretation of their experience, later generations defined themselves by it. Israel was re-created in each generation by its faith in YHWH, and by its fidelity to the way of life implicit in that faith. This was the core of what it meant to be Israel.

By the time of the postexilic restoration, Israel's way of life had been defined by observance of the ritual practices prescribed in the priestly laws of the Torah, notably the sabbath rest, circumcision, dietary regulations, and annual festivals, in addition to faith in one God and commitment to the ethical principles taught in the Torah and Prophets. These ritual observances, coupled with the dominant (though not universal) custom of endogamous marriage, made the Jewish people easily recognizable among the peoples of the Greco-Roman world. Prior to the exile, the Israel of God—not only the apostate, those who "mixed [themselves] with the peoples" (Hos 7:8) cultically, but also the faithful—was less easily distinguishable. Yahwistic rituals were not so different from the non-Yahwistic, except that they employed no images of God. Most characteristic of Israel, the people of YHWH, was its faith. Israel's understanding of the nature of God, and the understanding of the world that accompanied it, determined its identity. This understanding was at once a disposition of mind and heart, a sense of the meaning of human existence, a way of perceiving other human beings, and a way of life. It was the sharing of this faith in God, and obedience to the moral demands implicit in it, that characterized the true and enduring Israel.

THE WORD OF GOD

The majority of the prophetic utterances are presented as the word of YHWH. This prodigious claim to speak for YHWH is not defended by theological argument; it is simply asserted. On what grounds did the prophets make it, and on what grounds was it believed?

The primary ground of this claim to speak for YHWH was the clear inner conviction of being called by YHWH to do so. Sometimes the development of this conviction was accompanied by an intense emotional experience with visual or auditory components. The description of Ezekiel's call is the longest and most sensory of the prophetic calls recorded in the Hebrew Bible (Ezek 1:1–2:7). Ezekiel's vision engaged his senses of sight, hearing, and taste. Isaiah's experience was also visual (Isa 6), while Jeremiah's was primarily auditory (Jer 1). Amos (7:14-15) and Hosea (1:2) alluded to their calls, but did not describe any accompanying psychic experience. The call of Moses, which may have functioned in the literary tradition as a paradigmatic model of the prophetic call, was auditory, except for the single, striking visual element of flames in the middle of a bush (Exod 3:1-6). Most important in this prophetic tradition is not the sensory component of the experience, but the intense and persistent conviction of being called by God to speak on God's behalf.

A prophet's personal certainty of a call was not sufficient grounds for the community's acceptance of a prophet's word as the word of God. There were norms by which to test a prophet's claim, and the deuteronomic tradition offers two such tests. The first is theological:

> If prophets or those who divine by dreams appear among you and promise you omens or portents, and the omens or the portents declared by them take place, and they say, "Let us follow other gods" (whom you have not known) "and let us serve them," you must not heed the words of those prophets or those who divine by dreams; for the LORD your God is testing you, to know whether you indeed love the LORD your God with all your heart and soul. The LORD your God you shall follow, him alone you shall fear, his commandments you shall keep, his voice you shall obey, him you shall serve, and to him you shall hold fast. (Deut 13:1-4)

The second deuteronomic test is empirical:

> I will raise up for them a prophet like [Moses] from among their own people; and I will put my words in the mouth of the prophet, who shall speak to them everything that I command. . . . But any prophet who speaks in the name of other gods, or who presumes to speak in my name a word that I have not commanded the prophet to speak—that prophet shall die. You may say to yourself, "How can we recognize a word that the LORD has not spoken?" If a prophet speaks in the name of the LORD but the thing does not take place or prove true, it is a word that the LORD has not spoken. The prophet has spoken it presumptuously; do not be frightened by it. (Deut 18:18-22)

This passage reiterates the test of orthodoxy stated in the first passage, and goes on to state the test of empirical verification. Prophecies claiming to be the word of YHWH must pass both tests; one alone was not enough.

This deuteronomic understanding of authentic prophecy is presupposed by the writers of the books of Kings, which are part of the Deuteronomic History. One of the major themes of the books of Kings is prophecy and fulfillment. On numerous occasions, according to the narrative, YHWH declared through a prophet what was to happen in Israel's history, and these prophecies were always fulfilled, though sometimes only after a long period of time.[7] The authors are making a double point here. On the one hand, "The Lord GOD does nothing without revealing his secret to his servants the prophets" (Amos 3:7). Therefore, one may infer, Israel should not be surprised when acts of God occur. On the other hand, the secrets of God revealed by the prophets are true, in that the events prophesied actually come to pass. Consequently, Israel should take heed of oracles proclaimed by YHWH's prophets.

This is a rather mechanical view of prophecy and fulfillment: The occurrence of a specific historical event is predicted, and it eventually comes to pass. The purpose of prophecy suggested here is a far cry from the purposes suggested by the books of the prophets. Nevertheless, we can see a similar understanding at work in the transmission of these writings, for almost all the prophecies that have been preserved reflect, in one way or another, the actual course of Israel's history.

Fortunately for the communities that have used the prophetic books as part of their canon of sacred scripture, fulfillment of historical predictions was not the only criterion operative in the preservation of these writings. If this were their only merit, they would not be a particularly edifying witness of faith in God. It is chiefly their other qualities that have commended them to the faithful. As even the writer of Deuteronomy 13:1-5 made clear, the mere fulfillment of a prophetic sign is religiously meaningless. Prophetic signs and oracles are meaningful because of their witness to God and God's commandments. Israel eventually believed the canonical prophets, because what the prophets said rang true, in relation to Yahwistic tradition and in relation to the continuing experience of the Yahwistic community. Tradition and experience combined to create the norm of religious truth—just as they do in the religious community today.

SELECT BIBLIOGRAPHY

Childs, Brevard S. *Introduction to the Old Testament as Scripture*. Philadelphia: Fortress Press, 1979.

Eissfeldt, Otto. *The Old Testament: An Introduction*. New York: Harper & Row, 1965.

Gottwald, Norman K. *The Hebrew Bible: A Socio-Literary Introduction*. Philadelphia: Fortress Press, 1985.

Soggin, J. Alberto. *Introduction to the Old Testament*. Philadelphia: Westminster Press, 1976.

A. The Historical Context

Ackroyd, Peter R. *Exile and Restoration*. Philadelphia: Westminster Press, 1968.

Blenkinsopp, Joseph. *A History of Prophecy in Israel*. Philadelphia: Westminster Press, 1983.

Bright, John. *A History of Israel*. 3rd Ed. Philadelphia: Westminster Press, 1981.

Clements, R. E. *Prophecy and Covenant*. Studies in Biblical Theology 43. London: SCM, 1965.

______. *Prophecy and Tradition*. Oxford/Atlanta: Basil Blackwell/John Knox Press, 1975.

Culley, Robert C., and Thomas W. Overholt, eds. *Anthropological Perspectives on Old Testament Prophecy*. Semeia 21. Chico, Calif.: Scholars Press, 1982.

Gottwald, Norman K. *All the Kingdoms of the Earth: Israelite Prophecy and International Relations in the Ancient Near East*. New York: Harper & Row, 1964.

Hayes, John H., and J. Maxwell Miller. *A History of Ancient Israel and Judah*. Philadelphia: Westminster Press, 1986.

Johnson, Aubrey R. *The Cultic Prophet in Ancient Israel.* Cardiff: University of Wales, 1962.

Koch, Klaus. *The Prophets.* 2 Vols. Philadelphia: Fortress Press, 1983, 1984.

Lindblom, Johannes. *Prophecy in Ancient Israel.* Oxford: Basil Blackwell, 1962.

Muilenburg, James. "The 'Office' of the Prophet in Ancient Israel." *The Bible and Modern Scholarship.* Ed. J. Philip Hyatt. Nashville: Abingdon Press, 1965.

Overholt, Thomas W. *Channels of Prophecy: The Social Dynamics of Prophetic Activity.* Minneapolis: Fortress Press, 1989.

Petersen, David L., ed. *Prophecy in Israel: Search for an Identity.* London/Philadelphia: SPCK/Fortress Press, 1987.

______. *The Roles of Israel's Prophets. JSOT* Sup 17. Sheffield: JSOT, 1981.

Scott, R.B.Y. *The Relevance of the Prophets.* New York: Macmillan, 1968.

Soggin, J. Alberto. *A History of Ancient Israel.* Philadelphia: Westminster Press, 1984.

Wilson, Robert R. *Prophecy and Society in Ancient Israel.* Philadelphia: Fortress Press, 1980.

B. The Theological Context

Buber, Martin. *The Prophetic Faith.* New York: Macmillan, 1949.

Clements, Ronald E. *Old Testament Theology.* Atlanta: John Knox Press, 1978.

Eichrodt, Walther. *Theology of the Old Testament.* 2 Vols. Philadelphia: Westminster Press, 1961, 1967.

Gammie, John G. *Holiness in Israel.* Minneapolis: Fortress Press, 1989.

Heschel, Abraham. *The Prophets.* New York: Harper & Row, 1962.

Terrien, Samuel. *The Elusive Presence.* San Francisco: Harper & Row, 1978.

von Rad, Gerhard. *Old Testament Theology.* 2 Vols. New York: Harper & Row, 1962, 1965.

Vriezen, Th. C. *An Outline of Old Testament Theology.* Oxford: Basil Blackwell, 1970.

NOTES

1. On the early history of prophecy in Israel, see Joseph Blenkinsopp, *A History of Prophecy in Israel,* and Klaus Koch, *The Prophets* (2 vols.). On the phenomenon of prophecy as a whole, see Johannes Lindblom, *Prophecy in Ancient Israel.*
2. See esp. A. R. Johnson, *The Cultic Prophet in Ancient Israel.* Also see Robert R. Wilson, *Prophecy and Society in Ancient Israel,* and Robert C.Culley and Thomas W. Overholt, eds., *Anthropological Perspectives on Old Testament Prophecy.*
3. The prophetic element in the psalms is discussed in Sigmund Mowinckel, *The Psalms in Israel's Worship,* Vol. II, pp. 53-73 (Oxford: Basil Blackwell, 1962).
4. E.g., Wilson, *Prophecy and Society in Ancient Israel.*
5. For recent discussion of the question, see Thomas W. Overholt, *Channels of Prophecy,* pp. 149-61, and Gerald T. Sheppard, "True and False Prophecy Within Scripture," *Canon, Theology, and Old Testament Interpretation,* ed. Gene M. Tucker et al. (Philadelphia: Fortress Press, 1988).
6. Where the consonantal Hebrew text has *'dny yhwh* (i.e., "the Lord Yahweh"), the MT substitutes the vowels of the word *'elohim* ("God") as the word to be pronounced aloud instead of "Yahweh," in order to avoid the repetition of "Lord" (i.e., "the Lord Lord"), and most of the English

versions follow suit, translating, "the Lord God." The use of small capitals for "God" in these cases indicates that the consonantal Hebrew word thus rendered is *yhwh*.

7. The list of fulfilled prophecies is as follows: 1 Kings 11:29-39 (fulfilled, 12:15-20); 13:1-2 (fulfilled, 2 Kings 23:15-20); 14:1-6 (fulfilled, 14:18, 15:29); 16:1-4 (fulfilled, 16:11-12); 21:17-24, cf., 19:15-18, 2 Kings 9:7-10 (fulfilled, 2 Kings 9:1-28, 30-37 and 10:1-31); 22:17 (fulfilled, 22:29-37); 2 Kings 1:1-4, 16 (fulfilled, 1:17); 2 Kings 21:10-15 (fulfilled, 24:2); cf., 2 Kings 14:25; 19:6, 20, 32-37; 20:5, 16-18; 22:16-20.

CHAPTER THREE

Isaiah 1–39

PART I

INTRODUCTION TO THE BOOK OF ISAIAH

In its theological depth, literary diversity, and historical development, the book of Isaiah parallels the rest of the prophetic corpus. It is a multilayered collection whose growth spanned a period of two hundred fifty years, from the eighth to the fifth century BCE. It is this range and wealth of material, in addition to its famous messianic oracles, that account for its enduring popularity and its great impact upon Christian thought and piety through the centuries.

The wellspring of prophetic witness in the book was Isaiah, son of Amoz, who prophesied in Judah in the eighth century. His testimony to the holy God as the central reality in Israel's life, which is embodied in his vision (Isa 6) and spelled out in his oracular poems of wrath and divine discipline (e.g., 2:6-22, 5:8-30), establishes the mood of the book and sets the direction of its thought. The contributions of later writers draw out other implications of God's holiness for the life of Israel, including reconciliation with a chastened people, but these do not violate the spirit or substance of Isaiah's own witness.

The somber mood of Isaiah's oracles gives way to one of expectancy in the poems of Second Isaiah, the anonymous prophet of the sixth century (Isa 40–55). Here the full theological implications of Isaiah's insights are explicated, and new dimensions of Israel's service to God are proclaimed. These are not the only prophetic witnesses in the book, although they are the chief ones, and surely the best known.

In the midst of the diversity of religious ideas, literary forms, and historical settings that characterize the book of Isaiah, are several unifying themes. I have mentioned the theme of God's holiness. Another notable example is the theme of Jerusalem/Zion, the city of God:

> Zion shall be redeemed by justice
>   and those in her who repent, by righteousness. (1:27)

> On that day . . . those who were driven out to the land of Egypt
> will come and worship the LORD on the holy mountain at Jerusalem. (27:13)
>
> I am laying in Zion a foundation stone,
> a tested stone,
> a precious cornerstone, a sure foundation. (28:16)
>
> Get you up to a high mountain
> O Zion, herald of good tidings. (40:9)
>
> For Zion's sake I will not keep silent,
> and for Jerusalem's sake I will not rest,
> until her vindication shines out like the dawn. (62:1)

Each of these representative texts is from a different stratum of the book. The development of this theme reflects the development of the message of the book as a whole. The people of Jerusalem are the audience of much of the book, and the theme of Zion, as city, sanctuary, community and symbol, runs through it from beginning to end. Strictly speaking, the theme is YHWH and Zion, for everything the writers say about Zion expresses an aspect of this relationship. Thus, the relationship between YHWH and Jerusalem/Zion is central to the thought of the book, just as the relationship between YHWH and the wider community of Israel is central to the thought of the Old Testament as a whole.

Although Jerusalem/Zion stands at the center of the book, the horizon is by no means narrow. It takes in a substantial part of the world, from Ethiopia to Persia. The theme of YHWH and the nations stands alongside that of YHWH and Zion, and together they provide the dual focus of the message. In general, the theme of YHWH and the nations is subordinate to that of YHWH and Zion, but comes to the fore in the collection of oracles against the nations (13–23). A third theme, YHWH and the Davidic king, is important in First Isaiah, and it too is closely associated with the theme of YHWH and Zion. In 40–55, the Davidic king is displaced by the servant of YHWH as the central Israelite figure. The servant is not a royal figure, but is still the mediator of YHWH's justice, like the king in First Isaiah, and therefore stands in a certain continuity with the earlier figure. In all three instances—Zion, the nations, and the king/servant—the unity imparted to the book by these motifs is thematic. The unity does not preclude diversity of thought or authorship. On the contrary, the variety in the development of these themes in the different parts of the book is one of its salient features. The unity of the message is not one of static consistency but of dynamic continuity.

The underlying foundation of the unity of the book of Isaiah is the unbroken continuity of the religious community, whose witness of faith it represents. Since Jerusalem/Zion was the political and cultic center of this community at the time the book was composed, it is the chief symbol of the community in the book. However, it is identified in other ways. Above all, it is "Israel."[1] This is the *people*

Israel, sometimes called the "house of Jacob" (2:5, 6; 8:17; 10:20; 14:1; 29:22; 46:3; 48:1; 58:1), not the northern kingdom of Israel, which is called "Ephraim," to distinguish it from the kingdom of Judah (7:2, 5, 8, 9, 17; 9:9; 11:13; 17:3; 28:1, 3). This people is often referred to as "YHWH's people" (e.g., 1:3; 2:6; 5:13), or simply as "this people" (6:9, 10; 8:6, 11; 9:16; 29:13).[2]

To call the people of Israel a religious community, as I have done, is to use a modern term that has no direct equivalent in the Hebrew Bible. However, it is the most adequate definition. The religious community of Israel was identified with other communities at various times in its history—especially the kingdom of David and Solomon (the so-called United Monarchy) and the kingdoms of Israel and Judah. Ultimately, however, it was not identical with these other communities or their political institutions, for it was essentially a community of faith. It was Israel's witness of faith in God that gave it its distinctive character and provided the real unity in its prophetic traditions—in particular, the traditions represented in the book of Isaiah.

Religious faith is a quality of individual human beings: an understanding of the mind, a disposition of the heart, and a commitment of the will. It is personal, inward, and existential. Strictly speaking, communities do not have faith; only individual persons can have faith. Therefore, the truly fundamental reality underlying the unity of the book of Isaiah was the faith of the persons who created it. However, their faith was a shared faith. It involved common perceptions of God—of God's gifts and demands—and a common moral commitment to one another and to the world. The faith of each individual was informed, and therefore, to a considerable extent, made possible by the witness of faith of others in Israel, past or present. In this sense, the experience of the community was the context, and its witness of faith the presupposition, of the individual's faith in God. But the community consisted of persons—individuals—who had faith in God. And it was their witness of faith that united them as a community.

I am not suggesting that in biblical times, Israel was a community of persons who made individual decisions, as free adults, to associate with others for religious purposes. This, of course, is the way many modern religious groups recruit new members. Affiliation with the Israelite community of faith usually did not come about in this way. Participation in the community of faith was a concomitant of birthright membership in a family, and therefore in a clan or village, that worshiped YHWH and gave Yahwistic sanction to its laws, mores, and sociopolitical programs and ambitions. But over time, this congeries of families, clans, and villages changed substantially, in size, location, and ethnic composition. It expanded greatly after the conquests of David and Solomon, contracted during subsequent centuries, was severely diminished after the destruction of the kingdom of Israel, and was left a scattered remnant after the destruction of the kingdom of Judah. Its forms of governance changed several times in the course of history, and there was considerable change as well in its cultic usage. At any given time, it was possible to characterize Israel in particular political, cultic, or sociological terms, rather than in, or at least in addition to, its shared witness of faith. However, in the long run, it was this witness of faith, above all, that provided the basis of continuity in Israel.

In order to expound the witness of faith expressed in the book of Isaiah satisfactorily, it is first necessary to describe the understanding of the book's composition on which the exposition is based.

THE STRUCTURE OF THE BOOK AND ITS INTERPRETATION

Most critical treatments of the book of Isaiah in the twentieth century have separated it into two or three parts: First (1–39) and Second (40–66) Isaiah; or First (1–39), Second (40–55), and Third (56–66) Isaiah. The break between 39 and 40 is a clear one. The historical allusions in 1–39 are preexilic (before 587 BCE), while those in 40–66 are exilic and postexilic (after 587). Chapter 39 brings the first part of the book to a close and points forward to the exile, while chapter 40 is a new beginning, set at the end of the exile. Furthermore, the break between 55 and 56 is substantial also. Chapters 40–55 are literarily and theologically unified, anticipating the restoration of the Jerusalem cultic community, while 56–66 are literarily and theologically diverse, presupposing the existence of the restored cultic community. These are sufficient grounds for treating the three parts of the book separately, and this is what I will do here.

Treatments of the book as a prophetic unity, created by a single author, approach it either from one end of its historical development or from the other. Some conservative interpreters date the composition of the entire book in the eighth century BCE, on the grounds of the traditional attribution of the book to the prophet Isaiah. They justify this procedure by supposing that, although large portions of the book deal with realities of the exilic and postexilic age, Isaiah was inspired by God to write about those things, though he had no experience of them himself. This theory of prophetic inspiration has an affinity to a theory of prophecy presented in the books of Kings (e.g., 1 Kings 13),[3] but it has no basis in the Isaian oracles themselves. Exegetically, it is neither warranted nor helpful. Theologically, it creates an unbridgeable gulf between the prophetic writings and the living human community, of which we are a part. There is no basis for such a theory in actual human experience, for the future is never, and never has been, knowable in the way this theory asserts. The future is always open, determined by myriad actors in the drama of life. To assert that the future was known by Isaiah ten generations in advance is therefore incredible. Only a theory that grounds the proclamation of the book of Isaiah in the experience and reflection of contemporary writers (and, of course, their appropriation of earlier traditions of witness and experience) can preserve the relevance of its witness of faith in God for us today.

The incredible dogmatic theory I have just referred to should be distinguished from the nondogmatic views of the unity of *First* Isaiah, which are based on historical-critical interpretation of the text.[4] I will comment on the unity of First Isaiah in due course.

At the other end of the theoretical spectrum is the view that the entire book of Isaiah was composed in the fifth century BCE—that is, at the time of its latest datable portions. This is the view of John D. W. Watts, presented in his recent commentary.[5]

Although in my judgment, this theory attributes too much of the production of the book to the final composer-redactor and assumes more unity in the book than is evident, it is, in principle, a credible hypothesis. Any complete interpretation of the book must deal with the latest literary strata and the final redaction, and this is one way to do it. However, I think the more conventional view of the composition of the book is still the most defensible, and I will organize my treatment accordingly. In this and the next chapter, I will consider First Isaiah (1–39).[6]

AN OUTLINE OF FIRST ISAIAH 1–39

Prophecies of restoration are italicized in the following outline, to highlight the mixture of oracles of judgment and oracles of restoration.

A. Prophecies concerning Judah and Jerusalem (1–12)
    1. Superscription (1:1)
    2. Introductory oracles (1:2-31)
    3. Oracles of restoration and judgment (2–5)
        a. Title (2:1)
        b. *The restoration of Zion* (2:2-5)
        c. The terrible day of YHWH (2:6-22)
        d. Oracles of doom against Judah and Jerusalem (3:1–4:1)
        e. *The restoration of Zion* (4:2-6)
        f. A song of YHWH's Vineyard (5:1-7)
        g. Six woe oracles (5:8-30)
    4. A booklet on divine and Davidic kingship (6:1–9:7)
        a. A vision of YHWH as King (6)
        b. Oracles and signs for the reigning king (7–8)
        c. *A new king* (9:1-7)
    5. Oracles of doom against Ephraim and Assyria (9:8–10:34)
        a. A serial oracle against Ephraim (9:8–10:4)
        b. An oracle against Assyria (10:5-19)
        c. *Prophecies of an Israelite remnant and the deliverance of Zion* (10:20-27*a*)
        d. The failure of an assault on Zion (10:27*b*-34)
    6. *The ideal king and the peaceable kingdom* (11)
        a. *The ideal king and his kingdom* (11:1-9)
        b. *Additional prophecies of redemption for Israel* (11:10-16)
    7. A psalm of thanksgiving (12)

B. Oracles of judgment concerning individual nations (13–23)
   1. Babylon (13:1-22; 14:3-23; with *a promise for Israel,* 14:1-2)
   2. Assyria (14:24-27)
   3. Philistia (14:28-31; with *an assurance concerning Zion,* 14:32)
   4. Moab (15:1–16:14)
   5. Damascus and Ephraim (17:1-6)
   6. Ethiopia (18:1-6; with *a promise for Zion,* 18:7)
   7. Egypt (19:1-15)
   8. *Eschatological promises of redemption for Israel, Egypt, and Assyria* (19:16-25)
   9. Egypt and Ethiopia (20)
   10. Babylon (21:1-10)
   11. Dumah (21:11-12)
   12. Arabia (21:13-17)
   13. Judah (22:1-14) and a Judean official, Shebna (22:15-25).
   14. Tyre (23:1-18)

C. An eschatological prophecy of judgment and redemption (24–27)

D. Prophecies of judgment and redemption for Judah and Jerusalem (28–32)
   Judgment: 28:1-4, 7-29; 29:1-4, 9-16; 30:1-17; 31:1-9.
   Redemption: 28:5-6; 29:5-8, 17-24; 30:18-33; 31:4-9; 32:1-8, 15-20.

E. Prophecies of judgment for the nations and redemption for Zion (33–35)

F. Narrative conclusion to First Isaiah (36–39)
   A prose excerpt from 2 Kings 18:13–19:20 (omitting 18:14-16 and adding Isa 38:9-20)
   1. Sennacherib's invasion of Judah (36–37)
   2. Hezekiah's illness (38:1-8, 21-22)
   3. Hezekiah's psalm of complaint (38:9-20)
   4. A Babylonian embassy to Hezekiah and Isaiah's prediction of the exile (39)

THE REDACTION OF FIRST ISAIAH AND ITS MESSAGE

The diversity of First Isaiah, in content and background, is nearly as great as that of the book as a whole; therefore, attention must be paid to each of its major components. However, the compilation of the parts is purposeful, not accidental, and communicates a message. This message, and the related question of the redaction of First Isaiah deserve comment before we turn to the earliest stratum of the section, the oracles of Isaiah.

The message of Isaiah 1–39, taken as a whole, tells of God's punishment of Israel, particularly the kingdom of Judah; punishment of the nations, for idolatry and injustice; and God's subsequent redemption of the people of Israel. Both the punishment and the redemption begin in Jerusalem/Zion, reaching from there to encompass the nations of the world. The message is universal in scope, but is never separated from its historic center, the people of Israel and Jerusalem, the "city of faith" (1:21).

This message of punishment and redemption is summarized in the first chapter, which thus serves as an introduction. The theme of Zion's eventual redemption, stated briefly in 1:26-27, is developed in 2:2-5; 4:2-6, and in chapter 11, and again, much more fully, in chapters 32–39. The primary affinity of chapter 1 is to chapters 2–11. The dominant motif of the chapter, like 2–11, is God's judgment of Israel. The promise of redemption in 1:26-27, tersely stated and modest in proportion, lacks the fullness and grandeur of the oracles of salvation in the later parts of 1–39. Therefore, chapter 1 appears to be a resume of the collected oracles of the eighth-century Isaiah, which by its placement at the beginning of that collection, also serves as an introduction to the larger collection of chapters 1–39 (and indeed to the entire book).

It is difficult to date the oracles of salvation in 1–39, particularly in relation to 40–66. Were they already a part of 1–39 before 40–66 was joined to it? Or were they added at the same time as 40–66, or later? There are affinities between 34–35 and 40–55, suggesting the possibility of literary dependence, but the other salvation oracles in 1–39 have no close links to Second or Third Isaiah. In spite of this uncertainty about the process of compilation, in their present form, both 1–12 and 13–39 contain oracles of salvation alongside oracles of doom, and therefore both subsections proclaim the twofold message of God's judgment and redemption. In short, this is the general message of 1–12, 13–39, 40–55, and 56–66, the four major segments of the book.

When the specific content of the promises of redemption in 1–39 is compared with that in 40–66, substantial differences can be seen. The promises in 1–39 are concerned with the restoration of the city of Jerusalem; the continuation of the Davidic dynasty; the survival of the people of Israel through a "remnant"; the cessation of warfare; and, to some extent, with the reversal of fortunes of the mighty and the lowly. The emphasis is on externals. In 40–66, there is a shift of emphasis to internal factors in the life of the people of God—faith, trust, confidence, joy—and to relationships among people, both within Israel and between Israel and other peoples. To be sure, externals are not left out of consideration—the fall of Babylon, release of Jewish exiles, restoration of the cultic community of Zion—but much more interest is shown in the inner quality of Israel's experience.

Obviously, this change in the writers' interests reflects the new insights and the recognition of new needs which came about as a result of the experiences of the religious community during a period of two centuries, especially the experience of the exile. But although there were significant changes in the definition of issues and the formulation of the witness of faith, there was essential continuity in the understanding of God's creative power and steadfast love. The moral earnestness of life in God's world—the reality of God's righteous demands and judgments—is acknowledged in numerous ways throughout the book of Isaiah, and at the same time, the endless possibilities of new life and new obedience through the workings of God's grace.

Since the authorship of the oracles of salvation in 1–39 is disputed, it is possible that all Isaiah's own oracles were oracles of judgment. Nevertheless, the redactors of the Isaiah tradition have chosen to present the prophet's words of judgment together with words of redemption. The ultimate word in 1–12 and 28–32, as in every other major subsection of the book, is a word of redemption. Nowhere are prophecies of God's punishment of Israel permitted to stand unmatched by a corresponding prophecy of God's redemption. It is redemption that is the overarching motif of the book.

Traditional Christian interpretation has always emphasized this message of redemption in the book of Isaiah. However, modern critical scholarship has called this interpretation into question, primarily on the grounds that it is biased christologically. While it is true that Christian interpreters have sometimes read their own convictions into the Isaian text, their general perception of the message of the book as a message of redemption and hope is certainly correct. This perception is as valid in principle for 1–12 as for the rest of the book, even though the promises in 1–12 are shorter and focused more narrowly than those in the latter parts of the book.

An important aspect of the message of redemption for Israel in First Isaiah is the promise of the destruction of the kingdom of Assyria. Assyria, of course, was the great empire of western Asia in the eighth and seventh century BCE. The kingdom of Israel was annexed by Assyria in 732–722, and the kingdom of Judah was her vassal from that time until the late seventh century, when Assyria's imperial power waned. The ultimate end of Assyria, interpreted as an act of God's justice, is proclaimed in strategically placed texts in all three sections of First Isaiah—1–12, 13–23, and 24–39 (10:16-19, 24-27; 14:24-27; 30:29-33; 31:5-9). These texts, providing commentary on the conviction, attributable to Isaiah himself, that Assyrian arrogance eventually would be punished by God (10:5-15), help to bind together chapters 1–39. First Isaiah, in its final form, thus speaks confidently of the elimination of Assyrian power as a factor in the life of Israel, and of a glorious era of peace and justice to come, in which Zion, the city of faith, would be the sign and center. This dual affirmation is the thematic framework of the message of First Isaiah.

The message of redemption in First Isaiah is based neither on natural optimism nor on national pride, but on faith in the sovereign God, the Holy One of Israel (1:4; 5:19, 24; 10:20; 12:6; 17:7; 29:19; 30:11, 12, 15; 31:1). The purpose of God transcends the purposes of nations and individuals, and frequently stands over against them in judgment. God's purpose, both of judgment and redemption, is effected in and through the interactions of persons and peoples—not in some separate realm as conceived in the religious imagination. Therefore, the working out of God's purpose is not immediately discernible as

God's work. It appears as God's work only to the eyes of faith, whether it is viewed in the prospect of unfolding events or in the retrospect of history. Thus, the prophetic message is both an interpretation of events and human experiences, and a summons to commitment in faith.

I will deal more fully with the promises of redemption after we consider the earliest stratum of the book, the core of Isaian texts around which chapters 1–39 were formed.

The Isaianic nucleus has been built up into three groups of oracles—1–12, 13–27, and 28–35—on Israel, on the nations, and on Israel, respectively, with a narrative conclusion, 36–39. On the whole, the oracles of judgment in 28–32 may be later than those in 1–12 (there is no reason to think this is true of the oracles of redemption); however, there are no clear indications of an overall chronological arrangement in chapters 1–39.[7] Except where there are clear indications of date, it is best to regard it as indeterminate. I will consider first those texts that contain such indications, but one more methodological issue must be mentioned before we turn to the texts themselves.

THE PROTECTION OF ZION

Critical interpretations of the message of Isaiah can be divided into two groups, depending upon whether they include the promise of divine protection for Zion/Jerusalem as an integral part of the prophet's message, or exclude it as redactional. The resulting views are radically different. Since the issue is complex and the scholarly debate extensive, only the briefest comment is possible here. However, since a decision on this question fundamentally affects one's interpretation of Isaiah's message, it is necessary to say something about it.

First Isaiah concludes with two imaginative stories excerpted from Second Kings—stories about King Hezekiah of Judah and the prophet Isaiah. Although they are set against a background of real historical events, the stories themselves are fictional, as are so many stories in the books of Kings. They are created for didactic purposes, depicting historical figures in quasi-historical settings. One story (36–37) is set at the time of the Assyrian invasion of Judah, 701 BCE. It tells of the arrogant boasting of the Assyrians as they threaten to besiege Jerusalem after devastating the rest of Judah, and of the miraculous deliverance of the city by an angel of YHWH, who slew 185,000 Assyrian soldiers in their sleep, without human assistance (37:36-37). The historical reason for the Assyrian withdrawal—Hezekiah's payment of a large indemnity, reported both in 2 Kings 18:14-16 and in the annals of Sennacherib[8]—is omitted from the Isaian version of the story, leaving the nocturnal visit of the angel as the sole explanation of the Assyrian departure and the resulting deliverance of the city.

The date of composition of this tale is impossible to fix precisely, but it could be no earlier than the reign of King Josiah of Judah, at the time the first edition of the books of Kings was composed and the Josian redaction of the book of Isaiah was done.[9] The idea of the miraculous divine deliverance of Jerusalem in this narrative is clearly a late legendary explanation of the historical fact that the Assyrians did not capture the city in 701. What is less clear, and therefore the subject of scholarly disagreement, is the extent to which the idea of divine protection of Jerusalem/Zion is present elsewhere in First Isaiah, and if it is there, whose idea it was. Gerhard von Rad popularized the theory that the idea of YHWH's miraculous protection of Jerusalem was the key to Isaiah's message.[10] However, the alternative view, that this idea is redactional in First Isaiah, has been reaffirmed persuasively by Ronald Clements, and this is the view I will defend here.[11]

THE MESSAGE OF THE PROPHET ISAIAH

I will begin the exposition with the earliest datable portion of the book, the narrative of a prophetic vision and commission, in chapter 6, and the closely associated narrative of Isaiah's communications to King Ahaz of Judah, in chapters 7–8. These three chapters, plus the oracle on the accession of a new king in 9:1-7, are considered by many scholars to be a compilation, a kind of little scroll, incorporated as a unit into the larger Isaiah scroll. All this material except the royal oracle is prose, while the rest of Isaiah 1–12 is poetry. Chapter 6 reports a dialogue between Isaiah and the divine king, YHWH; chapters 7–8 report a dialogue between Isaiah and the Judean king, Ahaz; and chapter 9 contains an idealized picture of the reign of a new king. Chapter 6 is dated "in the year King Uzziah died"—about 742 BCE—while Isaiah's first encounter with King Ahaz (7:1-9) is dated about seven years later, at the time of the Syro-Israelite invasion of Judah.

HOLY GOD AND SINFUL PEOPLE

The message of Isaiah is theocentric from beginning to end. It is proclaimed as the word of God, and its whole substance is about God: God's purposes, God's acts, God's demands, God's relationship with Israel and the nations. More specifically, it is about YHWH, for this is the way God is usually named. And the message, in I-thou speech, is addressed directly to the people of Israel, as the word of YHWH to them. Here YHWH is presented as the living speaker to a listening audience, not merely as a character in a third-person story. This mode of communication intensifies the theocentricity of the writing. Most of the Bible is theocentric to one degree or another, but none of it more intensely so than the oracles of Isaiah.

The parties to the prophetic communication are YHWH, the God of Israel, and Israel, the people of YHWH. Of course, YHWH is not the God of Israel only, but is first the God of Israel, and is known and acknowledged as such. The traditional Israelite name for God is the one employed nearly 90 percent of the time in First Isaiah. The generic *'elohim* ("God") is used occasionally, but usually in apposition to *YHWH*. It seems to me that greater intimacy between God and the worshipers is implied in the use of the proper name *YHWH* than in the use of the word *God*, although *God* can become a proper name, in effect, for those who understand their relation to God to be intimate.

The theocentricity of Isaiah's oracles is symbolized perfectly in his vision of YHWH, the Holy One, enthroned above the seraphim (6:1-13). This vision provides a good point of entry into the prophet's thought because of its theocentricity, and also because most of the major themes of Isaiah's oracles are present here, and the image of YHWH in the vision is the most important clue we have to Isaiah's understanding of God.

Whether the vision describes Isaiah's initial call to prophesy is not stated. The account differs in this respect from similar prophetic texts (Hos 1; Amos 7:10-17; Jer 1; Ezek 1). A few scholars have inferred that Isaiah's vision represented a turning point in his public ministry, rather than its inception.[12] However, it seems more likely that this was indeed his initial call, since the report resembles other prophetic call-narratives, and it is the earliest dated material in the book. Furthermore, a call-narrative does not necessarily appear at the beginning of a prophetic book, as Amos 7:10-17 shows.

The narrative is a report of Isaiah's personal experience of the presence of God, or more precisely, of the intense awareness of the reality of God. He perceived himself as being in the immediate company of the sovereign holy God. He could "see" and "hear" God. Initially, God did not speak directly to him, nor did God "touch" him, but a third "person" mediated between them, by act and word. Then when Isaiah was prepared by the atoning touch and absolving word of the angelic "priest," God spoke to Isaiah and gave him his prophetic commission. This is highly metaphorical language, an attempt to describe the indescribable, to depict the simultaneous awareness of the real presence and the majestic otherness of God.

The experience resulted in Isaiah's prophetic vocation, which produced many words spoken to others about God, but the event itself was an experience of the real presence of God in the world and in his own life; or, to put it the other way around, of his own participation in a reality suffused and controlled by the power of God. This is the foundation of Isaiah's message and, in the end, its primary content. Essentially, it is the same message as that of the patriarchal and Mosaic traditions, the psalmists, and, of course, the rest of the prophets. Whatever the particular circumstances in which the recognition of God occurred, or the particular words and deeds to which it gave rise, it was this personal recognition that was the source and goal of Israel's witness of faith.

In his vision, Isaiah perceived the enormous incongruity between the holiness of YHWH and his own "uncleanness" and that of his people, who were supposed to be the people of YHWH. He imagined YHWH as a great king, enveloped in mystery and attended in adoration by all his courtiers, ready to do his bidding. In

YHWH's presence, Isaiah felt lost. He immediately sensed that his lips were unclean. This was no trivial thing in the circumstances, since his lips were symbolic of the prophetic vocation he was about to undertake and, therefore, of his whole being. Indeed, the symbol is appropriate for any human being, since speech is characteristic of human beings. Uncleanness of speech meant uncleanness of person, and this meant being lost before the majestic holiness of God.

In the vision, the seraphic host surrounding YHWH sang the mighty chorus, "Holy, holy, holy is YHWH of hosts. The whole earth is full of his glory." The "glory" of YHWH—weighty and radiant, full of energy and light—is not localized in the "throne room," the image of the temple of YHWH, but fills the whole earth. The whole earth is the setting and the measure of the glory of YHWH.

This notable assertion has important theological implications. The prophet declares that the glory of YHWH and the power it symbolizes are to be known not only in a sanctuary or in a prophet's vision, but over all the earth. The whole earth is filled with YHWH's glory. But YHWH is not to be identified with the earth or its powers, for YHWH is the most Holy One (this is the meaning of the threefold affirmation, "holy, holy, holy") whose holiness distinguishes this One from everything else. The seraphic chorus was thus an affirmation of both the transcendence and the immanence of God.

Kabod, "glory," denotes honor, weight, majesty, radiance, and power. "Presence" (NJV), too, is a suggestive translation, in the sense of a great or weighty presence. The presence of YHWH was no mere presence, like a human being's, but an awesome presence. *Kabod* is something that can be perceived. In Isaiah's vision, it was royal majesty and power, as these were symbolized by the trappings of the great King and embodied in the seraphic host that surrounded him. In fact, it is precisely the host of subjects commanded by a king (Isa 8:7; 10:16; 21:16) or the populace of a nation (16:14; 17:3, 4) which constitutes a king's or a nation's *kabod.* Of course, YHWH is not really a king on a throne, surrounded by his minions. This is only a symbolic vision. In reality, YHWH is the invisible God who created the earth and sustains it, and whose glory is manifest to the eyes of faith, throughout the whole earth.

The term *kabod* is used of YHWH only once more in First Isaiah, in the phrase *majestic glance* (3:8 NJV). This infrequent use of a term that is so important in 6:3 suggests the possibility that the seraphic cry in 6:3 may not have been Isaiah's own construction, but a quotation from a liturgical source. Such a quotation would have been natural in a visionary scene modeled after a temple service. Be that as it may, we have little to go on in trying to explicate the concept of YHWH's *kabod* in First Isaiah. The assertion in 6:3 serves as a corrective to the idea that YHWH's *kabod* is manifest only in the sanctuary; and it is a suggestive statement concerning the relation of God to the world. However, in the absence of parallel texts in Isaiah's oracles, it is doubtful that we should infer much more.

Being lost before the holy God is not Isaiah's last word in the vision. He also declares that he is forgiven and his guilt removed. Once again, the statement is terse to the point of being cryptic. We could wish for much more, some elaboration of the meaning of sin, for example; but the visionary drama is brief. It moves quickly from action to action, with only the barest dialogue. The prophet is forgiven and his guilt is removed, and that is all.

The pronouncement of Isaiah's forgiveness was made by a minister of YHWH, identified as a seraph. As the seraph made the pronouncement, he purged Isaiah's unclean lips with a burning coal. The fact that this ritual act has no parallel elsewhere in the Bible should not surprise us, because in life, such a burn would be an excruciating, disfiguring experience. Thus it occurs only in the prophet's vision, and it is left to our imaginations to interpret the seraph's act. We think at once of a surgical cauterization of a wound, an act that causes pain while producing healing, but this is admittedly speculative. Much more objective is the observation that the burning of Isaiah's lips in the vision has a parallel in the burning of the remnant of Israel. This occurs in YHWH's pronouncement of the judgment against the nation (6:13). The parallel between the burning of the nation and the burning of the lips is a crucial factor in determining the significance of the prophetic mission authorized by the commission, but I will come to that in a moment.

Holiness, at least in First Isaiah, is not merely an ontological category, but is also ethical. The ontological indications are in the depiction of YHWH as high and lifted up, enveloped in smoke, surrounded by a seraphic host, and shaking the foundations. Exaltation, separation from the mundane, and great power characterize this figure. The gulf between YHWH and Isaiah is enormous. If the holy is that which exhibits uncanny power, then the figure in Isaiah's vision is holy indeed. Human beings fall on their faces before such a One.

In this case, Isaiah does not actually fall on his face, but cries out, "Woe is me!" Ezekiel falls on his face in similar circumstances (Ezek 1:28), but Isaiah's response to the vision of the Holy One is an acute feeling of guilt. It is not his finitude that he decries, but his guilt, as represented by his unclean lips. When his lips are purged by the seraph's burning coal, it is his sin that is forgiven, his guilt that is removed. Nothing is said about his finitude.

If we take our cue from the vision, we will not be surprised to find elsewhere in First Isaiah that the use of the title "Holy One of Israel" for YHWH is always associated with recollections of Israel's sin (1:4; 5:19, 24; 30:11, 12, 15; 31:1). Sin can be cultic as well as ethical, of course, but the clear emphasis in all these passages is on the ethical aspects of sin, not the cultic. Clearly, therefore, holiness was primarily an ethical category for Isaiah. The Holy One of Israel required righteousness and faithfulness; therefore, to despise the Holy One (5:24) was an act of profound infidelity and waywardness.[13]

The title Holy One of Israel is used also in the secondary stratum of the book (10:20; 12:6; 17:7; 29:19), but in these texts some of the sharp ethical force of the prophet's usage is missing. Here the title has become a simple synonym for YHWH, without the same stress on the qualifying word *Holy*.

When the envisioned Lord asks for a messenger, Isaiah volunteers instantly: "Here am I. Send me." Understandably, his willing compliance has been offered as a model in myriad sermons. Amos seems to have been equally responsive (Amos 7:14-15), and so was Hosea (Hos 1:2-3); but Jeremiah was reluctant (Jer 1:6), and if the story of Moses' call (Exod 3) is an amalgam of classical prophetic-call experiences, then reluctance was a more frequent response than compliance. Ezekiel's response was the most complex of all those recorded. On the one hand, when he was shown the scroll of God's words, it was "sweet as honey" in his mouth (Ezek 3:1-3), despite its calamitous contents ("lamentation, and mourning, and woe," 2:10); but on the other hand, he required the special activity of YHWH's spirit to empower him (2:2; 3:12, 24), and he was overwhelmed by it (3:15). The human appeal of Isaiah's example is irresistible homiletically, but a balanced sampling of biblical examples is sobering. Even in Isaiah's case, the lectionaries stop short after his first words, "Here am I. Send me," omitting the sobering commission and Isaiah's further distraught response: "How long, O Lord?" (6:11).

It is no wonder that Isaiah exclaimed in dismay and the lectionaries omit any mention of his commission, for the commission was to harden the hearts of the people of Judah against the possibility of repentance, and thus, according to the logic of divine retribution, to assure the people's ruin (6:9-13). Many commentators, doubting that a prophet of God would view his mission so negatively at the outset, have discerned the influence of hindsight on this account. This judgment may be correct, for it would have been difficult for any scribe or redactor, in recounting Isaiah's experience, to avoid being influenced by the knowledge of subsequent events, particularly in view of the tragic history of Judah during the following century.

Given the possibility that the canonical version of Isaiah's commission recounts the result, rather than the purpose, of his prophesying, and even interprets it in the light of much later events, we should guard against a simplistic explication of the message of this chapter. We should regard it as a compound of Isaiah's own and others' insights. With this caveat, we can take note of the substantial inner consistency of the whole chapter.

The drama of the prophet's vision is mirrored in the drama of the nation's history. Like the prophet, the nation must acknowledge its unclean lips, be purified by the fire of God, be forgiven and restored; but unlike the prophet, the nation does not willingly confess its sin and submit to the purgation. Nations do not repent; only individuals repent. Nations are reformed only when they are forced by circumstances to do so. Usually it requires a catastrophe to provide the necessary understanding and moral courage to bring about reformation, and it is exactly such a catastrophe that is prophesied in Isaiah's commission. Only after the catastrophe—the burning, through which everyone, even the remnant, must pass—will there be a genuine prospect of new life (6:11-13). The healing to which the nation is accustomed, and which Isaiah's prophesying is intended to prevent, is a shallow, routine healing. Verse 10 does not say that the prophet's work will impede repentance; it says that it will impede the people's being "healed again"—that is, healed in the habitual, ritual fashion to which they have become accustomed ("healed again" is the more usual rendering of the Hebrew idiom employed here; the construction is identical to "be burned again" in 6:13).[14]

Did Isaiah himself prophesy the possibility of new life, the "holy seed" (vs 13*b*)? The majority of critical scholars think not, and take this to be the word of a redactor. This judgment may well be correct, although as I have said elsewhere, it is possible that it is not securely founded.[15] The strongest reason for judging the line to be secondary is that it accords so well with the many other secondary words of promise in Isaiah 1–39. In this case, the redactor has seen, in the report of Isaiah's visionary experience, an ultimate implication for the remnant of Judah that was not a part of the prophet's own message. The redactor offered to the "people of unclean lips" the same possibility of forgiveness and reconciliation to God that is offered to the prophet in his vision. This is the theological unity of Isaiah 6, in its final canonical form. Pragmatically, of course, there was an enormous difference between the restoration of the prophet and the restoration of the nation. According to the testimony of Isaiah, only a remnant of the nation would survive to learn the lesson of divine judgment and redemption.

FAITH AND ROYAL POLICY IN JUDAH

I have said that Isaiah 6 is part of a group of texts, a little scroll, dealing with royal policy in Judah. It includes chapters 7 and 8, and the royal oracle in 9:1-6 has been appended to this scroll, thereby giving it a future dimension. Isaiah's response to the Syro-Israelite invasion of Judah in 735, including his counsel to the Judean, King Ahaz, is the subject of the central section of the little scroll, which is in two parts of roughly equal length. The first part, chapter 7, contains two words from Isaiah to Ahaz, concerning the invasion (7:1-9, 10-17), followed by four brief additions on the coming day of YHWH (7:18-25). The second part, chapter 8, contains two further words of Isaiah concerning the invasion (8:1-4, 5-8), followed by two rather loosely related pieces (8:9-10, 11-15) and a self-admonition to record and preserve the message for a future time (8:16-18).[16]

The message of Isaiah to Ahaz is simple, and it is expressed consistently in all four oracles concerning the Syro-Israelite invasion: The threat posed by Syria and Israel is so fleeting and inconsequential that the king of Judah should stand fast and not be afraid. This straightforward message has provoked remarkable commentary—secondary interpretations with far-reaching messianic and theological implications. I will comment on the interpretations after discussing the texts themselves.

The political situation that called forth Isaiah's oracles is described in 7:1-6. King Rezin of Syria, and Pekah of Israel were threatening to invade Judah for the purpose of deposing King Ahaz and installing a king of their own choice, presumably in order to provide a united front in rebellion against their Assyrian overlord. This was the moment when Isaiah offered his counsel to Ahaz. The historical statement at the beginning of the scroll (7:1) summarizes the whole event, including the eventual failure of the invasion, but the account of Isaiah's encounter with Ahaz dates the encounter early in the event, before the outcome was known (7:3-6).

Isaiah's first word to Ahaz told him the threatened invasion would fail because of its leadership (vss 7, 9), concluding with the memorable pun, "If you do not believe [this] (*ta'aminu*), surely you will not be secure (*te'amenu*)" (vs 9, JMW). This statement often has been construed as a promise of God's protection of the Judean king as a reward for his faith in God, or even more generally, a promise of protection to anyone who has such faith. However, such constructions are much too broad. The sense of the statement is more specific. Ahaz is to believe what Isaiah is telling him as a word of YHWH—that the invasion must fail. If he believes this word, he will be secure in the circumstances. Parallels to this use of the verb, in the sense of believing a word of God as delivered by a prophetic messenger, are numerous in the Hebrew Bible (e.g., Exod 4:5, 31; 1 Kings 10:7; Isa 43:10; 53:1; Hab 1:5), while there are no examples of the kind of usage assumed in the more general interpretations of Isaiah's famous pun.[17] Isaiah wanted his oracle to be believed. He was not propounding a theory concerning the political consequences of religious faith.

At the same time, believing the prophet's oracle was tantamount to trusting the God on whose authority it was proclaimed.[18] This did not mean that God could be trusted to give Ahaz whatever he wanted in the circumstances; it did mean that God could be trusted to be God, in these, as in all circumstances and, therefore, could be trusted to sustain and vindicate every true service of God. Isaiah did not offer God's support in Ahaz's cause, but in God's own cause.

According to the little scroll, Isaiah was not content to deliver just one oracle to Ahaz at this time of national crisis. He delivered a second, in the form of the symbolic naming of a yet unborn child (7:10-17). This sign of Immanuel is the most famous prophetic word in the Hebrew Bible and also one of the most controversial. The identity of the child and its mother is unknown, and so is the significance of the curds and honey the child was to be fed. If one tries to imagine the actual situation in which Isaiah spoke to Ahaz, I believe the most plausible conclusion one can reach is that the child was Isaiah's and that it was he who would give the child the symbolic name and food. This would explain the significance attributed to these acts. The one who would perform them and the one who interpreted them were one and the same—the prophet himself.

Nevertheless, any reconstruction of the original scene is hypothetical. The only meaning of the Immanuel sign we know, or can know, for reasons I explain in the excursus on prophetic signs below, is the meaning it is given in the text. The two parts of this double sign—the naming of the child Immanuel and the feeding of the child with curds and honey—are not given separate meanings, but together they mean one thing, explained in verses 14-17: that the kings of Syria and Israel will be forsaken by the time the child is old enough to distinguish good (food) from bad.

In the original explanation, there are glosses on verses 8 and 17, made by someone who knew what happened later: that Assyria had invaded Syria and Palestine, and had administratively incorporated Syria, Israel, and part of Judah into the Assyrian empire. These events are alluded to also in the four additions in 7:18-25. In the minds of the redactors, these historical developments confirmed, without any lingering doubt, the validity of Isaiah's counsel to the Judean king. Their expansion of the original words of Isaiah gave new significance to those words in a new historical setting, showing once again the dynamic quality of the canonical process. Isaiah's prophecy was a prophecy of "Immanuel"—that is, of God's presence—based on his own experience, in his call vision, of being brought to full awareness of the reality of God's presence. And it testified to an awareness that could come to anyone, in Isaiah's time or in any other. The various layers in the prophetic tradition of the book of Isaiah are expressions of the continuity of this witness.

EXCURSUS ON THE MEANING OF PROPHETIC SIGNS

The sign of Immanuel is the first prophetic sign in the books of the prophets, but there are many more, especially in Jeremiah, Ezekiel, and Hosea. These signs are an important part of the prophetic tradition, and since they have provoked considerable critical discussion with divergent interpretations, I will explain the grounds of my approach to these narratives.

There are two types of prophetic signs—acted and verbal. Going about in public in one's underwear (Isa 20) is an acted sign. Reporting an omen (Jer 1:13-16) is a verbal sign. Reporting that a baby will be fed curds and honey (Isa 7:15) is a verbal sign, though it describes an act to be performed at a later time. Naming someone with a sentence-name, such as "A Remnant Will Return" (Isa 7:3), is a special kind of verbal sign; it has intrinsic meaning, while other verbal signs do not.

Regardless of their type, prophetic signs are not self-explanatory. They must be explained, and this is true even of sentence-names, for while these have some meaning, they are equivocal. Their range of possible meanings is wide, but not as wide as it is for other signs, for which the range can be virtually unlimited. "God Is With Us," for example, can signify many different things. So in every case, it is the explanation of the sign that communicates the prophet's point. There is no "original" meaning, apart from the explanation given explicitly in the text. The sign cannot make the point it is intended to make until it is explained. Presumably, the function of the sign is to draw people's attention to the explanation of the meaning, and also to make sure they remember the meaning. This is an inference, since the text never explains why prophets chose this way to make their point, but it is difficult to imagine any other reasons. Nevertheless, the meaning of the sign is the meaning it is given in the explanation in the text.

It is possible, of course, that the original explanation of a sign, its original meaning, could have been lost or deliberately set aside and another put in its place. In that case, the sign would acquire a new meaning. It is always legitimate to ask whether the explanation reported in the text is the original. This is an exegetical question, to be answered on the basis of any evidence that can be found in the text.

But this is a different question from, for example, that of the relationship of the secondary interpretation of Jesus' parable of the sower (Mk 4:13-20 and parallels) to the parable itself (Mk 4:1-9). This parable, like all parables, makes its own point. Some may miss that point, but that is because they do not "have ears to hear" (Mk 4:9). To add a secondary interpretation, as the Gospel tradition does in this case, is to add something extraneous, unnecessary. So this is not at all like explaining a prophetic sign, since every sign must be explained in order for it to be understood. The only question is, Who is going to explain it? If it is the prophet, then it is the original explanation, and the sign conveys the prophet's meaning. If someone else explains it differently from the way the prophet explained it, or would have explained it, then the sign is no longer the prophet's, but belongs to the one who gives it meaning.

If the original explanation is no longer known, it is futile to speculate about the original meaning. For example, if "God Is With Us" did not mean what the text says it meant, at the time Isaiah announced it to Ahaz (presuming this actually occurred), then there is no way to guess which of its many possible meanings was intended. Nevertheless, commentators, myself included, have speculated at length about what the sign meant originally—the "meaning" of the virginity (or maidenhood) of the mother-to-be, the meaning of the name Immanuel, the meaning of the curds and honey. Yet I have become convinced that none of these, or all of them together, mean anything until they are explained. And if the prophet intended the sign to mean something other than what the explanation in the text says it meant, then that meaning is completely lost. To discover the significance of virgins (or maidens) in other contexts, whether mythical, cultic, literary, or historical, would tell us nothing about the actual significance of the virgin (or maiden) in Isaiah's sign, though this way has been taken by interpreters. To discover the significance of curds and honey in some other context would tell us nothing about the actual significance of the curds and honey in Isaiah's sign, though this way too has been taken (beginning with the writer of Isaiah 7:21-22!).

Since parables make their own point, the few parables in the prophetic books are different from signs, in the narrow sense. Thus the report in Jeremiah 18:5-11 of the potter's reshaping of misshapen clay is a parable. It makes the point that misshapen clay can be reused by a potter. But the act of breaking a pottery flask in Jeremiah 19:10-11 is a sign. It makes no point (the point that a clay pot can be broken is hardly a significant point), unless or until the prophet tells why he is breaking the pot. In this case, Jeremiah tells why before he does it; but it is still the explanation that makes the point and not the breaking. In Jeremiah 13:1-11, the order is the reverse. There the prophet first performs the act, in this case the burying of a clean loincloth in a muddy riverbank, and later he explains why he did it. Apart from his explanation, the act makes no point at all. But a parable makes a point, and an allegory, of which there are several in the prophetic literature (e.g., Ezek 16; Hos 2), makes more than one. These texts do not present the same problem of interpretation as the signs.

There is another question to be asked about a prophetic sign: Was the sign ever performed in real life, or did it exist only in the story told about it? The answer to this question does not affect the meaning of a sign, because in either case, a sign's only meaning is the meaning given in the explanation. Nevertheless, whether or not a sign was performed in real life is an interesting historical question. Did the prophet really do it? Did Isaiah really walk about in public in his underwear? Did Jeremiah really bury a loincloth in a riverbank? If we could answer these questions, we would know something about these prophets, about the original setting of the action, and whether it was merely an imaginative story or happened in real life. But we would not know anything more about the meaning of the signs than we already know.

TWO MORE SIGNS FOR AHAZ

The message Isaiah gave Ahaz twice in their dialogue on Fuller's Field Road (7:1-17) was repeated a third and a fourth time, according to the little scroll on the Judean crisis. The third time, it was given by means of another symbolic name—Maher-shalal-hash-baz ("Speedy-Spoil-Quick-Plunder")—which Isaiah gave his son (8:1-4). Thus Maher-shalal-hash-baz joined his brother Shear-ya-shub ("A Remnant Will Return," 7:3) and perhaps a second brother, Immanu-el ("God Is With Us"), as living signs from their father Isaiah. Each of these sentence-names has a meaning so equivocal that it requires an explanation of the prophet's intention in order to convey a significant message.

The final word of Isaiah to Ahaz in the Judean crisis was a sign, or similitude, of two streams (8:5-8). One was the mighty river Euphrates; the other, the small stream Shiloah. The first symbolized Assyria; the second, Syria and Israel, according to Isaiah's explanation. Ahaz, rejecting Isaiah's counsel, was terrified by the Syro-Israelite invaders, weak waters though they were. So Isaiah was convinced that YHWH would engulf the invaders in the flooding river—

Assyria—which would rush on to inundate Judah also, thus proving Ahaz foolish for disbelieving the prophet. The prophecy of Judah's inundation is clearly secondary to the assurance of the failure of the Syro-Israelite invasion. The assurance of the invasion's failure was intended to strengthen Ahaz in the face of this threat. The prophecy of Judah's inundation is a response to Ahaz's refusal to accept Isaiah's counsel as the basis of royal policy, and therefore presupposes what happened after Isaiah's encounter with Ahaz. Yet this subsequent prophecy probably also was Isaiah's; it is consistent with the message of his commission (6:10-12).

The stream of Shiloah in this passage sometimes is understood to symbolize quiet confidence or trust in God, perhaps because the stream was close to the temple of Jerusalem, but this interpretation is subjective and beside the point. The only meaning of the stream in the parable is the meaning stated. This quiet little stream is contrasted to the mighty Euphrates, and the contrast between them is likened to that between the Syro-Israelite invaders and the Assyrians. And then Ahaz is invited to choose which military force to face. This is the only meaning of either the Shiloah or the Euphrates in the sign.

But the point of this fourth sign, the same point made three times before, is actually not the main point of the little scroll in its present form. It is only the lead-in to the main point: the promise of salvation to the faithful remnant of "the house of Jacob" (8:17), those who would survive the crisis of Isaiah's time. The devastation that would befall both Israel and Judah, including even Jerusalem, as a result of Ahaz's wrong choices, might appear to be the work of foreign powers, but in actuality, it was the work of YHWH (8:11-15). The Lord YHWH was a stone of stumbling for those who feared other powers, but a sanctuary for those who feared YHWH, and it was for those few that Isaiah preserved his testimony (8:16-22).

What were the implications of Isaiah's counsel for political action in the kingdom of Judah? Several possibilities have been proposed by interpreters. The most popular inference is that Ahaz was supposed to do nothing but wait calmly for YHWH to intervene miraculously against the conspirators. This idea of faithful inaction for the salvation of Jerusalem informs the later account of YHWH's deliverance of the city from the Assyrians in 701 BCE (Isa 37:33-38), but this idea is not stated in Isaiah 7–8. Another possible inference is that Ahaz was to defend himself and his kingdom, in the sure confidence that YHWH would support him as a descendant of the chosen line of David (cf. 2 Sam 7). This interpretation, too, is purely inferential.[19] The fact is that the text does not indicate what Isaiah wanted Ahaz to do. It says only that the Syro-Israelite invasion would fail because of the weakness of its leaders, and that was the word Isaiah wanted Ahaz to believe; no political or military strategy is suggested.

To this point in our exposition of Isaiah 1–39, we have been dealing with texts attributed by almost all scholars to Isaiah himself, the firm core of the earliest stratum of the book, the central proclamation to the leaders of the kingdom of

Judah in the eighth century BCE. Here we have not only the words most likely to have been spoken by Isaiah, but also a standard by which to judge the Isaian character of the other oracles in the book. In the next chapter, we will be dealing with texts whose origins are diverse. Some are attributable to Isaiah (e.g., 2:6-20); others are uncertain (e.g., 9:2-7); still others are very likely the work of later hands (e.g., 36–39). This material is sometimes baffling in its complexity; yet theologically, it is immensely suggestive. It is the legacy of several generations of writers, and the proof of the generative power of Isaiah's prophetic witness.

SELECT BIBLIOGRAPHY

Barton, John. "Ethics in Isaiah of Jerusalem." *Journal of Theological Studies* 32 (1981): 1-18.

Blank, Sheldon H. *Prophetic Faith in Isaiah.* New York: Harper & Row, 1958.

Clements, R. E. *Isaiah 1–39.* New Century Bible Commentary. Grand Rapids: Eerdmans, 1980.

______. *Isaiah and the Deliverance of Jerusalem. JSOT* Sup 13. Sheffield: JSOT, 1980.

Davies, Eryl W. *Prophecy and Ethics: Isaiah and the Ethical Traditions of Israel. JSOT* Sup 16. Sheffield: JSOT, 1981.

Fohrer, Gerhard. "Zion, Jerusalem." *Theological Dictionary of the New Testament,* ed. G. Friedrich. Vol. VII: 292-319. Grand Rapids: Eerdmans, 1971.

Gray, George B. *A Critical and Exegetical Commentary on the Book of Isaiah, I–XXVII.* The International Critical Commentary. Edinburgh: T. & T. Clark, 1912.

Hamborg, G. R. "Reasons for Judgment in the Oracles Against the Nations of the Prophet Isaiah." *VT* 31 (1981): 145-59.

Hayes, John H., and Stuart A. Irvine. *Isaiah—The Eighth-Century Prophet.* Nashville: Abingdon Press, 1987.

Holladay, William L. *Isaiah: Scroll of a Prophetic Heritage.* Grand Rapids: Eerdmans, 1978.

Interpretation 36/2 (1982).

Jensen, Joseph. "Weal and Woe in Isaiah: Consistency and Continuity." *CBQ* 43 (1981): 167-87.

______. "The Age of Immanuel." *CBQ* 41 (1979): 220-39.

Kaiser, Otto. *Isaiah 1–12.* 2nd Ed. Philadelphia: Westminster Press, 1983.

Review and Expositor 65 (1968): 395-482.

Roberts, J.J.M. "Isaiah 2 and the Prophet's Message." *Jewish Quarterly Review* 75 (1985): 290-308.

______. "Yahweh's Foundation in Zion." *JBL* 106 (1987): 27-45.

Roth, Wolfgang. *Isaiah.* Atlanta: John Knox Press, 1988.

Scott, R.B.Y. "The Book of Isaiah, Chapters 1–39." *The Interpreter's Bible.* Vol. 5. Nashville: Abingdon Press, 1956.

Sheppard, Gerald T. "The Anti-Assyrian Redaction and the Canonical Context of Isaiah 1–30." *JBL* 104 (1985): 193-216.

Vermeylen, Jacques, ed. *The Book of Isaiah*. BETL 81. Leuven: University Press,1989.

Ward, James M. *Amos and Isaiah*. Nashville: Abingdon Press, 1969.

Watts, John D. W. *Isaiah 1–33*. Word Biblical Commentary. Waco, Tex.: Word Books, 1985.

Welch, Adam C. *Kings and Prophets of Israel*. London: Lutterworth Press, 1952.

Whedbee, J. William. *Isaiah and Wisdom*. Nashville: Abingdon Press, 1971.

NOTES

1. "Zion" appears 47 times in the book of Isaiah, as many as in all the other prophetic books combined. In addition, Jerusalem is mentioned 49 times, although the frequency of reference is not distinctive in Isaiah; it occurs 104 times in Jeremiah, for example. It is the frequency of reference to Zion that is distinctive in Isaiah. "Israel" appears 90 times, compared with 93 in Jeremiah and 177 in Ezekiel, for example.

2. The full list: Isa 1:3; 2:6; 3:1, 12, 13, 14, 15; 5:13, 25; 10:2, 24; 22:4; 30:26; 32:13, 18; 40:1; 43:20, 21; 47:6; 49:13; 51:4, 16, 22; 52:4, 5, 6, 9; 53:8; 56:3; 57:14; 58:1; 63:8, 14, 18; 64:9; 65:10, 19.

3. The author of the books of Kings has created a series of alleged prophetic predictions in order to illustrate his theory of the significance of the prophetic word in the life of Israel (1 Kings 11:29-39; 13:1-2; 14:1-16; 16:14; 21:17-24; 22:17; 2 Kings 1:1-4, 16; 14:25; 19:6, 20, 32-37; 20:5, 16-18; 21:10-15; 22:16-20).

4. For example, the view advocated by Hayes and Irvine in *Isaiah—The Eighth-Century Prophet.*

5. Watts, *Isaiah 1–33*, pp. xxiii-xxxiv.

6. The question of the redaction and unity of the book of Isaiah has received renewed attention from critical scholars since the publication of Brevard Childs' *Introduction to the Old Testament as Scripture* (Philadelphia: Fortress Press, 1979). Its main thesis is that the final, canonical form of the biblical books is the primary context for interpreting the component texts. For a useful survey of proposals made to date concerning the redaction of the book of Isaiah, and especially the relationship between First and Second Isaiah, see G. I. Davies, "The Destiny of the Nations in the Book of Isaiah," *The Book of Isaiah*, ed. J. Vermeylen, pp. 93-120.

7. The treatments of Watts and Hayes-Irvine, based on the assumption that almost everything is in chronological order, involve a great many arbitrary decisions about the date of the material, and a corresponding number of interpretations that beg the question of setting and purpose.

8. See *ANET*, 287-88.

9. On the composition of the books of Kings, see any of the standard commentaries on Kings, or introductions to the Old Testament/Hebrew Bible. On the Josian redaction of Isaiah, see especially Clements, *Isaiah 1–39*, pp. 5-6, and the works of H. Barth referred to there.

10. von Rad, *Old Testament Theology* (New York: Harper & Row, 1962, 1965), Vol. 2, pp. 118-44; see also Ben C. Ollenburger, *Zion, the City of the Great King*. *JSOT*Sup 41 (Sheffield: JSOT, 1987), pp. 104-130.

11. Clements, *Isaiah 1–39* and *Isaiah and the Deliverance of Jerusalem*. See his telling criticism of von Rad on pp. 24-25 of the former work. See also Ward, *Amos and Isaiah*, pp. 228-56.

12. A. C. Welch made a case for this view in *Kings and Prophets of Israel*, pp. 210ff.

13. On the whole concept of holiness in Isaiah, see John Gammie, *Holiness in Israel* (Minneapolis: Fortress Press, 1989), pp. 71-101.

14. Cf. E. Kautzsch, ed., *Gesenius' Hebrew Grammar*, 2nd English ed., ed. A. E. Cowley (Oxford: Clarendon Press, 1910), p. 120d, and the Isaiah commentaries of Gray and Kaiser. The basic sense of the line as I have rendered it is conveyed also in the NJV.

15. Ward, *Amos and Isaiah*, pp. 159-60. Neither the formal argument (that the short line disturbs the stylistic unity), nor the textual argument (that the line was missing in the Hebrew Vorlage of the LXX), stands up under close scrutiny. The short line which concludes the second half of the vision ("A holy seed is its stump," v 13*b*) is exactly parallel formally to the short line which concludes the first half of the vision ("Here am I, send me," v 8*b*). And the LXX of v 13 actually seems to presuppose the same Hebrew text as the MT, but a portion of the verse has been omitted by homoeoteleuton.

16. On the structure and significance of this section of the book, see Bernhard W. Anderson, " 'God with Us'—in Judgment and in Mercy: The Editorial Structure of Isaiah 5–10 (11)," *Canon, Theology, and Old Testament Interpretation*, ed. Gene M. Tucker et al. (Philadelphia: Fortress Press, 1988), pp. 230-45.

17. See Ward, *Amos and Isaiah*, pp. 184-88, and *IDBS*, pp. 329-31.

18. The translation of the NRSV, "stand firm in faith," is therefore not illegitimate, though in my opinion it is interpretive.

19. Hayes and Irvine have a novel theory (*Isaiah—The Eighth-Century Prophet*): that Isaiah believed the people of Judah and Jerusalem would be punished by Assyria for supporting the Syro-Israelite conspiracy, but that the line of the Davidic kings itself would be preserved by YHWH because of the dynastic promise to David. However, it seems to me that the authors have repeatedly arbitrarily interpreted, and even translated, the text, in order to get this meaning from it.

CHAPTER FOUR

Isaiah 1–39

PART II

The kings of Judah and Assyria, who, more than anyone else, determined the destiny of Isaiah's people, ruled by a different set of principles from those of the prophet. In the bitter conflict of values recorded in the book of Isaiah, Isaiah's witness was largely ignored by the kings of Judah, and probably was unknown to the kings of Assyria. In historical perspective, however, it is Isaiah's witness that has endured, while the royal absolutism of Judah and Assyria has been rejected almost everywhere. The texts we will consider in this chapter provide commentary on this historic conflict of principles.

THE IDEAL RULER

The little scroll on the Syro-Israelite invasion of Judah concludes with an admonition to preserve Isaiah's testimony for a future time (8:16-22). This is followed by the first of two famous royal oracles (9:1-7; 11:1-9), which promise Judah a better, more effective ruler in that future time. The authorship and date of these oracles are unknown. Scholars are about evenly divided as to whether they come from Isaiah in the eighth century or from later anonymous writers. My own judgment concerning their date is that they were composed during the time of the monarchy (up until 587) or soon afterward, since the later prophetic writings (Isaiah 40–66, Ezekiel, and the later portions of the book of the Twelve Prophets) show little interest in the restoration of the monarchy. Apparently the hope for a restoration was fostered as long as there were active royalists in Judah and the realization of the hope was possible, and then it faded away. Monarchical self-rule ceased to be an option for postexilic Judaism, and other issues came to occupy the interest of the community. If 9:1-7 is Isaiah's, it probably is an oracle on the occasion of the birth, or more likely the accession, of a new Judean king—Hezekiah.

The lasting significance of the royal oracles in Isaiah lies in their ethical content, not their predictive value. As prophecies of the restored sovereignty of the Judean kingship, they were not fulfilled, but as expressions of an ideal of leadership, they have had a profound influence on Judeo-Christian thought. Of all the royal texts in the Hebrew Bible, they most fully reflect the ethical norms of prophetic Yahwism. When compared with the dynastic promise to the Davidic line (2 Sam 7) and the royal psalms (Pss 2, 18, 20, 21, 45, 72, 89, 101, 110, 132, 144), the messianic oracles in Isaiah represent nothing less than a radical reordering of values. The primary purpose of the Judean dynastic texts was to establish the Davidic line in the hearts of the people of Israel and in the power of YHWH; the primary purpose of the Isaianic oracles was to foster the ideals of peace and justice.

Justice is the platform of every government, ancient and modern. Therefore, we should expect to find it as a criterion of rule in the Davidic tradition, and we do indeed find it there (e.g., Pss 72; 101). However, the interest in self-preservation was so powerful in the Judean royal house, as in every ruling establishment, that it inevitably swallowed up any commitment to the Yahwistic ideal of justice. One need only read the books of Samuel and Kings to see what happened in the history of the Israelite monarchy.

The oracle of Nathan (2 Sam 7) and the royal psalms probably express the understanding of the Davidic monarchy held within official Judean circles.[1] The oracle of Nathan acknowledges that Judean kings were liable to divine punishment for their iniquities (7:14), but it makes the divine grant of kingship itself irrevocable. In this view, the dynasty had an unconditional right to rule, regardless of the behavior of the particular incumbents. Consequently, the monarchy ultimately was invulnerable to criticism from prophets or anyone else. Without a constitutional basis for termination of the dynasty, there was no ultimate political sanction for the misbehavior of the kings.

The Israelite monarchy was not unique in this regard, of course. This radical deficiency was characteristic of all monarchies prior to the modern era. The Israelite monarchy was more vulnerable to moral criticism than many others in the ancient Near East, however, since everyone knew that the institution was a relatively recent historical development—not, as in other societies, an immemorial fixture of communal existence. Therefore there was less foundation in Israel for the belief in the divine right of kings.

The royal oracles in Isaiah presuppose the same dynastic promise as the other texts I have mentioned, so in this sense, they do not represent a different understanding of the divine right of the Judean kings. However, they shift the emphasis in the relationship of YHWH and the kings from YHWH's maintenance of the royal line to the kings' service of YHWH in the pursuit of peace and justice, and they prophesy the granting of special gifts for this purpose. The oracle in 9:1-7 speaks first of the achievement of peace (vss 4-6) and then of "justice and righteousness" as the foundations of kingship (vs 7). The oracle in 11:1-9 presupposes a state of peace and focuses upon the qualities of leadership, which are grounded in personal knowledge of YHWH and faith in YHWH (vss 2-3). Only a deeply committed servant of God can fulfill the role intended for the Israelite king; this loyalty cannot be superficial but must extend to the very core of the king's being. He must be possessed not only of wisdom and discernment, but by the very spirit of wisdom and discernment, which is nothing less than the spirit of YHWH.

And from these inner qualities of knowledge, faith, wisdom, and discernment, righteous rule will result. The king will not be deceived by hearsay or appearances. Knowing the truth in himself, he will recognize it in others and will govern accordingly. Thus the "peaceable kingdom" will be fostered from the center outward (vss 6-9). This prophetic image of the righteous ruler is a royal image in these oracles, but the moral insights suggested are relevant to other forms of leadership as well. Of all the royal or "messianic" images in the Hebrew Bible, this one from the book of Isaiah has had the greatest impact upon christological thought in the New Testament, and therefore upon subsequent Christian thought. First Isaiah's image of the messiah was transformed in Christian usage when it was identified with Second Isaiah's image of the suffering servant of YHWH (esp. 52:13–53:12), but the identification of these two images was not made in the book of Isaiah itself. The servant is not a king in Isaiah 40–55.

ASSYRIA, ROD OF YHWH'S ANGER

In Isaiah's time, the small kingdoms of Syria-Palestine were vassals of Assyria. Isaiah's confidence in the weakness of the Syro-Israelite conspiracy against Judah (7–8) may have been linked to his awareness that Assyria would not tolerate such a treasonable act. The specter of Assyria looms large in 7:17-25. The picture of Assyria in this passage is partly retrospective and redactional, but since the threatening power of Assyria was also a theme of the sign of the two streams (8:5-8), which may well be Isaiah's, it seems that the redactors have expanded Isaiah's point in the light of subsequent events. This same combination of prophetic insight and editorial hindsight is shown in the treatment of Assyria throughout the book. It is impossible to sort out the two completely, though there are places where the editorial intrusion is obvious (e.g., 7:8*b*).

A deep foreboding of national disaster permeates the oracles of Isaiah. The principal agent of disaster in western Asia throughout the eighth century was Assyria, so there is no reason to doubt that Isaiah himself prophesied the destruction of Judah and Israel by this power, just as the other eighth-century prophets did. However, three decisive events in the period after Isaiah's time influenced the final shaping of his transmitted oracles:

1. The inconclusive Assyrian siege of Jerusalem in 701;
2. The destruction of the Assyrian kingdom, 615–612; and
3. The destruction of the Judean kingdom, including the city of Jerusalem, 598–587.

The first of those events gave rise to superstitious trust in YHWH's miraculous protection of Jerusalem against a godless invader (14:24-27; 31:6-9; 37:33-37). This belief continued to blind the Judean people until Jeremiah's time (Jer 7:1-15), although it is unknown how widely it was held or what impact it had on the conduct of public affairs in the kingdom. However, the belief in Jerusalem's physical inviolability dissolved with the Babylonian destruction of the city.

The decline of Assyrian power after the death of Asshurbanipal (ca. 626) and the destruction of the Assyrian kingdom in the following decade had a profound effect on Judean politics and theology. Politically, King Josiah was encouraged in his national reform by the power vacuum created by the Assyrian decline. Theologically, the fall of Assyria made a deep impression on the prophetic tradition, especially the books of Nahum and Isaiah. Prophetic judgments of Assyrian arrogance were seen to be vindicated in these events.

The destruction of Jerusalem in 587 gave final confirmation to Isaiah's prophecy of YHWH's judgment against the Judean kingdom, even though Assyria, the agent of wrath for two centuries, had by then been superseded by Babylonia. So it was Babylonia, rather than Assyria, that fulfilled the prophetic threat—not only of Isaiah, but also of Micah, Zephaniah, Jeremiah and Ezekiel. The Babylonian destruction of Judah was an event of unparalleled importance for prophetic theology, for it validated the prophetic interpretation of Israel's history. It is unlikely that the prophetic oracles would have been preserved if this event had not occurred.

Though Isaiah's oracles may owe their preservation to the fall of Judah, their merit is not determined solely by the correlation between his prophecies and the subsequent events of history. Their intrinsic value exceeds their predictive worth, though the latter is not unimportant. Isaiah's chief oracle on Assyria is in 10:5-19, its poetic felicity and moral perception standing out among the canonical oracles on foreign nations. It presupposes that the ultimate authority behind the Assyrian rule is YHWH, and it interprets the Assyrian conquest of Samaria and Jerusalem as YHWH's judgment against a godless nation. It is not necessary for the conqueror to interpret his conquest as YHWH's work in order for him to fulfill YHWH's purpose. On the contrary, according to Isaiah's oracle, the conqueror puts quite a different construction on his victory, imagining himself a godlike personage autonomous in his power, with lieutenants who are the equal of kings. Obviously YHWH, regarded by the Assyrian as one of the lesser deities among "the kingdoms of the idols" which he has conquered, means nothing to him. Thus the prophet depicts a figure of overweening pride, the supremely arrogant ruler.

The original Isaian oracle ends with a probing question which penetrates to the heart of the issue of the source and limit of political power.[2] Its rhetorical effectiveness is due in part to its understatement:

> Shall the ax vaunt itself over the one who wields it,
> or the saw magnify itself against the one who handles it?
> As if a rod should raise the one who lifts it up,
> or as if a staff should lift the one who is not wood! (10:15)

The moral is pointed in verse 12:

> When the Lord (*'adonay*) has finished all his work on Mount Zion and on Jerusalem, he will punish the arrogant boasting of the king of Assyria and his haughty pride.

This last line, prose in an otherwise poetic oracle, may be an expansion of the original oracle. It links the fortunes of the Assyrian king (who is assumed to be, but never specified as the proud speaker in the poem) specifically to the fortunes of Zion/Jerusalem. By contrast, the poem views the Assyrian's treatment of Jerusalem as one among many of his arrogant deeds. Isaiah 10:16-19, a further expansion, describes the eventual punishment of the Assyrians in detail. It does not contradict the intention of the poem, but it is a somewhat prosaic explication. The biting sarcasm of verse 15 is rhetorically economical. The poem ends with a question that is stark in formulation and probing in intent. In exactly the same way, the prophetic commission in Isaiah 6 and the dialogue with Ahaz in 7:1-9 conclude—with a rhetorically simple but provocative statement. This economy of expression is obscured by the prose expansion, even though the meaning of the poem is not altered.

The ultimate and, in many ways, most interesting example of the redactors' work on the Assyrian motif is the inclusion of the story of Hezekiah and Sennacherib in Isaiah 36–37, a duplicate of 2 Kings 18:13–19:37, with one significant omission. Second Kings attributes the Assyrian withdrawal from the siege of Jerusalem not only to a nocturnal assault by "an angel of YHWH" on the Assyrian camp (19:35-36), but also to Hezekiah's payment of a huge tribute to Sennacherib (18:14-16). Isaiah 36–37 contains no mention of this tribute, but explains the withdrawal entirely on the grounds of YHWH's miraculous intervention.

The story deals with Sennacherib's siege of Jerusalem in 701. The question of what really happened, and how the complex biblical traditions are to be unraveled, is one of the most vexing questions in biblical historiography. The problem exists in part because the biblical story is not a simple historical record, but an imaginative re-creation of such an encounter; it deals with real events and real people, but in an imaginative way. Reconstructing history from the story is difficult if not impossible, but it is possible to make sense of it as a prophetic narrative. Its purpose in the book of Isaiah is to support faith in YHWH as the Lord of all people and the only power worthy of ultimate trust; in this respect it resembles the stories in Esther, Judith, and Daniel 1–6, although it has a firmer basis in history.

The story in Isaiah 36–37 is based on motifs contained in Isaiah 10:5-15. It also echoes 10:16 ("Therefore the Lord, YHWH of hosts, will send wasting sickness among his stout warriors . . . ." cf. 37:36). But 10:16, part of the secondary expansion (vss 16-19) of the original oracle, could be dependent upon the prose tale, rather than the other way around. However, the Assyrian's boasting and his condescension toward the God of Israel in the prose story are developments of the two principal themes of Isaiah's older poetic oracle (10:5-15).

The tale is well told and filled with drama. We are never really in doubt that the conclusion will be a victory for YHWH and all loyal worshipers of YHWH, but confidence in the outcome does not diminish the emotional tension of the narrative. The climax comes suddenly, and all at once the story is over. In a single night, 185,000 Assyrian soldiers are struck down, and Sennacherib goes home to Nineveh the following morning (37:36-37). Soon afterward, while worshiping an idol, he is assassinated by his sons, a fitting end for a king who mocked YHWH.

The theological point of this story is essentially the same as the one in the oracle in 10:5-15. The difference is that 10:5-15 does not say how long it might take for YHWH's judgment to fall upon the arrogant Assyrian, while in chapter 37, it falls at once. This idea of immediate divine retribution is found also in Deuteronomy 7:9-10:

> Know therefore that the LORD your God is God, the faithful God who maintains covenant loyalty with those who love him and keep his commandments, to a thousand generations, and *repays in their own person those who reject him.* (italics added)

This statement is a deuteronomic adaptation of an old affirmation; the oldest form is found in Exodus 34:6-7 and Numbers 14:18. The deuteronomist modified the affirmation in the same way the deuteronomic writer of Isaiah 36–37 (2 Kings 18–19) modified the prophecy in Isaiah 10:5-15. Both the creedal statement in its oldest form and the Isaianic oracle testify to the righteousness of YHWH in punishing iniquity, but neither attempts to spell out how or when this punishment comes about. By contrast, both Deuteronomy 7:9 and Isaiah 36–37 do exactly that—they chart the workings of divine justice. Between Isaiah's oracle in 10:5-15, with its understated, probing question ("Does the ax vaunt itself over the one who wields it?"), and the prose narrative in 36–37, with its notion of immediate retributive justice, there are several other texts in First Isaiah on YHWH's judgment of Assyria (14:24-27; 30:31; 31:8). These texts express the assurance of divine judgment, but they do not contain a timetable for it. Isaiah 14:24-27 is significant because it specifically prophesies the end of Assyrian control of the land of Israel. This was a major point of Judean and prophetic concern, probably more important than the question of Assyria's status among the great powers.

A PROPHETIC MONTAGE

The interpretation of the fortunes of Judah and Assyria in First Isaiah is a prophetic montage created by successive generations of writers. No single historical situation can account for it; thus we must imagine a series of situations marked by major events in Judah's history. First there was the Syro-Israelite invasion of Judah in 735, which failed because of Assyrian intervention and led to the Assyrian annexation of Syria and Israel (732–722). Next, there was the Assyrian siege of Jerusalem in 701, which was interrupted before the city was destroyed. Then there was the fall of the Assyrian empire itself in 615–612. Finally, there was the destruction of the Judean kingdom and the city of Jerusalem in 598–587. We can imagine a prophetic writer, after each of these events, asking two questions:

What *response* to this event should be made by the people of Judah and their leaders, in order to be faithful to YHWH?

How should we *interpret* what has happened, in light of YHWH's righteous purpose?

The message of First Isaiah focuses on these two questions. The message is consistent throughout Isaiah 1–39 in its theological presuppositions, but it reflects changing responses to the successive events in history. Both these features of the message—continuity and adaptability—are evident in the book. However, we cannot separate the constituent images of the montage neatly, since each image incorporated and adapted previous images in order to create a new unity at each stage. The wonder is that the message retained any coherence at all through this long process.

We can see the montage as a whole and reflect on it at a distance, far removed from the concrete situations of the writers. The images of Syria and Israel, Assyria and Judah, have faded, leaving a relatively simple message: God empowers great kingdoms to rule over peoples, but these kingdoms are short-lived and extremely vulnerable to the devastations of arrogance. The people of YHWH are not called to rule over other peoples, but to pursue quite different goals. Kings in the line of Jesse and David are empowered by YHWH to achieve justice and peace in Israel. At its most authentic, this Davidic rule is noncoercive, relying on the wisdom and insight derived from the knowledge and spirit of YHWH. However, this does not mean that YHWH's rule among the peoples of the world is wholly noncoercive, because rulers need coercive power in order to govern nations. At the same time, peace among nations is both a political hope and a moral responsibility of godly nations and their rulers. That is the essence of the message of First Isaiah.

ZION

The book of Isaiah can be described as the book of YHWH and Zion; that is the theme of the first chapter, and it recurs regularly through the whole book. It is one of the main elements that binds the three Isaiahs together. Since Zion, as place and symbol, is central in the thought of the redactors of the book, it is difficult to identify the specific contribution of Isaiah to this tradition. The Zionism of the later strata is so strong that it has influenced the transmission and redaction of Isaiah's oracles. Particularly important was the conviction that Zion enjoyed the special favor and protection of YHWH, which would cause it to flourish among the peoples of the world and to endure the assaults of its enemies.

From what I have said about the interpretation of the fortunes of Judah and Assyria in First Isaiah, it should be clear that I regard the conviction as expressed in the book, that Zion enjoyed the special favor and protection of YHWH, to have been generated by the termination of the Assyrian siege of Jerusalem in 701 and the decline of the Assyrian empire after 626. The alternative possibility, which some scholars have endorsed, is that the belief in YHWH's protection of Zion against physical assault was adopted by Isaiah from the existing ideology of the Jerusalem cultus. However, this hypothesis is less likely than the other. Among other things, it requires the further hypothesis that Isaiah first endorsed this belief and later abandoned it to prophesy YHWH's punishment of Jerusalem. But whatever may have been the origin of this belief, it was dashed by the Babylonian capture and destruction of Jerusalem in 598 and 587. In its final form, First Isaiah presupposes the destruction of the city and promises its restoration (e.g., 1:24-31; 2:1-5; 4:2-6). The message of Isaiah and that of the Josian redactors have been taken up into the message of the final redactors. Ultimately, this is a more perspicuous message, because it adds to the prophetic insights of Isaiah the lessons drawn from the entire history of the kingdom of Judah.

The place to begin the discussion of the Zion theme is Isaiah 1, not only because it is the first Zion text in the book, but because it contains a summary of what the book says about this theme. From there, we can proceed to examine its further development.

WAYWARD CHILDREN: ISAIAH 1

Isaiah's oracles, like those of the prophets generally, are concerned with social issues more than with personal ones; with Israel's corporate responsibilities more than with the private responsibilities of individuals. The ethics of these oracles are social ethics, and as a result, they seldom deal with the inner dynamics of morality and faith. The primary concern is not with the psychological dimensions of religious behavior, but its public manifestations; deeds take precedence over motives. Nevertheless, Isaiah's oracles do have something to say about the inner workings of faith. This is certainly true of the account of Isaiah's vision, and it is true also of the opening chapter of the book.

The theme of the hardening of Israel's heart, the central theme of YHWH's commission to Isaiah, points to the larger question of the psychology of guilt and, by implication, the psychology of redemption. Chapter 6 does not expound the writer's understanding of the inner dynamics of guilt and redemption, but it does hint at this aspect of religious experience. And so does chapter 1, which traces the process of estrangement from God, as well as reconciliation to God, employing the metaphor of the family:

> Hear, O heavens, and listen, O earth,
> for the LORD has spoken:
> I reared children and brought them up,
> but they have rebelled against me.
> The ox knows its owner,
> and the donkey its master's crib;
> but Israel does not know,
> my people do not understand. (1:2-3)

In these and the following lines, the whole course of the development of the attitudes and manifestations of sin is suggested. The "offspring of evildoers," deeply influenced by their forebears, inwardly "despise the Holy One of Israel" and outwardly "deal corruptly," until "they are utterly estranged" from YHWH (vs 4). Here, in two sentences, is the whole story of moral perversion and religious apostasy, stated so tersely it is easily missed. Let us trace the argument again. Environment and behavior shape disposition, and disposition hardens behavior into habit. This is the spiral of progressive alienation from God, and the end result is total "sickness," from head to toe and inside out (vss 5-6). Obviously, the worship rendered by such people is vain—mere empty ritual, without critical self-awareness or moral earnestness (vss 10-15). Far from promoting knowledge of God and righteousness, it reinforces self-delusion and iniquity.

How can the spiral of alienation be reversed and reconciliation be brought about? The writer was clear about the terms but pessimistic about the prospects, at least as far as Judah was concerned:

> Come now, let us argue it out,
> says the LORD . . . .
> If you are willing and obedient,
> you shall eat the good of the land. (1:18-19)

The sources are dialogue and willingness, the positive disposition of the heart and mind; just behavior is the manifestation (vs 17).

> Zion shall be redeemed by justice,
> and those in her who repent, by righteousness. (vs 27)

This is a future redemption, prophesied for the remnant of the Judean kingdom. Isaiah did not expect the kingdom of Judah to repent; he expected it to fall. The redactors knew that it had already fallen, and they had no difficulty understanding that the promised redemption would be confined to a remnant that repented. The repentance of the remaining Judean community was a genuine possibility in these circumstances; thus Isaiah's personal experience of forgiveness and redemption, which was described in his vision, could be shared by other faithful people.

These texts which relate the inner dynamics of sin and redemption (6:1-9 and 1:2-9) are far too brief for our liking. Nevertheless, they give us some idea of the fundamental aspects of Isaiah's understanding, which, it seems safe to say, is presupposed in his other oracles.

INJUSTICE AND WORSHIP IN ZION

Isaiah 1 continues with a commentary on the ritual of the altar in the temple of Jerusalem. This oracle is Isaiah's clearest word concerning the quality of worship in his time, and since the cultus of the Jerusalem temple was an important factor in the development of the Zion tradition, the oracle is clearly relevant to that theme.

The oracle repudiates the prevailing Judean worship as being unacceptable to YHWH. Tellingly addressed to Jerusalem as "Sodom" and "Gomorrah" (vs 10), the repudiation covers not only the blood sacrifices which formed the core of ritual in the temple (1:11), but the entire system of worship, including the sabbath observance (vs 13) and even public prayer (vs 15). All the religious assemblies are denounced in YHWH's name (vss 13-14).

How is this denunciation to be interpreted? Surely Isaiah was not fundamentally anticultic. On the contrary, his own experience of prophetic call was expressed entirely in cultic imagery. Obviously, his piety was deeply and positively shaped by the liturgies of the temple, yet he denounced that ritual piety. The reason given in the oracle was that the people's "hands [were] full of blood" (vs 15). In one sense, this was exactly what could be expected, since they were offering blood sacrifices (vs 11); yet this allusion is purely ironic, for it is the blood of oppressed persons that the prophet has in mind: When he admonishes the people to "wash" off the blood, he adds, "seek justice, rescue the oppressed, defend the orphan, plead for the widow" (vs 17). The implication is that those whose ritual performances the prophet repudiates are those who are responsible for the subversion of justice and the neglect of the helpless. If they believe that punctilious ritual is all that is required of them as the people of YHWH, then they misconstrue the nature of their special status among the peoples of the world.

Israel's relation with YHWH was marked, and fostered, by ritual observances of various kinds. Few if any of these typical cultic acts were unique in the ancient world. Their uniqueness was solely the result of Israel's unique understanding of the being of YHWH. It was Israel's theology, not the form of their cultic actions, that was distinctive, and their theology, properly understood, had important ethical implications. It was not possible to be truly the people of YHWH and not take responsibility for the fair treatment and well-being of all the members of this community. Blatant disregard of social justice, coupled with punctiliousness in worship, was an abomination in the eyes of the prophetic defenders of Yahwistic faith. This did not mean that individual worshipers must be sinless in order to participate in public worship. On the contrary, elaborate provisions were included in the cultic traditions of Israel for dealing with sin and guilt by means of public worship. What it meant was that the congregation that did not perceive the moral and social dimensions of its service of YHWH did not understand that service at all, and therefore could not be formed and nurtured as the people of YHWH through worship. The worship of such a community was inherently empty (1:13).

Isaiah 1:18-20 proposes a remedy for this emptiness. It involved dialogue with YHWH (vs 18), which meant morally earnest engagement with the Yahwistic tradition, and resolute obedience to YHWH's will (vs 19). The consequence of the people's commitment would be to "eat the good of the land"; if they refused, they would "be eaten by the sword" (vs 20). This conditional understanding of Israel's occupation of the land is expressed most fully in the book of Deuteronomy, and it informs much of the prophetic interpretation of Israel's history.

The remainder of chapter one consists of a prophecy of judgment against the "harlot" city of Jerusalem (1:21-24), corrupted by murder, robbery, and oppression, plus a promise of redemption after the judgment (1:27-31). The judgment is viewed as purging the city of its unrighteous leaders; the redemption is reserved for the repentant righteous ones, from among whom new leaders will be installed. This sequence of events is assumed in most of the references to Zion/Jerusalem in First Isaiah. The redemption comes only after the punishment of the existing populace of the city, and the nation of which it is the capital; thus the redemption presupposes destruction and restoration. Zion is never thought of as invulnerable to military assault (except of course in the legendary account of the Assyrian siege of Jerusalem in Isa 37), but the promise of a new Zion, replacing the old, is a prominent feature of the book, and there is no compelling reason to doubt that it was rooted in the thought of Isaiah himself. Indeed, even in the midst of a prophecy of total desolation for the existing kingdom (8:16-22), he mentions that YHWH dwells on Mount Zion (vs 18). The link between YHWH and this place was clearly very strong in his mind.

The basis of the special relationship of YHWH and Zion in the oracles of Isaiah is primarily moral rather than cultic. There is nothing in 8:16-22 or elsewhere to suggest that the relationship depended upon the temple or the sacrificial cultus. It did depend upon righteousness and justice (cf., e.g., 1:21, 27; 3:1-15; 5:1-7) and prophetic testimony (8:16). Thus it was Isaiah's own words, among others, which needed to be preserved in order to provide a continuous witness to the reality of YHWH's acts and YHWH's demands, upon which the renewal of Zion as YHWH's city depended. It was the witness of faith in the judging and redeeming God, a witness made in Zion, made in Isaiah's time and to be made in the coming age, which forged the link between YHWH and Zion. Without this witness there was nothing special about Zion, but with this witness there was something quite special—it was the very city of God. It is probable that Isaiah, like everyone in ancient Israel and its environment, took for granted that ritual would be performed as a regular part of the life of any community. Therefore, there was no need to make a point of it in his oracles. But the dedication of a community to the moral and social principles of Mosaic Yahwism could not be taken for granted, and it was this that Isaiah made his cause.

Isaiah's conviction that Zion's distinctiveness lay in the righteousness of its people and its testimony to the righteousness of God is echoed in the eschatological oracle in 2:1-4. This oracle appears again in Micah 4:1-4. Its origin and date are unknown, but its teaching is consonant with that of both Isaiah and Micah. It speaks of the exaltation of the "mountain of the house of YHWH," which is, of course, Mount Zion, and of the pilgrimage of many people to this place. At the mountain, the ways and word of Yahweh are taught, and people are judged accordingly; all this is entirely prophetic. There is no mention of a ritual cult, but even if the existence of a temple on Mount Zion is assumed, it is clear that the prophetic word has taken precedence over the sacrificial cult as its raison d'être. And from the teaching and the judging flows the abolition of warfare and the achievement of world peace—that is, the moral fruits of moral education and moral discipline.

The composer of 1:21-31, part of the introductory précis of Isaiah's message, captured one side of the prophet's understanding of redemption well: "Zion will be redeemed by justice, and those in her who repent, by righteousness" (1:27). The other side of the prophet's understanding of redemption was complete trust in the righteousness of God. Isaiah 1:21-31 expresses only the negative, punishing aspect of God's righteousness, not the positive, redemptive aspect that is prominent in most of the oracles of promise in First Isaiah. Thus it is not a fully adequate summary of Isaiah's message, or that of the redactors. Moreover, the text goes on in verse 28 to express an ethical dualism, a rather simple division between the righteous and the unrighteous, which seems to contradict Isaiah's understanding of the universality of sin ("Woe is me! . . . for I am a man of unclean lips!" 6:5). By contrast, the opening line of the passage could have been uttered by the prophet himself.

The prophets' elevation of ethical above ritual factors in the relationship of Israel and God, coupled with their rejection of all forms of magic and idolatry, represented a desacralizing of much that was sacred in popular religious practice, but a sanctifying of the ordinary realm of morality and social interaction. To secular eyes, the process may appear to be a mere secularization of the sacred, but to the eyes of faith, it is one aspect of the prophetic sanctification of the world.

Isaiah's critique of the immorality and injustice in the city of Jerusalem is incisive and thorough, and it culminates consistently in a prophecy of doom. Chapter 3 is the fullest example: Arrogant selfishness, greed, and oppression of the poor are the main charges against the dominant class of the city (3:9-15); the consequences predicted are social upheaval (3:1-8) and captivity (3:16-26). The prophecy of captivity was a conventional feature of prophetic oracles of judgment, but since it was not often fulfilled, it probably lacked credibility in the minds of the national leaders to whom it was directed. It does present an oversimplified picture of the relation of social morality to world events, but this imprecision in the analysis of historical cause and effect does not invalidate Isaiah's moral critique or the ethical ideals that it presupposes. The whole point of Isaiah's witness was not to change the course of action in the kingdom of Judah, but to inform and motivate faithful Yahwists in days to come. According to the report of his call (Isa 6), he knew his prophesying would not redeem the hard hearts in contemporary Judah, but harden them further. The benefits of his work would accrue only to the faithful remnant, and it was for them that his testimony was preserved.

There are two Zion-prophecies in the later chapters of First Isaiah (29:1-8; 31:4-9). These are a composite of Isaianic ethical critique, retrospective reflection on the deliverance of Jerusalem in 701, and idealistic eschatology. Once again, the purpose of these oracles is to instruct and inspire the faithful in succeeding generations. They underscore the importance of righteousness among the people of God and the reality of God's work in their lives. For this reason, and because they have been revised and expanded over time, their historical allusions are blurred and their authorship indeterminate. Taken together, the oracles of Zion in First Isaiah affirm that God can be trusted to preserve and empower a community of faithful people "in Zion," who seek justice and bear prophetic witness to the righteousness of God. The keynote of this Isaian Zionism is sounded in 28:16:

> See, I am laying in Zion a foundation stone,
>   a tested stone,
> a precious cornerstone, a sure foundation:
>   "One who trusts will not panic."
> And I will make justice the line,
>   and righteousness the plummet;
> hail will sweep away the refuge of lies,
>   and waters will overwhelm the shelter.

This is ethical rather than nationalistic Zionism. Elements of the latter are present in First Isaiah, but they reflect the views of other writers, not those of

Isaiah himself; they are inconsistent with the view so powerfully expressed in oracles that have the strongest claim to be his own.

THE DAY OF WRATH

The oracles of Isaiah contain words of redemption, but they are relatively few, and they point to a redemption that follows a time of destructon. The dominant word is the word of God's wrath. The tone of Isaiah's message was established unmistakably by the narrative of his call (Isa 6). Only after every last bit of the sinful nation had gone through the fire of judgment could a purified sapling—a remnant—spring from the charred stump. So Isaiah's work was mainly a labor of wrath—redemptive in the end for a few, but laden with doom for the nation. The wrath of which he spoke, in a brilliant series of woe and doom oracles, was not a personal sentiment, but a response to the quality of the age in which he lived, an expression of the wrath of God.

Those oracles are found in 2:6-22; 5:8-24; and 9:8–10:4, each of which is a serial composition. The first is formed by the refrain in 2:10, 19, and 21; the second by the sixfold "Woe!" in 5:8, 11, 18, 20, 21, 22; and the third by the refrain in 9:12, 17, 21, and 10:4. The repetitions intensify the emotional impact of the oracles, deepening the sense of foreboding. Consider sections of the oracles in chapter 5:

> Woe to those who join house to house, who add field to field!
> Woe to those who rise early in the morning to run after strong drink!
> Woe to those who draw iniquity with cords of falsehood!
> Woe to those who call evil good and good evil!
> Woe to those who are wise in their own eyes!
> Woe to those who are heroes at drinking wine . . .
> who acquit the guilty for a bribe and cheat the innocent of his right!
> (vss 8, 11, 18, 20, 21, 22 RSV)

More somber still is 9:8–10:4, which denounces the northern kingdom of Israel (9:9), partly, it seems, for its role in the Syro-Israelite invasion of Judah (vs 21), but for much else as well, especially oppression of the poor and needy (10:1-2). Each section of the poem ends with the dread refrain, "For all this (YHWH's) anger is not turned away; his hand is stretched out still!" The wrath of God proclaimed in these oracles is to be seen not only in the eventual end of the nation, but in the moral dissolution of Israelite society in Isaiah's time. Wrath is not primarily a sentiment attributed to God, but a reality of history, the fateful progress of injustice and oppression in social relations and international affairs, which eventually make life a hell.

The evils decried in these oracles run the gamut from intertribal violence (9:20-21), land-grabbing (5:8), and perversion of justice (5:23; 10:1-2), to arrogant self-assurance (9:9-10) and denial of the reality of God (5:12, 18). Similar accusations occur elsewhere in Isaiah's oracles, but these have the special mark of the drumbeat of doom sounding through them, the relentless repetition of God's determination to destroy.

Isaiah's supreme expression of wrath is the poem on the day of YHWH in 2:6-22. The objects of that wrath are human arrogance (vss 12-17) and its manifestations: militarism, amassing of wealth, and idolatry (vss 6-8). The concreteness of these accusations contrasts with the vagueness of later eschatological prophecy, including Isaiah 24-27, with which Isaiah 2 has certain affinities, including the idea of universal judgment. The repetitions heighten the rhetorical effect. Note the threefold repetition in the accusation: "Their land is filled with . . . and there is no end to their . . . ." This repetition is echoed in the threefold repetition of the verbs *humble/bring low* in verses 9, 11, and 17, and again in the threefold warning to hide before YHWH's terror, in verses 10, 19, and 21. The tenfold repetition of *against* in the middle of the poem sounds like the voice of doom itself (the following translation is mine).

Surely you have forsaken your people, the
house of Jacob;
for they are filled with eastern soothsayers
like the Philistines,
and they swarm with alien offspring.
Their land is filled with silver and gold,
and there is no end to their treasures.
Their land is filled with horses,
and there is no end to their chariots.
Their land is filled with worthless gods.
They worship their own handiwork,
the things their fingers have made.
So humans are humbled and people brought low.
Do not forgive them! (2-9)

Get behind rocks and hide in the dirt,
before the terrible presence of YHWH,
and before his exalted majesty.
The lofty countenance of human beings will fall,
and the pride of people bow down.
And YHWH alone will be exalted in that day. (10-11)

Surely YHWH of hosts has a day,
against everything proud and exalted,
against everything lofty and [high],
against all the cedars of Lebanon, exalted and lofty,
against all the oaks of Bashan,
against all the exalted mountains,
against all the lofty hills,
against every tall tower,
against every fortified wall,
against all the ships of Tarshish,
against all the elegant fleet. (12-16)

And the pride of human beings will bow down,
  and the arrogance of people be brought low.
And YHWH alone will be exalted in that day,
  and the idols will vanish completely. (17-18)

Get into caves in the rock and holes in the ground,
    before the terrible presence of YHWH,
    and before his exalted majesty,
  when he rises to shake the earth. (19)

In that day human beings will throw away
  to the moles and the bats
their idols of silver and idols of gold,
  which they made for themselves to worship,
to get into holes in the rocks and cracks in the cliffs,
    before the terrible presence of YHWH,
    and before his exalted majesty,
  when he rises to shake the earth. (20-21)

Leave humans alone, in whose nostrils is breath,
  for of what account are they? (22)

Here the negative implications of YHWH's holiness, expressed also in the commission of Isaiah (6:9-13), are described in a scene of universal terror. The image of YHWH "rising to shake the earth" is a metaphor suggested by the great military conquerors who terrorized the ancient world. In fact, the prophet must have expected the agent of YHWH's terror to be a military conqueror. It is significant that in his view, this act would be an act of YHWH. Everything that happened to the "house of Jacob"—that is, the whole people of Israel—in the great events of their history was the working out of God's righteous will for them. In this case, God's righteousness expressed itself in wrath against a godless and unjust society. In other circumstances, the outcome might be quite different; yet in all circumstances, Israel's life was an engagement with YHWH. The people's existence was inescapably theocentric.

Apart from the reference to the house of Jacob in the first line, this scene involves not only Israelites, but human beings generally. Thus the day of wrath is universal; or, in nonmetaphorical terms, the existence of all human beings is theocentric. This certainly was Isaiah's view, as, for example, his oracle against the Assyrian king shows (10:5-15). Nevertheless, understanding one's existence theocentrically and responding appropriately to the reality of God are acts of faith; therefore Isaiah's oracles make sense only to those who have faith in God, and it is to such persons that they are addressed.

Isaiah believed that he lived in an age of wrath, and his oracles were heavily weighted with moral accusation and divine judgment. The fundamental theological assumptions upon which they were based, however, were not negative, but the positive foundations of a just society and authentic human existence. His oracles emphasize moral responsibility, the limits of human freedom, and the consequences of inordinate pride. There is little mention of blessings, or the benefits of being the people of YHWH. Certainly in his view, the religious community had no special political advantage over others. The favor of God was not something to be manipulated for a nation's aggrandizement. The clear implication of his message is that blessing comes primarily in the quest for social justice and in righteous service of the common good.

ISAIAH 13–23

This group of oracles on foreign nations has its counterpart in Jeremiah 46–51 and Ezekiel 25–32. The theme of YHWH and the nations, and its corollary of Israel and the nations, run through most of the Hebrew Bible; therefore the general subject of these oracles is not distinctive, and neither is the theme of national judgment, since it is the theme of nearly half the prophetic oracles concerning Israel. What is distinctive about these oracles is that they are not balanced by oracles of salvation for the foreign nations. Although the theme of salvation for the nations occurs in a few places in Second and Third Isaiah, and in one notable passage in Isaiah 13–23 (19:19-24), it is not characteristic of Hebrew prophecy. The overarching message of the prophets concerning the foreign nations is a message of judgment and doom.

The origin of such oracles may have been the ritual cursing of enemies (cf. Balak's engagement of Balaam for this purpose, Num 22:1-6 and following chaps), though this is only a hypothesis. The meaning of the extant oracles would not be affected by a determination of the original setting of the genre, but it would give us a better understanding of their purpose.

The first cursing of a foreign people in the Bible is Noah's curse of Canaan in Genesis 9:25-27. From this point in the bibical story, the conflict between Israel and the nations is a constant theme, though it is interwoven with the theme of accommodation between Israel and the nations. The stories of Jacob and Esau, Jacob and Laban, and Joseph and the Egyptians illustrate the interplay of these two themes in the early traditions of Israel, and the entire Deuteronomic History (Joshua–2 Kings) carries it on until the time of the Babylonian destruction of Jerusalem. The climax of the Pentateuchal story, which became the paradigm of the redemptive work of YHWH in the Hebrew Bible, is the story of YHWH's deliverance of Israel from Egypt through the destruction of the Egyptian oppressors. The pharaoh in the book of Exodus is the prototypical enemy of God and oppressor of God's people. The destruction of the pharaoh's forces is justified morally on the grounds of his enormous cruelty to the Hebrew slaves and his refusal to relent.

The conflict with the Canaanites has a different motivation, though the dispossession of the Canaanites is linked to the exodus story by means of the promise of settlement in the land (e.g., Exod 3:8). But the religious motive of the anti-Canaanite polemic is to eliminate Israel's greatest temptation to idolatry. The elimination of idolatry in Israel and Israel's environment is one of the main themes of the Deuteronomic History. Not surprisingly, the elimination of idolators is one of the themes of the prophetic oracles against foreign nations.

The Judean royalist tradition provides a further background for these oracles. The imperial aspirations of the Davidic kings were sanctioned by the royal psalms (Pss 2, 18, 20, 21, 72, 89, 101, 110, 132, 144:1-11), which may have been recited in the temple of Jerusalem. YHWH's promise of hegemony over the nations is celebrated (Ps 2), sometimes in reference to Syria-Palestine (72:8; 89:25), and YHWH's support against the enemies of the Israelite kings is sought and expected (18:34-45; 21:8-12; 144:1-11).

All the nations that appear in Isaiah 13–23 appear also in Jeremiah 46–51 or Ezekiel 25–32, or both, except Assyria, which is mentioned very briefly in Isaiah 14:24-27. It is omitted from the other two collections, perhaps because Assyria ceased to be a factor in international politics before the oracles in Jeremiah and Ezekiel were composed. The virtual omission of Assyria and the prominence of Babylon in Isaiah 13–23 (13:1-22; 14:3-23; 21:1-10) suggest a date long after the time of Isaiah. Isaiah's own oracle on Assyria is contained in 10:5-15. The order of the oracles does not appear to have great significance, though the ones in 13–21 are arranged in an approximate geographic order from east to west, with oracles on Babylon at the beginning and the end. The Tyre oracle in 23:1-18 is separated from the rest by an oracle against Judah in chapter 22, so it may be a later addition. The oracles in Jeremiah 46–51 and Ezekiel 25–32 also are arranged in approximate geographic order—in Jeremiah, from west to east; in Ezekiel, as in Isaiah, from east to west—but this principle appears to be merely aesthetic. The date of the oracles is indeterminate.

We may distinguish between oracles concerning the imperial nations—Egypt and Babylon—and those concerning the small neighboring nations—Philistia, Edom, Moab, Ammon, and Aram (Damascus). There are major Egypt-oracles in all three collections, and major Babylon-oracles in Isaiah and Jeremiah, but strangely, none of the latter in Ezekiel. Oracles on Israel's neighbors appear in all three books, though there are more in Jeremiah (5) than in the other two (3 each). With these groups, we also should compare the oracles against six neighboring nations in Amos 1–2.

There are many similarities between the oracles on the imperial nations and those on the smaller ones. The principal difference relates to the parts these nations played in international relations. Egypt and Babylon are denounced repeatedly because they display the colossal arrogance of the very powerful, and because of their abuse of power in the wholesale oppression of other nations. The crimes of the small nations are similar in kind, but on a much smaller scale.

Throughout these long stretches of denunciation, the nations essentially are accused of only three crimes: The two most frequent are pride and international violence; the third is idolatry, which is much less frequent than in the oracles of judgment against Israel. This seems appropriate, since in prophetic perspective, Israel, knowing the will of YHWH, had no excuse, while the other nations did not have such knowledge. The punishment imposed by YHWH for the nations' wickedness is always the same—death and destruction, sometimes including mockery by other nations.

This summary shows that essentially, the content of these oracles is sharply focused upon one idea—that YHWH punishes nations for arrogance, violence, and idolatry by destroying them. The importance of this idea here is that it is an affirmation of the universality of YHWH's sovereignty over the peoples of the world, and therefore, implicitly, of the ultimate unity of the peoples. Thus the oracles of YHWH's judgment on the nations reaffirm what is asserted in the story of Noah (Gen 6–9) and in the table of the nations (Gen 10): All humankind is one family, created and ruled by one God.

Whether it is true that nations fall for the reasons mentioned in these oracles is both a historical and a theological question, closely related to whether the fall of Israel and Judah occurred for the reasons adduced by the prophets. Undoubtedly, the oracles on the foreign nations apply the formula of divine retribution too simply; the factors in the fall of nations are complex and not always the same. However, the main point of the oracles is not to analyze history, but to remind Israel of the destructive effects of arrogance, oppression, and idolatry in the life of a nation, and in relations among nations. Thus the oracles serve the purpose of instruction, but they also provide reassurance for victims of international conflict and oppression, and confirmation of their trust in the righteousness of God.

Isaiah 13–23 contains some vivid poetry. Particularly impressive are the taunt song on the Babylonian tyrant in 14:4-21 ("How the oppressor has ceased, the insolent fury ceased!" vs 4); the lamentation over the destruction of Moab in 15:1–16:11 ("My heart cries out for Moab," 15:5); and the poem on Ethiopia in 18:1-7 ("a land of whirring wings . . . a nation tall and smooth," vss 1-2).

The sympathetic attitude expressed in the lamentation over Moab contrasts sharply with the vindictiveness of the oracle on Philistia in 14:28-31—"The first-born of the poor will graze, and the needy will lie down in safety; but I will make your root die of famine, and your remnant I will kill" (vs 30). Were Judah's relations with Moab so much better than those with Philistia, or were these simply the sentiments of two different writers?

The prophetic sign in Isaiah 20 is a classic. It is one of only two concerning foreign nations (Jer 51:59-64 is the other), though it is actually a warning to Judah not to get mixed up in an anti-Assyrian alliance with Egypt and Ethiopia.

The most remarkable of all the oracles on foreign nations is the one on Egypt in Isaiah 19:16-24, a series of five prose statements, all beginning with the eschatological formula, "In that day." The first is typically antiforeigner, but the rest are entirely positive. The second speaks of the existence of five Hebrew-speaking cities in Egypt—that is, Jewish cities. The third speaks of an altar to YHWH in the middle of Egypt and of YHWH's self-revelation to the Egyptians, who will thus come to know and be healed by YHWH. The fourth speaks of an international highway between Egypt and Assyria, which will promote religious ecumenism. Finally, the fifth makes this astonishing prophecy:

> On that day Israel will be the third with Egypt and Assyria, a blessing in the midst of the earth, whom the LORD of hosts has blessed, saying, "Blessed be Egypt my people, and Assyria the work of my hands, and Israel my heritage."

This is a radical word, especially in the midst of so many denunciations. The author of this text is unknown, and so are its date and historical setting, but its theological and ethical implications are important.

ISAIAH 24–35

The message of deliverance in First Isaiah is largely the work of later writers. Isaiah spoke of Israel's future beyond the day of wrath only in terms of a purified remnant; for him, the main function of Israel's enemies, in YHWH's plan, was to carry out YHWH's judgment against Israel. However, other oracles, primarily in 24–35, express different expectations. In these, YHWH takes the side of Israel against the enemies and saves even the city of Jerusalem from foreign conquest. These materials reflect, in part, the optimism generated by the deliverance of Jerusalem from Assyrian siege in 701 and, in part, the eschatological longings of the exilic age. The optimism of the seventh century is evident, particularly in the redaction of 28–32 (e.g., 29:1-8; 31:4-9) and the longings of the exile in 24–27 and 33–35. Because there is so much Isaianic material worked into 28–32, this section shares the same moral earnestness that is the hallmark of the first part of the book (1–11)—specific moral criticism of the people of God, and the general impression that the historical destiny of the people is tied up with the moral quality of its life.

This ethical perspective is not completely alien to 24–27 or 33–35, but the emphasis and mood of these sections are quite different. These chapters express a firm faith in a righteous God, and their immediate intention appears to be to encourage such faith. For example, see 26:3, "Those of steadfast mind you keep in peace—in peace because they trust in you," and 33:2, "O LORD be gracious to us; we wait for you." Both these examples focus on individual believers. The kingdom of Judah has receded from view. The judgment of God which is prophesied is universal, and therefore emotionally distant and irrelevant to the historic concerns of the kingdom of Judah. In 24–27, the coming judgment is so vast that it includes even "the host of heaven in heaven" (24:21; cf. 34:4).

There is an occasional note of discriminating justice in these chapters (e.g., 33:1; 25:10-12; 26:5-6), but usually justice takes the form of oppressing the oppressor—that is, reversing injustice rather than abolishing it. An even stronger motif is judgment for all, a leveling, undiscriminating judgment:

> Now the LORD is about to lay waste the earth and
>   make it desolate,
>   and he will twist its surface and scatter
>   its inhabitants.
> And it shall be, as with the people, so with the priest;
>   as with the slave, so with his master;
>   as with the maid, so with her mistress;
> as with the buyer, so with the seller;
>   as with the lender, so with the borrower;
>   as with the creditor, so with the debtor.
>   (24:1-2; cf. 24:17-23; 34:1-4)

On the surface, there is an affinity between such texts and Isaiah 2:6-22, but there are major differences as well. Isaiah 2:6-22 is directed against human pride, while Isaiah 24 is directed against human beings as such. In addition, 2:6-22 is bracketed by chapter 1 and chapter 3, filled with sharply focused criticism of concrete social evils. Isaiah 24–27 and 33–35 condemn sinful humanity in abstract, general terms, while the oracles of Isaiah condemn specific sins. Isaiah was aware that all human beings, including himself, were "unclean" in the presence of the holy God (6:5-7). However, this awareness did not overwhelm his moral discrimination. His oracles display keen, discriminating ethical judgment. The writers of 24–27 and 33–35 had completely different interests and sensibilities, arising out of a completely different historical situation. The theological questions that preoccupied the Jews of the exilic and postexilic periods were not the same as those that preoccupied Isaiah and his contemporaries in the eighth century, or even their followers in the seventh.

Isaiah 24–27 is important to most readers of the Bible primarily because of its allusion to resurrection of the dead in 26:19 and the abolition of death in 25:8. If 26:19 does indeed affirm resurrection of the dead, it is the only text in the prophetic literature to do so. The other prophetic text that is popularly thought to do so is Ezekiel 37, the famous vision of the dry bones. However, Ezekiel 37 actually is a parable of the restoration of the community of Israel and has nothing to do with the resurrection of physically dead persons. The enfleshing of the bones is purely metaphorical: The "bones" are the defeated, discouraged Jews who were suffering in Babylonian captivity. The only other passage in the Hebrew Bible to affirm resurrection is Daniel 12:2, an apocalyptic text from the second century BCE, when ideas of life after death began to enter Jewish thought from the religious environment. In the book of Job, the suffering Job asks wistfully whether one might live again after dying (14:14), like a sapling sprung from a dead tree (vss 7-9). The notion is attractive to him because, if it were possible, he might have an extension of time to be vindicated in the eyes of God (vss 15-17). However, he can answer the question only negatively (vss 18-22). As far as we can tell from the Bible, this was the conviction of all the writers in the age of the prophets.

In any case, it is clear that neither Isaiah himself nor his redactors were concerned with the question of individual mortality; they were concerned with the moral life and death of the community of Israel. Even Isaiah 26:19, when it is read in context, expresses concern for the community of the faithful, not the mortality of the individual. In verse 14, the revival of physically dead persons, in this case the alien lords who have ruled the people of YHWH, is denied, and consolation is drawn from this fact. Therefore, when the writer soon afterward affirms that "the dead will live, my body will rise" (vs 19 MT), he is speaking metaphorically. The death that he and other faithful Yahwists suffer is social and political, and also moral and religious, like the "death" suffered by the "bones" in Ezekiel's vision. On the other hand, 25:7, "[YHWH] will swallow up death forever," does appear to refer to physical death, though here the idea is not life after death through resurrection, but life without any death at all. The wish for such life is natural, though the actual expression of that hope is extremely rare in the Hebrew Bible.

THE LAST WORD IN FIRST ISAIAH

The redactor had the last word in Isaiah 1–39 by placing the historical excerpt from 2 Kings at the end. As a result, the last word, strictly speaking, is the prophecy of the Judean exile in Babylon (39:5-8), reportedly delivered by Isaiah to King Hezekiah. This word sets the stage for the great proclamation of deliverance from exile in 40–55.

In another sense, the last word of the redactor is the overall impression created by the ordering of 1–39. The composition begins with the précis of Isaiah's message about Jerusalem/Zion in chapter 1, and comes to a climax in the story of the miraculous salvation of Jerusalem from the Assyrians in 36–37. The effect of this inclusive arrangement is to highlight all the anti-Assyrian and pro-Zion texts in the intervening chapters. These themes constitute the double cord that laces the whole garment together. When we consider the centrality of Jerusalem/Zion in 40–66, it is not surprising to find that it dominates 1–39 too. The last part of the book, 56–66, was written in and for the religious community centered in the second temple of Jerusalem. Evidently it was someone in that community who compiled the whole book and gave it its character as a book of Zion, and the religious and political impact of that remarkable achievement is still being felt today.

FROM FIRST TO SECOND ISAIAH

At several points in this and the previous chapter, I have referred to the seventh-century redaction of Isaiah's oracles, in response to the deliverance of

Jerusalem from the Assyrian siege in 701 and the fading of Assyrian imperial control in Syria-Palestine later in the century. I have also mentioned the possibility of a seventh-century date for the composition of the royal oracles in Isaiah 1–39. These literary developments expressed the confidence of Judahites in God's succor of the kingdom and its Davidic sovereign, the anointed of YHWH. Despite Judah's small size, or perhaps because of it, the kingdom survived the remainder of Hezekiah's reign (to ca. 687) and the nearly half-century reign of Manasseh (to ca. 640), thanks to its acceptance of its status as a vassal of Assyria.

When Assyria's power waned after the death of Ashurbanapal (ca. 625), Judean hopes soared, and Josiah, zealous for YHWH, seized the day by asserting Judean control over the territories once ruled by David and purging them of idolatrous cult practices. This was the era of Zionistic and messianic optimism, and it is most likely that the principal redaction of the Isaiah tradition occurred at that time. This was a significant phase in the development of the prophetic witness, although it did not rank in importance with the contribution of Isaiah or that of his exilic successor, Second Isaiah. That anonymous poet of the sixth century brought the prophetic faith to its fullest theological expression, and it is to his achievement that we now turn our attention.

SELECT BIBLIOGRAPHY

Jenkins, A. K. "The Development of the Isaiah Tradition in Isaiah 13–23." *The Book of Isaiah*, ed. J. Vermeylen. Leuven: University Press, 1989.

Johnson, Dan G. *From Chaos to Restoration: An Integrative Reading of Isaiah 24–27*. *JSOT*Sup 61. Sheffield: *JSOT*, 1988.

Kaiser, Otto. *Isaiah 13–39*. Philadelphia: Westminster Press, 1974.

Miller, William R. *Isaiah 24–27 and the Origin of Apocalyptic*. Harvard Semitic Monographs 11. Missoula, Mont.: Scholars Press, 1976.

See also Select Bibliography at end of previous chapter.

NOTES

1. On the subject of monarchy in Israel, esp. its religious dimensions, see John Gray, *The Biblical Doctrine of the Reign of God* (Edinburgh: T. & T. Clark, 1979), and A. R. Johnson, *Sacral Kingship in Ancient Israel* (Cardiff: University of Wales, 1955).

2. See R. E. Clements, *Isaiah 1–39*, New Century Bible Commentary (Grand Rapids: Eerdmans, 1980), p. 113.

CHAPTER FIVE

Isaiah 40–55

SECOND ISAIAH

Biblical prophecy achieves its highest development in Isaiah 40–55. Formally, the book, as I will call it for convenience, is a great artistic achievement, and theologically, it is unsurpassed. Here the prophetic interpretation of Israel's story reaches its climax. The writer draws out the full implications of prophetic faith in an all-encompassing vision of human redemption. In time, the vision ranges from the remote past to the unseen future. In scope, it reaches from Jerusalem to Babylon and the ends of the earth. The prophet never loses sight of Israel's unique role in the drama of history, but he interprets it in a daring new way. Traditional national concerns are transmuted into a universal perspective, and Israel's tragic experience is interpreted as an aspect of the service of God.

The prophet announces a turn of the ages that is taking place before Israel's eyes. A millennium is drawing to a close and another is breaking forth. Astonished by the prospect, he summons the people of Israel to share in the proclamation and, as servants of God, to take part in the unfolding events. The new age will be a time of renewal for the people of Israel, survivors of the fall of Judah and their descendants living in scattered communities in Palestine, Egypt, and Mesopotamia; but more, it will be the age of the universal revelation of God as creator and ruler of all things. This revelation is bound up with the impending collapse of Babylon and its empire (Isa 46; 47), the restoration of Jerusalem (44:27; 51:3ff.; 52:1ff.), and the revival of Israel's corporate existence under the torah of God (42:4; 51:4). But it portends the acknowledgment of God by all peoples (40:5; 41:20; 45:3, 6, 14, 22-25) and God's universal offer of deliverance from injustice and idolatry, fear and despair (42:6-7; 45:22; 49:6; 55:1). It begins at the level of military engagement (41:2ff.) and the longing of prisoners for release (42:7; 49:9, 25); it ends with the promise of the definitive self-disclosure of the one true God (40:8, 27-31; 52:10; 55:1-13). In short, it is both historical and eschatological.

The writer prophesies a world conquest by Cyrus, king of Persia, and the return of Jewish exiles from Babylon to a restored Jerusalem. However, the significance of Cyrus and the return should not be exaggerated. Though these are the principal political elements of the prophet's message, the message is not primarily political. Fundamentally, it is a summons to Israel to serve God in new ways, in a new world situation, defined by the decline of Babylonian power and the rise of Cyrus. But the situation itself is neither the ground of the prophet's hope nor the goal of his summons; it is merely the setting for Israel's service. To be sure, the new historical moment is not to be missed: Obedience in the present situation is crucial for Israel's service, and for its continued service in new situations that emerge. Any change in circumstances may affect the mode and scope of that service, but it does not alter its fundamental quality. And that quality is defined in religious terms. Cyrus's military success and political policies provide the present occasion for the service, but its motivating force and rationale are Israel's knowledge of God. Moreover, although God can be known only through the actuality of human experience, God's being is never exhausted by it. On the contrary, God is the transcendent eternal ground of all experience. It is God who gives meaning to history, not the other way around. And it is Israel's knowledge and service of God that constitute the focus of the prophet's message. Everything else is subordinate.

IDOLATRY AND FAITH

The moral condition of Israel which the prophet addresses is one of futility and despair, coupled with the persistent temptation to idolatry. In the face of this temptation, he calls for a renewal of faith in God as God really is. The prophet's decisive response to Israel's discouragement is a theological response, a critique of idolatry. This is a radical response, since it deals not with pragmatic social policy or concrete political action, but with the foundations of authentic existence. In the circumstances, this seemingly impractical message is the most practical message possible. Beneath the need for release from prison, or for better economic opportunity, or for new social integration, lies the need for religious understanding, the truth about ultimate reality, the knowledge of God.

The interpreter of Isaiah 40–55 is likely to take the writer's understanding of God for granted and concentrate on his interpretation of history, as if God were well known and history a puzzle. But this emphasis is misplaced, for knowledge of God never can be taken for granted. For the prophet's audience, for the prophet himself, and indeed, for everyone, however great the mystery of history, the being and activity of God are a greater mystery. Ultimately at stake in the writer's analysis of history and summons to obedience is his construal of ultimate reality, his doctrine of God. The crisis of Israel's existence was first a crisis of faith: Idolatry was the root problem.

Israel's temptation to idolatry was not new in the exilic period, but perennial, from the time of its constitution as the people of YHWH. However, during the era of Israel's settlement in Palestine, the Yahwistic religious establishment had been a bulwark against idolatry. This establishment had been corrupted from time to time, but it had always produced advocates of authentic Yahwism who made it impossible for the people to worship worldly gods unchallenged. These advocates were not all cultic officials, but the Yahwistic tradition they defended presupposed cultic institutions and was nourished by them. Since these institutions were largely destroyed along with the Israelite kingdoms, for most of the survivors, the cults of alien gods were the only available options for their regular religious practices. Therefore, Israel's situation during the exile was unprecedented. It was not the introduction of Babylonian gods that was new, for these were already well known to many Israelites, and were, in any case, largely interchangeable with the Assyrian gods, which had been known for a century and a half, and even with the Canaanite gods, which had always been known. Of the many references to idolatry in Isaiah 40–55, only one mentions Babylonian deities specifically (46:1). All the other references are indefinite.

Idolatry was not a superficial thing, the innocent employment of plastic images as aids to devotion. It was an orientation of the mind, a disposition of the heart, a set of values, a way of life. Thus the prophet's attack on idolatry was not merely an attack on images; though some passages in the text satirize the manufacture of images (41:6-7; 44:9-20), the whole point of the satire is to ridicule by trivializing. Under the surface, idolatry was not trivial at all.

A further incentive for Israelites to apostatize from YHWH, in addition to the loss of their traditional cult, was disillusionment over the capacity of YHWH to sustain them. It was a common ancient belief that the fall of a nation demonstrated the weakness of its gods. Also, because national gods generally were localized, for many Israelites, exile from "YHWH's land" would have meant exile from YHWH's sphere of influence, and both these notions were idolatrous, in the deeper sense of the word.

The writer's account of God's way with Israel is a repudiation of idolatrous explanations of their experience. He draws upon convictions expressed by the preexilic prophets, but he draws out implications of Yahwistic faith which his predecessors had not developed. And all this he casts into a new form of prophecy that is persistently positive. It sings in acclamation, calling the faithful to accept God's gift of a new beginning and shape the future by their obedient service.

The dominant theme of preexilic prophecy was interpretation of the dissolution of the Israelite kingdoms as a punishment for religious apostasy and social injustice. Prior to the fall of the kingdoms, the prophetic message included a warning of impending disaster and an exhortation to reform (e.g., Amos 5:6; Isa 1:18-20). However, the oracles of Amos, Hosea, Micah, and Jeremiah were dominated by a foreboding of disaster for the two national states and their cultic establishments. The prophets' call to obedience was predicated on the sure expectation of the fall of the Israelite monarchy. Sometimes their oracles explicitly mentioned a surviving remnant (Amos 5:15; Isa 7:3; 10:20-23), but even when they did not, they presupposed that only a part of the populace would survive the fall. Apart from the question of its cause, the moral issue for these prophets was how to respond to the will of God during and after the fall. The destruction of the kingdom was, at the same time, an opportunity for renewal through the removal of obstacles to Israel's covenantal obedience. This understanding of the fall of the kingdom pervades the book of Hosea and is present in other prophetic writings as well (e.g., Jer 31:31-34; 32:9-15; Isa 8:16-18; 20:20ff.).

In Second Isaiah, the same interpretation of Israel's history is assumed, but the emphasis is different. The new situation of the audience required a new proclamation, with the emphasis upon the new opportunity. The previous history of idolatry and disobedience, which resulted in Israel's oppression by the great powers, is accepted as a record of sin and punishment (Isa 40:2; 42:24-25; 43:24-28), but this history is now to be put out of mind so that every thought can be concentrated upon the new beginning (40:1ff.; 42:9; 43:1ff.). Preoccupation with the past and passivity toward the future were temptations for Israel. The prophet's mission was to counter such attitudes (40:27; 41:10; 42:18-25; 49:14; 50:1-3):

> Do not remember the former things,
>   or consider the things of old.
> I am about to do a new thing;
>   now it springs forth, do you not perceive it?
> (43:18-19)

THE FORMER THINGS AND THE NEW THINGS

This is a major theme in Second Isaiah. The "former things" (41:22; 42:9; 43:9, 18; 46:9; 48:3) and the "new things" (42:9; 43:19; cf. "what is to come" 41:23) are keys to the prophet's interpretation of history; indeed, they point to one of his central arguments for faith in YHWH, the argument from history. Nothing is more important in his theological apologetics, yet the meaning of these terms is not self-evident. Consider beside the lines I have just quoted ("*Do not remember* the former things"), this line: "Remember this and consider . . . *remember* the former things of old" (46:9)!

Many commentators have identified the "former things" and the "new things" with events in the career of Cyrus. In the principal variation of this theory, the former things are the early victories of Cyrus, and the new things apply to his eventual conquest of Babylon.[1] According to this interpretation, the prophet's argument would be that, since YHWH had predicted Cyrus's early victories through a prophet (or prophets), and these had come to pass, therefore the Jewish community should believe the prophecy of Cyrus's conquest of Babylon and trust YHWH to bring that event to pass also.

This theory seems improbable to me. There is no evidence in extant writings that Cyrus's early victories were predicted by a prophet of YHWH before the time of Second Isaiah. Moreover, this explanation trivializes the prophet's grand argument from history, which, as we shall see, encompasses the whole sweep of Israel's experience, from patriarchal times to the present.

An alternative version, which interprets the former things as Cyrus's conquest of Babylon and the new things as his repatriation of the Jewish exiles, is stronger.[2] Some biblical prophecies of Babylon's fall may reasonably be dated earlier than Isaiah 40–55 (e.g., Isa 13; 15:22-23; Jer 51:1-58). One of these cites "the king(s) of the Medes" as conqueror(s) of Babylon (Jer 51:11, 28). Although Cyrus was a Persian, not a Mede, he did become king of the Medes.

This theory is correct in that the prophet's "new things" included the release of imprisoned Jews in Babylon and the rebuilding of Jerusalem, but it is incorrect, I believe, in interpreting the "former things" as Cyrus's conquest of Babylon. All the references to Babylon's fall in Isaiah 40–55 are in the future. The city's fall is not one of the former things, but one of the new things. The scope of the former things, I am sure, is much wider than this interpretation allows.[3]

A much more plausible interpretation is that the former things are the prophecies of First Isaiah.[4] A variation on this view is that they are "the rescues of Jerusalem in the eighth century, as declared beforehand by the prophet [Isaiah]."[5] However, I see nothing in Second Isaiah's references to tie them specifically to the prophecies in First Isaiah, though he may have had those prophecies in mind as a part of the witness which made the former things of YHWH known. Most important in the prior prophetic witness was YHWH's punishment of Israel through destruction of the kingdom and the exile (Isa 40:3). These were the events which marked the end of the former age and the beginning of the new.

The full horizon within which these allusions to the past and future must be viewed—the world-horizon of God's work as creator and sovereign—is sketched by the writer in the opening chapter (Isa 40). Israel has been told "from the beginning . . . from the foundations of the earth" (40:21) of the unique effectiveness and sole sovereignty of God. Allowing for a measure of hyperbole in this assertion, we must surely take it to mean that God has made known to Israel, throughout the entire span of its life, God's relationship to this people and to the rest of the creation. Beside God, the nations, even the great powers that had oppressed Israel, are ephemeral (40:23-25). God's word alone stands forever, while the peoples perish overnight (40:6-8). Therefore, they can trust the God who declares Israel's sin forgiven and the punishment ended (40:1-2), and summons the people to wait in strength (40:31) for the coming revelation of God's glory (40:5). It is the eternal word of God that gathers up the past redemptively and points creatively to the future.

The first and last is YHWH (41:4; 44:6; 48:12), so YHWH alone is God (44:6). He has called the generations of Israel from the beginning (41:4)—that is, from the time of Abraham (41:8; 41:2), and the exodus (52:4), or even from the time of Noah (54:9). God has "declared and saved and proclaimed" (43:12). Of old, God made known "the former things" and then performed them, lest Israel should attribute them to idols (48:3-5). Now God declares "new things" before they come to pass, so that Israel will understand those things too as acts of God (48:6-7). In 43:15-19, the new event is clearly modeled on the exodus from Egypt, through which Israel had come to be the people of YHWH (43:15, 21). In the new exodus, the people would be re-created and given a new commission as witnesses to God's historic salvation.

By contrast, the alien gods stand silent through the changes of history, unable to interpret events or give them moral significance (41:21-24), so that those who worship these gods are incapable of making sense of what has been or is to be (43:9). Only Israel bears witness to the meaning of history and the transcendent sovereignty of the creator (43:10-13). Israel has known the saving acts of God from the beginning as a people. Indeed, Israel is the people whose very existence and self-understanding have been defined by God's saving words and deeds. Now Israel is to be re-created by the same God, in a way that recalls their original creation, but goes beyond it in new dimensions of service.

The injunction not to remember former things (43:18) is a poetic device to call attention to the new things, to concentrate thought and action upon them. However, as models of God's revelation and redemption, the former things must be remembered (41:21; 44:21; 46:8-10; 51:1-2), for they provide indispensable clues to the meaning of Israel's life, for the present and future, as well as in the past.[6] If the former things are the saving and judging acts of God, from ancient times to the downfall of Judah, interpreted by prophets in Israel and thus made morally relevant for the faithful, then the new things, which God is even now beginning to perform (42:9; 43:19), are the whole series of events which mark God's renewal of Israel as servant and witness. This is the essence of the entire prophecy of Isaiah 40–55.

Something important is at stake in the choice among the theories I have described, not only for our understanding of what the writer was saying, but important also for the appropriation of the prophetic witness in our own witness. If the first theory is correct, then the prophet was basing his appeal for faith on the fulfillment of a particular prophecy (of Cyrus's victory). If the theory I have defended is correct, he was basing his appeal on the long tradition of Yahwistic proclamation. Those are two quite different foundations for commitment. The first is a slender reed; the second, the most solid foundation available in human experience. To be sure, to say this does not make the one wrong and the other right, exegetically. But I believe this can be established solely on exegetical grounds, along the lines I have just laid down. And having established it exegetically, we then may properly make capital of it theologically.

The point is sufficiently important to be repeated: The prophet is appealing to believing Yahwists to renew their faith in God and commit themselves in a new way to God's service—that is, to trust that God is doing a new thing; or to put it another way, that it is God who is doing a new thing. The prophet bases his appeal in part on the testimony of history. But the history to which he appeals is the history of faith, that understanding of God and the world which brought Israel into being in the first place, and which sustained Israel as a religious people, from generation to generation. The basis of faith is the story of faith, not some prophecy that turned out to be correct. That kind of argument is weak, as the deuteronomists realized when they conceded that even prophets of false gods could sometimes predict events (Deut 13:1-3). No, the argument used by Second Isaiah involves a deeper understanding of the nature of prophecy. In this argument, prophecy is the theocentric interpretation of all human experience, especially the experience of Israel. It is truly an argument "from faith to faith."

THE REVERSAL OF FORTUNES

In prophetic perspective, God is sovereign in all dimensions of human life. Therefore, God is capable of transforming not only the hearts and minds of people, but also their social and material circumstances, and the promise of such a transformation in Israel's life runs through Isaiah 40–55. It includes the promise that the desert would bloom and the wilderness run with streams of water (41:17-20). However, this should not be taken as the assurance of an instant change in the conditions of soil and climate, but as a poetic celebration of an anticipated improvement in the people's well-being, a general revival of the moribund Israelite community. To interpret the poetry in this way is not to deny the material aspects of the prophet's picture of restoration. At the least, he seems to have envisioned the relief of physical suffering and the satisfaction of common needs (49:9-10; 44:1-3; 42:15-16; 43:19-21).

But beyond this, the recurring suggestion of a dramatic change in the physical condition of the earth (40:4; 42:15-16; 49:11) seems intended as an affirmation of God's freedom as creator. God is not bound absolutely to maintain things as they are, but is able to alter them to serve God's purpose. That God will level mountains and make rivers flow in the desert is surely poetic metaphor, but it is no mere metaphor to assert God's intention to uplift the oppressed and humble the proud (49:7-10, 22-26; 51:7-8, 13-14, 22-23). These and other descriptions of the imminent reversal of peoples' fortunes proclaim the justice of God. God does not abide human injustice and cruelty forever, but finally redresses those wrongs.

This seems to me to be the meaning of the humiliation of kings in 49:22-26. This and related passages in the book (43:3-4; 45:14; 49:7; 51:21-23) have been interpreted by some scholars as straightforward expressions of nationalism,[7] but the sentiments expressed seem more complex than that. The poems do express patriotic pride, and even a certain vengefulness against the despoilers of Israel, yet the chief motives behind these visions of the future must have been disgust at the abuse of the weak by the strong, and a longing for God's justice.

The comment of Morna Hooker on the image of subjugated foreigners in Isaiah 40–55 is exactly to the point. Criticizing Johannes Lindblom's view that the prophecies of subjugation were written early in the prophet's life, and then were superseded by prophecies of salvation for the foreign peoples, she writes, "Lindblom surely underestimates, here, however, not only the considerable element of exaggeration in Hebrew prophecy, but also the different feelings which the author of these oracles must have had for Babylon, the cruel tyrant, on the one hand, and for the rest of the nations, subject like Israel, on the other."[8]

A further consideration in interpreting this imagery of subjugation is that much of it was simply traditional, representing the conventions of the old Israelite cult, which also are preserved in the royal psalms.[9] This imagery also includes exodus typology: Egypt is called a ransom for Israel in the announcement of the new exodus (43:1-2). These images were familiar to the prophet's audience and therefore were useful for kindling their hopes. Talk about the future is couched in terms drawn from the past, so symbols used to interpret the old era (43:16-17; 48:21; 51:9-10) were used to interpret the new as well.

The conquest of nations by a champion empowered by YHWH is a central feature of the prophet's proclamation. We come upon it early in the book (41:1-29). The conqueror in this poem (41:2, 25) is not identified by name, but most commentators conclude that Cyrus was intended, since he is named as the conqueror in a subsequent poem (45:1-7). At one time it was common to see an allusion to the call of Abraham (Gen 12:1) in the reference to the "one aroused from the east" (41:2), and to interpret 41:2-3 as a prophecy of the ultimate reversal of Israel's present political fortunes and the fulfillment of the messianic hopes. However, for some time, only Charles Torrey and James Smart have defended this view. Although there is merit in their arguments, a stronger case can be made for the majority view.[10]

The coming salvation proclaimed by the prophet is the work of YHWH from beginning to end. In accomplishing it, YHWH utilizes two kinds of human agency. One is the military conqueror and political ruler, identified in 45:1 as YHWH's anointed one; the other is the religious leader, variously represented as prophet, teacher, counselor, and lawgiver, and identified in 41:9 (and frequently thereafter) as YHWH's servant. Both these roles are crucial in the unfolding plan of YHWH. The first role is performed by the Persian king, Cyrus; the second by "Jacob"—that is, Israel, the offspring of Abraham (41:8-9). Both are spoken of in extravagant, poetic terms in chapter 41, and are explicated in more realistic terms later. The role of Cyrus is the political implementation of God's justice in the present era of world history, while Israel is the interpreter of history in the light of God's purpose. No other people can perform this service of Israel's, because no one else has the right understanding of the nature and purpose of

God. All the other nations misconstrue reality in idolatrous, polytheistic, and ahistorical terms (41:21-24). Only in faith in YHWH can the meaning and end of history be rightly understood (41:25-29).

Cyrus, anointed by YHWH as ruler, subdues nations and kings so that people throughout the world may know that YHWH alone is God (45:1-7). However, knowing YHWH is not simply a result of the ruler's conquest, but the ultimate result of the historic work of YHWH, which includes Cyrus's conquest, but much more as well. Most important, it includes the creation of a new Israel to be the herald and servant of YHWH, and whose witness to the nations concerning the continuity and scope of YHWH's activity, from the beginning to the present, will put the conquest of Cyrus within a total theological perspective. It is in this sense that the ruler's victories are "for the sake of my servant Jacob, and Israel my chosen" (45:4). Without the witness of Israel to the nations, the ruler's achievement cannot be truly understood. Military conquest by itself demonstrates nothing about God.

Recognizing the ruler's conquest of nations as an act of YHWH presupposes belief in YHWH. Therefore, one is tempted to conclude that the prophet was concerned only with Israel. Undoubtedly he was concerned with Israel first. By identifying the power beyond the world conqueror as none other than YHWH, the prophet meant to reawaken Israel's faith in the covenantal God; but in chapter 45, as elsewhere, the prophet points beyond Israel to all people. The repeated stress in 45:1-7 on the uniqueness of YHWH as creator of all things has universal implications, and the climactic lines mark the final goal of Cyrus's conquest as the acknowledgment of YHWH by all nations (45:6-7). Once again, it should be said that this goal could not be achieved simply by means of a world conquest. This conquest could be no more than the occasion for a worldwide proclamation of God. It is the prophecy, the preaching, the instruction, the law of and about God, that gives religious and moral substance to the historical event. Without these, it remains a mere happening. Kings rise and fall, and yesterday's empire is swept away in a new wave of military power. Where, in this shifting struggle for supremacy, is the clue to ultimate meaning, security, and value? To realize at last that it is not there at all is to be prepared for a word about the origin and purpose of life that is different from the usual word uttered in the name of the gods of the nations. To speak this unique word is the mission of Israel, the servant of YHWH.

If the ultimate goal of the conquest by Cyrus is to prepare people everywhere to acknowledge YHWH, one of the immediate goals of that conquest is to end Babylon's oppressive rule and rescue its victims (43:14; 45:13; 47:1ff.; 48:14, 20). The conquest of Babyon is not mentioned explicitly in the Cyrus passages (44:24–45:13), though it is mentioned in other passages that deal with the conqueror empowered by YHWH.[11] Therefore, the fall of Babylon is understood to be part of the political upheaval described in 44:24–45:7. Babylon's fall would be the just humiliation of an arrogant, idolatrous tyrant (46:1–47:15) and, at the same time, rescue the exiles and political prisoners (48:20).

The promise of return for the Jewish exiles in Babylon has long been regarded as the central feature of Second Isaiah's message. However, it is important to view this event in the perspective of Second Isaiah, not in that represented by Ezra 1–2. The picture of the return of Jewish exiles from Babylon to Jerusalem in Ezra is not the fulfillment of Second Isaiah's hopes; the prophet's vision was large, and his expectation was grand. This is not to say that a return of exiles was incompatible with Second Isaiah's hopes. On the contrary, any real redemption of the Jewish people in the sixth century would have had to include liberation of the important group exiled in Babylonia. For some of them to return to Jerusalem to participate in rebuilding the city would not have been unthinkable to those who cherished the hopes of Second Isaiah, for he promised the rebuilding of Jerusalem (44:26-27; 45:13; 49:14-21), the revitalization of the religious community of Zion (46:13; 51:3; 52:1-2, 7-12; 54:11-14), and the repopulation of Judea (54:1-3). However, the picture in Ezra 1–2 differs from Second Isaiah's in several ways. First, it is a detailed, prosaic description of events after the fact, while Second Isaiah's vision is a lyrical promise. Second, and this is the truly important difference, Ezra 1–2 points toward the creation of an exclusive cultic community in Judea, while Second Isaiah's prophecy points toward the creation of an inclusive society. In this respect, the two are fundamentally incompatible.

The redemption proclaimed by Second Isaiah was not merely religious. It involved marching armies and broad dislocations in political and social life. It was truly worldly, material, historic, and also radically religious. Most wars are religious, in the minds of those who fight them. God is invoked on all sides, and feelings of sanctity and righteousness inspire the warriors. But the new order prophesied in Isaiah 40–55 involved much more than a partisan triumph, sanctioned and empowered by God; it involved the transformation of the minds of people to a new understanding of human existence. It also involved the reordering of human relationships in accordance with the justice of God. In this process of transformation, Israel was to play a prominent part, as both the object and the agent of God's saving work.

ISRAEL, SERVANT OF YHWH

First and last, Israel is "the servant of YHWH," the prophet's characteristic term for the people of God (41:8, 9; 42:19; 43:10; 44:1, 2, 21, 26; 45:4; 48:20; 50:10; 54:17). The term has a long prior history,[12] but Second Isaiah invested it with new meaning and, in doing so, profoundly affected all subsequent biblical theology.

The attention of Christian and Jewish interpreters has centered traditionally on chapter 53;[13] and, during the past century, on the so-called servant songs

(42:1-4; 49:1-6; 50:4-9; 52:13–53:12), which Bernhard Duhm separated from the rest of the book in his commentary of 1892. Most commentators in Germany still follow Duhm's lead, but a growing number of scholars elsewhere regard the four passages as integral parts of the book. This is my own position. The servant motif is prominent in the rest the book, as the list of passages cited above indicates, and I see no adequate grounds for treating the four songs separately. Doing so yields a simpler picture of the servant, both inside and outside the songs, but this does not justify the procedure. The thought of the book is subtle, nuanced, and complex in most respects, and it would be surprising if it were not so in this respect.

The "songs" are not songs, but speeches. Two are spoken by the servant himself (49:1-6; 50:4-9); two are spoken by YHWH about the servant (42:1-4; 52:13–53:12). They are, of course, poetry, like most of the book; I use the term *songs* because it is conventional.

An enormous literature is devoted to the identification of the servant. Jewish interpreters once considered him to be the messiah, but his identification with Israel, collectively, has been the dominant Jewish view since the Middle Ages. The collective interpretation is also the most popular among Christian scholars today, though a few continue to think of the servant primarily in relation to Jesus. Many biblical figures have been proposed over the years, from Moses to Second Isaiah, but none of these identifications is persuasive; the servant has affinities with many other figures, but identity with none. If the writer had anyone in particular in mind, he obviously did not disclose the person's identity, so the relevant question for interpretation is that of the nature of the servant's service. What were the source, shape, and goal of his ministry?

THE TRIAL OF THE NATIONS AND THE FIRST SERVANT SONG

The first servant song (42:1-4) forms the climax of the second major section of the book (41:1–42:4). This section is styled as a trial of the nations and their gods, before YHWH, the God of Israel. Before we continue with this text, however, we must examine the one before it, upon which it depends.

The book begins with four prophetic messages from YHWH to YHWH's people (40:1-11). First, unnamed messengers are ordered to announce to Jerusalem that the sin which caused their captivity has been forgiven and their atoning service is completed (40:2). The second message announces the coming revelation of God's glory to "all flesh" (40:3-5). The third message, given by the prophet, proclaims the eternity of God's word, which contrasts with the transiency of humankind (40:6-8).[14] Finally, Jerusalem is exhorted to convey to all the cities of Judah the "good news" it has heard (40:9-11).

For our present purpose, two features of this poem stand out. First, the responsibility to transmit the good news is given to many among God's people—that is, they are to act as prophetic messengers to ever-widening circles of people, some of whom become messengers in turn. The news is relayed from the unnamed "voice" to the prophet, to Jerusalem, and then to all the surrounding cities.

Second, the news is all about God. The full report is only hinted at in the opening lines: God's glory, soon to be revealed; God's eternal word; God's power; and God's will to forgive, bless, and nurture God's people. In the remainder of the first chapter (40:12-31) and in many subsequent poems, this message is stated in its fullness. The prophet assures the people Israel that their life is known and understood by YHWH and encompassed within YHWH's sovereign power, even though they are exiled and scattered, living in humble and humiliating subjection to proud Babylon. The God who knows them is not merely Israel's God, but the creator of all things, the ruler of nations, and the judge of all people. It is YHWH who is this God. The gods of the nations are creations of human beings, themselves creatures of God. Therefore, Israel must not envy or emulate other peoples, abandoning their faith in resignation to present realities, but must accept instead the renewal of faith which the creator offers, on the basis of a wider perspective. Israel is reminded to consider history, as interpreted by the prophets, in relation to their present opportunity, as interpreted by a prophet, and to set this understanding against that of the nations, who cannot make sense of history.

The trial of the nations (41:1–42:4) brings YHWH and Israel into confrontation with the foreign nations and their gods. The nations are judged impotent to oppose YHWH's purpose and ignorant of its meaning (41:5-7, 11-12, 22-24, 28-29). Implicitly, Israel is also judged and called to test its faith in YHWH in interaction with the nations (41:8-16; 42:1-4).

In 41:8-16, Israel is addressed as YHWH's servant and assured of YHWH's support, which cannot fail. However, the servant's task is described here in figurative terms: He is to thresh and winnow mountains and hills (41:15-16). In 42:1-4, his task is described literally: He is to "bring forth justice to the nations" (vss 1, 3, 4). Although the specific content of this justice is not indicated, it is said that it will be achieved quietly (vs 2), without violence, and as the complement of *torah* (vs 4). Torah is law, of course, but it is more. It is teaching, instruction, revelation. It is the moral and religious foundation of law, as well as law itself. Consequently, it provides the motive power for the pursuit of justice, as well as its rationale. Everything the servant of YHWH performs is informed by the word of the prophet, or the torah of the counselor, and it is interpreted to the peoples by similar means, in order to make it morally effective. The source of torah, like the source of the prophetic word, is the spirit of God (42:1), and its range is universal (vs 4).

Verse 4*a* seems to imply that the servant's mission will require patience, though it actually is a word play on the preceding line: The servant will not extinguish a dimly burning wick or crush a bent reed (vs 3), and he himself will not burn dimly or be crushed (vs 4). The use of these verbs suggests the vulnerability of the servant, and thus anticipates the servant's suffering in the third and fourth songs.

A striking feature of the great court scene (41:1–42:4) is the contrast between the nations and the servant. The nations respond to the upheaval that is about to seize the world (41:2ff.) by frantically making sacred images to bolster their confidence (41:5-7). The chosen servants of the foreign peoples (vs 24), then, are idols created by those peoples. The servant of God, on the contrary, is the creation of God, chosen and inspired by God (42:1), and commissioned to accept the great changes taking place in the world as opportunities for justice among peoples (42:1-4). The servant of God does not resist the future in the interest of security, but welcomes it in the interest of justice, trusting God to provide the resources necessary for a secure life (41:17-20).

The world empire of Persia, established by Cyrus, was perceived by Second Isaiah as the setting for the people Israel to perform their service to God and the nations (42:4). Israel was not to respond to the change of empires by resorting to idols (41:5-7), but by having confidence in God, the power behind both Israel and Cyrus (41:10). Thus, Cyrus and Israel were to be the joint instruments of God's justice. One was to establish a new political order; the other was to teach the ways of God. The actual defeat of Israel's oppressors, the enemies of God, was to be accomplished by Persian armies. Israel's triumph (41:11-16) was to be simply a moral vindication.

The new age would be marked by the fulfillment of the promises of God, "declared from the beginning" (41:26). In my judgment, this statement does not mean that Cyrus's ascendancy was predicted by an Israelite prophet. It means that God would use the new empire as the setting within which to fulfill the promises made to the ancestors of Israel, promises inherent in Israel's call as the people of God. God had "declared it from the beginning" (41:26) and "called the generations from the beginning" (41:4); this declaration and call were bound up with God's choice of Abraham, when he was called from the ends of the earth to be God's servant (41:8-9). The servant who stepped forth in the present age (42:1) would stand in direct continuity, in order to complete the work of God begun in Abraham. The goal of the whole historical drama is to bring all people to the knowledge of God (41:20; 42:4). To know God requires instruction in God's word, God's justice, and God's law, and it is the responsibility of Israel, the servant, to provide this teaching. Therefore, at the climax of the dramatic scene in 41:1–42:4, after the nations fail to present an advocate to interpret the meaning of history, YHWH presents his advocate, the agent of justice and torah.

THE SECOND SERVANT SONG

In the second song (49:1-6), the peoples are addressed again in a dramatic setting, but now the speaker is the servant himself. In words reminiscent of Jeremiah 1:4, he asserts his total dependence upon God (49:1). His whole life, from birth, has been set within the providence of God, and God's purpose has been the decisive factor in his vocation. And yet the work God intends to accomplish through him seems to be fruitless. The results remain hidden (49:2), and the servant has become skeptical of the outcome (vs 4*a*), although he has not yet despaired (vs 4*b*).

His complaint to God (vs 4) reminds us of the complaints of Jeremiah (Jer 11:18–12:6; 15:10-21; 17:14-18; 18:19-23; 20:7-12, 14-18). Here, as there, God responds—not with permission to relinquish the difficult vocation, but with a larger commission (Isa 49:5ff.; Jer 12:5-6; 15:19-21). In addition, the prophet/servant is given assurance that God is the true source of strength in his work and the only reliable judge of its worth.

The servant has understood his mission to be the renewal of Israel's relationship to YHWH, the revival of the people's flagging faith and fitful obedience (49:5; cf. 40:27; 41:10; 42:18-20; 43:8, 22). But now he is told that his mission is much wider than this; indeed, that it has no national limits. He is the "light to the nations" (49:6). This same commission was also indicated in 42:6-7, immediately after the introduction of the servant in the first song (42:1-4).

The specific content of the salvation mediated by the servant is not described in the second song (49:1-6), so we must look at the context to discover it. First of all, the new age will bring the restoration of Israel from exile, followed by the people's reconstitution as a community in the land of their ancient heritage (49:8-19). This reversal of their present destiny is imagined as an exchange of positions with the ruling nations of the present oppressive age. Proud, prosperous kings and their retinues will pay homage to Israel (49:7, 22-23), and the tyrannical oppressors will be utterly humbled (49:26). Here as elsewhere, the writer has drawn heavily upon forms of expression familiar to his audience from the liturgies of the Judean community.[15]

The ultimate goal of the reversal of fortunes among the nations is to produce knowledge of God—God's justice, righteousness, and liberating power—and praise of God (49:13; cf. 42:10ff.; 44:23), both in Israel (49:23) and among the nations (49:26). The nations will come to know God as Israel performs its service as teacher; and in teaching, Israel will come to know God more fully.

ISRAEL AND THE SERVANT

In the second song, the servant is called Israel (49:3) and is immediately given a mission to Israel (vss 5-6). How should we explain this apparent contradiction?

This is the only time in the four songs, in which the servant otherwise is personified as an individual prophetic figure, that he is called Israel. Outside the songs, the identification with Israel is frequent (41:8; 44:1, 2; 45:4; 48:20), but there is no personification as an individual. Therefore, one way to resolve the problem is to delete *Israel* as a gloss in 49:3 and regard the four songs as a separate strand in the book, with a different message. This strand can then be attributed to a second writer, or to a second stage in the work of the first writer. Both variations of this theory have been advocated.

The theory has merit, especially in the second, two-stage, version, and further evidence supports it, in addition to the facts already mentioned. All the references to the servant as Israel, except the disputed reference in 49:3, are in chapters 40–48, while the ones in which the personification is strongest are in chapters 49–55. Thus a shift in the identity and in the mission of the servant occurs between 40–48 and 49–55. The explanation of this shift would be that the writer's initial expectation of a positive response to his message from the whole Jewish community was frustrated, so he revised his expectation and focused it upon an individual, or a cadre of individuals.

Some evidence exists that the writer may have changed his mind about Cyrus, too, for there is no mention of the conqueror, either by name or by role, in chapters 49–55. Yet, the role of the conqueror is a central feature of 40–48. According to the two-stage interpretation of the development of the writer's thought, he became disillusioned with Cyrus, as well as with Israel. Presumably the change would have occurred after 538 BC, when the prophet realized that Cyrus would not "call on [YHWH's] name" (41:25 MT; cf. 45:3), but would persist in worshiping alien gods, particularly Marduk, the god of Babylon. By that time, according to this theory, the prophet saw that the mission of "the servant" would be much more difficult than he had first imagined. It would involve misunderstanding and rejection, even persecution. And it would fall to a heroic individual or individuals to perform the service faithfully. It was not a service the general Jewish populace would perform.

This interpretation may be correct. The only textual obstacle is the reference to the servant as Israel in 49:3. This could be scribal gloss (even though it is present in all the ancient versions), but even if the reference to Israel is original, this interpretation still may be correct. It only requires that we understand *Israel* here to mean the true Israel, rather than the actual Jewish community.

The alternative to this two-stage interpretation is a two-level one. In that view, the two representations of the servant are simultaneous and complementary, rather than sequential and contradictory. The references to the servant as Israel are understood to be literal, and those to the servant as an individual are understood to be figurative, or representational. No inherent difficulty lies in accepting such a possibility, though the immediate juxtaposition of the two kinds of reference in 49:3-6 is somewhat jarring. I have always preferred this alternative to the two-stage interpretation, because the two-stage interpretation is speculative, and the two-level interpretation takes fuller account of the manifest unity of the book.

The message that emerges is not essentially different in the two cases. In the first case, there is a development in the definition of the role of the servant from the wider to the narrower, from the communal to the individual. The one supersedes the other. In the second case, the two definitions are operative throughout; the one interacts with the other. However, in either case, one of the goals of the individual servant's task is to lead the community to perform its task. This is ultimately the same task, the true service of God, and therefore the outcome is the same.

THE THIRD AND FOURTH SERVANT SONGS

The servant speaks again in the third song (50:4-9), but now the scene has changed. The servant's mission has become clearly hazardous. A somber note was sounded in the second song (49:7), and now we are told that the servant is despised by the nations and enslaved by their rulers. He has been persecuted—beaten and spat upon (50:6)—and he interprets this treatment as divine instruction, enabling him to "sustain the weary" (vs 4). He receives such instruction daily, without feeling ashamed or attempting to retaliate (vss 4*b*-6). His suffering is not a sign of weakness, but the fruit of hearing and speaking the word of God (vs 4*b*), and thus is "for the gospel" (2 Tim 1:8). The servant's life is an expression of his commission to proclaim who God is and what God is doing in the world, and this alone makes sense of the servant's patience, rejection, confidence, humiliation, and vindication.

In the second part of the song (50:7-9), the servant reasserts his confidence in God, who has given him his vocation and will surely vindicate him (vs 8). The declaration by God of his innocence (his "right") will finally silence his tormentors (vs 9). These lines anticipate the confession made by the tormentors in 53:7-9.

Two voices speak in the fourth song—YHWH at the beginning and the end (52:13-15; 53:11*b*-12), and a group of people in the middle (53:1-11*a*). The people are observers of the servant's life, but otherwise are not clearly identified.

A great reversal in the fortunes of the servant is announced by YHWH. This is the climax in a series of divine reversals, which include metaphorically watering the desert (44:3), drying up the sea (44:27), and literally humbling Babylon (chap 47) and gathering scattered Israelites. But nowhere is a divine reversal more startling than this one. It is the complete vindication and exaltation of one who has been condemned and destroyed. Furthermore, it produces a complete change of understanding in the observers, which constitutes a reversal of their fortunes, too.

To the observers, the servant was deformed (52:14) and ugly (53:2), and not only did they despise and spurn him (53:3), but they persecuted, tried, condemned, and led him to execution. They considered him a criminal and thus justified his suffering and death as punishments of God (53:4). But now in retrospect, they hold a totally different evaluation of the servant. They confess that it was they, not he, who deserved affliction as punishment for their iniquity. Nevertheless, they believe that God had willed what happened—not to punish him, but to benefit them. They have been made whole as a result of the servant's experience (53:5-6).

In the concluding speech, YHWH confirms the observers' confession. The servant's suffering has indeed been undeserved, but it was willed by God in order to bring others into a right relationship with God (53:10-11). Therefore, "the many" will behold YHWH's final exaltation of the servant (vs 12). A full interpretation of this text requires that we answer the following questions: Who are the observers? What did the servant do to be treated as he was? Did the servant die? Will he be resurrected? What is the significance of the sacrificial imagery? What exactly did the servant's suffering accomplish for the observers? How did this come about?

Though the speakers are not identified in 53:1-9, the clue is given in the opening speech of YHWH (52:13-15), where it is said that "many nations . . . kings" will be amazed at the reversal of the servant's fortune. Therefore, since the very next statement in the dialogue is the observers' confession of surprise at the discovery of the true meaning of the servant's life (53:1), the speakers can be none other than the "many nations/kings" of 52:15.[16]

The speakers could include Jews, too, if the servant is understood to be the representative Israelite. However, we surely must think of them first as Gentiles. "Many nations" can hardly mean less than this, and the "kings" cannot be Israelites. Thus the scope of the writer's intention is wide. It is perhaps not too much to say that it is worldwide.

The picture of foreign peoples and kings turning toward Israel and Israel's God has appeared before in the book, and yet a profound development has taken place. Earlier, the writer used the image of a triumphal procession to proclaim the humbling of the oppressors and their acknowledgment of YHWH (45:14-15; 49:22-26; cf. 49:7). In those prophecies the fortunes of the nations and their kings were reversed, their idols were repudiated, and the injustices done to Israel were redressed. But the humbling of kings was a humiliation, and the vindication of Israel smacked of pride. Thus, though the image of a triumphal procession was a vivid poetic device, it was deficient as a prophetic parable.

In the fourth servant song, there is no humiliation of peoples, but only the emergence of a new understanding on their part. They have pondered the inner meaning of the servant's oppression, in relation to their own behavior, and have reached a new understanding of the moral dynamics of human existence. They anticipate the exaltation of the servant, but it will not come at the expense of others (53:10-12). From this point until the end of the book (chap 55), there is no recurrence of the earlier note of vindictiveness. In 54:2-3, for example, the picture is of a restored Israel, repopulating the cities and lands from which the old Israel was exiled. In the climactic celebration of the drama of redemption (chap 55), the nations are gathered around Israel and the new "David," but they are not put to shame.

In the present time, according to the observers (53:1-9), it is the servant who is abased, not they, although by their own admission, he does not deserve such treatment (53:9). On the other hand, they are laden with guilt (53:5-6). What does this part of their confession mean?

First of all, it is important to remember the poetic character of this material. It is highly metaphorical, with one metaphor fading into another: the trespass offering (53:10), the criminal (vss 8-9), the victor (vs 12). Levels of meaning overlap, and the identity of the speakers is not always clear; are they the same in 53:7-9 as in 53:1-6, or is this a new voice? The text of verse 8 makes it uncertain. The Masoretic Text reads, "The blow upon him (was) for the transgression of my people"; the Qumran Isaiah scroll (1 Q Is[a]) has "his people"; and the LXX says, "For the iniquities of my people he was led to death." Emendations have been proposed, but the uncertainty remains. Again, who is the speaker in 53:10? Is it the same as in verses 7-9 (or in 1-9)? This is possible, since YHWH is referred to in the third person. Or is verse 10 part of the concluding YHWH speech (vss 11-12)? This too is possible, since it is not uncommon in Hebrew poetry for speakers to refer to themselves in the third person (e.g., 54:13). In short, we must not push any feature of the poem too far as the key to its meaning. A riot of images inhabit this pericope, and the possible implications are numerous.

The work God accomplishes through the life of the servant is full of surprises—reversals of human value and expectation. The weak and ugly one, considered deserving of God's punishment, is ultimately exalted and vindicated, while those who have despised and condemned him discover their own guilt and unworthiness. But at the same time—and this is the miracle—they find themselves in a new situation before God, a condition of wholeness (vs 5) and righteousness (vs 11), brought about precisely by the servant's obedience.

This obedience, which is unto death, is likened to the traditional trespass offering (*'asham*). This metaphor is intriguing, but because we know so little about the meaning of the trespass offering to the ancient Israelites—that is, its interior, moral meaning—its meaning here is unclear. By and large in the Hebrew Bible, the *'asham* is a sacrifice offered over and above any material compensation for a measurable offense (Lev 5:14-16). As such, it does not, in itself, suffice to effect atonement for the offender, but provides a necessary ritual accompaniment of the restitution, the latter being in money or kind. However, in some circumstances, the *'asham* is considered atoning (e.g., Lev 19:20-22). Did Second Isaiah have one of these regulations in mind, and if so, which one?

Deep in the consciousness of ancient people there lay the conviction—or better, the assumption—that a broken relationship between human beings and God, brought about by either willful or inadvertent sin, could not be restored (healed, "covered over," atoned for) without a ritual sacrifice. We can only guess why they believed this, since the literary sources, including the Hebrew Bible, do not explain the belief. This belief and the rituals that accompanied it were far older than the extant literature. Doubtless the "original" meaning of the various forms of sacrifice was long forgotten by the time the biblical books were written.

Some fragmentary clues to old meanings can be found in the Hebrew Bible: "The life of the flesh is in the blood" (Lev 17:11, 14; Deut 12:23; cf. Gen 9:4). Does this mean that blood sacrifice establishes a living relationship between the offerer and God, by means of a third, or substitute, life? The Bible does not explain it. Perhaps sacrifice was a mystery to the Israelites, too. In any case, they performed it and regarded it as an effective means of restoring vital relations between God and themselves.

And that is the result of the "sacrifice" described in Isaiah 53. There is an analogy between the servant's life of obedience unto death and the obligatory ritual of the trespass offering. And yet to the modern reader, the ancient trespass offering is more obscure than the servant's offering. This may not have been true for Second Isaiah's audience, but it is true for us. His use of the analogy gives new significance to the *'asham*, for it transforms it into a morally coherent act. It is this text, not the ancient law of sacrifice, which turns the *'asham* into a powerful religious symbol for us. Whatever it meant before, it has come to mean the self-conscious offering of one's life for the sake of others, in obedience to the word of God.

We have mentioned the reversal of human values and calculations brought about by the revelation of God's purpose. One such calculation upset by the career of the servant concerns the relation between outward appearance and inward merit. The servant is ugly and afflicted; therefore he is judged to be sinful, and his material misfortune is considered a just reward for his lack of virtue. This cruel doctrine was widely held in the ancient world, and it has continued to plague religious communities to the present day.

THE DEATH OF THE SERVANT

Does the servant's suffering end in death? And if so, is his exaltation a resurrection from the dead? In asking this, we should remember that we are dealing with a parabolic figure, a symbolic role in a poetic drama, not with an actual historical person. Therefore it is irrelevant for us to speculate about whether it was possible for Second Isaiah to hope for the resurrection of an individual. He may or may not have done so, but we need not debate the issue, since the servant here is not a particular individual but the representation of the people Israel in their role as messengers of God. Nevertheless, the questions remain: In 53:4-9, was the servant depicted as dying? And was his restoration to full vitality, as described in 53:10-12 (and 52:12), tantamount to resurrection?

The verb "to die" is not used explicitly in the Masoretic Text, so it is possible to regard the servant as being brought to the point of death but not actually dying.[17] The analogy commonly cited in support of this interpretation is that of the pious sufferer in the psalms of lamentation, whose suffering is said to be in, or in the power of, the pit, or *sheol*—that is, the realm of death (e.g., Pss 18:4-5; 30:3; 88:3-6). On the other hand, "He was cut off from the land of the living" (Isa 53:8) certainly implies that the servant has died, and this meaning is confirmed by an examination of other biblical passages in which the phrase "land of the living" is employed.[18] (Note esp. Pss 52:7; 116:9; Isa 38:11; Jer 11:9; and texts cited in Ezekiel.) In all these, "land of the living" means life as opposed to death, in the usual meaning of those terms. Jeremiah 11:19, in which the prophet complains about a plot to kill him, is particularly telling. Here, "Cut him off from the land of the living," clearly means "to kill him," in the ordinary sense of the word.[19] It is noteworthy that the same metaphor of the sheep led to the slaughter is used in both Jeremiah 11:18-19 and Isaiah 53:7-9.

Other factors support the conclusion that the servant is put to death, although they are less decisive than the one just considered. The LXX of 53:8*b* reads, "Because of the iniquities of my people he was led to death." This rendering presupposes a Hebrew word which contains only one more letter than the word in the Masoretic Text—*lmwt* instead of *lmw*. It is easy to imagine that an original *lmwt* might have been shortened inadvertently to *lmw*. However, since the Greek translation of this verse is generally somewhat free, this evidence is not conclusive.

The Masoretic Text of 53:9*a* ("and with the rich [or, as some propose, the rabble] *in his deaths*") appears textually corrupt. Many scholars today revocalize the final word of this clause, following the Dead Sea Isaiah Scroll, reading, "and *his tomb* with the rich," or the like, which produces a good parallelism with the preceding line.[20] The meaning in this case is that the grave/tomb was prepared for him. This does not necessarily mean that he died, though it suggests it, I think. Of course, the possibility still remains that verse 9 should be read, "and with the rich in his death," as the RSV and others do. North translates, "and with the dregs of men when he died."[21] Finally, there is the reference to the servant's life as a trespass offering (53:10). The usual *'asham* was a ram (or male lamb) slaughtered ritually (cf. Lev 5:15, 18; 7:1ff.; 14:10ff.). The obvious implication is that the servant, too, has died sacrificially.

In sum, it seems to me that the picture of the servant's fate in Isaiah 53:7-9(10) includes his death. The evidence is not absolutely unambiguous, but it is clear enough to make this conclusion probable.

The servant's ignominious condemnation and death are not the last word, for the prophet anticipates his glorious revival and vindication by God (53:10-12; cf. 52:13). This is a dramatic poem, and many of the images are symbolic, so it is not germane to ask whether a sixth-century BCE Jewish prophet could have expected the physical resurrection of a person after death.[22] It is enough to realize that he could have imagined such an event, and this is proved by Job 14:7-17. The writer of Job does not himself believe in the possibility of a person rising again out of *sheol,* but he certainly is able to imagine it, and to have Job wish for it. Thus, there is nothing inherently incredible about Second Isaiah's use of similar imagery in his poem.

I have said nothing so far about the possible influence of the ancient myths of dying-and-rising gods, or the ritual humiliation of ancient kings, upon 52:13–53:12. If there was an influence from the revivification myths, it was indirect and merely formal, for the servant is not a divine figure in any respect. Also, considering the writer's vigorous polemic against the foreign gods, we can hardly suppose that he made conscious use of an alien mythology. The possibility of influence by the royal rituals is greater, because it is possible to construe the servant as a royal messianic figure, as some scholars have done. Such influence would have come directly from the Mesopotamian cultural environment of the Jewish diaspora, and not from the traditions of the proexilic Israelite monarchy, since there is no evidence that the royal rituals of Israel contained a mock humiliation of the king, in the fashion of the Babylonian Akitu festival.[23] But in any case, the mock humiliation of a Babylonian king in the New Year's festival, in which the symbols of rule are first removed and then restored, after his face has been slapped by the high priest,[24] is a far cry from the picture of the servant in the fourth song. The supposition of influence in this case is meaningless. A closer analogy is perhaps to be found in the language of the Hittite vassal treaties from the second millennium BCE, where "to kill" a king often means to depose him, and "to raise to life" means to reinstate him as king.[25]

We may pass quickly over the material symbols of the servant's exaltation—his long life (53:10) and his sharing in "the spoil with the strong" (vs 12). The latter, in particular, carries forward the series of vignettes in which the poet describes the future reversal of Israel's material deprivation (e.g., 41:17-20; 45:14). This aspect of the prophet's hope is not unimportant, but in the fourth song it is secondary to another theme—the moral outcome of the servant's obedience. And this brings us to the last two questions framed at the beginning of this discussion: What did the servant accomplish for others? and, How was it accomplished?

The people confess that they have completely misunderstood the servant's relationship to God, as well as their own (53:1-10), and they now see these relationships in an entirely new light. They realize now that they have been wrong and the servant has been right about their behavior and its consequences, about God and God's justice, about good and evil, reward and punishment, life and death, and this new understanding constitutes their religious and moral conversion. They have been "justified," brought into a right relationship with God. This is the meaning of the climactic affirmation of verse 11: "The righteous one, my servant, shall make many to be accounted righteous."[26] The servant's life, teaching, and example thus have been an indispensable element in the transformation of the people at the level that matters most, their moral consciousness and their knowledge of God.

The conversion of the people is the essential content of the servant's exaltation. His triumph is to see the fruits of his travail (53:11)—the success of his ministry, his teaching, and his "intercession for transgressors" (vs 12). Nothing else need be added, for anything else would be extraneous and irrelevant to the entire purpose of his vocation. The "spoils" he is to receive are, in reality, nothing more and nothing less than the people's proper acknowledgment of the way of God and of valid service to God.

In the poetic drama of the fourth song, the peoples acknowledge the meaning of the servant's life and its consequence for the many, but in the actual world of the writer, the success of the servant's mission was yet to come. Therefore the prophet spoke of the servant's exaltation in the future (52:12; 53:11-12). When it came, its content would be like that in the prophetic drama—that is, the transformation of the peoples' moral and religious understanding. And this transformation would be not so much a response to the servant's exaltation as the very exaltation itself.

The peoples would learn that the servant was right in the only way possible—by discerning the truth of his teaching, exemplified in his life. This point is implied by the poem as a whole, and it is made explicit in verse 11, if the RSV translation is correct: "By his knowledge shall the righteous one, my servant, make many to be accounted righteous."[27] It was for this knowledge that the servant was willing to die and that the people initially persecuted him. It was his proclamation about God as the creator and source of all natural blessing and the judge of all nations, who demands justice among people as the condition of life, who forgives former transgressions in order to bring about new possibilities, and who commissions his servants to serve people without violence. This message and the life which exemplified it were the very antithesis of the convictions and behavior of the peoples, and therefore the fundamental reason for their persecution of the messenger.

The alternative translation of the first word in that verse as "affliction," rather than "knowledge," advocated by D. W. Thomas and adopted by NEB and others, yields a somewhat different though not incompatible point.[28] However, the traditional translation is the better one, as I have argued elsewhere.[29]

The poet does not say what made the people change their minds about the servant. What made them finally acknowledge what they initially had spurned? Perhaps it was the servant's death, or his willingness to die for the sake of his vocation. Yet neither the death of the servant, nor his faithfulness unto death, could by itself validate the truth of his teaching. Countless people have been martyred for false causes. In the last analysis, the knowledge of God, which was the foundation and substance of the servant's teaching, could be authenticated only by itself. The servant's suffering and death may have shocked the people into reexamining the meaning of his life, and of their own, but these alone could not explain why they had come to interpret his life in an entirely new way. The prophet describes the people's conversion, but he does not explain it fully.

The servant's discipline by the hand of God (his *musar*, or remedial chastening) brings about the wholeness of the people (their *shalom*, or well-being, health, peace) (53:5). Through his knowledge (or devotion, or travail), the righteous servant helps to make many righteous (53:11). Wholeness and righteousness are not fully attainable without the knowledge of God, of

God's gifts, and of God's demands. The demand placed upon Israel, as the servant of God, is to be the bearer of God's *torah* to the nations. Therefore, being made righteous means taking on the servant's vocation as one's own. This, it seems to me, is the meaning of the people's confession (53:1-9), when viewed in relation to all the servant passages in Second Isaiah. It is only in the four servant songs that the servant is personified as an individual prophetic figure. First and last—and in reality—the servant is Israel, the people of God; and for them, being in a right relation to God means acting as God's witnesses, God's messengers, God's prophets.

It is crucial to realize that the life, suffering, and death which bring about the people's atonement—their right relation to God—are the experiences of one who is a witness to God. What he was and what he was doing when he died made all the difference, for it was only when his special work and prophetic proclamation were acknowledged and accepted by others, including those responsible for his death, that they were brought into a right relation with God. This relation involves knowledge, commitment, and faith, and no merely mechanical (or forensic) transfer of penalty from one to another could produce this kind of atonement. The transaction is thoroughly moral and religious—a matter of the mind, the will, and the affections.

The servant will "divide the spoil with the strong" (53:12), but not at others' expense. His victory will not be a defeat for anyone else, but the simultaneous victory of all. "*Everyone* who thirsts" will be satisfied with the waters of God (55:1).

SEEKING YHWH

The collection of Second Isaiah's poems concludes with that universal summons to share in the benefits of God's grace. In slightly different words, that summons is an admonition to seek YHWH (55:6). In the Hebrew Bible, seeking YHWH refers first to worshiping YHWH, both individually and together as a people. The service of God begins and ends in praise, and praising God includes acts of corporate worship, though it certainly is not limited to these. We will conclude our explication of Second Isaiah's message by considering this theme.

Isaiah 55 is the joyous climax to an astonishing series of poems. One experiences it first as the eschatological song of salvation which accompanies the conversion of the nations, an exuberant counterpoise to the dreadful picture of the suffering servant in chapter 53. Its scope is universal, its mood ecstatic! It is hard to imagine a more joyful conclusion than "the mountains and hills before you shall burst into song, and all the trees of the field shall clap their hands" (55:12)!

However, the chapter is more than a sequel to the fourth servant song. It draws together many of the motifs of the collection as a whole, though it does so without any obvious repetition of what has been said before. In particular, it recapitulates the opening poem (chap 40), bringing the beginning to completion, in both form and substance. The word of God, which God will not permit to go forth uncreatively (55:10-11), is the same word that stands everlastingly midst the transient creatures of flesh (40:8). The mountains, hills, trees, and fields, which celebrate the fulfillment of God's redemptive purpose (55:12), recall the mountains and hills leveled into a highway for God's coming (40:3-5), in contrast to the desert that borders the highway in the opening poem. "Why do you say, O Jacob . . . 'My way is hidden from the LORD'?" (40:27) is echoed by "Seek the LORD while he may be found, call upon him while he is near" (55:6). The transcendent mystery and power of God, to which the opening poem alludes in spatial metaphors (40:12-17), is interiorized in the concluding poem as divine wisdom, which expresses itself in mercy and forgiveness (55:7-9). The last word of all is an assurance of joy and peace (55:12), just as the first word was one of comfort and pardon (40:1-2).

Thus, from beginning to end, Isaiah 40–55 is a book of affirmation and encouragement. Addressed to a defeated and scattered people, burdened with guilt, restricted in movement, and tempted to idolatry, these oracles are both a testament of faith and a summons to action. In every line they reflect an undeviating trust in the purpose of God—in the lives of people and in the destinies of nations; trust in the will of God—to displace death, bondage, and injustice with life, freedom, and righteousness. And yet, for all its emphasis upon the positive aspects of God's activity and Israel's historic opportunity, Second Isaiah is neither utopian nor sentimental. Its realism is perhaps most clear in the last servant song, but it is evident on every page. The writer was steeped in the prophetic tradition and the sober memories of Israel's past, and his promise of renewal and his exhortation to obedience reflect his awareness of the frailties of people and the historic obstacles to the fulfillment of righteousness. His poetry is often lyrical and hyperbolic, but his assurances are never maudlin or cheap.

SECOND ISAIAH AND WORSHIP

The words *poem, song,* and *lyric* have appeared again and again in our discussion, and we need to consider now whether the literary quality denoted by these terms is a clue to the social setting of the work, particularly a setting in public worship. The affinity of Second Isaiah to the book of Psalms has long been recognized. Until recently the direction of influence was thought to be from Second Isaiah to the psalms, because the psalter was regarded as later in date. Twentieth-century form-criticism of the psalter changed this, and the critical consensus today is that a great many of the extant psalms, and most of the forms and language utilized in the rest, were created for worship in preexilic times.

It is not our task to examine in detail the literary affinities between Second Isaiah and the book of Psalms, or to describe the history of criticism on this subject. We may simply accept the critical consensus, which seems well founded to me, and refer the reader to the commentaries.[30] Our interest here is restricted to the theological implications of the liturgical qualities of Isaiah 40–55, in the light of the allusions to worship in the poems themselves.

Second Isaiah proclaimed nothing less than the creation of a new people of God, in a new era of world history. Since well-regulated worship of YHWH had characterized Israel's life from the beginning, we may be curious as to what role the prophet assigned to public worship in Israel's coming age. A priori, we would expect it to be significant. The contemporary book of Ezekiel places the cult at the center of life of the restored Israel (Ezek 40–48), and we would expect to find a similar picture in Isaiah 40–55. It is surprising, therefore, that Second Isaiah hardly mentions the cult in his poems.

The temple of Jerusalem is mentioned once, as being destined for reconstruction along with the rest of the city (44:28), but the authenticity of this reference is open to question, as I have indicated, and at most, it is a casual allusion. Considering the importance of Zion/Jerusalem in the writer's vision (a subject to be treated below), his silence concerning the temple must be regarded as deliberate.

Aside from the metaphorical description of the life of the servant of YHWH as a trespass offering (53:11), only one passage in Isaiah 40–55 even mentions Israel's sacrificial cult (43:23-24), and that mention is by no means an affirmation of its worth. This passage is part of an oracle (43:22-28)—one of two in the book (the other is 50:1-3)—in which the writer engages in the kind of polemic against Israel so characteristic of the preexilic prophets, and echoes their sharp criticism of the sacrificial cult.

Verses 22-24 may be translated as follows:

> It is not to me that you called, O Jacob,
>   for you have wearied of me, O Israel.
> It is not to me that you have brought sheep
>   for your offerings,
>   and your sacrifices have not honored me.
> I have not made you serve with offerings,
>   nor have I wearied you with frankincense.
> It is not for me that you brought sweet cane with silver,
>   and the fat of your sacrifices has not satisfied me.
> Surely you have served me with your sins,
>   wearied me with your iniquities!

The connotation of these lines, according to some translations, is that Israel did not bring sacrifices to YHWH, but should have done so,[31] but this cannot be correct. Throughout the preexilic period, there was a continuous sacrificial cult dedicated to YHWH. How, then, could Second Isaiah have asserted that sacrifices were not brought to YHWH? The effort to avoid this problem by relating the charge specifically to the period of the exile founders on verse 28, which makes it clear that the failure indicated was preexilic. No, the nuance of the passage is quite different: It is that, despite the fulsomeness of Israel's offerings to YHWH, YHWH was not honored by them and did not want them. Torrey's translation is satisfactory: "Hast thou not brought me thy sheep for burnt-offerings?"[32] The prophet is scornful of the preexilic sacrificial system, which merits nothing but sarcasm. He never once mentions its restoration in the coming age. The "vessels of YHWH" that are to be carried in procession by the returning exiles (52:11) are probably cultic paraphernalia, but we can only guess what the writer had in mind, and again, this is a casual allusion. He is not recommending the transport of the vessels, but assuming it. This is merely a detail of the reversal of fortunes in the coming era.

A telling clue to Second Isaiah's understanding of the preexilic cultus is contained in the final strophe of this oracle (43:25-28), where two points are made: The cult was powerless to expiate guilt and was corrupted by the participants' transgressions (vs 27); and God forgives, "blots out your transgressions, forgets your sins" (43:25), for God's own sake—that is, freely, out of love—not because of anything done by the people. This, the prophet asserts, God has already done for Israel (40:1-2; 44:22), prior to any atoning act by the people.

The only other reference to sacrifice, though it does not specifically refer to the Israelite cult, is 40:15-16. This text declares that YHWH's being is so vast that all the timber and animals of Lebanon could not provide an appropriate burnt offering. So by implication, any ordinary sacrifice would be completely gratuitous.

Second Isaiah's polemic against idolatry—the religious use of graphic images—is well known, for it is a prominent feature of his oracles.[33] Not usually observed, however, is that most of this polemic applies not only to foreign cults, but also to the syncretized cult of preexilic Israel. The practices described are not ones that tempted Israel for the first time during the Babylonian captivity, but the same ones that had attracted the people for generations. The attraction was all the more powerful after the fall of Judah because of the widespread belief that the fall proved YHWH to be a powerless god. Idolatry was an ancient attraction after all, as were the omens and divinations (44:25), enchantments and sorceries (47:12), which the prophet ridiculed. Second Isaiah's theology points to the de-ritualization of Israel's life, at least in relation to what had been normative throughout its previous experience, and to what was universal in its environment.

The promise in 52:1 that the uncircumcised and unclean would not inhabit Jerusalem in the future is less a prescription of ritual acts than an acknowledgment that the city is currently overrun by the enemies of Israel, who have trampled the people into the dust (vs 2) and desecrated their capital. Nevertheless, if this line is Second Isaiah's, it does suggest that he took some of the traditional marks of Israel's character for granted. However, this statement hardly consititutes a picture of a restored cultus. A further clue to the prophet's thought is the absence of any allusion to a cultic function in the servant's role. Yet the servant's office is the only mediatorial one depicted in the prophet's vision of the new Israel. In addition, the prophet never laments the absence of a "legitimate" Yahwistic cult in the life of the exiles, in the fashion of Psalm 137 or the book of Lamentations. Surely this silence is indicative.

The aspects of corporate worship which Second Isaiah does affirm are prayer and praise: "Sing unto YHWH a new song!" (42:10ff.); "The ransomed of YHWH shall return to Zion singing" (51:11; cf. 51:3; 52:8-9); "Seek YHWH while he may be found, call upon him while he is near" (55:6)—that is, in prayer. Since neither psalms nor prayers require a temple, a system of corporate worship could be formed around these two principal elements without any resort to the sacrificial rites of the old Israelite sanctuaries, or to those of the second temple of Jerusalem. This was essentially what Jeremiah told the Judean exiles in Babylonia (Jer 29:12-13). This word is in keeping with the ancient theophanic tradition of Yahwism, which acknowledged the presence of YHWH with the people, apart from any cultic setting. This tradition, which centers in the memory of the exodus from Egypt and the covenant-making in the wilderness, is echoed in Isaiah 40, and appears again in 41:10 in the use of characteristic words from the old story of salvation, "I am with you" (Exod 3:12). This tradition may be compatible with a temple cultus, but not without a certain amount of tension (2 Sam 7:4-7). When the theophanic tradition is accommodated to a fixed cultus, something essential in the tradition is threatened.[34]

Of course, we must remember the eschatological quality of Second Isaiah's proclamation. When one is overwhelmed by a vision of the glory of God that is about to be made visible to all the world (40:3-5), one is not likely to think about sanctuaries, with their interest in the ritual assurance of God's presence. In any case, questions of the shape, setting, and function of corporate worship in the new Israel are not dealt with in Second Isaiah.

JERUSALEM / ZION

The situation is quite different with Jerusalem/Zion, for the city is prominent in the prophet's proclamation.[35] The "holy city," (52:1) is the goal of the coming great pilgrimage, which will begin with the exodus of the exiles from their places of captivity (40:3; 43:5-6,16-21; 48:20-21; 49:12; 51:9-11), and move through the wilderness (40:3-4) to the land of promise. The model for this pilgrimage is, of course, the old exodus. The ancient Song of the Sea (Exod 15:1-18) concludes:

> You brought them in and planted them on the mountain of your
> own possession,
> the place, O LORD, that you made your abode,
> the sanctuary, O LORD, that your hands have established.

The "mountain" in the song was probably the central highlands of Palestine or Mount Ephraim, since the song was composed long before David's capture of Jerusalem, but in the minds of the inhabitants of the kingdom of Judah, it eventually was localized in Jerusalem/Zion. Thus for them, there was a primordial link between the deliverance from Egyptian captivity and the procession to the holy mountain of God in Jerusalem. Furthermore, the whole scenario probably was reenacted liturgically in the pilgrimage festivals, thereby becoming embedded in the religious consciousness of Judah.[36]

In Second Isaiah, the purpose of the events, from the exodus to the entry into Zion, is to glorify God in the eyes of the world. In this too the writer follows ancient tradition, for God's deliverance of Israel from Egypt was, above all, a demonstration of God's sovereignty and glory in the eyes of Pharaoh and the world (e.g., Exod 7:5; 14:4, 18; 15:14-15). Second Isaiah made explicit the universalism implicit in this tradition.

Jerusalem, which is nearly synonymous with Zion in these poems (40:9; 41:27; 52:1, 2), is a specific place, and yet it is representative of all the cities of Judah (44:25; cf. 51:3; 52:9), and even symbolic of the whole people of God (51:16; cf. 40:2; 52:9). When the writer envisions the manifestation of God's power in Zion as the climax of the return (46:13; 51:11; 52:8), his intention is not restrictive. On the contrary, Zion is the commissioned herald of the good news to all the world (40:9)! Thus, the geographic concreteness of the prophet's vision serves his universalism.

CONCLUSION

The construction of the prophetic traditions recorded in the book of Isaiah rests upon two foundations: the work of Isaiah in the eighth century BCE; and of Second Isaiah in the sixth. Isaiah's oracles are the foundation of chapters 1–39, while Second Isaiah's are the foundation of chapters 40–66. The nucleus of chapters 56–66, to be found in 60–62, owes much to the language and thought of 40–55—so much, indeed, that many commentators refer to the author of 60–62 as a disciple of Second Isaiah. There is much to appreciate in the chapters appended to Second Isaiah's poems; nothing there quite matches these poems in theological depth, although some parts do rival them in rhetorical effect. Most readers of the Hebrew Bible over the centuries, beginning with the writers of the New Testament, have made no distinction between the prophetic witness of Isaiah 60–62 and that of 40–55. Both testify to the redemptive work of the servants of God and to the source and goal of their work in the power and praise of God. Close scrutiny of chapters 56–66 discloses diverse understandings of the scope and conditions of redemption, but at least one of these understandings manifests the same essential spirit as does Second Isaiah.

SELECT BIBLIOGRAPHY

Blenkinsopp, Joseph. "Second Isaiah: Prophet of Universalism." *JSOT* 41 (1988): 83-103.

Clements, R. E. "Beyond Tradition-History: Deutero-Isaianic Development of First Isaiah's Themes." *JSOT* 31 (1985): 95-113.

Clifford, Richard J. *Fair Spoken and Persuading: An Interpretation of Second Isaiah.* New York: Paulist Press, 1984.

Hooker, Morna D. *Jesus and the Servant.* London: SPCK, 1959.

Kaufmann, Yehezkel. *The Babylonian Captivity and Deutero-Isaiah.* New York: Union of American Hebrew Congregations, 1970.

Lindars, Barnabas. "Good Tidings to Zion: Interpreting Deutero-Isaiah Today." *BJRL* 68 (1986): 473-97.

McKenzie, John L. *Second Isaiah.* Anchor Bible. Garden City, N.Y.: Doubleday, 1968.

Melugin, Roy F. *The Formation of Isaiah 40–55.* BZAW 141. Berlin/New York: Walter de Gruyter, 1976.

Mowinckel, Sigmund. *He That Cometh.* Oxford: Basil Blackwell, 1956.

Muilenburg, James. "The Book of Isaiah: Chapters 40–66." *The Interpreter's Bible.* Vol. 5. Nashville: Abingdon Press, 1956.

North, C. R. *The Suffering Servant in Deutero-Isaiah.* Oxford: Oxford University Press, 1956.

______. *The Second Isaiah.* Oxford: Clarendon Press, 1964.

Orlinsky, Harry M., and Norman H. Snaith. *Studies on the Second Part of the Book of Isaiah. VT* Sup 14. Leiden: Brill, 1967.

Robinson, H. Wheeler. "The Cross of the Servant." *The Cross in the Old Testament.* London: SCM Press, 1955.

Scullion, John. *Isaiah 40–66.* Old Testament Message 12. Wilmington, Del.: Michael Glazier, 1982.

Simon, Ulrich E. *A Theology of Salvation: A Commentary on Isaiah 40–55.* London: SPCK, 1953.

Smart, James D. *History and Theology in Second Isaiah.* Philadelphia: Westminster Press, 1965.

Southwestern Journal of Theology. 11/1 (1968).

Stuhlmueller, Carroll. *Creative Redemption in Deutero-Isaiah.* Analecta Biblica 43. Rome: Biblical Institute, 1970.

______. "Deutero-Isaiah: Major Transitions in the Prophet's Theology and in Contemporary Scholarship." *CBQ* 42 (1980): 1-29.

Torrey, Charles C. *The Second Isaiah.* New York: Scribner's, 1928.

Watts, John D. W. *Isaiah 34–66.* Word Biblical Commentary. Waco, Tex.: Word Books, 1987.

Westermann, Claus. *Isaiah 40–66.* Philadelphia: Westminster Press, 1969.

Whybray, R. N. *Isaiah 40–66.* New Century Bible Commentary. Grand Rapids: Eerdmans, 1975.

NOTES

1. H. L. Ginsberg has called this theory the "formerly regnant one." See *The Book of Isaiah: A New Translation* (Philadelphia: Jewish Publication Society, 1973), p. 20, and the earlier treatment of the issue by Menahem Haran in *VT* Sup 9 (1963): 127-55, which Ginsberg follows.
2. See Ginsberg.
3. So Muilenburg, McKenzie, and Westermann, among others.
4. B. S. Childs, *Introduction to the Old Testament as Scripture* (Philadelphia: Fortress Press, 1979), p. 329.
5. Wolfgang Roth, *Isaiah* (Atlanta: John Knox Press, 1988), p. 17.
6. Among the standard commentaries on Second Isaiah, Muilenburg, McKenzie, and Westermann adopt a position concerning the meaning of "the former things" similar to the one presented here (see their discussion of 41:22; 42:9; 43:9, 18; 46:9; 48:3). North sees an allusion to Cyrus's early victories in 41:22 and possibly 42:9, but not elsewhere.
7. See, e.g., Orlinsky and Snaith, *Studies on the Second Part of the Book of Isaiah*, pp. 154-65.
8. Hooker, *Jesus and the Servant*, p. 180.
9. Pss 2, 18, 20, 21, 45, 72, 89, 101, 110, 118, 132, 144.
10. Torrey, *The Second Isaiah*, pp. 38-52, 135-50; Smart, *History and Theology in Second Isaiah*, pp. 115-30. The view of Torrey and Smart depends upon the deletion of the name of Cyrus in 44:28 and 45:1 as a scribal gloss, an exegetical move which other scholars consider arbitrary. Smart makes much of the prophet's assertion that the conqueror "shall fulfill all [YHWH's] purpose" (44:28), contending that this purpose comprehended far too much for Cyrus to have been imagined as the agent. However, Smart's interpretation of this line is not the most likely one (see the discussion of 45:1-7 below).
11. "The man of [God's] counsel," 46:11, and "the one whom YHWH loves," 48:14.
12. See *IDB:* "Servant."
13. See North, *The Second Isaiah*, and Orlinsky and Snaith,, *Studies*.
14. In the MT, it is human *hesed* (covenantal loyalty) that is contrasted with God's word. The word is frequently emended to *hemed* (beauty, glory, or strength).
15. See esp. Pss 2, 21, 47, 72, 96, and the discussion in Frank M. Cross, *Canaanite Myth and Hebrew Epic* (Cambridge, Mass.: Harvard University Press, 1973), pp. 99-111.
16. This is true, whether or not a new literary unit begins with 53:1 (Smart; Orlinsky), for the movement of thought from the end of 52 to the beginning of 53 is so clear and immediate that the two cannot reasonably be read separately. However, the case for regarding 52:13–53:12 as one unit is persuasive. See Torrey, Muilenburg, Westermann, North, McKenzie, among others.
17. See Torrey; G. R. Driver, "Isaiah 52:13–53:12: The Servant of the Lord," BZAW 103 (1968): 104-5; and Orlinsky and Snaith, *Studies*, pp. 59-63.
18. Pss 27:13; 52:7; 116:9; 142:6; Job 28:13; Isa 38:11; Jer 11:19; Ezek 26:24, 25, 26, 27, 32.
19. The Hebrew verb "to cut off" is different from the one in Isa 53:8, but the meaning is the same. Orlinsky's observation that Jeremiah did not die is beside the point. The statement in question refers to the plan to kill Jeremiah. It is irrelevant to the meaning of the verb that the plan failed.
20. See JB, NEB, NAB, CBAT, JPS 1917, NRSV, Westermann, and McKenzie, among others.
21. Cf. NJV.
22. See, e.g., G. R. Driver, "Isaiah 52:13–53:12."
23. See J. M. Ward, "The Literary Form and Liturgical Background of Psalm LXXXIX," *VT* 11 (1961): 321-39. For an alternative viewpoint, see Ivan Engnell, "The Ebed-Yahweh Songs and the Suffering Messiah in 'Deutero-Isaiah'," *BJRL* 31 (1948): 54-93. For another study of royal motifs in Second Isaiah, see Sigmund Mowinckel, *He That Cometh* (Nashville: Abingdon Press, 1956), pp. 187-257.
24. See *ANET*, pp. 331-34.
25. See J. Wymgaards, "Death and Resurrection in Covenantal Context," *VT* 17 (1967): 226-39.
26. Cf. NAB and JB ("justify many"), RSV ("make many to be accounted righteous"), NJV ("makes the many righteous"), and CBAT ("bring righteousness to many").
27. Cf. McKenzie.
28. D. W. Thomas, "A Consideration of Isaiah LIII in the Light of Recent Textual and Philological Study," *Ephemerides Theologiae Lovaniensis* 44 (1968): 79-86. See CBAT, JB, NAB, NJV, and NRSV

("Out of his anguish he shall see light; he shall find satisfaction through his knowledge").

29. J. M. Ward, "The Servant's Knowledge in Isaiah 40–55," *Israelite Wisdom*, ed. J. Gammie et al. (New York: Union Theological Seminary/Scholars Press, 1978), pp. 128-29.

30. E.g., Westermann, pp. 23-27 and throughout.

31. E.g., RSV, NEB, NAB, and NRSV.

32. See Torrey's comments and those of North and Smart.

33. Isa 40:18-20; 41:5-7, 21-24, 28-29; 42:17; 44:9-20; 45:16, 20-21; 46:1-7; 48:5.

34. Cf. Jer 7; 26.

35. Zion in 40:9; 41:27; 46:13; 49:14; 51:3, 11, 16; 52:1, 2, 7, 8; Jerusalem in 40:2, 9; 41:27; 44:26, 28; 51:17; 52:1, 2, 9.

36. See Mowinckel, *The Psalms in Israel's Worship* (Oxford: Basil Blackwell, 1962), I, pp. 106-92; A. R. Johnson, *Sacral Kingship in Ancient Israel* (Cardiff: University of Wales, 1955); and Hans-Joachim Kraus, *Worship in Israel* (Oxford: Basil Blackwell, 1966), pp. 179-238.

CHAPTER SIX

Isaiah 56–66

THIRD ISAIAH

After studying Second Isaiah, with its unity of style and prophetic witness, we find ourselves once again, in chapters 56–66, in the kind of diversity we encountered in 1–39. It is clear that the scroll of Isaiah was the repository for most of the anonymous prophetic writings preserved in Judah over a period of two hundred years. At times, the diversity of idea and spirit in Third Isaiah becomes outright conflict. Part of Third Isaiah resembles Second Isaiah and seems dependent upon it, yet there are enough differences to set these sections apart as the work of different writers. Other parts differ drastically from the first in language and attitude. Some of these voices represent rival factions in the Judean religious community during the period of the second temple (after 516 BCE). It is impossible to date these texts closely, but it is enough to be able to place them in this general setting.

It is clear that in most of these texts, the Babylonian captivity is no longer the setting, and the reestablishment of the religious community in Jerusalem, which Second Isaiah anticipated, has taken place. Isaiah 63:7–64:12 is an exception. It is a communal lamentation which presupposes the conditions of the exilic period. Otherwise, the perspective of the writers of these texts is quite different from that of Second Isaiah. Their concerns are generally more mundane and practical, like those of soldiers when the war has ended and the celebration of their return is over. How should the sabbath be observed? What constitutes proper fasting? Who should be allowed in the sanctuary? How should foreigners be treated? These are some of the questions addressed in these chapters.

More than two voices are heard in this dissonant chorus. However, they group themselves into two principal parts, which can be heard antiphonally. The first part is affirmative in spirit, and its message is redemptive and inclusive; the second part is negative in spirit, and its message is retributive and exclusive. The parts never blend into a harmony, but remain discordant to the end.

Scholarly views of the composition of Isaiah 56–66 vary, as one would expect with material as diverse as this. The reconstruction presented in Westermann's widely used commentary is elegant, though aspects of it are speculative.[1] He discerns four strands, which are more or less concentric and chronological in order, beginning with 60–62, the earliest, in the center. The first is the work of Trito-Isaiah, who revived Deutero-Isaiah's message of universal salvation (60–62) in a framework of popular laments (58:1-12; 63:7–64:12), but modified Deutero-Isaiah's universalism by making the foreign nations servants of Israel (60:3-4, 9; 61:9; 62:2; 66:12). The second strand reflects the view of one of the rival parties in Judea, which deemed itself devout and denounced its opponents as transgressors (59:1-8; 65:1-16*a*, plus two shorter additions, 57:20-21 and 66:3-4). Three preexilic oracles of doom were used to support their view (56:9–57:13). A third writer revived the old idea of the judgment of foreign nations, in an apocalyptic key, to counteract the universalism of Deutero and Trito-Isaiah (60:12, 19-20; 63:1-6; 65:17, 25; 66:6, 15-16, 20). The fourth hand brought all this material together, framed in the spirit of Deutero-Isaiah (56:1-8; 66:18-21). However, a final word from the apocalyptic group was added at the very end to correct this view (66:22-24).

Whether this is the correct chronology of the formation of these chapters is debatable, as are certain other features of the reconstruction. In particular, chapter 66 looks like a string of short, independent additions, rather than parts of coherent strands. Nevertheless, Westermann's analysis identifies the major elements of the message of these chapters effectively, and therefore serves as a useful introduction to a discussion of them.

The first part in the chorus I described above includes Westermann's first and fourth strands; the second part includes his second and third strands. The first part, I have called affirmative-redemptive-inclusive; the second part, negative-retributive-exclusive, and our discussion will focus on these two parts. Christian interpreters and makers of lectionaries naturally have been drawn to the first and repelled by much of the second. But it is not only Christians who have responded to the inclusive message. My first knowledge of Judaism came from the inscription engraved across the pediment of the Reform temple in the city where I grew up. From Isaiah 56:7, it read: My House Shall Be Called a House of Prayer for All Peoples. I was impressed by this statement even as a child, but I did not appreciate it fully until I discovered, many years later, what a radical statement it was for the time in which it was written, and even for our time.

REDEMPTION AND RESPONSIBILITY

In the message of the Torah and the New Testament, obedience to the commands of God is a response to God's creative and redemptive love. The imperative of the commandment always presupposes the indicative of the gospel. And this is also the message of the prophets. Third Isaiah's little scroll of lyrical prophecies (60–62) begins characteristically: "Arise, shine; for your light has come, and YHWH's glory has risen upon you!" (60:1). The imperative for the Judean community is to reflect the light of God's redemption in their life and in their witness of faith. The light is God's, and it has shone already. This scroll is in the spirit and style of Second Isaiah, and parts of it are among the best loved passages in the entire book of Isaiah. But first we will look at two of the preceding texts, which also represent the inclusive, redemptive perspective—56:1-8 and 58:1-12.

Isaiah 56:1-8 challenges the notion that there can be a physical or ethnic test of admission to the religious community. It asserts that eunuchs and foreigners who keep the sabbath and "hold fast to [YHWH's] covenant" have a full place in the community. Specifically, it says of the eunuch that he will have "a monument and a name" in the temple of YHWH, better than sons and daughters (vs 5). This is the text from which the name of the present holocaust memorial in Jerusalem, Yad Vashem, was taken. This affirmation of the status of eunuchs in the house of God contrasts with the negative attitude toward physically "blemished" persons in the priestly code of the Pentateuch. There is no mention of eunuchs there, but Leviticus 21:20, which is roughly contemporary with Third Isaiah, prohibits any man with crushed testicles from approaching the altar; this text is referring to priests who officiate at the altar, so it is not fully parallel to Isaiah 56:7. However, it is an example of the same attitude of tabu addressed by the writer of Isaiah 56. The list in Leviticus 21:16-24 of all the disabled to be excluded from the service of the altar is extensive; it is clear that the framers of the priestly code wanted only physically perfect males, "in the full glory of their manhood," to minister at the altar of God. This entailed the exclusion of women, of course, an exclusion that persists in many Christian churches today.

The participation of foreigners in worship is also restricted. The foreigner mentioned in Isaiah 56 is the *nekar*, not the *ger*, or "resident alien." The first was the real ethnic outsider, while the second had taken up permanent residence in Israel and become a citizen. The law gave the *ger* cultic privileges, but not the *nekar*. For example, the *ger* could share in the Passover meal, provided he was circumcised (Exod 12:48), but the *nekar* was excluded (Exod 12:43). Isaiah 56 welcomes into the sanctuary the foreigner "who joins himself to YHWH"—that is, who obeys the commandments, especially the observance of the sabbath (vs 6)—where his offerings will be accepted on the altar of God (vs 7). "For my house shall be called a house of prayer for all peoples" (vs 8). But this voice did not prevail in Palestinian Judaism in the biblical period. By Herod's time, foreigners were excluded from the temple on pain of death.

Isaiah 58 could serve as a commentary on the famous line in Micah 6:8, "Do justice, love kindness, and walk humbly with your God," which answers the question about the kind of offering God requires. Isaiah 58 asks what kind of fast God desires, and gives a fuller answer than the one in Micah, which is an important affirmation, to be sure, but is very general. The answer in Isaiah 58 offers specific guidance. The fast, or self-denial, which God desires is to free the oppressed, feed the hungry, shelter the homeless, and clothe the naked (vss 6-7). More, it is to "*pour yourself out* for the hungry and satisfy the needs of the afflicted" (vs 10 MT, RSV).[2] This is the righteousness that will go before one, trailing YHWH's glory as a rear guard (vs 8). This idea of service is in the tradition of the great prophets.

The central cluster of poems in 60–62, by far the best known portion of Third Isaiah, is filled with famous quotations. The opening lines, "For behold, darkness shall cover the earth . . . ," are familiar to anyone who has heard Handel's *Messiah.* The promise that "nations shall come to your light, and kings to the brightness of your shining" (vs 3), one of many similarities to Second Isaiah, is reminiscent of the fourth servant song, where many nations and kings are brought to the knowledge of God by the servant's witness (53:1ff.). Chapter 60 is a lyrical promise of a prosperous, peaceful Jerusalem, full of righteous people (vs 21) and lighted by the glory of YHWH (vss 19-20), with gates always open to the world (vs 11).

For all its similarities, this is not quite the message of Second Isaiah. The status of foreign peoples in the redeemed city is different, and the difference is ethically significant. The foreign peoples, clearly subordinate to Israel, come bringing treasure to YHWH's temple (vss 6-7), the "wealth of nations" (vs 11), but they "come bending low" (vs 14). Those who refuse to serve in the new Jerusalem will be "utterly laid waste" (vs 12).

The picture in Second Isaiah is not the same. It is true that in the chapters that herald the fall of Babylon and the release of Jewish captives, there are images of humbled oppressors being led in a triumphal procession to acknowledge YHWH (45:14-15; 49:22-26; 49:7). Nevertheless, in the final chapters, this image does not recur, and at the end, the nations simply join in the universal celebration of redemption, without any subordination (55:4-5). In Isaiah 60, the focus of the foreign peoples' service is the sanctuary of YHWH, not the Israelite people as such, for this chapter is addressed to the city of Jerusalem. However, the subordination of foreigners is made clear later. The Israelites will be priests and ministers of YHWH, enjoying a double portion of the wealth of nations, while the aliens do the menial work (61:5-7). However, this is not the sectarianism that resulted from Ezra's reform. Foreigners are included in the redeemed community.

These central chapters of Third Isaiah are best known for this passage, which comes right in the middle:

> The spirit of the Lord God is upon me,
> because the Lord has anointed me;
> he has sent me to bring good news to the oppressed,
> to bind up the brokenhearted,
> to proclaim liberty to the captives
> and release to the prisoners,
> to proclaim the year of the Lord's favor,

and the day of vengeance of our God,
to comfort all who mourn. (61:1-2)

According to the Gospel of Luke, Jesus began his ministry in the synagogue of Nazareth, reciting this text (Lk 4:16-21). Luke conflates several passages from Isaiah (cf. 42:7; 58:6), but 61:1-2 is the main one. Among Christians today, these are among the most frequently quoted lines of the Old Testament; they are second only to Exodus 3:7-8 in the usage of liberation theologians. Obviously, these words are a powerful formulation of the social ethic of the Bible.

Since Third Isaiah is postexilic, the prisoners referred to here are not the exiles in Babylon, but ordinary prisoners. Whether the writer was thinking of all prisoners or only of persons unjustly imprisoned, is not stated. As the text is worded, it is quite general.

Who exactly the afflicted (*'anawim*) are in 61:1 and elsewhere is a difficult question, on which considerable literature is accumulating. The modern versions differ: "afflicted" (RSV, NJB), "lowly" (CBAT, NAB), "humble" (NEB, NJV), "poor" (NIV). Liberationists argue that the afflicted are the oppressed poor, not the religiously humble, but the Hebrew term can mean either. The NRSV, apparently responding to the argument of liberation theologians, now reads "the oppressed." In Luke, as in the LXX of Isaiah, the word is *ptochois*, whose range of meaning is similar to the Hebrew; it certainly includes beggarliness and often economic poverty. The other sufferings mentioned in Isaiah 61:1-2 are both physical (imprisonment) and spiritual (heartbreak and mourning). On the other hand, the sufferings mentioned in the related text in 58:6-9 are physical. It would be wrong, I think, merely to spiritualize either of these passages; the principal connotations are social and physical.

There is a second shift in emphasis from the message of Second Isaiah, less obvious than the first I mentioned—the subordination of foreigners—and also less significant ethically. This rather subtle shift from the radical theocentricity of Second Isaiah to a greater Zion-centeredness is most evident in chapter 62. There it is said that kings will see Zion's glory (*kabod,* vs 2), and Jerusalem will become the praise of the earth (*tehillah,* v 7; cf. 60:18). The glory is reflected, to be sure, since the source and goal are YHWH (60:1, 2); nevertheless, this language jars a bit alongside Second Isaiah's, who uses these words only for YHWH (40:5; 42:8, 10, 12; 43:21; 48:9, 11).

TWO COMMUNAL COMPLAINTS

As the text is now arranged, 60–62 is an answer to the communal complaint in 59, linked to it by 59:20-21. A second communal complaint (or lamentation) is found in 63:7–64:12, composed while the temple and city of Jerusalem were in ruins (63:18; 64:10-11). The setting of the complaint in 59 is unclear. It bewails the sin and injustice that grip the community, but its allusions are so general that it could have been recited at any time. In this respect it resembles the complaint psalms of the psalter, but its protracted recital of iniquities is more like a prophetic accusation than a complaint psalm. Isaiah 63:7–64:12, on the other hand, is very similar to the communal psalms of complaint. As far as the subject matter and historical setting are concerned, the sequence of chapters would be more logical if 60–62 followed 63:7–64:12, while 59 would make equal sense wherever it were placed. The redaction seems haphazard to me, and not as orderly as Westermann claims.

Isaiah 59 expresses the idea of divine retribution, but Isaiah 63:7–64:12, a carefully wrought complaint psalm, presents quite a different view.3 Its considerable length suggests that it was intended for nonliturgical reading, rather than liturgical recital. It rehearses the ups and downs of the community's fortunes, all understood in relation to the acts of YHWH. Moreover, it bases its appeal on the community's long, intimate relationship with YHWH and the love of YHWH that makes that relationship possible (63:7). The community is languishing under the double weight of its own guilt (64:6) and the desolation of its cities (vss 10-11). The psalmist recalls YHWH's previous redemption of the people after they had sinned (63:9, 14), and pleads for the same redemption again (63:15; 64:1): "For you, O YHWH, are our father; we are the clay, and you are the potter" (64:8; cf. 63:16). Two things are important to note here. The first is the explicit use of the metaphor of the father for YHWH. This is not common in the Hebrew Bible, so the texts that contain this language have played a large role in Christian usage. I will not discuss at this point the critical hermeneutical problem created by this language for Christian witness today; that will be reserved for the discussion of Hosea 11. The second thing to note about Isaiah 64:8 is the theological implication of the metaphor of the clay and the potter. How different it is from that suggested by the retributive language of 59:18-20! The writer of 63:7–64:12 understood guilt and redemption as it was understood by Isaiah, Jeremiah, and Hosea.

The contrast in the understanding of redemption contained in these two communal complaints, Isaiah 59 and 63:7–64:12, illustrates the kind of contrast of idea and spirit that exists throughout Third Isaiah. Nowhere is the contrast in spirit more evident than in the concluding chapter. The last part of chapter 66 is a disjointed string of last words, accumulated on the scroll of Isaiah at its most vulnerable point, its trailing edge. Verses 18-21 prophesy that YHWH's glory will be declared among peoples who have never heard of YHWH before; these peoples will be gathered into Jerusalem, together with the surviving Israelites from all nations, and there they will make offerings to YHWH; and some of them will even become priests and Levites. This is the inclusive, redemptive spirit of Second and Third Isaiah, and it would have been a fine last word for the book, but it is followed by another last word:

For as the new heavens and the new earth,
which I will make,
shall remain before me, says the LORD,
so shall your descendants and your name remain.
From new moon to new moon,
and from sabbath to sabbath,
all flesh shall come to worship before me,
says the LORD. (66:22-23)

Here is a fitting final response to the prophecy in verses 18-24. Unfortunately, however, a mean-spirited scribe scratched in the last word—the wish for the perpetual torment by worms and fire of the corpses of those who rebelled against YHWH. This is retributive theology run out to the bitter end. In Jewish usage, verse 24 is not permitted to be read as the last word of the book of Isaiah. Instead, verse 23 is repeated.[4] Happily, it is the redemptive voices in the chorus of Third Isaiah that stand out.

CONCLUSION

We have completed our journey through the book of Isaiah, attempting to take account of the unity in its message without obscuring the diversity in its several messages. The unity stands out best when we view it from a distance, in its gross configuration. Seen closely, it is the diversity that most impresses us. In a brief interpretation like this, however, it is impossible to do full justice to the diversity—the rich complex of ideas—which becomes evident when the text is scrutinized thoroughly. These three chapters on the book of Isaiah have been merely an introduction to this greatest of all prophetic books.

SELECT BIBLIOGRAPHY

Achtemeier, Elizabeth. *The Community and Message of Isaiah 56–66*. Minneapolis: Augsburg Press, 1982.

Beuken, W.A.M. "Servant and Herald of Good Tidings: Isaiah 61 as an Interpretation of Isaiah 40–55." *The Book of Isaiah*, ed. J. Vermeylen. Leuven: University Press, 1989.

Carroll, Robert P. "Twilight of Prophecy or Dawn of Apocalyptic." *JSOT* 14 (1979): 3-35.

Hanson, Paul D. *The Dawn of Apocalyptic*. Philadelphia: Fortress Press, 1975.

Knight, George A. F. *Isaiah 56–66: The New Israel*. International Theological Commentary. Grand Rapids: Eerdmans, 1984.

Polan, Gregory, OSB. *In Ways of Justice Toward Salvation: A Rhetorical Analysis of Isaiah 56–59*. American University Studies, Series 7: Theology and Religion, 13. New York: Peter Lang, 1986.

Westermann, Claus. *Isaiah 40–66*. Word Biblical Commentary. Waco, Tex.: Word Books, 1987.

See also Select Bibliography for previous chapter.

NOTES

1. Westermann, *Isaiah 40–66*, pp. 295-308 and throughout.
2. The idea is weakened in the LXX, which is adopted by the NRSV.
3. Westermann calls it the finest in the Old Testament.
4. See, e.g., NJV.

CHAPTER SEVEN

Jeremiah

THE POETIC TRADITION

Jeremiah experienced at first hand the ruin of Judah that Isaiah had prophesied. He, too, prophesied this ruin, in vivid pictures of destruction joined to trenchant statements of its cause. Once it began to occur, Jeremiah turned to the future and gave expression to dimensions of prophetic faith that became a source of hope for the survivors of the fall. He also internalized the suffering of Israel and, in a bold assertion of identification, the suffering of God. The resulting struggle of the heart is described in a series of personal laments that are unique in the prophetic literature. All this is framed by an extensive narrative of Jeremiah's public acts, giving a longer, more detailed picture of him than any comparable narrative in the prophetic tradition.

The book of Jeremiah is large and rather disorderly, so before we can attempt to make sense of the development of its complex message, we must describe the major options for explaining the literary growth of the book, and declare which of these options informs the present interpretation.

INTRODUCTION TO THE BOOK OF JEREMIAH

The book of Jeremiah is quite unlike the book of Isaiah. Isaiah is a series of collections of poetic oracles, placed end to end without a narrative framework; the only prose narrative is the excerpt from 2 Kings (Isa 36–39). Jeremiah is a montage of poetry and prose; the poetic oracles are set in a substantial narrative framework which unifies and dominates the book. Although the text of Jeremiah is even longer than that of Isaiah, Jeremiah appears to represent only one prophetic voice, while Isaiah can readily be seen to represent many. Obviously, the book of Jeremiah requires a different approach from the one employed with the book of Isaiah.

In spite of initial appearances, both the unity and the authorship of the book of Jeremiah are disputed by many scholars today. I will outline the principal positions on these questions and indicate which one seems strongest to me.

The range of positions is illustrated dramatically by three major commentaries published in the same year, 1986.[1] At one end stands William Holladay, who treats both poetry and prose as reliable representations of the words and deeds of Jeremiah. At the other end stands Robert Carroll, who regards the prose as the work of postexilic deuteronomic writers and the poetry as the work of anonymous prophets of the exilic period. In Carroll's view, both the story and the persona of Jeremiah are creations of the prose writers. William McKane stands between these two extreme positions. He, too, attributes the prose to exilic deuteronomic writers, but treats the poetry as substantially originating from Jeremiah. If Holladay is correct, the message of the book was created for a preexilic audience in the kingdom of Judah; if Carroll is correct, it was created for a Jewish audience in the diaspora. Clearly, a gulf separates these two views, and the position one takes on the critical questions will affect the way one interprets the message. Of the three I have sketched, my own position is closest to McKane's.

The difference between the poetry and the prose in the book of Jeremiah is not always fully appreciated by interpreters. This difference involves much more than mere words or ideas; it is a difference of artistic creations, of integral products of the literary imagination. The two kinds of writing are radically unlike in form, structure, and style, and they have distinct theological emphases. Therefore, it seems to me that the proper way to undertake an interpretation of the thought of the book is by treating the two separately. Once one has done this, it is desirable to compare the two, to consider what kind of unity they may exhibit together. But the right way to start, I am convinced, is with the two strata separately.

I will treat the *poetic oracles of judgment* as communications to the religious community of Jerusalem before 587; the *longer prose narratives and prose speeches* will be treated as communications to the postexilic Jewish community. The reasoning for this is simple. The closest literary affinities of the poetic oracles of judgment are to the oracles of the preexilic prophets, addressed to the religious communities of Bethel/Samaria and Jerusalem (Amos, Hosea, First Isaiah, Micah, and Zephaniah); the closest literary affinities of the prose narratives and speeches are to the writings of Ezekiel, addressed to Jews in exile. These are the best controls we have, although a second control for the prose is provided by the latest stratum of the book of Deuteronomy (especially the speeches in Deut 5–11) and the books of Kings. The close affinity of the Jeremiah prose to this deuteronomic literature has long been recognized. This is an important relationship, but a comparison of the prose of Jeremiah with the prose of Ezekiel is at least as telling, since both are prophetic traditions.

The continued attribution of the prose, or the traditions embodied in the prose, to the preexilic Jeremiah (Holladay) seems arbitrary to me, in the face of recent textual and redactional studies.[2] Not only is the mounting weight of text-critical and redaction-critical evidence against this hypothesis, but it does not account adequately for the radical formal difference between the poetry and the prose. On the other hand, I see no persuasive reason not to attribute the poetic oracles of judgment to Jeremiah. These oracles show great unity of language, style, and thought, and they fit the setting of preexilic Jerusalem admirably. We do not need an alternative hypothesis (Carroll) to explain them.

The remaining materials in the book require special treatment. The *brief reports of the symbolic actions* of Jeremiah (e.g., 13:1-11) are prose narratives, and thus belong stylistically with the other narratives in prose. However, the actions they report are typical of the behavior of preexilic prophets (e.g., Isa 20:1-6; Hos 3), and thus they belong kerygmatically with the poetic oracles of judgment. The *oracles of promise* contained in Jeremiah 30–31 could be preexilic (insofar as they are addressed to the descendants of the kingdom of Israel), but they could just as well be exilic. I will leave the question of their authorship open, but treat them separately from the other poetic oracles. Finally, I will comment briefly on the *oracles of judgment concerning foreign nations* (Jer 46–51), of unknown authorship.

THE FLUID TEXT OF JEREMIAH

The individual units of the text of Jeremiah contain many indications of a long process of literary development, most of which, as McKane has shown in his commentary, was piecemeal. He finds few indications of systematic editing or extensive "sources" and concludes that an indeterminate number of hands was involved in the process of composition and emendation, over an indeterminate period of time. He considers it impossible to identify definite stages in the growth of this "rolling corpus" when taken as a whole, though he does believe it possible to discern stages in the growth of individual units. If his analysis is correct, it would be misleading to interpret all the oracles of judgment simply as the message of Jeremiah, composed during the last decades of the kingdom of Judah. What we are dealing with, instead, is a tradition about that message. Consequently, when we speak of "Jeremiah" in this context, it must be remembered that what we really refer to is the Jeremiah tradition. Nevertheless, there is an important difference between the tradition of the poetic oracles of judgment and the tradition of the prose speeches and narratives. Though both exhibit similar scribal operations in the extant texts—and this I take to be the basis of McKane's disclaimer about the presence of distinct sources—I believe we must posit different origins for the two kinds of literature. It is this difference I have in mind when I refer to Jeremiah as the source of the poetic oracles of judgment and the anonymous exilic writers as the source of the prose narratives and speeches. Both these literary traditions underwent modification and expansion in the course of time, and these alterations show up across the whole expanse of the text; therefore close exegesis of any portion of the text must consider the evidence of such alterations. Beyond this, though, interpretation of the book in its larger configuration must take account of the probable origin of its major literary components—that is, the setting and purpose of the major traditions in their earliest form.

Whoever the original audience was, the entire book as it now stands is an interpretation of the fall of the kingdom of Judah, for the benefit of surviving Judeans and their descendants. It contains a message for postexilic Jews. The meaning and truth of its witness of faith must ultimately be judged by the credibility of its interpretation of the fall of Jerusalem and the understanding of God's relationship to Israel which undergirds it. Determination of its credibility will not depend primarily upon conclusions about the date and authorship of the component parts, but these conclusions probably will affect one's judgment of the historical accuracy of the description of the acts of Jeremiah. What it says about these acts is more likely to be true if the writers were contemporaries of Jeremiah. And though this is an important consideration which should not be minimized, it does not gainsay the fact that *theologically*, the witness of the book does not depend upon its historical accuracy in these details.

To summarize the main points of my approach: I regard *the principal source of the poetic tradition* to be Jeremiah, prophesying in the religious community of Jerusalem in the last decades of the kingdom of Judah. The poetic oracles of judgment (accusations and threats) in Jeremiah 1–23 are the primary stratum of this tradition. The poetic oracles of promise in Jeremiah 30–31 are a second, perhaps secondary (i. e., non-Jeremian), stratum. The poetic oracles on foreign nations in Jeremiah 46–51 are a third stratum, from an unknown author. I regard *the principal source of the prose tradition* to be anonymous writers living in the Jewish community after the exile. Both the poetry and the prose were subjected to scribal emendation and expansion over a long period of time; consequently, the understandings—historical, theological, and ethical—expressed in both traditions are an amalgam of the understandings of many persons, over several generations.

ORACLES OF JUDGMENT CONCERNING JUDAH AND JERUSALEM

According to the historical notices in the book, Jeremiah was called to prophesy in the thirteenth year of Josiah in the kingdom of Judah (ca. 626; Jer 1:2; 25:3), and was last reported prophesying to Judean refugees in Egypt after the assassination of Gedaliah, the governor of Judah (after 586; Jer 44). If the initial date is right, his career lasted forty years, spanning the reigns of five kings—Josiah, Jehoahaz, Jehoiakim, Jehoiachin, and Zedekiah—and four major phases in the life of the kingdom—the last years of Assyrian domination, the Josianic revival, the period of Egyptian influence, and the Babylonian conquest.

The oracles concerned with this period are collected in Jeremiah 1–23, together with a series of complaints (11:18–12:6; 15:10-21; 17:14-18; 18:18-23;

20:7-12, 14-18). This material in poetic form is interspersed with occasional sermons and sign narratives in prose, but our concern for the moment is the poetic oracles.

With few exceptions, the materials in this collection are undated and devoid of clear indications of their setting. We are told that the oracles composed prior to 605 were recorded in a scroll delivered to King Jehoiakim in that year (Jer 36), and that these and other oracles were recorded in a second scroll after the king burned the first one (36:28, 32). However, we do not know which of the extant oracles, if any, were included in these scrolls. It is generally assumed that the second scroll contained the oracles that now appear in Jeremiah 1–23, but this is only a theory, so it it is impossible to date most of the oracles. Since nothing in the book is explicitly dated during the reign of Josiah, and there are no clear allusions to Josiah's reform, it is doubtful whether Jeremiah prophesied during Josiah's reign, in spite of the dating of his call in 1:2 and 25:3. That date has been much discussed by scholars, but with inconclusive results. The best approach for us to take here, since we cannot date the individual oracles precisely, is to treat the collection as a whole against the general background of the last years of the Judean monarchy.

Two themes dominate the oracles in Jeremiah 1–23: the proclamation of Judah's religious apostasy and moral corruption, and a resulting punishment by God; and the description of a terrifying horde about to descend upon Judah from the north. The theme of the foe from the north appears first in the narrative about the spilling kettle (1:13-19), which follows Jeremiah's call (1:1-11). This omen narrative, and its companion narrative on the *shaqed* tree (1:11-12), affirm YHWH's determination to stand by his word and thus confirm Jeremiah's call. At the same time, they provide an introduction to the announcement of an impending invasion by "all the kingdoms of the north" (1:14-15 LXX). For the prophet, the spilling kettle is the sign of the invasion, and it gives the first indication of the specific content of his message. This word about the invader is followed at once by an explanation of the calamity as a divine punishment for Judah's apostasy from YHWH and the people's worship of idols (1:16). Thus, the two major themes of the first part of the book, stated at the beginning, are subsequently intertwined throughout ten chapters. Chapter 10 ends with a final coda on the theme of the northern invader (vs 22). The invader is described in graphic terms:

> A lion has gone up from its thicket,
> a destroyer of nations has set out . . .
> to make your land a waste. (4:7)

> A hot wind comes from me out of the bare heights in the desert
> toward my poor people, not to winnow or cleanse. (4:11-12)

> Look! He comes up like clouds,
> his chariots like the whirlwind. (4:13)

It is an enduring nation;
it is an ancient nation . . . .
Their quiver is like an open tomb;
all of them are mighty warriors.
They shall eat up your harvest and your food;
they shall eat up your sons and your daughters. (5:15-17)

They grasp the bow and the javelin,
they are cruel and have no mercy,
their sound is like the roaring sea. (6:23)

The snorting of their horses is heard from Dan;
at the sound of the neighing of their stallions
the whole land quakes . . . .
See, I am letting snakes loose among you,
adders that cannot be charmed. (8:16-17)

Hear, a noise! Listen, it is coming—
a great commotion from the land of the north
to make the cities of Judah a desolation,
a lair of jackals. (10:22)

In recent years, scholars have abandoned the once popular theory that Jeremiah, reacting to a Scythian raid through Palestine, first thought the invader would be the Scythians, but revised his prophecy after the rise of the Neo-Babylonians. Most interpreters now relate the prophecy simply to the Babylonians. Certainly in the present form of the tradition, there is no doubt that the destroyer is Nebuchadnezzar of Babylon. But it would not have required a Scythian raid through Palestine or the rise of Neo-Babylonia to evoke the idea of an impending conquest of Judah by a great Mesopotamian power. Since Judah had been a vassal of Assyria for more than a hundred years, the idea of subjugation by Mesopotamian forces must have been ever present in prophetic minds. The Josian interlude between the decline of Assyria and the rise of Babylonia was brief. Effective Assyrian control of the West ended only after the death of Asshurbanapal (ca. 626), which coincided with the reported date of Jeremiah's call (1:2). The specter of an alien horde sweeping down from the north over the little kingdoms of western Asia was not the creation of an overactive prophetic imagination, but the legacy of five generations of invasion and vassalage. Indeed, we may wonder whether Jeremiah's persistent use of this image in his early oracles was not intended deliberately to counter national optimism engendered in Judah by Asshurbanapal's death and Josiah's reform (621). In any case, it stands in stark contrast to the confident spirit that permeated Judah in the age of Josiah (cf. Jer 7:1-4; 2 Kings 22:1–23:26). By 609, when Josiah was killed by Pharaoh Necho (2 Kings 23:9), the interlude of Judean self-determination was over, a few years after it began, and Judah was forced once again to reckon with the threat of foreign domination. Jeremiah's prophecy of invasion was therefore entirely realistic.

Interleaved with the oracles on the invader from the north are the oracles that diagnose the moral illness of Judah at the close of the seventh century:

> Thus says the LORD:
> What wrong did your ancestors find in me
> that they went far from me,
> and went after worthless things,
> and became worthless themselves? (2:5)

Here in a single line, the prophet characterizes the moral and psychological consequences of idolatry!

> I brought you into a plentiful land
> to eat its fruits and its good things.
> But when you entered you defiled my land,
> and made my heritage an abomination. (2:7)

It was YHWH's land, held by Israel in trust, like all of YHWH's gifts, and that land had been made an abomination—a morally polluted environment. Words of comparable force abound in the chapters that follow:

> Be appalled, O heavens, at this,
> be shocked, be utterly desolate, says the LORD,
> for my people have committed two evils:
> they have forsaken me,
> the fountain of living waters,
> and dug out cisterns for themselves,
> cracked cisterns that can hold no water. (2:12-13)

> Thus says the LORD,
> Stand by the crossroads, and look,
> and ask for the ancient paths,
> where the good way lies; and walk in it,
> and find rest for your souls.
> But they said, "We will not walk in it." (6:16)

> O LORD . . .
> You have struck them,
> but they felt no anguish;
> you have consumed them,
> but they refused to take correction. (5:3)

> They were well-fed lusty stallions,
> each neighing for his neighbor's wife. (5:8)

> Look up to the bare heights, and see!
> Where have you not been lain with? (3:2)

There was idolatrous worship "on every high hill and under every green tree" (2:20) and unrighteousness in every town and village. The lines we have quoted are matched manyfold in the oracles of Jeremiah 1–23. They cover in rich detail the features of idolatry and injustice, and the motives from which these arise. There is no question about the rhetorical power of this poetry. The question is what to make of it theologically.

Taken by themselves, the prophecies of the invasion from the north are more political than theological. They show Jeremiah's practical astuteness, or his prescience, or, if the poems are prophecies after the fact, his descriptive power. But do they have any theological content? Coming from a society that regarded practically everything that happened as an act of God, do they say anything more than that the invasion was expected and finally occurred? We would be hard pressed to find anything more, were it not for the fact that they are interleaved with the oracles that accuse Judah of idolatry and apostasy. It is only because the invasion is interpreted as a divine punishment for Judah's sin that the announcement has any theological significance. Have the redactors understood it properly? Was the prophet's intention as straightforward as their arrangement of his oracles suggests? These questions have been debated for a long time.[3]

Scholars who regard the prophets primarily as defenders of covenantal righteousness accept the redactors' interpretation of the oracles. In this view, the covenant between YHWH and Israel was a conditional agreement, in which Israel's infidelity would be punished by loss of the divine gifts, especially possession of the land of Canaan. Thus the deeper the people's guilt, the more sure a prophet like Jeremiah would have been of their eventual loss of the land.

This view of Jeremiah's prophecy of the foe from the north is supported by a great many passages, both in the prophetic books and elsewhere in the Bible (especially in Deuteronomy), and has been reinforced by comparing the prophetic oracles with certain international treaties of the time, which in many respects resemble covenantal forms in the Bible. They are remarkably like the prophetic oracles of judgment, in that they pronounce devastating curses upon the treaty signatories for violation of the terms of agreement.[4] The resemblance extends even to details of the curses, for many have almost exact parallels in the divine judgments announced by the biblical prophets. The purpose of the curses in the treaties is to enforce the vassal's fidelity to the suzerain, who grants and enforces the relationship. The curses stand as threats, and the normal expectation is that the vassal will remain obedient. Similarly, many prophetic oracles in the Hebrew Bible are stated conditionally, with the threatened disaster presumably intended as a means of provoking repentance and renewed obedience to God, the suzerain in the covenantal relationship.

There would be little reason to question the adequacy of this interpretation of Jeremiah's oracles, were it not for the fact that many are not conditional threats or calls for repentance, but unconditional prophecies of doom. Certainly this is true of the oracles about the foe from the north (4:19-22, 23-26, 28, 29-31; 5:14-17; 6:22-26; 9:10-11, 17-22). These are not mere threats, made to reinforce a plea for obedience, but descriptions of ineluctable disaster. Could it be, therefore, that these prophecies represented the prophet's primary conviction, and the accusations of sin were formulated to give a moral explanation of the expected event? Such an interpretation, though a minority view, has been suggested. According to this theory, Jeremiah reasoned from his certainty of the coming calamity to a presumption of the nation's sin. The dominant theory, which I sketched above, is that he reasoned from the sin to the calamity. It is possible, of course, to combine the two explanations. Thus, Thomas Raitt has argued that Jeremiah was led to announce the people's punishment partly from a conviction of their guilt, and partly from a wish to justify the expected disaster as a righteous act of God.[5]

I am not sure that all the oracles in the collection express a single, consistent view of the relation of the people's guilt to the political events of the time. The oracles vary in content and must have been composed over a period of time, so it is unlikely that all of them were composed for exactly the same reason. Furthermore, we do not know whether the prophet cared about the logical consistency of his oracles or was aware of all their implications. Many seem to be passionate statements arising from intuitive visionary experiences, or deeply felt responses to the critical events of the time (e.g., 4:19-22, 23-26; 8:18–9:1). An attempt to fit them into a tight logical scheme might distort them.

The particular features of Jeremiah's oracles that are most difficult to balance logically are, on the one hand, the recurring suggestion of conditionality in the warnings of disaster—with the corresponding appeal for repentance—and on the other hand, the frequent note of unconditionality in the prophecies (or visions) of national destruction. It is theoretically possible to resolve the contradiction by dating the unconditional oracles later than the conditional, as many interpreters have done, but there is no real evidence in the book to support this theory. On the contrary, the oracles on the foe from the north, which are unconditional, seem to be among the earliest. Accordingly, some interpreters conclude that Jeremiah prophesied the invasion from the north early in his ministry, was ridiculed when it did not occur, and republished the oracles years later after the Babylonian conquest of Judah.[6] This theory is not wholly implausible, but it is subjective.

There is a better way to deal with the tension between the conditional and unconditional announcements of disaster, although it too involves a number of assumptions which cannot be demonstrated conclusively. First, we need not conclude that the conquest prophesied unconditionally was expected to involve annihilation of the entire population of Judah, even though it was depicted in terrible terms. The prophet and his audience surely would have realized that the city of Jerusalem and the leadership of the nation would be the principal victims of the conquest. Most of the people would survive, only to deal once again with the fundamental social and religious issues they had confronted all along. Thus even an oracle of unconditional disaster was implicitly a summons to decision, insofar as it anticipated the event it announced. On the other hand, the conditional threats, those that exhort the hearers to renew their faith in YHWH and their obedience to the covenant, should not be understood as offering a sufficient means of controlling the destiny of the whole Judean kingdom—that is, of saving the kingdom by repentance. Many forces were shaping the destiny of the kingdom, and several of these were beyond the people's control. Even if they responded to the prophet's exhortations, the kingdom still might fall.

In short, there is a complex set of factors to consider in interpreting the relations among the various oracles of Jeremiah. Furthermore, they were delivered over a considerable period of time and they were edited later. Therefore we should not expect complete uniformity and logical consistency in what they assert or imply.

WAYWARD ACTS AND WAYWARD HEARTS

Jeremiah's picture of Israel's life in the preexilic period is a picture of unrelieved infidelity to God. In his view, the nation simply had abandoned YHWH to worship other gods (2:4-13). He characterized these gods in terms familiar from earlier prophets, especially Hosea: the deities of the Canaanite cult (2:23), worshiped "on every high hill and under every green tree" (2:20); and the spirits of sacred trees and stones (2:27). All these deities were mere emptiness to Jeremiah, and they made those who worshiped them empty (2:4).

Another aspect of Israel's apostasy was her reliance on foreign nations as a source of security (2:18). Such reliance may have entailed the adoption of the religious cults of these nations, but this does not seem to have been the main reason for Jeremiah's condemnation. Rather, he believed that trust in foreign powers was illusory and would lead to humiliation and captivity (2:36-37).

Like Hosea, Jeremiah regarded the entire time of Israel's settlement in the land of Canaan as a time of religious apostasy (Jer 2:7, 20). He allowed for only a brief moment of "bridal devotion" in the era before the settlement (cf. Hos 2:15; 11:2).

Was the notion of an original time of fidelity—however brief—an illusion, and if so, did such an image of original innocence lead the prophet to exaggerate the faithlessness of Judah in the present time? Most eras of human history are times of mixed good and evil. Was this epoch in the history of Judah an exception? Was life in Jeremiah's time as evil by comparison as his oracles suggest?

In interpreting the prophets' unqualified condemnations of Israel and Judah, we must take into account their use of conventional forms of speech, which had become fixed during many generations. Evidence of the early stages in the development of these conventions is fragmentary, and it does not tell us why the condemnations are so simplistic. Perhaps the reason is that they used stereotypes, and stereotypes tend to involve unqualified, either/or judgments. Many of the biblical proverbs are like this, contrasting the wise person and the fool in either/or terms. In this case the categories make sense, and we are not bothered by the oversimplified characterizations. These are types, not actual persons. It is when we consider the complex ambiguous behavior of actual persons that we realize how difficult it is to make simple moral judgments, and consequently how dubious it is to make evaluations like the ones in conventional prophecy. To perceive human behavior in ways defined primarily by these traditions is to see in stereotypes. We cannot be certain that the Israelite prophets themselves viewed their contemporaries only in this way. However, because their oracles constitute such a large part of the literature surviving from their times, it is inevitable that we think of their contemporaries in stereotypes, if we allow ourselves to be guided uncritically by these oracles.

Turning again to the oracles of Jeremiah, one is struck by the note of incredulity running through them (e.g., 2:4; 14). Israel's apostasy from YHWH was incomprehensible to the prophet, for he could not conceive of Israel except as the people of YHWH. Just as the prophet's own life had been formed from the beginning by the reality of the word of YHWH (1:4-8), so Israel's life had been shaped and nourished from the beginning by faith in YHWH. Using metaphors made familiar by Hosea, Jeremiah spoke of Israel as the child or the bride of YHWH. Without YHWH, Israel would not have existed. Israel was, by definition, the people of YHWH. Therefore it made no sense to Jeremiah for them to try to live as if they were something else (2:4-13, 31-32).

The only possible explanation of the nation's senseless behavior was that it had lost its heart to idolatrous powers. "I have loved strangers, and after them I will go," Israel boasted (2:25). Compelled by passion, the faithless bride of YHWH had given herself to others, believing they could satisfy her desire (4:30; 3:1-2, 6-10). But since passion without discipline is a fickle thing, this devotion too was inconstant. Thus she moved from lover to lover in a futile search (3:28, 36), even turning back to YHWH when she thought she would benefit from it (3:4-5). "The heart is devious above all else, it is perverse—who can understand it?" the prophet asked (17:9).

The bridal metaphor used by Jeremiah and Hosea has become problematic in Christian usage today because of its sexist connotations. For the moment I simply note the problem; I will deal with it more fully in the discussion of Hosea.

It was easy for the prophets to use the names "YHWH" and "Baal," blessing those who worshiped YHWH and cursing those who worshiped Baal, but it was not easy to define the point where worship of one became worship of the other. This was a matter of opinion. One index the prophets used was the quality of justice practiced by the worshipers. Without persistent concern for the rights and welfare of all the people, and perseverance under the moral standards of the covenant, Israel's religion was a godless thing in the eyes of the prophets, whether or not it was nominally Yahwistic.

The catalogue of social evils in the oracles of Jeremiah is short, and not many oracles speak of them at any length. However, there are enough to place Jeremiah securely within the prophetic tradition of social criticism. Adultery and fornication were commonplace, he said (5:7-11), not only in the figurative sense of baalized cultic practice, but apparently in the literal sense as well. Jerusalem was filled with oppression, violence, and destruction (6:6-7). Treachery and enslavement of others had made some people wealthy and powerful (5:26-27), and with their power, they had corrupted the courts and neglected the fatherless and the poor (5:28). Lust, greed, deceit, and slander were rife, so that no one dared trust anyone else. Thus, the whole fabric of social relations was torn to shreds (9:2-8). The prophet searched Jerusalem for one righteous person (5:1), and finding none among the poor—where crime flourishes in ignorance and misery—he turned to the rich, who were trained in the law of God and could afford to be just. But he found none there either—not one (5:2-5).

Naturally, we protest this condemnation of the entire population of Jerusalem. Not only is it unlikely on the face of it, but it contradicts the evidence of the prose narratives of the book, which give a more balanced and realistic picture of the people of Judah. In Jeremiah 26, for example, the princes defend Jeremiah's innocence and his life against the cultic officials, who are incensed at his threats against the temple (26:10-16). In later incidents, Jeremiah is shown using the Rechabites as an example of covenantal loyalty (chap 35), and even characterizing the Judean leaders exiled in 598 as "good figs" (24:1-7). Thus it seems clear that the writers of the prose have described the moral situation in Judah more realistically than did the prophet in his oracles of judgment. The Judean situation must have been morally ambiguous, like most situations at other times and places. Nevertheless, the responsibility of the interpreter is not to reject the prophetic oracles as unhistorical, but to acknowledge them for what they are—words addressed to the will and conscience of a religious community. Seen in this way, the oversimplification and exaggeration make sense. Jeremiah's account of the moral engagement between YHWH and Judah is passionate and intense, and it concentrates on the heart as the site of the encounter. Thus the style of his oracles matches the substance.

DIVINE PASSION

In a series of poems unique in the prophetic literature, the prophet pours out his anguish over the debacle that engulfed Judah before his eyes (4:19-22; 8:18–9:1; 9:10-11; 9:17-22; 10:19-20; 14:17-18; 14:19-22). The first (4:19-22) comes immediately after the prophet sounds the alarm for the approaching siege (4:13-18). The reason for the siege is given in the last line: "Your ways and your doings have brought this upon you!" (vs 18). Then at the actual sight of war, the prophet cries out, "My anguish, my anguish! I writhe in pain!" The emotional pitch of the passage is so high that many commentators regard it as a vision. This too closes with an explanation of the reason for the event: "For my people are foolish, they know me not. . . . They are skilled in doing evil, but how to do good they know not" (4:22). There is no identification of the speaker in this last verse, or in 4:19-21. The "me" in "they know me not" (4:22) must be God, as all commentators recognize. However, the preceding lines are usually assigned to the prophet, also on internal grounds. "My heart is beating wildly. . . . Suddenly my tents are destroyed . . . . How long must I see the standard?" This can only be the prophet's own cry. Or can it? Formally, there is no break at all between the cry (vss 19-21) and the explanation (vs 22). The obvious conclusion would be to take the "I" of the two parts as one and the same, were it not for the vivid pathos described in the first part. Commentators therefore have concluded that the prophet was speaking for himself here, but it seems to me that there is an intentional confusion of speakers. The prophet is not conveying his own private response to the tragedy of Judah, but the response of a messenger of YHWH —one who is YHWH's mouth. It is not too much to say that in his mind, his own pathos is also the pathos of God.

This same confusion between Jeremiah and YHWH is found again in 8:18–9:1, one of the best known passages in the book. It is generally assumed that Jeremiah is voicing his own grief here, and this judgment is probably correct, as far as it goes. The poem is a complaint in five parts. It opens with a brief expression of grief and heartsickness (8:18), then the puzzled cry of the one called, literally, "my daughter, my people" (NRSV, "my poor people"): "Is YHWH not in Zion?" (8:19). This is followed by a response from YHWH: "Why have they provoked me to anger with their . . . idols?" (8:19). The fourth part is another quotation of the people's words: "The harvest is past, the summer is ended, and we are not saved" (8:20). Finally, the poem ends with a long lament over the sick (8:22) and the slain (9:1) of "my daughter, my people."

The response of YHWH in 8:19 is sometimes regarded as a scribal addition, incongruous with the remainder of the lament (Hyatt; JB), but this conclusion presupposes that Jeremiah is expressing his own grief over the people's calamity and not speaking as the mouth of YHWH. It seems to me that just the opposite is true. Jeremiah is speaking for YHWH throughout the lament; therefore the middle section there is not incongruous.

The two quotations of the people (8:19, 20) are brief laments. The second looks as though it may have originated in a ceremony of complaint over a bad harvest; it has a certain affinity to the complaint over a drought that appears in Jeremiah 14:1-9. However, in the present context, the popular sayings in 8:19 and 20 have a wider reference. The calamity is more than agricultural: the people are wounded (8:21), they are desperately ill (8:22), and some of them have been slain (9:1). These assertions, placed in juxtaposition to passages that describe the invasion from the north (8:14-17) and the moral corruption of the people (9:2-3), have to do with the final "harvest" of the Judean kingdom.

We may note here, by the way, that the indignant speaker in 9:2-3—"O that I had in the desert a traveler's lodging place, that I might leave my people and go away from them"—also is not so obviously Jeremiah as is usually assumed. The closing formula, "says YHWH" (9:3), appears to cover the whole speech, not merely the last line of it. Thus, in boldly anthropomorphic terms, the prophet represents YHWH as wishing for a wilderness retreat where he can get away from his treacherous people. God's grief has turned to rage.

Another reason to think that the poet speaks for God in the lament of 8:18–9:1 is the fourfold use of the phrase "my daughter, my people" (8:19, 21, 22; 9:1). This phrase and the related one, "my people," occur a total of forty-four times in the book. In thirty-six instances, spread over all the literary strata of the book, the speaker is YHWH.7 In eight instances, it is uncertain whether the speaker is YHWH, or the prophet, or both.8 In *no* instance is it unambiguously the prophet. This evidence surely indicates that the "I" presupposed in the phrase "my people" is YHWH and that any employment of this style by the prophet (or by his imitators) is derivative, in the sense that he is taking it upon himself solely as the spokesman of YHWH. Commentators frequently have understood Jeremiah's reference to "my people" as an indication of his fundamental identification with them, but this is not Jeremiah speaking. It is YHWH.

In 9:10-11 and 9:17-22 the situation is altered somewhat. Here the speaker is not lamenting, but calling for others to do so. Even here, the lament to be taken up is intended to cause the speaker's "eyes to run down with tears" (9:18), and as the opening formula, "Thus says YHWH of hosts" (9:17), makes clear, the speaker is YHWH. Everyone joins in the lament over the destruction of Jerusalem—the people, the prophet, and God.

In the two remaining poems in this series, we hear the lament of the prophet in one (10:19-20) and the lament of YHWH in the other (14:17-18). In the first, again the identification between prophet and God is close. At one moment the prophet appears to be speaking ("Truly this is my punishment, and I must bear it" 10:19), but in the next moment, it appears to be YHWH ("My children have gone from me, and they are no more" vs 20). Thus the third-person reference to YHWH in vs 21 is made by YHWH himself, in yet another vivid anthropomorphism (cf. 4:20).

In summary, it seems likely that the passion expressed in these oracles—grief, indignation, anger—is not only Jeremiah's but God's as well. It is a divine pathos that expresses itself through the chosen messenger, one whose existence is so closely bound to the word of God that his whole life is shaped by his calling (1:5).

JEREMIAH'S COMPLAINTS

Jeremiah was not a fanatic, so identified with God that he forgot his limitations. This is clear from his complaints (11:18–12:6; 15:20-21; 17:14-18; 18:18-23; 20:7-12, 14-18). The complaints, once called "confessions," today are often called "laments" because of their similarity to the psalms of lament (or lamentation). However, *complaint* is more descriptive of their contents, as it is of the related psalms. Jeremiah's complaints show him to be vulnerable to the assaults of his enemies and to the resulting vindictiveness and self-doubt. They show him questioning the justice and power of God and doubting his call, but they also show him receiving new strength and assurance from this inner dialogue.

There are different views of the origin of these texts. Their affinity to the individual complaint psalms has long been recognized, but it has been variously explained. Prior to the rise of form criticism, Jeremiah's authorship of his "confessions" was accepted as a matter of course, and the complaints in the book of Psalms were regarded as imitations of his style, or possibly his own compositions. His confessions were treated naturally as expressions of his personal struggle.

Thanks to form criticism and the comparative study of the hymns and prayers of the ancient Far East, the genres and language of the psalms came to be recognized as older than the book of Jeremiah, and scholars concluded that Jeremiah's complaints were formally dependent upon the psalms. For a long time, no one doubted that the content of Jeremiah's complaints was based upon his personal experience.[9] This view was challenged finally by H. G. Reventlow, and as a result, commentators on Jeremiah have been forced to reexamine Jeremiah's complaints. Reventlow argued that the complaints had nothing to do with Jeremiah's personal experience, but were liturgical texts spoken by Jeremiah on behalf of Judean worshipers as he fulfilled his responsibility as a cultic prophet.[10] They are really communal psalms of complaint, although they have been styled as complaints of the individual; the "I" is the corporate "I" of the Judean cultic community, and the language of the complaints is entirely conventional. However, these proposals have not been accepted by most scholars.

An attractive alternative has been proposed by A.H.J. Gunneweg.[11] Rejecting both the individual-psychological and cultic theories of the origin of Jeremiah's complaints, he regards them as part of a retrospective interpretation of Jeremiah as the exemplary sufferer depicted in the complaint psalms. Although Jeremiah's complaints reflect genuine Jeremiah tradition, they are not biography, but proclamation. What Jeremiah suffers as a result of his vocation is the embodiment of what the complaint psalms express: He is the righteous sufferer. However, Jeremiah is not a private individual here, suffering because of his personal fidelity to God. Rather, as a prophet of disaster, he suffers because he is already experiencing the suffering that he believes God will bring upon the people. The calamity is fulfilled in Jeremiah's life, so it must be experienced by the reader. In this interpretation, the complaints of Jeremiah are not so much cries of the heart as expressions of horror at the threatened disaster. Jeremiah shares the disaster with the people and he suffers with them. His life is prophecy fulfilled, and as a result, his complaints are to be understood as proclamation.

The strength of this interpretation is that it does justice both to the genuine prophetic elements in the complaints (Jer 15:16-17, 19; 17:15; 20:8-9) and the conventional form in which they are cast. It avoids Reventlow's confusion of the allusions to prophetic vocation with more general religious language, yet it recognizes the rest of the language of Jeremiah's complaints as the conventional language of the psalms. The most debatable aspect of Gunneweg's work is the judgment that the interpreter of Jeremiah's life was not Jeremiah himself, but a later writer. Unfortunately, this question cannot be settled on the basis of present knowledge. We can be sure that the later traditioners interpreted Jeremiah's life by means of these complaints, but we cannot be sure that Jeremiah did so himself.

Acknowledging, then, that we are dealing with a picture of Jeremiah drawn by tradition, and not necessarily with a self-portrait, we can consider the message communicated by the complaints. In the book, the complaints presuppose the call of the prophet (Jer 1); however, in keeping with our procedure of treating the poetry separately from the prose, here we will consider only the complaints themselves and will take up the question of their relation to the prose framework of the book later.

The first complaint of Jeremiah is a response to a threat against his life (11:18-23). Several theories have been advanced to explain the source and nature of the threat, some of which involve a rearrangement of the text of 11:18–12:6, but none of the proposed arrangements is fully satisfying. There is general agreement that the present text combines at least two originally separate pieces (11:18-23 and 12:1-6) and that both of these have been expanded in transmission. However, the steps in the process are untraceable. In the canonical edition, the occasion for Jeremiah's complaint was the discovery, interpreted as a revelation of God (11:18), that people in Anathoth, his native town, were plotting to kill him (11:19, 21). If 12:6 belongs with 11:18-20, as many scholars believe, then members of Jeremiah's own family were involved in the conspiracy. The motive for their murderous intent was to stop Jeremiah from prophesying in YHWH's name (11:21). Naturally, interpreters have not been content with these meager facts, but have speculated about the background of the conspiracy.

A theory once popular was that Jeremiah incurred the wrath of the rural priesthood by supporting Josiah's reform, which closed up the rural sanctuaries and put the priests out of work (2 Kings 23:8-9). A second theory is that Jeremiah *opposed* the reform and thus incited the Jerusalem hierarchy. According to yet another theory, Jeremiah initially supported the reform and then opposed it when he saw the results. All these theories are speculative, since nothing at all is said about Josiah's reform in the book.

The only reason given in the book for the threat on Jeremiah's life was that he prophesied the destruction of the temple and the city of Jerusalem, the termination of the kingdom of Judah, and the deportation of the court and leading citizens. According to the prose tradition, opposition to Jeremiah began among the cultic officials when Jeremiah proclaimed (about 609) that the temple was in danger of destruction (Jer 26; cf. 7:1ff.). The opposition became general as time went on and Jeremiah's conditional message of disaster gave way to one of unconditional destruction and exile (36:1ff.; 27:1ff.; 37:1ff.; etc.). The poetic oracles fit into this prose picture fairly well. Most prophesy doom, but a few are calls to repentance (notably 3:1-5, 12*b*-14, 19-25; 4:1-4). It is doubtful whether the chronological sequence presupposed by the prose narrator is historical. Nevertheless, the picture of Jeremiah's persecution for prophesying judgment suits the poetic oracles well enough for us to interpret the conspiracy in 11:18-23 in this way.

The situation is different in several other complaints. In 17:15 and 20:7, the cause of the complaint is public ridicule of Jeremiah for the failure of his prophesies to come to pass. No physical harm is mentioned, but in 20:7, there is a reference to "overcoming" and "taking revenge" against him, which sounds harmful. In 18:18, the people's attack is a reaction to his prediction that law, counsel, and word would perish from priest, wiseman, and prophet, but their abuse is only verbal.

Jeremiah's conflict with other prophets (cf. 27–28) is mentioned in 14:13-16, which the editors have placed in proximity to the complaints. Jeremiah's rivals prophesied peace while he prophesied disaster. In the circumstances, the audience's response was not surprising. They were bothered by his threat of doom (11:19, 21; 15:20; 18:20; 20:10*b*) but mocked him over its delay (15:15; 17:15; 18:18*b*; 20:7-8).

The most serious threat to Jeremiah occurred during the final Babylonian siege of Jerusalem (588), when the Judean princes put him in a cistern, ostensibly to starve, because he counseled surrender to the attackers (38:1-6). He had been imprisoned previously for alleged desertion (37:11-15). Thus the charges varied, and so did the treatment he received. At the base of all this conflict was Jeremiah's prophecy of destruction and exile; everything else was derivative.

It is futile to try to date Jeremiah's complaints in relation to specific events in his life, as was formerly done as a matter of course. We can only guess which, if any, of the experiences of persecution mentioned in the prose narratives might have been the background for the complaints. Furthermore, if we cannot date them, we cannot trace any development in them, as many interpreters have tried to do, so we must confine ourselves to the contents of the complaints as they are given to us by the tradition. The Jeremiah we encounter everywhere in the book is a figure interpreted, perhaps even transfigured, by tradition. This is true above all in the complaints.

The most striking feature of Jeremiah's complaints is the petition to God to take vengeance on his enemies. It appears in every one (11:20; 12:3; 15:15; 17:18; 18:21-22; 20:12). Some commentators are offended by this, wondering how such words were possible on the lips of a man of God. But Jeremiah was powerless; his only recourse was to pray for relief from his persecutors. The way one did this in ancient Israel was the way indicated in the psalms of complaint.

Jeremiah's wish for vengeance against his enemies was closely related to his belief that they would fall when the nation fell. In fact, only one statement in his complaints specifies the vengeance he hoped for, and it is precisely that his enemies would suffer in the nation's fall (11:22). The oracles against Pashhur and Shemaiah (20:3-6; 29:31-32), as vengeful as the complaints, make the same point.

In his commentary on Jeremiah, W. Rudolph contrasts Jeremiah's spirit of vengeance toward his enemies with Jesus' spirit of forgiveness toward his executioners (Lk 22:34), and adds that this illustrates the difference between New Testament and Old Testament piety. However, this comparison is unfair. To be sure, there is a radical difference between the love of one's enemies and the desire for vengeance, but it is not fair to the Old Testament writers to use the words of Jesus against them in this way. More comparable New Testament texts would be Paul's admonition to the Philippians to "look out for the dogs, look out for the evil-workers" (Phil 3:2), or the words of wrath against the enemies of God in the book of Revelation (e.g., 9:4-6), or even the words of judgment attributed to Jesus in the Gospels (e.g., Mt 25:29-30, 41-43). Love of the enemy is the ultimate quality of redemptive love, but that is divine love, not human love, and it transcends the ordinary piety of the people of the New Testament as much as that of the people of the Old, as Paul, for example, continually affirmed.

There is no common pattern of ideas in Jeremiah's complaints, nor is there a progressive development in them. All five contain a petition for God's justice, but most of the other components are varied. Two complaints contain responses by God (11:21-23 plus 12:5; 15:19-20), and two contain curses of the prophet's life (15:10; 20:14-18). Other features vary considerably from complaint to complaint. God's responses are particularly significant. In the first case, the response has two parts: the assurance that those who sought to kill Jeremiah will fall in the day of disaster (11:21-23); and that Jeremiah cannot expect relief from trouble, but must be prepared for even greater tests of strength (12:5). This second part is the more interesting of the two, for we expect the denunciation of the enemies, but the other word comes as a surprise. It presupposes two things: that conflict over the word of God is not occasional, but perennial; and that messengers of God cannot expect extrinsic rewards for their service, but must find their reward in the service itself. God provides no shelter from the contest, but only the courage to endure it. This point is made even more clearly in 15:19-20, and it is particularly telling there because of the mood of the accompanying complaint (15:10-18).

In the first complaint the fact of the prophet's persecution is mentioned, and in the piece that has been joined to it (12:1-6), the general question about the prosperity of the wicked is put to God, with no attempt to answer it theoretically. However, in the second complaint (15:10-21), the tone is much more personal. Here the problem is the inner agony of one who has devoted himself gladly to

God, and who feels betrayed by the God who sent him. He curses his life (15:10) and groans in pain (vs 18); then, amazingly, we read that the problem is not with God but with himself (15:19-20): "If you turn back, I will take you back. . . . If you utter what is precious, and not what is worthless, you shall serve as my mouth." The worthless words are not the public oracles, obviously, but the charge of God's infidelity. Is the cry of vengeance against his persecutors also a worthless word (15:15)? That it may be is suggested by the next lines of God's reply: "It is they who will turn to you, not you who will turn to them" (vs 19*b*). The natural way to understand this line is as a directive not to treat his opponents as they treat him. Let them conform to his behavior, not the other way around. And the following lines confirm this interpretation: "They will fight against you, but they will not prevail against you, for I am with you to save you and deliver you, says the LORD" (15:20).

After the antithetic parallel in verse 19*b* ("It is they who will . . . not you who will"), we expect a similar parallel in verse 20: "It is they who will fight against you, not you who will fight against them." The antithesis is implied, but instead of putting it this way, the writer shifts the thought to another level. The Lord YHWH is with Jeremiah to preserve his life, so by implication, the prophet need not fight against his enemies, for they cannot prevail against him. The prophet has committed his cause to God (11:20), so all fighting is out of his hands. Thus the directive in verse 19*b*, "It is not you who will turn to them," must be a prohibition of direct action against the persecutors, not a prohibition of petitions to God for justice.

"If you turn back, I will take you back," is the word Jeremiah hears from God, meaning, "Repent and you will be restored to service." Is repentance then first, and restoration second, or does restoration require God's healing initiative before repentance can occur? According to Jeremiah's understanding of the human heart, it does: "The heart is devious above all things, it is perverse—who can understand it?" (17:9). "Can Ethiopians change their skin or leopards their spots? Then also you can do good who are accustomed to do evil?" (13:23). Though Jeremiah might not be reckoned among those accustomed to do evil, he shared with them the fundamental human problems of finitude and bondage of the will. Therefore he cried out, "Heal me, O LORD, and I shall be healed; save me, and I shall be saved!" (17:14).

We might expect this appeal—the opening line of the third complaint (17:14-18)—to include a wish for a change of heart toward the enemy, but no such wish is spoken. The problem is that Jeremiah is being made to suffer for faithful service to God's word. The word did not come from his own heart (17:16); it came from "before the face" of God. If this were true, then the prophet could only expect the word to be fulfilled and not allowed to pass away (17:15). And if the word were fulfilled, it would put the scoffers to shame and vindicate the prophet (17:18).

The central issue in the complaints is Jeremiah's relationship with God. The issue is put most sharply in the last complaint: "O LORD, you have enticed me, and I was enticed" (20:7). This cry of betrayal echoes the words of the second complaint—"Truly you are to me like a deceitful brook, like waters that fail" (15:18)—but goes even further, to show a deeper level of the man's struggle to extricate himself from his predicament. Caught between his prophetic calling and the people's derision (20:8), he has tried to abandon his vocation (vs 9*a*). But the effort has been futile, for he has been wracked with torment over his failure to obey his commission, and thus driven to speak out again (vs 9*b*). His commission, and the suffering bound up with it, were inescapable. His only comfort was the conviction that he would be sustained in his work and that his witness would be vindicated in time (vss 11-12).

This expression of ultimate confidence is not put in the form of divine address to Jeremiah, like the responses to the first two complaints (11:22-23 plus 12:5-6; 15:19-20), but the substance of the statement is closely related to these responses. All three mark a turning away from self-concern—his loyalty to God, his sympathy for the people, his sacrifice of human satisfaction for the sake of his calling, his undeserved suffering at the hands of his countrymen—to concern for the calling—its transcendent ground and authority, its urgency, its validity. At the end of his struggle, he returns again to the point from which he began in interpreting his call—the conviction that his existence was bound inseparably to the word of God; that no obstacle, within or without, could keep him from performing his service as a prophet. The experiences reflected and interpreted in the complaints were rooted in the prior experience of the call to prophecy, and they served as a reaffirmation of that call in the active course of an arduous life.

Jeremiah's curse upon his own life (20:14-18) which accompanies the fifth complaint (20:7-12) is unique in the prophetic literature. Its only parallel in the Hebrew Bible is the self-curse of Job (Job 3), which some scholars regard as an imitation of Jeremiah's curse. The similarities are undeniable. Both begin by cursing the day of birth and end by asking why one should have been born only to live a life of suffering. If there is literary dependence involved, since Job 3 is much more elaborate, it is reasonable to suppose it is dependent upon Jeremiah 20:14-18. In its compactness, Jeremiah's curse is even more powerful than Job's, particularly in its closing question. The impact of Job's question is diluted somewhat by the fulsomeness of the poem. But Jeremiah's question is fired at heaven like a single shot: "Why did I come forth from the womb to see toil and sorrow, and spend my days in shame?"!

Here is the deep point of despair. The arrangement of the book, which places this self-curse with the last complaint, suggests that the moment of deepest agony came after the moment of renewed confidence in the preceding complaint (20:11-12), that the cry of despair was the prophet's last word about his own life. However, this is a hazardous inference to draw, since the arrangement may be fortuitous. Certainly the last word of the Jeremiah tradition was that he persevered in prophecy for forty years in spite of his anguish. When he disappears from view among the Judean fugitives in Egypt, he is still prophesying (Jer 44)!

Jeremiah rejected the role of intercessor for his people in the days of the kingdom (7:16; 11:14; 14:11), but the figure remembered and portrayed in the tradition became genuinely intercessory in behalf of the remnant who survived the fall of Judah and renewed the Yahwistic community in the next generation. The purpose of intercession is to bring about reconciliation between the people and God. For reconciliation to be real, it must be mutual. But in the age of wrath, even a penitent people could not turn away the judgment of God (14:11); so meaningful reconciliation was impossible, intercession futile. In the aftermath of judgment, new possibilities were nourished by new understandings. A chastened remnant, truly penitent, was open to reconciliation with God; discerning more deeply the terms of the relationship, the people could see, as they could not before, that the question of reconciliation was never really one of God's turning to them, but of their turning to God. This was what Jeremiah had discovered in his anguished dialogue. Jeremiah began by believing that God would do what he wanted—avenge him against his enemies and vindicate him in the eyes of the people—if he fulfilled his prophetic calling. But he learned that God did not work on Jeremiah's terms, but only on God's terms. The same lesson was learned on a communal scale, by those who had ears to hear, from the fall of Judah. The rewards of faithful service to God were different from those imagined in the ordinary religion of Israel, or in most popular religion. Jeremiah had to learn to serve God for God's sake alone, not for the things he believed God should do for him. Once he had learned this lesson and appropriated it into his consciousness, he was reconciled to God. His acceptance of the real terms of his relationship with God was the basis of his reconciliation. It was Jeremiah, not God, who changed in this process.

And so it was for the remnant of Judah. God was the same after the fall as before it. It was the the remnant's understanding of God that had changed. Viewing God through the eyes of Jeremiah, the chastened prophet, the people were enabled to discern the truth about the ways of God: the life God gives and sustains, the vocation of service God offers, and the personal flourishing God makes possible within the community of righteousness and faith. The old understanding of God as the guarantor of Israel's political integrity and supplier of material needs could be set aside in favor of a more profound understanding of God's grace. Jeremiah's oracles expressed these truths, and his experience exemplified them. In this way he became the reconciled reconciler of God and Israel, an authentic intercessor.

APOSTASY AND REPENTANCE

I have suggested that the prophets' obedience to their calling was not contingent upon their achievements. They persisted, whether or not their words were heeded. Indeed, the preexilic prophets hardly expected national reformation prior to the fall, but viewed the fall as the necessary precondition of genuine reformation. This does not mean they were not concerned with repentance and reform. On the contrary, they were profoundly concerned, but they clearly had no illusions about the conditions of renewal. Nations do not repent; only individuals. National changes take place gradually, or are forced by great events. The forces that determine the destiny of a nation are so vast and complex that any simple appeal to individuals to transform a nation's life is bound to fail.

Jeremiah perceived the depth and universality of sin and understood the enduring struggle between good and evil. His vain search throughout Jerusalem for a single righteous person (5:1ff.) was his testimony to the universality of sin. His question, "Can Ethiopians change their skin or leopards their spots?" and the added statement, "Then also you can do good who are accustomed to do evil," were his testimony to the depth of sin. Surprisingly, repentance was also a part of his message.

The relation of repentance to punishment, forgiveness, and salvation in the book of Jeremiah is complex, and it is understood differently in the poetic oracles and in the prose sermons. A call to repentance as the means of assuaging the wrath of God and averting destruction of the kingdom appears in the prose (7:3-15; 26:3-6, 12-13; 36:2-3; cf. 18:11). According to 25:3-9 and 35:15, this call was made both by Jeremiah (25:3-9) and by other prophets (35:15), but was rejected by the people, who thus sealed their doom. A summons to an unidentified king to repent in order to ensure the continuation of the Davidic dynasty is made in 22:3-5, again in the prose. The wickedness alluded to in these passages is very general, but in two other prose texts, it is more specific: In 34:15 it is slavery; in 38:20-23, it is misguided military policy. In these texts, too, repentance is understood to be a means of averting doom. By contrast, in the poetic oracles, a straightforward assurance that the kingdom of Judah could be saved by repentance is never made. Repentance is an important theme in these oracles, but it is treated more subtly than in the prose.

Apostasy and repentance—turning aside and turning back—are the subjects of the great oracle in Jeremiah 3:1-5, 12*b*-13, 19-23, and 4:1-4. Using the metaphor of Israel's marriage to YHWH, learned perhaps from Hosea, Jeremiah rejects the notion that the unfaithful wife who has been justly divorced by her husband can return to him when it pleases her, even as she persists in adultery (3:1-5). However, forgiveness and restoration of the bond between God and Israel are still possible for those who are truly penitent and abandon their evil ways (3:12*b*-13; 4:1-4). Indeed, God will heal their faithlessness (3:22). In context, this assurance means that a persistent effort by Israel to be faithful to the covenant with YHWH will be met with sufficient resources of divine grace to overcome the lingering inclination to embrace the tangible gods of nature.

Divine punishment is correlated to human infidelity in this poem, where it is suggested that Israel has been chastised for idolatry by lack of rain (3:3). The discipline has been futile, since Israel has persisted in pursuing alien gods. This idea of chastisement by drought, found elsewhere in the prophetic corpus (e.g., Amos 4:7), is based on the ancient view that rainfall, like all natural phenomena, occurred at the specific direction of God. The notion is incredible to most people today, but it is a minor motif in the present oracle. The dominant motif is an appeal to the people to accept a restored relationship with YHWH. The promise made to reinforce the appeal is that other nations will bless themselves in YHWH's name and glory in YHWH, as a consequence of Israel's fidelity (4:1-4). No material benefits are offered. What Israel will gain is a vital bond to the true God, and since all that is meaningful and necessary in life depends upon that bond, this is the ultimate promise. Any other would be contingent and uncertain.

I am arguing that the poetic oracles do not correlate human sin with divine punishment, or human virtue with divine blessing, in the simple fashion of the prose sermons. However, a correlation of a different sort is suggested in the oracle in 3:1–4:4. An end to God's anger is promised if Israel will return to God (3:12), and a heightening of anger is threatened if Israel will not return (4:4). This is a kind of correlation of repentance with forgiveness and unrepentance with wrath. But there is no simple correlation here between Israel's repentance and the fate of the Judean kingdom, as there is in the prose. Here the prophet has not tried to map out the future in concrete detail. He is convinced that the people's moral and social well-being are at stake, that the terms of their engagement with God are life and death. However, he does not try to chart the exact course of Israel's future under God.

This is the only poetic oracle in the book where the main theme is an appeal to Israel to repent. Several others mention Israel's unrepentance as a factor in her worsening situation (5:3; 8:4-7; 9:5-6 [LXX]; 13:22-23; 15:7; 23:14). However, the idea that repentance would change the course of the kingdom's destiny is not mentioned in these oracles, and is mentioned only once in the poetry, in 4:11-22. The main theme of this poem is the invasion of Judah by a ravaging army, and it concludes with a cry of anguish (vss 19ff.). The disaster is explained as being a punishment for Israel's evil deeds (vss 18, 22). It is not a disciplinary stroke (vs 11) given in the hope of reform, but a punitive one, required by the severity of the crime. Therefore, when the poet pleads with Jerusalem to cleanse her heart from iniquity in order to be saved (4:14), we should take this as an invitation—not to head off the invasion, but to preserve a faithful remnant beyond the evil day. Whether or not this is the correct interpretation of this text, it is clear that there is little in the poetic oracles to compare with the calculus of repentance and salvation contained in the prose sermons. Jeremiah, like all the prophets, was deeply interested in the moral reformation of the people of Israel, and therefore "preached repentance." But moral reformation can take place in all kinds of political and material circumstances. Jeremiah was just as concerned with repentance during and after the political collapse of the Judean monarchy as he was before it occurred. His concern transcended the political vicissitudes of the nation, even though he was not indifferent to the social well-being of the people. It was simply that his ultimate concern was obedience to God's word and trust in God's love.

PROMISES OF RESTORATION

The collection of oracles in Jeremiah 30–31 is commonly called the book of comfort, or consolation. It contains several of the finest poems in the Jeremiah tradition and a number of prophetic affirmations, notably the prophecy of a new covenant (31:31-34), which have figured prominently in modern interpretation of Jeremiah's work.

Commentators agree that the collection has been edited and amplified by an exilic redactor, but there is no unified scholarly judgment concerning the extent of the Jeremianic component, its specific historical setting, or its audience. The references to Samaria (31:5), Ephraim (31:6, 9, 18, 20), Ramah (31:15), and Rachel (31:15) lead some scholars to conclude that Jeremiah addressed these oracles to the exiles of the northern kingdom, although these scholars date the oracles variously. Some assign them to the earliest period of Jeremiah's ministry, before Josiah's reform (621), some to the age of the reform itself (621–609), some to the decade between the first and second Judean deportation (598–587), and some to the time of Jeremiah's residency at Mizpah, while Gedaliah was governor of Judah (after 586). Still others doubt that Jeremiah had any interest in the restoration of the northern kingdom, and therefore regard the Jeremianic words in this section as intended for the survivors of Judah in 586.

Most critics regard the prose segments of these chapters as redactional, though some are inconsistent in this, attributing the prose prophecy of the new covenant to Jeremiah himself, on the ground that it is too good to have been composed by a redactor. But if the critics are agreed that Jeremiah's own words are to be found primarily in the poetry, they are not agreed on the extent of those words. The range of opinions stretches roughly from that of Hyatt, who includes about twenty verses, to that of Rudolph, who includes twice as many.[12]

All in all, the work of redaction has been done so thoroughly that the collection can hardly be read any longer, except as a proclamation to the remnant of the two kingdoms, after 586. Little information exists in the Bible about the fate of the survivors of the fall of the northern kingdom in 721. However, Josiah's program of national reform in 621 extended into the territory of the old Israelite kingdom (2 Kings 23:15-20), probably with the intention of restoring the Davidic monarchy to its original limits, in the political vacuum created by the waning of Assyrian power in the west. Therefore, it is not surprising to find oracles in the book of Jeremiah addressed to people in that territory. Their destiny would have been closely linked to Judah's after 621. This judgment is confirmed for the period after 586 by the report of "eighty men from Shechem, Shiloh, and Samaria" who went to worship at the temple of YHWH (Jer 41:4ff.). Heads shaved, clothes torn, flesh cut, they must have been lamenting the fall of Jerusalem; intercepted at Mizpah by the assassins of Gedaliah, they too were slain. Thus it seems that during Jeremiah's time there were active Yahwists living in the former kingdom of Israel who would have been appropriate subjects of his preaching, along with the Yahwists of Judah.

Jeremiah was from Anathoth (1:1), a town in the traditional territory of Benjamin. According to the ancient tribal genealogies, Benjamin was the son of Jacob and Rachel, and the full brother of Joseph, whose son Ephraim became leader of the dominant tribe in the north. Therefore, it is natural to suppose that Jeremiah was interested in both Rachel tribes and that this interest endured through the changing fortunes of these territories. If this was the case, when the redactor directed Jeremiah's promises to the remnants of the kingdoms of Israel and Judah (30:3, 4; 31:27, 31—all in prose), he simply was expressing what already was implied in the oracles of Jeremiah, for we know from other parts of the book that Jeremiah was keenly interested in the future of Judah's survivors.

It is much less clear, however, that the redactor was expounding the message of Jeremiah in everything he said to the remnant. The unconditional promise of repossession of the land (30:3); restoration of the city of Jerusalem (31:38-40) with its royal palace (or citadel, 30:18), its "holy hill" (31:23; cf. 31:12), and its Davidic dynasty (30:9); and especially the unqualified assurance that the city would never again be overthrown (31:40)—all lack the ethical content of the oracles of Jeremiah, and even of the prose speeches (e.g., 7:1ff.). And the notion that the nation would be restored in the future just as it used to be (30:18-21) seems incompatible with the expectation of new dimensions of divine/human interaction in other parts of the book (even 31:31-34). That notion came not from Jeremiah, but from the same circle that produced 33:7 ("as they were at the beginning"). We are forced to agree with the scholars who attribute these mutations in the Jeremiah tradition to the exilic redactors.

Another sign of editorial activity is the arrangement of the book of consolation. Poems that describe the people's present distress are followed in every case by promises of future restoration, so that a regular pattern of alternation is established, with a crescendo in the arrangement. The first description of distress (30:5-7) is complemented by a single oracle of promise (30:8-9).[13] The second description (30:12-15) is followed by two oracles of promise (20:16-17; 30:18-21), and the third (30:23-24) is followed by three (31:1, 2-6; 31:7-9; 31:10-14). Next, there is a return to the simple pairing of a word of distress (31:15) with a word of consolation (31:16-17). Finally, after the final description of the present distress (31:18-19), the book concludes with a climactic series of promises, most of them in prose (31:20-40).

Discerning the stages in the redactional process is less important than describing the theological themes of the collection. Uppermost among these themes is the idea that Israel was under the care and discipline of a righteous and loving God, best imagined as a devoted parent: "I have become a father to Israel, and Ephraim is my firstborn" (31:9); "I have loved you with an everlasting love; therefore, I have continued my faithfulness to you" (31:3).

The metaphor of father and son is used again in 31:20; that of father and daughter, in 31:21-22, recalling the oracles of Hosea. It may be significant that in both passages in Jeremiah in which God is referred to as father, Ephraim is the focus of concern, for "Ephraim" was Hosea's favorite designation of his audience (the name is used 36 times in Hosea and only 24 times in the rest of the books of the prophets). For example, he used this name for the northern kingdom four times in the famous parent-child oracle in Hosea 11. Thus, Jeremiah 31 shows signs of indebtedness to Hosea similar to those in the early chapters of the book (esp. Jer 2; 3; cf. "the grain, the wine, and the oil" in Jer 31:12; Hos 2:8, 9, 22).

The idea of divine discipline suits the metaphor of God as parent, although it also suits the metaphor of teacher and judge. It is used effectively in Jeremiah 30:11 and 31:8. The discipline of God is just (30:11), even though it may be *experienced* as cruel and merciless (30:14). Its aim is the reformation of the child, as the child itself may eventually attest (31:18). The Hebrew term employed in these texts (*yasar*) is important in prophetic theology (see *IDBS*, "Divine Discipline"). It is a key element in the fourth servant song of Second Isaiah (52:13–53:12), where it is asserted that the disciplining of the servant of YHWH brings about redemption for others. This idea of vicarious discipline is not present in Jeremiah 30–31, where the idea is the moral transformation of people through direct discipline.

The cry of the repentant Ephraim in Jeremiah 31:18, "Bring me back, let me come back," echoes the plea of 17:14, "Heal me, O Lord, and I shall be healed." Both petitions rest on the conviction that God's gracious initiative is needed to break through the armor of human self-deception, in order to make genuine reformation possible. The basis of God's redemptive action is God's own being. It is simply God's nature to work for the moral fulfillment of God's creatures. Thus the writer supports his petition by declaring, "For you are the Lord, my God" (31:18).

The ultimate dependence upon God for moral healing is underscored in another poem (30:12-17), where the foreground is filled with images of apostasy and judgment, but the image of God as healer is in the background and eventually comes to the fore. Israel sought her well-being through international politics (and its corollary, syncretistic religion), but God the Judge and Savior brought calamity upon Israel, both in and through their misguided quest. The nations that devoured Israel in this process were not the final arbiters of Israel's destiny; they would be consumed in turn, and Israel would be restored by God the Healer. "We have heard a cry of panic, of terror, and no peace. . . . It is a time of distress for Jacob; yet he shall be rescued from it" (30:5-7). The last word in this line, *mimmenah,* can mean either "from it" or "by it," and perhaps both meanings are intended.

The affinity between Jeremiah 30–31 and Isaiah 40–55 has long been noted. It is particularly evident in the promise of the ingathering of Israelites from the ends of the earth (31:8), the renewal of Zion as the mountain of God, the procession of Israel to the mountain (31:12), and the rejoicing of the redeemed in the new era (30:19; 31:4, 12-13). It is also evident in the use of images from nature to speak about the coming renewal and the changelessness of God's being and purpose (esp. 31:35-37). Whether this affinity is due to literary dependence is a question that cannot be answered with assurance. However, both compositions express the hopes of exilic prophets. Finally, we must comment on the adage in 31:29-30:

> In those days they shall no longer say:
> "The parents have eaten sour grapes,
> and the children's teeth are set on edge."
> But all shall die for their own sins; the teeth of everyone
> who eats sour grapes shall be set on edge. (31:29-30)

The belief that God punished the children of sinners as well as the sinners themselves was deeply rooted in Israel. It is expressed in the creedal formula that appears fairly often in the Pentateuch, especially in conjunction with the Decalogue (Exod 20:5-6; 34:6-7; Deut 5:9-10; cf. Num 14:18). This formula, which includes positive as well as negative assertions about God, is the nearest thing to an explicit "doctrine of God" to be found in the Hebrew Bible. The fullest version of it appears in Exodus 34:6-7:

> The Lord, the Lord,
> a God merciful and gracious, slow to anger,
> and abounding in steadfast love and faithfulness,
> keeping steadfast love for the thousandth generation,
> forgiving iniquity and transgression and sin,
> yet by no means clearing the guilty unpunished,
> but visiting the iniquity of the parents upon the children,
> and the children's children,
> to the third and the fourth generation.

The first part of the affirmation is repeated in Psalms 86:15; 103:8; 145:8; Joel 2:13; and Jonah 4:2. We will have occasion to discuss it more fully in connection with the book of Jonah. For now we need only take note of this important creedal tradition as a background to the saying quoted in Jeremiah.

The saying is quoted again in Ezekiel 18:2-4, where it is the text for a sermon on divine retribution. The question of literary dependency between Jeremiah and Ezekiel is interesting but unanswerable. The saying was evidently popular in exilic times, and it provoked reactions from both writers. Both rejected the people's blaming their forebears for their fortunes, but there is a difference in what they said. Jeremiah 31 asserts that the saying will not be repeated "in those days," because it will have no validity then. This is eschatological; the tacit admission is that it may be valid in the present time. However, Ezekiel 18 simply asserts that the saying is false; God does not treat people this way. Every son is requited for his own acts, not for his father's, and he is requited in his own lifetime. There is no need to wait for "those days."

Jeremiah 31:29-30 is one of a series of eschatological prophecies which express belief in the ultimate righteousness of God, the judge of human history, but which presuppose a realistic assessment of existence in the present age. Today it is still possible to say, "The parents have eaten sour grapes, and the children's teeth are set on edge," for the evidence on every side shows that this is true. The opposite observation could also be made—that the children enjoy the fruits of their parents' virtue. However, this was not the problem for Jeremiah's generation. They were burdened with the legacy of a dead kingdom, and Jeremiah, or a disciple of Jeremiah, never would have denied that the destruction of the nation was brought on by the fathers, although he denied the implication that the current generation was not responsible at all. Furthermore, he hoped for the day when every generation would be solely responsible for its own fortunes.

ORACLES ON FOREIGN NATIONS

Jeremiah 46–51 is a collection of anonymous oracles of judgment against foreign nations, similar to Isaiah 13–23 and Ezekiel 25–32. In the LXX, these chapters follow 25:13 and are in a different order: 49:34-39; 46:2-28; 50; 51; 47; 49:7-22, 1-6, 28-33, 23-27; 48. Commentators are divided on which of these is the older placement and the older sequence. There are two reasons to prefer the placement in the LXX. First, chapter 25 is a logical introduction to the oracles; second, this placement corresponds to the placement of the oracles on foreign nations in Isaiah and Ezekiel—between the oracles of judgment against Israel and the oracles of salvation for Israel. On the other hand, the internal order of the oracles in this group is more logical in the Hebrew Bible than in the Greek Bible. The Hebrew contains a geographic ordering from southwest to northeast, with the oracle on the great powers, Egypt and Babylon, bracketing the middle group on the smaller Syro-Palestinian nations.

Having already discussed the general questions concerning oracles on foreign nations in chapter 4, I will make only a few comments here on the oracles in Jeremiah 46–51.

The theme of the foe from the north, so important in Jeremiah 1–10, appears in these oracles also, and in a curious way. Babylon, the foe from the north in 1–10, is to be destroyed by a similar foe, according to 50:3 and 9. This certainly suggests that the phrase was a conventional formula referring to a mysterious, ominous region and could be used in any doom oracle. It appears again in 47:2 in the oracle against Philistia. Oddly, the redactor has added a note to this last oracle, saying that it refers to the Pharaoh's assault on Gaza—an assault from the southwest!

The Jeremiah collection contains a more complete group of oracles against Israel's Syro-Palestinian neighbors than does either Isaiah or Ezekiel. Jeremiah lists Philistia, Moab, Ammon, Edom, and Damascus (47:1–49:27), the same list, except for Tyre, which appears in Amos 1:3–2:3; and since the Tyre oracle in Amos is perhaps secondary, the two lists may originally have been the same. Amos's oracles are much older, of course, and this fact, plus the quotation of Amos 1:4 in Jeremiah 49:27 suggests the possibility of imitation by the writer of the Jeremiah oracles.

The long lamentation over Moab in Jeremiah 48:1-46 appears to be derived from the poetically superior lamentation in Isaiah 15–16. The Jeremiah text is noteworthy because it prophesies the restoration of Moab's fortunes (48:47), and so too does a gloss on the oracle on Ammon (49:6). However, in the section on Edom, the third member of this traditional triad, there is no corresponding word of promise; this silence reflects the unremitting attitude of hatred toward Edom expressed throughout the Hebrew Bible, about which I will have more to say in the discussion of Obadiah. Ethically, the content of the oracle on Ammon is similar to the one on Edom. The key line:

> (Rabbah) shall become a desolate mound,
>   and its villages shall be burned with fire;
> then Israel shall dispossess those who dispossessed him,
>   says the LORD. (49:2).

Finally, in 50:1–51:58, we note the long, long tirade on Babylon—all 104 verses of it! The great length of the composition suggests that one of the purposes of its publication must have been emotional catharsis. I do not mean to imply that the writer was not serious in condemning the tyrannical Babylonians. They were violent oppressors of many peoples, including Israel; and the outcry of the oppressed, heard so eloquently in oracles like this, was fully justified. As a comment on the fall of a tyrant, this oracle is parallel to the book of Nahum, which celebrates the fall of Nineveh with equal fullness, and in my judgment, in even more effective poetry.

We turn next to the prose tradition in the book of Jeremiah. Although this tradition contains rich memories of the prophet's life and witness, as literature, it is the product of the next phase of Israel's historic journey, the exilic age, and its message is shaped by the circumstances and needs of that age.

SELECT BIBLIOGRAPHY

Blank, Sheldon H. *Jeremiah, Man and Prophet.* Cincinnati: Hebrew Union College, 1961.

Boadt, Lawrence. *Jeremiah 1–25*. Old Testament Message 9. Wilmington, Del.: Michael Glazier, 1982.

Bright, John. *Jeremiah*. Anchor Bible. Garden City, N.Y.: Doubleday, 1965.

Brueggemann, Walter. *To Pluck Up, To Tear Down*. International Theological Commentary. Grand Rapids: Eerdmans, 1988.

Carroll, Robert P. *From Chaos to Covenant: Prophecy in the Book of Jeremiah*. New York: Crossroad Press, 1981.

______. *Jeremiah*. Philadelphia: Westminster Press, 1986.

Clements, Ronald E. *Jeremiah*. Interpretation. Atlanta: John Knox Press, 1988.

Crenshaw, James L. *Prophetic Conflict: Its Effect upon Israelite Religion*. BZAW 124. Berlin/New York: Walter de Gruyter, 1971.

Holladay, William L. *Jeremiah*. Two volumes. Hermeneia. Philadelphia/Minneapolis: Fortress Press, 1986, 1989.

Hyatt, J. Philip. "The Book of Jeremiah." *The Interpreter's Bible*. Vol. 5. Nashville: Abingdon Press, 1956.

______. *Jeremiah: Prophet of Courage and Hope*. Nashville: Abingdon Press, 1958.

McKane, William. *The Book of Jeremiah*. Vol. I. International Critical Commentary. Edinburgh: T. & T. Clark, 1986.

O'Connor, Kathleen. *The Confessions of Jeremiah: Their Interpretation and Role in Chapters 1–25*. SBLDS 94. Atlanta: Scholars Press, 1988.

Overholt, Thomas W. *The Threat of Falsehood: A Study in the Theology of the Book of Jeremiah*. Studies in Biblical Theology. Second series, 16. London: SCM Press, 1970.

Perdue, Leo, and Brian W. Kovacs, eds. *A Prophet to the Nations: Essays in Jeremiah Studies*. Winona Lake, Wis.: Eisenbrauns, 1984.

Raitt, Thomas M. *A Theology of Exile: Judgment/Deliverance in Jeremiah and Ezekiel*. Philadelphia: Fortress Press, 1977.

Robinson, H. Wheeler. "The Cross of Jeremiah." *The Cross in the Old Testament*. London: SCM Press, 1955.

Skinner, John. *Prophecy and Religion: Studies in the Life of Jeremiah*. Cambridge: Cambridge University, 1922.

Thompson, J. A. *Jeremiah*. New International Commentary on the Old Testament. Grand Rapids: Eerdmans, 1980.

Unterman, Jeremiah. *From Repentance to Redemption: Jeremiah's Thought in Transition*. *JSOT* Sup 54. Sheffield: JSOT, 1987.

Welch, Adam C. *Jeremiah: His Time and His Work*. Oxford: Basil Blackwell, 1955.

NOTES

1. Robert P. Carroll, *Jeremiah;* William L. Holladay, *Jeremiah;* and William McKane, *The Book of Jeremiah*, vol. 1.

2. See esp. E. W. Nicholson, *Preaching to the Exiles* (Oxford: Basil Blackwell, 1970); J. Gerald Janzen, *Studies in the Text of Jeremiah*, Harvard Semitic Monographs 6 (Cambridge, Mass.: Harvard University Press, 1973); Sven Soderlund, *The Greek Text of Jeremiah*, *JSOT* Sup 47 (Sheffield: JSOT Press, 1985); Louis Stulman, *The Prose Sermons of the Book of Jeremiah*, SBLDS 83 (Atlanta: Scholars Press, 1986); and McKane, *Book of Jeremiah*, pp. xiv-xvix.

3. See, e.g., John Skinner, *Prophecy and Religion,* pp. 74-88.

4. See Delbert H. Hillers, *Treaty Curses and the Old Testament Prophets,* Biblical et Orientalia 16 (Rome: Pontifical Biblical Institute, 1964).

5. "Function, Setting, and Content in Jeremiah's Oracles of Judgment," unpublished paper read at the annual meeting of the Society of Biblical Literature, Toronto, December 1970.

6. Skinner, *Prophecy and Religion,* pp. 35ff., 231ff.; H. H. Rowley, "The Early Prophecies of Jeremiah in Their Setting," *BJRL* 45 (1962): 198-234.

7. In poetic oracles of judgment: 2:11, 13, 31, 32; 4:11, 22; 5:26, 31; 6:14, 27; 8:7, 11 (MT); 9:2, 7 (MT); 15:7; 18:15; 23:13, 22; in prose: 7:12; 23:27, 32; 29:32; 50:6; in late prose additions: 12:16; 33:24; in the "book of comfort": 30:3; 31:14; in the oracles against foreign nations: 51:45, cf. "They shall be to me a people"; in prose: 7:23; 11:4; 13:11; 24:7; 32:38; in the book of comfort: 30:22; 31:1, 33.

8. In prose: 12:14; 23:2; in poetry: 6:26; 8:19, 22, 23; 9:1; 14:17.

9. See, e.g., Skinner, *Prophecy and Religion,* pp. 201-30; and Sheldon H. Blank, *Jeremiah: Man and Prophet,* pp. 105-42.

10. H. Reventlow, *Liturgie und prophetisches Ich bei Jeremia* (Güterslow: G. Mohn, 1963).

11. "Konfession oder Interpretation im Jeremiabuch," *Zeitschrift für Theologie und Kirche* 67 (1970): 395-416.

12. Hyatt's list: 30:3-7, 12-15; 31:2-6, 9*c*, 15-22; Rudolph's list: 30:5-7, 10-24; 31:2-22, 31-37. See their commentaries.

13. Verses 10-11 are absent in the LXX and appear to have been added in the MT from 46:27-28; see John G. Janzen, *Studies in the Text of Jeremiah,* Harvard Semitic Monographs 6, p. 49.

CHAPTER EIGHT

Jeremiah

THE PROSE TRADITION

The powerful figure of the prophet Jeremiah that is so well known to faithful readers of the Bible is described retrospectively by the exilic authors of the prose portions of the book. The best analogy to this creation of a religious personage from the memories of associates of the historical person is the creation of the personage of Jesus Christ in the Gospels, from memories of the historical Jesus. The story is both a story of the religious leader and a story of the authors' faith.

The book of Jeremiah is slightly more than half prose. The most substantial prose sections are biographical narratives, which cover major episodes in Jeremiah's life (19:1–20:6; 26–29; 36–45) and sermons (7:1–8:13; 11:1-14; 18:1-12; 21:1-10; 25:1-11; 34:8-22; 35:1-19; 44:1-14). Naturally, it is the sermons, straight theological discourses in sermonic form, that are the most explicit theologically. It is the biographical narratives and prose sermons that will be the main subject of our discussion in this section. Another type of prose material includes prophetic signs, omens, and parables; a number of these are in the book, and I will discuss them as a group early in this section. In addition to these three types of prose material, all of which are important theologically, there are many short prose pieces which we need not discuss. Most of these are brief editorial introductions and the like, which serve merely to tie the book together. Then finally, two promises of the restoration of the monarchy (23:1-8; 33:1-26) are late, independent additions, which I will discuss at the appropriate point.

The prose tradition is post-Jeremian in perspective and theology. I do not mean that it is anti-Jeremian, but rather that it builds upon remembered words and deeds of Jeremiah to make its own points. Some of these points agree with those made in the poetic oracles; others differ, to a greater or lesser degree, and it is the distinctive points to which we will give our primary attention.

The narratives and speeches can be distinguished on formal grounds, but this does not justify separating them as two independent sources; often they are so intermixed that any separation is arbitrary. Vast stretches of the biographical narratives are, in fact, nothing more than speeches (e.g., most of 19:3-15; 28:2-16; 42:9-22; 44:21-30), and all but one are set in a narrative framework. The only speech without a narrative introduction is 11:1-17.

The vocabulary and style of the speeches are different from those of the narratives, but the difference is due largely to the difference in subject matter. The speeches are theologically explicit, rhetorically fulsome, and repetitious, just as one might expect. The narratives use different language and a different style to accomplish a different purpose. Since the differences between the two types of material do not necessarily imply different authors, or sources, I will treat the two kinds of material as components of a single complex tradition.

The book of Jeremiah was composed for an exilic audience, and it is the prose that unites the diverse materials into a book and enables us to identify its intended audience. The poetic oracles were composed for a preexilic audience, and the exilic community received their message at second hand. Most of the oracles are accusations of apostasy and moral corruption in the kingdom of Judah, or announcements of the kingdom's imminent destruction. In other words, the poetic oracles presuppose the concurrent existence of the kingdom. Whatever lesson they contain for a later generation is implicit, and it is dependent upon the readers' knowledge of subsequent events. The prose sermons are explicitly hortatory—that is, they are made up primarily of admonitions. Thus they contrast with the poetic oracles, which are primarily accusations and announcements. Moreover, the prose sermons deal largely in moral generalizations applicable to a wide range of situations. The oracles usually proclaim unconditional disaster, while the sermons are conditional. The oracles declare the nation morally helpless ("Can the leopard change its spots?"), while the sermons plead for repentance. All these differences imply different authors.

The biographical narratives occupy a middle ground between the poetic oracles and the prose sermons. They are a means for transmitting the message of the preexilic oracles, and they do this by describing the setting in which the oracles were proclaimed and telling the story of Jeremiah's interaction with the leaders of Judah. Further, the narratives are the vehicle for expanding the themes most relevant to the exiles. I will discuss the narratives first and then the sermons.

THE CALL NARRATIVE

Jeremiah 1 has generally been assigned by critics to the primary stratum of the book. However, Carroll and McKane, among others, recognize the whole chapter, one of the most intensely dialogical passages in the Bible, as an editorial introduction to the book. Unaided by a vision of the sort experienced by other prophets (Amos 7:1-9; 8:1-3; Isa 6; Ezek 1), Jeremiah understands his existence as being shaped by the word of God. At the moment when he feels compelled to become a prophet, he realizes that his whole life has been a preparation for his calling; therefore, he has no choice but to accept it. To refuse would be to reject his destiny as determined by the wisdom and purpose of God. He has been consecrated—set aside—for God's use from the very beginning. And so, after a momentary protest on the grounds of his youth (1:6), he accepts the commission, with the assurance that God will support him in his work (1:8). He need not fear those to whom he is sent, for God will deliver him. This assurance is repeated at the end of the chapter, where Jeremiah's opponents are identified: kings, princes, priests, and people (1:19). Thus we have a picture of a prophet of YHWH, who lives his life through his special relationship with God and finds himself sustained so that he can fulfill his calling. "I am with you" (1:8) was YHWH's promise to the prophet, as it was to Moses and Israel (Exod 3:2; Isa 7:14). This promise was basic to prophetic faith and prophetic hope.

The promise of God's presence is not the only motif common to Jeremiah 1 and Exodus 3. Both narratives exhibit the same literary structure. As Norman Habel has shown (1965), these are two examples of an established literary form, the prophetic call narrative. The elements of the complete form, shown in Exodus 3, are (1) divine encounter, (2) introductory word, (3) commission, (4) objection, (5) reassurance, and (6) sign. Not every call narrative contains all these elements. Jeremiah 1:4-10, which follows the Exodus 3 pattern most closely, lacks an integral sign, though two signs have been appended to the account (1:11-12; 1:13-19).

Fashioning a call narrative according to a conventional pattern does not imply any inauthenticity in the experience. On the contrary, this was the way one spoke in Israel about an authentic prophetic call. To have spoken differently would have made it suspect. At the same time, the narrative is sufficiently distinctive to show that Jeremiah's experience was his own and not a mere imitation of someone else's. Despite the formal similarities among the call narratives, each is unique in substance, echoing the main themes of the prophet's message. This was certainly true of Isaiah's call, as we have seen, and it was also true of Jeremiah's. Jeremiah 1 anticipates the oracles of judgment and promise for Israel, and even the oracles on foreign nations. Thus it is a suitable preface to the whole book.

The report that Jeremiah was set aside by God from birth to be a prophet, and thus separated from worldly associations, anticipates the report of his refusal to marry, have children, or participate in social activities (16:1-9). The purpose of this refusal was not to isolate the prophet from the life of Judah, but to enable him to live out proleptically the calamity of Judah which he prophesied. To a degree unmatched by the other prophets, Jeremiah's life was the symbol of his message.

Jeremiah was set "over nations and over kingdoms, to pluck up and to pull down, to destroy and to overthrow, to build and to plant" (1:10). First to destroy, and then to rebuild. This motto of Jeremiah's ministry is repeated several times throughout the book (12:17; 18:7, 9; 24:6; 31:38, 40; 42:10; 45:4), always in the prose stratum. It is a feature of the final compilation of the book, and it helps to unify the whole.

Being set over nations and kingdoms is a grand commission. In the finished book it covers the oracles on foreign nations. But this is not its only meaning. Since all Jeremiah's oracles were addressed to Israelites, being set over nations and kingdoms is figurative language; but his oracles interpreted the crisis of his time, and this crisis involved many nations. He also spoke about the God who shaped the destinies of nations, and it was crucial for his audience to believe this, or nothing he said would make sense to them. It was also crucial for the exilic audience of the book to understand it, since the rest of the world interpreted the destinies of nations and the ways of the gods differently. In prophetic perspective, one could not be a faithful witness to the ways of God without being a prophet "over nations and kingdoms."

"Do not be afraid of them, for I am with you to deliver you," is the assurance given the prophet in his commission (1:8). Like the other motifs in the call narrative, this one anticipates—or recapitulates—a feature of Jeremiah's ministry, in this case his persecution by his fellow Israelites. The admonition not to fear one's enemies is an ancient word, rooted perhaps in the tradition of holy war (e.g., Josh 8:1; 10:25; 11:6) and certainly in the exodus tradition (Exod 14:13). Words once spoken in the face of a threat from outside the covenant community are spoken here in the face of a threat from within it. This was an unusual development in an age out of joint.

SIGNS, OMENS, AND PARABLES

The prose reports of signs, omens, and parables have affinities with both the poetic and the prose traditions. Their message is generally of a piece with the poetic oracles, but many have been interpreted in the manner of the prose tradition, or have been taken up as integral parts of that tradition.

The omens of the almond branch (1:11-12) and the spilling kettle (1:13-16) come immediately after the call narrative. The first, which is a pun on the name of the almond tree (*shaqed*) and the word *watching* (*shoqed*), is a confirmation of the call and expresses the assurance that YHWH watches over the prophetic word in order to perform it. The kettle omen introduces the theme of the foe from the north, so prominent in chapters 1–10. The third omen concerns baskets of good and bad figs, in Jeremiah 24. This omen is the occasion for a lengthy discourse on the exile and the remnant, which is part of the regular prose tradition, and which I will comment on presently. An omen means nothing to anyone but the one who "sees" it, so it must be explained by that person, just as these three omens are explained, for they would seem far-fetched to anyone but the seer. Jeremiah saw them as omens because he was so preoccupied with his message that associations came freely to his mind. Once linked to the message in this way, the omens become fine mnemonic devices.

Jeremiah's enacted signs are inventive. Here as always, prophetic signs mean something only when they are explained (see the discussion of Isa 7). Several of Jeremiah's signs are dramatic flourishes to accent a speech, so in these cases, the meaning becomes evident at once. He shatters a clay pot while prophesying Jerusalem's destruction (19:1-13), wears a wooden yoke while prophesying vassalage to Babylon (27:1-22), makes a throne platform for Nebuchadnezzar while prophesying the Babylonian conquest of Egypt (43:8-13), and orders the sinking of a scroll in the Euphrates as soon as it has been read. However, one other sign is much more elaborate—the sign of the loincloth (13:1-11).

The meaning of the sign is clear enough: Just as Jeremiah spoils a clean loincloth by burying it in a muddy bank of the Euphrates, so Babylon will spoil Judah and Jerusalem, the "loincloth" of YHWH. Commentators have debated whether Jeremiah actually made two 800-mile round trips to the Euphrates to make a point, or whether he went to some other river nearby. The improbability of the whole drama leads me to conclude that it was only a parable and never acted out. In any case, it is a memorable parable.

Another parable in the book is clearly a verbal parable and not an acted sign, and that is the parable of the potter (18:1-17). It involves no action by Jeremiah. Instead, he makes an example of the action of the potter. The potter's freedom to start over again when a pot he is making becomes misshapen becomes a parable of YHWH's freedom to do the same thing with YHWH's people. In another place, Jeremiah also uses the example of the Rechabites' loyalty to their ancestral covenant to point out the contrast with Israel's disloyalty to their covenant with YHWH (35:1-19); this too is a prophetic parable. Finally, Jeremiah's purchase of his cousin's field in Anathoth during the siege of Jerusalem (32:1-44) is interpreted as a sign of hope. It expresses the confidence that "houses and fields and vineyards will again be purchased in this land" (vs 15). Some of these narratives exhibit the interests and style of the later prose tradition, but the signs, omens, and parables they report are entirely believable as words and deeds of Jeremiah. They are so distinctive, they could easily have been remembered.

GOOD AND BAD FIGS

The omen of the two baskets of figs signals a comparison between the worth of the "good figs," the Judeans deported to Babylon in 597, and that of the remnant in Judah, the "bad figs." This is a drastic contrast, and it vests the hope of a postexilic restoration entirely in the exiles. Several inferences are possible: One is that king Jehoiachin and the other exiles were more capable than Zedekiah and the rest of the puppet government; another inference is that the writer favored the policies of the exiled leaders; a third possibility is that the omen of the figs refers to Jehoiachin's legitimacy.

The text tells us nothing about Jehoiachin's capabilities or policies, but quite a lot about Zedekiah's ineptitude and vacillation. Second Kings 24:9 calls Jehoiachin an evil king, like his father, but this summary condemnation is a cliché of the writers and thus useless as an indication of Jehoiachin's real interests or competency. On the other hand, there is evidence that Jehoiachin, not Zedekiah, despite his enforced exile, was considered the rightful king of Judah, both by Jews and by the Babylonian court.[1] This consideration supports the third interpretation.

Another possibility is that the writer's evaluation had less to do with Jeremiah's generation than with the next one; Jeremiah 24 may reflect the judgment of exilic or postexilic Jews. It is possible that Jeremiah shared the judgment expressed here, of course, yet the passion expressed in 24:6-10, especially in the intemperate condemnation of the Judean remnant (vss 9-10), sounds more like partisan bias than prophecy. A priori, we would expect Jeremiah to have been equally critical of both groups of leaders. Harsh words about Jehoiachin are recorded in 22:24-30 (and in 13:18-19), although these admittedly deal more with his destiny than with his character. However, even if 24:1-20 preserves some recollection of Jeremiah's view, then in the light of 22:24-30, we must see his hope for the future as being grounded in the work of other exiled leaders and their descendants, not in that of Jehoiachin himself, whom Jeremiah expected to die, childless, in exile. Be that as it may, this is a historical and not a theological issue; therefore we need say no more about it here.

FALSE PROPHECY

The story of Jeremiah's symbolic yoke in chapters 27–28 is a story of prophetic conflict. This is a major issue in the prose tradition, just as it is in the poetic oracles.

The book of Deuteronomy contains three tests of authentic prophecy. First, the prophet or dreamer of dreams must not induce people to worship gods other than YHWH (13:1; 18:20). Second, the prophecy must be commanded by YHWH and not delivered presumptuously. Finally, the prophecy must come to pass (18:21-22). On the surface, these tests do not appear very helpful. The third one is actually proposed simply because the first two do not settle the hard cases—the disputes between prophets of YHWH who possess the accepted credentials. However, the third test also is useless at the moment of dispute.

The story of King Ahab and the 401 prophets, told in deuteronomic perspective and affirming the deuteronomic test of prophecy, illustrates the problem (1 Kings 22). Four hundred prophets told Ahab that if he attacked Ramoth-gilead, YHWH would give him victory. Micaiah ben Imlah told him that YHWH had put a lying spirit in the minds of the four hundred in order to entice Ahab so that he would be killed. Ahab ordered Micaiah jailed, and Micaiah, invoking the deuteronomic test of prophecy, replied, "If you do indeed return victorious [in *shalom*], the LORD has not spoken by me" (vs 28 CBAT). Ahab attacked and was killed.

It is easy to see why the deuteronomic historians told this story, for it illustrated their understanding of prophecy and also described the death of a king they despised. However, the story also illustrates the weakness of the deuteronomic test. The test worked, but not for Ahab. At the moment of decision, the test was worthless.

The concerns of the deuteronomists are evident in Jeremiah 27–29, a booklet about Jeremiah's conflict with the prophets of peace. Chapter 26 is related to 27–29 by means of the reference to the prophets Micah and Uriah (26:16-24). This may account for the side-by-side placement of 26 and 27–28. However, the incidents recounted were widely separated in time (609 for 26:1; 598 for 27:3 and 28:1; the mention of Jehoiakim in 27:1 is obviously an error, perhaps influenced by 26:1), and the issues treated were quite different.

The warning against "prophets, diviners, dreamers, soothsayers, and sorcerers, who say, 'You shall not serve the king of Babylon'" (27:9; cf. 29:8-9), reflects the prohibition of divination, soothsaying, and sorcery in Deuteronomy 18:10. In addition, the deuteronomic test of historical fulfillment is cited explicitly in Jeremiah 28:6-9. Furthermore, loss of the land, the penalty cited in 27:10-11 for heeding false prophets, is one of the principal deuteronomic penalties for disobedience of the torah (e.g., Deut 28:63-68).

The test of historical fulfillment is cited also in Jeremiah 28:6-9, though it is applied there only to the prophecy of peace (*shalom*). A prophecy of doom is not subject to the same test, because it is validated by ancient tradition (vs 8). This is the principle to which the princes of Judah appealed as the reason to spare Jeremiah's life in the incident described in Jeremiah 26 (cf. vss 16-19). Jeremiah was merely doing what prophets of YHWH had done before. That was the reason Ahab hated Micaiah, for Micaiah never prophesied anything but evil against him (1 Kings 22:8). Perhaps that was also the reason he disregarded Micaiah's prophecy about Ramoth-gilead. Ahab may have believed the four hundred prophets because he wanted to, but why should he believe Micaiah when Micaiah seemed to prophesy evil as a matter of course? That was the problem when prophets always prophesied the same thing: They lost their credibility. Requiring the deuteronomic test of historical confirmation was just as relevant to Jeremiah as it was to the prophets of peace, since he too had only one message. But the narrator, writing many years later, knew that Jeremiah had passed the test, so he invoked it only for the prophets of peace.

Were the prophecies of Jeremiah and Micaiah true only because the doom they prophesied came to pass? Was this the only reason the traditioners believed them to be true? It was the only reason in Micaiah's case, obviously, for the only thing he said was that Ahab was doomed. But was this the only reason in Jeremiah's case? Were his oracles preserved only because his prophecy of doom was fulfilled? This was surely one of the most important reasons, perhaps the most important. However, I would like to believe they were preserved also because of the depth of their ethical insight and the power of their witness of faith in God.

What is the didactic intention of Jeremiah 27–29? According to the narrative, the issue between Jeremiah and his prophetic opponents was the duration and extent of Babylonian sovereignty over Judah, following the capture of Jerusalem in 597 BCE. Jeremiah was convinced that the exile would last a long time, while his opponents were convinced it would be brief. Whether they counseled rebellion, we do not know. The text does not accuse them of doing so, but only of lying, committing adultery, and prophesying falsely (29:21-23). Their main error was prophesying a speedy return of the exiles.

What was the message of Jeremiah 27–29 to Jews in the sixth century, and how does it compare with the message of the prose sermons? The answer, in a word, is that the message of this booklet is quite different from that of most of the prose sermons. In 27–28, the message is an admonition to the Judeans to submit to the yoke of the king of Babylon for as long as God grants him sovereignty over the nations. If they submit, they will be permitted to stay in the land and live, but if they refuse, they will be expelled from the land and perish (28:10-11). The message of the letter to the exiles (Jer 29:1-14) is based on the same premise, the continued dominion of Babylon. It counsels the exiles to make a new life in Babylon, to seek the welfare of the city, and to accept it as their own city (29:5-11).

None of the main themes found in the principal group of prose sermons (7:1ff.; 11:1ff.; 17:19ff., etc.) appears here. These themes are the condemnation of idolatry, and the warning to (1) obey the torah of God, (2) observe the sabbath, (3) protect the rights of helpless Israelites, and (4) maintain an undefiled worship of YHWH. Some of the phrases in Jeremiah 27–29 are used in the sermons: "my servants the prophets" (29:19; cf., e.g., 7:25; 25:4; 44:4); "sword, famine, and pestilence" (27:8, 13; 29:17, 18; cf., e.g., 21:7, 9; 34:17; 38:2); and the literary style is not unlike that of the sermons. However, the theme of these chapters is different from the themes of the sermons.

Nevertheless, the exhortations in 27–29 continued to be relevant to the exiles, as well as to the Judean remnant, long after the events of 597–586. The same choices had to be made for at least two generations, until the "yoke of Babylon" was broken by the Persians in 539. To be sure, there was no possibility of rebellion in Jerusalem after 586, but the question of how to respond to Babylonian supremacy continued to be the decisive question. There was every reason for the redactors to continue to give a prominent place to this booklet, for it provided vital counsel to the Jews of the exilic era. Unlike the preexilic oracles of Jeremiah, it required no reinterpretation or adaptation in order to be applied meaningfully to the social issues of the mid-sixth century. Furthermore, the conditional formulation of the prophetic proclamation was self-evident in this material, as it was read in the exilic situation; therefore, it did not need to be made more explicit, in the manner of the prose sermons.

THE BIOGRAPHICAL NARRATIVES

The first half of the book of Jeremiah is a collection of poetic oracles, with a few prose sermons. The second half of the book (disregarding the oracles on the foreign nations in 46–51) is a collection of prose narratives (26–45), with a few poetic oracles (30–31) and a brief appendix (52). When the narratives are read in chronological order, they give the impression of a connected account of Jeremiah's career, from the death of Josiah (609 BCE) to the assassination of Gedaliah (after 586 BCE). The order is roughly as follows:

1. Jeremiah's sermon in the temple of Jerusalem at the beginning of Jehoiakim's reign (Jer 26; 609 BCE).
2. The symbol of the broken pottery flask and the sermon at the Potsherd Gate (19:1–20:6; 605).
3. The example of the Rechabites' covenantal loyalty (35; 598?).
4. The response to the summit meeting of nations; the dispute with Hananiah over the duration of the Judean captivity; and the letter to those who were exiled in 597 BCE (27–29; ca. 596).
5. The omen of the two baskets of figs (24; ca. 595).
6. Zedekiah's conference with Jeremiah and Jeremiah's arrest (37; 588).
7. Jeremiah's purchase of his cousin's field near Anathoth (32; 588).
8. The siege of Jerusalem and the temporary release of the Judean slaves (34; 587).
9. Jeremiah in the cistern and his rescue by Ebedmelech (38; 587).
10. The fall of Jerusalem and the deportation of Zedekiah (39; 587).
11. Jeremiah's release and Gedaliah's appointment as governor of Judah (40; 587/6).
12. The assassination of Gedaliah (41).
13. Jeremiah's prophecy to the Judean remnant (42).
14. The abduction of Jeremiah and Baruch, and the flight to Egypt (43; after 586 BCE).
15. Jeremiah's prophecy in Egypt (44).

This narrative is commonly called the biography of Jeremiah, though only for convenience, since the story is not a biography in the modern sense, but a chronicle of Jeremiah's encounters with the leaders of Judah. As such, it is a story of rejection, abuse, and persecution, but the intention of the narrative does not seem to be to record the sufferings of a just man so much as to represent the message of a prophet, against the background of his public ministry. The account is not merely antiquarian; it is prophetic, as is shown by the reiteration of a few principal themes. The writer wanted Jeremiah to speak to new generations.

The prophet's message is presented in much the same terms as the speeches in 7:1–8:3; 11:1-17; and 18:1-12. Two long, summarizing speeches in deuteronomic style are especially notable (32:17-44; 44:2-14) as they draw out the implications of the fall of Judah. Speeches are fairly evenly distributed throughout the book, and this helps to unify it; the parallel placement of 25:1-13 and 44:2-14 is particularly significant. The first is a sermonic summary of the prophet's preaching at the end of the first part of the book; the second is a sermonic summary of his preaching at the end of the second part.

In addition to explaining the fall of Judah, the narratives answer a number of questions that troubled the exilic community. Who would share in the eventual renewal of Israel? How could Babylonian dominion be reconciled with faith in the rule of God? How should faithful Jews respond to Babylon? What leaders should they heed? What could they expect of God in the years ahead?

Several pronouncements in the narratives locate the hope for the renewal of Israel's life in the leaders deported to Babylonia in 597 and, to a lesser extent, in the remnant left in Judea after 586; they also pronounce God's judgment on certain persons. The list of those denounced contains no surprises: (1) Jehoiakim, the king who reversed the achievements of Josiah's reform, spurned the counsel of Jeremiah, and precipitated the Babylonian conquest of Judah (36:30); (2) Pashhur ben Immer, priest, policeman, and professional prophet, who harassed Jeremiah and offered easy counsel to the Judean establishment (20:6); (3) Shemaiah of Nehelam, exiled in 597, who nourished the fantasy of a speedy return and counseled additional persecution of Jeremiah (29:24-32); (4) the exiled prophets Ahab and Zedekiah, who were accused of false prophecy and adultery (29:21-23); (5) King Zedekiah, the puppet of pro-Egyptian revolutionaries, who presided over Judah's last debacle (34:1-5; 37:17; 38:17-23; 39:4-7); (6) Jeremiah's abductors, who fled to Egypt after the assassination of Gedaliah, fearing a Babylonian reprisal (42:7-18; 44:24-29).

The surprising feature of this catalogue is the number of specific individuals named, because such allusions are not all that common in the prophetic literature; for the most part, this literature speaks about types of people and general causes. It is one thing to analyze patterns of behavior and the course of history, but quite another to predict the fate of specific individuals. Among the few other examples of oracles against individuals in the Hebrew Bible, the best known is Nathan's condemnation of David for his crime against Uriah (2 Sam 12:1-15). Claus Westermann contends that this is the oldest form of judgment oracle and the model from which the communal oracle of judgment developed.[2] The problem with this conclusion is that almost all the extant examples of oracles against individuals are in the Deuteronomic History or in secondary strata of the prophetic books, so one cannot be confident of the antiquity of the type. The curious thing about these oracles is that all are found in narrative accounts of prophetic activity. None occurs in a poetic oracle! One must wonder, therefore, whether they are not the product of the historical imagination of the exilic writers.

Prophetic judgments about the groups that would take part in the new Israel are more prominent in the prose tradition of Jeremiah than are judgments about particular officials of the old regime. The narrative of the two baskets of figs (24) invests the hope for the future in the exiles deported to Babylon in 597 (vs 6) and excludes the court of Zedekiah and the Palestinian remnant from the inheritance (vss 8-10). I have argued above that this judgment reflects the prejudice of the prose writers more than it reflects Jeremiah's own view. Although Jeremiah seems to have had little use for the puppet government of Zedekiah, it is improbable that he would have made a blanket condemnation of the people who remained in Judah after 586. His decision to remain in the land and cast his lot with the Judean remnant (40:1-6), his advice to the elders of Judah to remain there and build it up (42:7ff.), his purchase of land there (32)—all weigh against the conclusion that he was responsible for the condemnation of the "rotten figs."

THE LETTER TO THE EXILES

According to the narrative in chapter 24, Jeremiah expected the exiles in Babylon to make a major contribution to the restoration of the Yahwistic community in Judah. However, since he did not expect this restoration to occur soon, he attempted to dispel the illusion of an immediate return (28:1-4) with his famous letter to the exiles (29:4-7). In that letter, he told the exiles to make a new life in Babylonia, to take spouses and have children, and to instruct their children to do the same, so that they could increase in their new homeland. Even more, he told them to seek the welfare of their new Babylonian neighbors and to pray to God on their behalf, because their neighbors' welfare was tied to their own.

This was a radical word during the sixth century. It presupposed faith in God's universal rule and accessibility, and it challenged the nationalism of zealous Judeans, as well as their regard for the Jerusalem temple as the exclusive place of approach to God. The text does not say whether the new spouses of the exiles might be Babylonians, but this possibility is not explicitly excluded, either. According to the biblical record, intermarriage was not prohibited until the age of Ezra (Ezra 9). By that time, the prohibition seemed necessary to Judean leaders, but it contradicted the spirit of Jeremiah's letter to the exiles, which shows confidence in the work of God beyond geographical, political, and cultic boundaries, the deepest expression of prophetic faith.

The duration of the exile is put at 70 years in 29:10. Obviously, the writer knew about the Persian conquest of Babylon in 539 and the subsequent edict of return for the Jewish exiles. The period of Babylonian sovereignty was 70 years, in round numbers (from the defeat of Pharaoh Necho in 605), but this is a relatively minor note in the prose tradition. A much greater concern was the interpreting of the meaning of Babylonian rule in the purposes of God (27:6-22; 32:4, 26-28; 34:2-3; 37:9-10; 38:17-18; 43:9-13). According to the prophet, the only sensible response to the events of the time was to submit to the yoke of Babylon, since Babylon ruled by the will of God.

THE PURPOSE OF THE PROSE WRITERS

The prose tradition of the book of Jeremiah makes the most sense when it is interpreted against the background of exilic and early postexilic Judaism. The earliest possible date of composition of the main prose narrative is 585, the approximate time of the last events mentioned (Jer 40-44); the latest possible date is uncertain. Jeremiah 52:31-34 mentions the Babylonians' release of King Jehoiachin from prison, which would have been about 561, but this passage could be an editorial addition to the main narrative. It may be significant that neither Cyrus's conquest of Babylon (539) nor the release of Jewish exiles (538) is mentioned explicitly, though 29:10 presupposes the fall of Babylon. However, the silence about Cyrus is not a sufficient ground for fixing the date of composition.

Clues to the residence of the writers are also scant. Nicholson argues for Babylon on the grounds of bias shown toward the exiles (24:1-10, e.g.), emphasis on sabbath observance (17:19-27), and interest in false prophecy (27–29), which, he claims, were particular concerns of Babylonian Jews.[3] This argument has merit but is not conclusive.

The political situation of the Jews in the sixth century was probably much the same throughout the ancient Near East. Whether they lived under Egyptian-Saite, Lydian, Neo-Babylonian, or Persian rule, they were subjects of alien powers, and they constituted a small religious minority in the midst of large populations. The basic condition of life for the people addressed by the exilic book of Jeremiah was their separation from one another and from the institutions and patterns of life they had known in the kingdom of Judah. They suffered severe culture shock, magnified by the fear that their loss would be permanent.

The Jeremiah prose explains the fall and exile of Judah as a divine punishment for religious apostasy, defined especially as cultic idolatry (5:18-19; 7:16-20; 7:21–8:3; 9:12-16; 11:9-13; 13:1-11; 16:1-13; 17:1-4; 19:1-13; 32:28-35; 44:1-30). This interpretation coincides with that of the oracles of Jeremiah (and all the other preexilic prophets), although there are differences in emphasis, particularly in describing the inner dynamics of idolatry. The poetic oracles vividly describe the activity of the apostate imagination and the way it controls behavior, whereas the prose is content to repeat the general truth that idolatrous behavior accompanies a stubborn heart. The concern of the sermons is not the "how" of moral waywardness, but the "why" of divine judgment. The deep psychological probing manifested in the poetry is totally lacking in the prose sermons. Compared to the inwardness of the oracles, the sermons are quite impersonal.

It is easier to recognize the differences between the oracles and the sermons than to explain them in relation to the historical circumstances of the writers. Obviously, the content of the preexilic oracles made sense to the exilic redactors or they would not have preserved them. They must have found a message there for the survivors of the fall, and not merely the message that Jeremiah's prophecy of the fall was correct. Conversely, the prose sermons would have made sense not only to an exilic audience but also to a preexilic audience. Not from the difference in their content, but from the difference in their form, we are led to infer that the two groups of writings originated in different social settings. The repetitive, didactic style of the sermons, their narrow concentration upon a few themes, and their uncomplicated notion of divine retribution suggest a new, pedagogical relation of writer to reader, not the old relation of prophetic critic to cultic establishment. The image they evoke is that of the school or the congregation, rather than the temple or the royal court.

When we turn from the question of the social setting of the prose tradition to that of its purpose, we find a significant clue in the final chapter of the story of Jeremiah, the account of his debate with the Jewish refugees who abducted him to Egypt (Jer 44). There the prophet and the Judean women propose opposite explanations of the fall of Judah: Jeremiah explains it as YHWH's punishment for infidelity to YHWH; the women explain it as the result of their neglect of the Queen of Heaven, the great mother goddess (44:18). They also reject Jeremiah's exhortation to save the remnant of Judah by remaining faithful to YHWH. The obvious implication of their response is that their worship of YHWH has not secured their welfare; what matters is worship of the Queen of Heaven. Both prophet and people agree that the fall was a consequence of religious apostasy, but they disagree over which god was offended.

The situation of the prose writers may be mirrored in the scene just described. The decisive issue for these writers was the theological interpretation of the fall of Judah. At stake was not merely an intellectual debate over a point of theology, but the identity of the people as a religious community. Had all the survivors of the fall interpreted their fortunes as did the women in the story, there would soon have been no people of YHWH. They would all have been assimilated into other communities.

The first question answered by the prose sermons is whether YHWH was in control of the fortunes of the Judeans, and the answer given is that YHWH was indeed in control. The destruction of the nation had come about by YHWH's decision. It was not at all the case that YHWH had been powerless to prevent it, in the face of the powerful gods of the nations. The LORD YHWH had made it happen as a well-deserved punishment for Judah's sin. Thus the prose sermons are, first, an apologia for faith in YHWH as the true God.

However, it was not enough for the writers to persuade the exiles that YHWH had the power to control their destiny. It was necessary also to persuade them that YHWH had the will to bless them. Otherwise, neither their hope nor their commitment would have revived. Two kinds of encouragement are given by the prose sermons: One is the simple promise of restoration; the other is the conditional promise of blessing.

The conditional promise of blessing occurs frequently (7:1-15; 11:1-8; 17:19-27; 18:1-12; 22:1-5; 25:3-14). Naturally, it is couched as a word addressed to the preexilic Judean community, so on the surface, these speeches are exhortations to the nation, especially its leaders, to repent in order to avert the doom that is threatening them. However, as soon as we compare the speeches with the poetic oracles of judgment, it becomes clear that the real audience of the speeches is not the preexilic nation, for most of the oracles are unconditional prophecies of destruction—Jeremiah's message to the Judean nation. The conditional exhortation was a message to the survivors of the fall.

Not all the prose sermons contain this conditional exhortation; many contain straightforward explanations of the fall as YHWH's punishment for apostasy (7:16–8:3; 21:1-10; 25:1-14; 32:6-16, 26-44; 34:1-22; 35:2-10; 44:1-14; cf. 3:6-10; 13:1-11; 14:11-16; 16:1-18; 19:1-13; 24:1-10). The point of these explanations is to assert that it was YHWH who was responsible for what had happened. The other sermons stress the additional point that reformation was the necessary condition of renewal.

The retrospective interpretation of the fall of Judah, with its implicit appeal to the survivors to return to YHWH and live, occurs more frequently in the prose than do explicit promises of future blessing, though there are some of the latter. As might be expected, the most common sort of promise concerns the restoration of corporate life in Judah (3:14-18; 12:14-17; 16:14-15; 29:4-14; 32:36-44). But as might not be expected, these promises are remarkably sober with respect to the material circumstances of the restored community. There are no extravagant assurances of prosperity or power. The writers were clearly less interested in vindicating Judah's national pride than in revitalizing her covenantal faith.

There is little emphasis on Zion in the prose tradition. Zion is mentioned only once (3:14), and then without the usual emphasis on an ingathering of exiles in the coming age. The full hope for the future of Zion is expressed in Ezekiel 40–48 and in several passages in the book of Isaiah, but not in Jeremiah. Some of the standard postexilic themes associated with Zion do appear in 23:1-8 and chapter 33, but without explicitly mentioning Zion; these texts seem to represent an independent strand in the book, introduced, in the judgment of most scholars, after the poetic oracles had been combined with the main prose tradition. They express what was perhaps the most natural way for the Judean leaders in exile to imagine the future restoration of their corporate life—as the reestablishment of the institutions of the preexilic era. The keynote of the promise was that God would "restore the fortunes of Judah and Jerusalem (LXX) and build them again *as they were before*" (33:7). This meant that there would be a Davidic king, a

Levitical priesthood, a restored temple, a sacrificial ritual, and sufficient national wealth to make the nations stand in awe (vs 9). The hope for national wealth and a Davidic king were not fulfilled, as things turned out, though the temple, the priesthood, and the sacrificial ritual were restored.

The writer of Jeremiah 33 was concerned not only with the material restoration of the Judean kingdom, but also with the elimination of evil and the forgiveness of sin (33:8). Shown here is a moral seriousness that is consonant with prophetic teaching. We might wish for some further word about the moral obligations of the citizens of the restored society, but it is perhaps unreasonable to expect every chapter of the book to affirm the whole range of promises and demands involved in the new relationship with God. Jeremiah 33 was added to a large corpus, in which ample attention had already been given to the divine demands. This text supplements the other parts of the book by supporting aspects of Jewish aspiration that were not mentioned elsewhere.

This chapter may have been written about the same time as the rest of the prose speeches. It reflects no knowledge of the actual restoration of temple, priesthood, and ritual (after 516), but it seems to be an encouragement for the first generations after the fall of Jerusalem.

RITUAL AND PROPHETIC INTERCESSION

The delight in the memory of the temple ritual shown in 33:14-26 is unmatched in the other prose sermons. In fact, it contrasts sharply with the antitemple polemic of the first and best known of the prose sermons, 7:1-15. This polemic has led many commentators to attribute the substance of 7:1-15 to Jeremiah himself, rather than to the deuteronomic writers. The premise upon which this judgment is based is that the deuteronomists favored the Jerusalem cultus and even were behind the cultic reform of Josiah. It is generally supposed that the torah scroll which inspired the reform was some form of the book of Deuteronomy (2 Kings 22; cf. Deut 12). Thus, the deuteronomists have been thought of as ritualistic, in contrast to the prophets, who have been thought of as severely critical of the temple cult. Some scholars have felt obliged to explain why the antitemple polemic in 7:1-15 was even preserved by the deuteronomic editors, rather than being suppressed. Hyatt, for example, has written, "If it is surprising that a deuteronomic editor has preserved the words of a prophet concerning the destruction of the Jerusalem temple, so dear to the heart of his school, we must remember that he wrote in 550, after the temple had been destroyed, and that Jeremiah's words made such a lasting impression that they could not be suppressed."[4]

Hyatt's statement presupposes that the words of the prophet were an embarrassment to the editor and were preserved reluctantly only because they were well known. But 7:1-15 is not a grudging report, but one written from the heart. This becomes clear when the speech is compared with the one in 26:4-6, a shorter version of a similar speech. The writer of 7:1-15 has extended himself on behalf of this criticism; this is not the grudging labor of a dutiful scribe but the sincere attack of a prophetic critic.

When we look elsewhere among the prose speeches, we find a fair number of other passages which condemn various forms of ritualism, and none of these contains any hint that the writer was apologizing for the Jerusalem cultus or exempting it from prophetic stricture.

> Thus says the LORD of hosts, the God of Israel: Add your burnt offerings to your sacrifices, and eat the flesh. For in the day that I brought your ancestors out of the land of Egypt, I did not speak to them or command them concerning burnt offerings and sacrifices. But this command I gave them, "Obey my voice, and I will be your God, and you shall be my people; and walk in all the way that I command you, so that it may be well with you." (7:21-23)

This passage is not a continuation of the temple speech (7:1-15) but a separate pericope loosely joined to it, together with two others (7:6-20; 7:29–8:3). It contains a radical criticism of the sacrificial system, as such (there is no mention of baalized worship here; it refers to the Yahwistic cult). To be sure, it echoes the oracles of Jeremiah (6:20; cf. Amos 5:25) and could conceivably preserve a word of the prophet. However, the passage as it stands is filled with characteristic deuteronomic phrases and ideas. If the editor did not share the prophet's opinion of the sacrificial cult, he has certainly hidden his own sentiment well!

Again, in the prose passage 3:14-18, which is also thoroughly deuteronomic, there is a sharp rejection of the ark of the covenant, the most sacred cult object in the preexilic Jerusalem temple, and no word at all about rebuilding the temple or reinstating the sacrificial cult, even though the passage is a promise of restoration. What is promised is that the city of Jerusalem will replace the old ark as God's throne (3:17). Here, as in 7:1-15 and 7:21-23, the concern expressed is purely moral, not cultic at all.

A further stricture against ritualism appears in the prose tradition in 14:10-13. Here again, it is not only idolatrous ritual that is rejected, but all ritual.

In all these passages, the futility of cultic efforts to appease the wrath of God is underscored, and none attributes superior status or sanctity to the ritual of the Jerusalem temple. In short, the attitude displayed in these prose texts is identical to that of the preexilic prophets.

Only once among the prose speeches do we encounter any affirmation of the temple, and that is in the speech about sabbath observance (17:19-27). The promise implicit in this conditional warning is ample; though most of the standard elements of the later Jewish hope are affirmed, including hope for the Davidic kingship, the emphasis is upon sabbath observance. What is important to the writer here is the ethical commandment to rest from work on the sabbath. This has nothing to do with temple ritual; the reference to the temple system is incidental, inserted because the speech is ostensibly a speech of Jeremiah to a preexilic Judean audience.

I am not arguing that the writers of the prose tradition repudiated the temple cultus. I am suggesting that they were aware of the dangers of ritualism, were sympathetic to the prophetic criticism of the sacrificial cult, and showed no trace of reverence for the Jerusalem temple, a reverence which seems to have characterized the piety of Judah in the sixth century (cf. 2 Kings 19; Isa 37).

The authors of the prose tradition had no illusions about the power of ritual acts to influence the will of God. And they were equally circumspect with regard to the power of prophetic intercessions; three times, the prose writer recounts YHWH's command to the prophet not to pray for the people (7:16; 11:14; 14:11). Commentators sometimes have interpreted these texts as expressions of the belief that prophetic intercession was so powerful that Jeremiah had to be stopped from interceding before it was too late—that is, before words had been mobilized which would alter the course of events or force God to act in a certain way. Such potency is often attributed to prophetic prayer in the Bible, not least in the Deuteronomic History (e.g., 1 Kings 17:17-24; 2 Kings 2:19-25). The best statement of such an idea is in the account of Amos's vision (Amos 7:1-9), where a prophetic intercession is twice depicted as capable of averting the wrath of God.

However, it would be incorrect to read the three passages in Jeremiah as simple illustrations of such a belief. Jeremiah 14:11-12 makes it clear that a prophet's plea on behalf of the people will have no more effect than the people's fasts or sacrifices, and the same point is made more briefly in 11:14. Finally, 7:16 makes explicit the point implied in the other two texts—that no human being can turn aside the divinely ordained consequences of idolatry. Jeremiah 15:1, also a prose text, puts it vividly: Not even the two greatest prophets of Israel, Moses and Samuel, could change the mind of God concerning contemporary Judah. Thus all the magical overtones in the ancient, popular view of the holy word have been removed in the Jeremiah tradition, in accordance with a purely ethical understanding of the authority of the prophet—the authority of an exhorter and teacher.

This understanding of the prophet as exhorter and teacher of the people also has displaced the old idea of the prophet as seer, according to the prose writers. For them, the prophets represented a long line of moral counselors, stretching back to the time of the exodus (7:25; 25:4; 29:19; 35:15; 44:4). They regarded the prophetic message as an appeal for repentance from idolatry as the condition for possession of the land of Israel. This notion is compatible with the idea of the prophet as predictor of disaster, an idea that is pervasive in the Deuteronomic History; but the History emphasizes the reliability of prophetic prediction more than does the Jeremiah prose, and it is less concerned with the prophetic appeal for repentance.[5] The Deuteronomic History is historical narrative with a didactic aim, while the Jeremiah prose is didactic preaching in a historical framework.

Both serve the purpose of religious education, and both probably originated in the same circle of exilic teachers.

THE COVENANT, OLD AND NEW

In marked contrast to the poetic oracles of Jeremiah, in which the word *covenant* never appears, the prose tradition makes much use of this term. The best known covenantal pericopes in the book are the sermon in 11:1-14 and the prophecy of the new covenant in 31:31-34. Both have received extensive critical attention. Indeed, the new covenant passage may be the one text in Jeremiah most frequently cited in the interpretive literature. Both passages are thoroughly deuteronomic in language and belong to the sermonic stratum of the book, whatever may have been their antecedents in the words of Jeremiah.

The other covenantal texts in the prose are 22:8-9; 32:40; 33:20-25; 34:12ff.; and 50:4-5, which deal variously with God's covenant made with Israel at the time of the exodus (22:9; 34:13; cf. 11:3ff.; 31:32), the new covenant to be made in the coming age (32:40; 50:5; cf. 31:31, 33), and God's covenant with the royal and priestly lines of David and Levi (33:20-25). This last passage is part of the long promise of future blessing, added to the book independently of, and later than, the main prose tradition, so it can be excluded from the present discussion. And several other texts which contain the term *covenant*, but which have nothing to do with God's covenant with Israel (34:8, 10, 15; 3:16; 34:20), also can be excluded.

All but one of the twenty-three occurrences of the term in the book of Jeremiah are in the prose. The one occurrence in poetry is not in an oracle of Jeremiah, but in a lament put in the mouth of the people on the occasion of a drought (14:21; cf. 14:1ff.). Thus, since the poetic oracles of Jeremiah make virtually no use of the term *covenant*, they stand in direct continuity with the oracles of the eighth-century prophets. A covenant between God and Israel is never mentioned in the oracles of Amos, Micah, or First Isaiah, and only twice in Hosea (6:7; 8:1). However, the term was certainly important to the writers of the Jeremiah prose. Let us look first at the covenant sermon in 11:1-14.

Although it describes a sermon by Jeremiah to preexilic Judeans, the text's own audience is made up of exilic Jews. This is shown by the acknowledgment that punishment for breach of covenant has already taken place (vs 8). The Judeans lost the land that YHWH gave to their ancestors in fulfillment of YHWH's covenant with them (11:5), because the Judeans violated their part of the covenant (11:6-8). Here, as always in the prose sermons, the writer describes the people's breach of covenant as a turning to other gods (11:9-13), although he also cites the moral consequences of the apostasy—refusing to obey and walking "in the stubbornness of an evil will" (vs 8). The writer appeals to the people in their deprived situation not to resort to futile idolatries in an effort to regain security (11:12-13). Thus, implicitly, the writer asks them to return to YHWH, who has taken away their security and who alone can restore it.

The two blessings conferred by the covenant, according to this speech, are the personal bond between God and people ("So you shall be my people, and I will be your God," 11:4) and the gift of the land (vs 5). The first is given "so that" the second can be given too. The implication is that the bond of faith between people and God is the means to a material end, possession of the land. This notion haunts the pages of Deuteronomy and the Deuteronomic History. The writers never succumb to crass materialism, to be sure, and they always attach moral conditions to the right of possession. Nevertheless, there is an ambiguity in the deuteronomic witness concerning the means and ends of religion. It is never quite clear whether Israel is to be religious in order to enjoy the blessings of the land, or whether it is the other way around. This witness contrasts with that of the book of Ezekiel, for example, in which it is absolutely clear that the end of religion is knowing YHWH as God. Everything else is secondary. "That you may know that I am YHWH" is the constant refrain of Ezekiel (e.g., 6:7, 10; 7:4; 11:10; 12:15; 15:7).

"I will not listen to them when they call to me in the time of their trouble" is another assertion of the covenant sermon (Jer 11:14). This is not the last word of God for all time, but the last word concerning the kingdom of Judah (cf. vs 11). While the kingdom is being dismantled, no cry of penitence or intercession will stay the hand of God. But when the dismantling is finished, there will be new possibilities.

The second great covenantal passage in Jeremiah comes near the end of "the book of comfort" (30–31). This collection is largely poetry, but the prophecy of the new covenant is in prose. The language and style of the pericope (31:31-34) are indistinguishable from that of the prose speeches generally; therefore, the unavoidable conclusion is that the writer of the speeches is also the writer of this prophecy.[6] Many scholars have preferred to believe that Jeremiah was the author of this text, because it has been so important in Christian usage. However, the worth or usefulness of the text does not depend upon the identity of its author, as the anonymous poems of Isaiah 40–66 demonstrate.

Jeremiah 11:1-14 speaks about the operation of the Sinaitic covenant—in this case, the punishment of infidelity. The new covenant prophecy in 31:31-34 speaks not about the operation of this covenant, but about its abolition. The writer promised the people a new covenant, but only at some time in the future. To him, the present time for the remnant of Judah was a time between covenants.

The promised covenant would involve every Israelite's deep personal knowledge of YHWH and of YHWH's torah. No one would require mediation of divine forgiveness or instruction in torah, but everyone would be forgiven directly, and everyone would know directly.

This proclamation is certainly eschatological, because it describes the fulfillment of the relation between people and God, the perfection of faith, the achievement of total commitment. In this sense, it is the goal of God's leading, God's ultimate desire for every human being, the aim of salvation history. What it describes is not humanly attainable, yet it is not simply illusory. It reflects an awareness of the relation of action to will, of behavior to the affections of the heart. The writer knows there is no obedience without the will to obey, and no will to obey without the knowledge of God.

The Sinaitic covenant, as it is described in the canonical Torah, is not the antithesis of the new covenant prophesied in Jeremiah 31:31-34. All the theological insights expressed in this prophetic text are expressed again and again in the narrative traditions of the Pentateuch. As a result, it is difficult for us to understand the contrast that existed in the author's mind between the old and new covenant. Perhaps he was not thinking of a contrast in principle, but of what the old covenant had become in the understanding of his contemporaries. In any case, the text does not explain why the old covenant failed, nor does it explain how the new covenant would differ in form, content, or instrumental means. The prophecy points to the two ultimate sources of human obedience, the grace of God and the disposition of the human heart. It tells us nothing about the proximate sources or concrete fruits of covenantal knowledge. Did the writer imagine that the knowledge of God could be infused directly into a person's mind, without the aid of education or the practice of religion? Or was he merely pointing to God's freedom from the limitations of conventional forms of schooling and worship, and God's power to do new, unprecedented things?

The more we ponder this prophecy, the more questions arise in our minds. It is a model of biblical prophecy in cutting to the heart of the religious question, yet it gives no programmatic help for dealing with the practical problems of the religious life. It is an indispensable but an insufficient word; it requires the counsel of the legislator, the priest, and the pedagogue to complete it.

We must not conclude our discussion of this passage without noting its affinity to the great rhetorical introduction to the code of Deuteronomy (Deut 5–11). Jeremiah is usually given credit for the insights contained in the prophecy of the new covenant, and perhaps this is fair. But it is not fair if one overlooks the close affinity between this prophecy and the sermons in Deuteronomy 5–11, or if one sets the two over against each other antithetically. When we study, for example, Deuteronomy 5:28-29; 6:4-6; 8:3-4; 9:4ff.; 10:12ff.; and 11:1ff., 13, 18, we find the same emphasis on the disposition of the heart and the unmerited love of God that we find in Jeremiah 31:31-34. Furthermore, Deuteronomy 5–11 contains programmatic words about education and the observance of law that are unparalleled in Jeremiah 31. These further words do not contradict the prophetic insights, but serve to implement them in the corporate life of Israel.

CONCLUSION

The story of Jeremiah is the longest, most detailed story of any person in the Hebrew Bible. It is subjective to speculate about the motives of writers in a culture and an age so remote from our own; however, it is hard to resist the conclusion that the writers of the book of Jeremiah knew of him as a compelling personality, as well as an articulate spokesman of the word of God. Surely, they have given us a portrait of such a person, whatever may have been the sources of their inspiration.

SELECT BIBLIOGRAPHY

Nicholson, E. W. *Preaching to the Exiles: A Study of the Prose Tradition of the Book of Jeremiah*. Oxford: Basil Blackwell, 1970.

Sheppard, Gerald T. "True and False Prophecy Within Scripture." *Canon, Theology, and Old Testament Interpretation*, ed. Gene M. Tucker et al. Philadelphia: Fortress Press, 1988.

Stulman, Louis. *The Prose Sermons of the Book of Jeremiah*. SBLDS 83. Atlanta: Scholars Press, 1986.

See also Select Bibliography at end of previous chapter.

NOTES

1. See *IDB*, "Jehoiachin."
2. Claus Westermann, *Basic Forms of Prophetic Speech* (Philadelphia: Westminster Press, 1967), pp. 137-68.
3. Nicholson, *Preaching to the Exiles*, pp. 122-33.
4. See *Interpreter's Bible* (Nashville: Abingdon Press, 1956), vol. 5, p. 789; cf. Wilhelm Rudolph, *Jeremia*, Handbuch zum Alten Testament (Tübingen: J.C.B. Mohr, 1958).
5. See 1 Kings 11:29-39; 13:1-2; 14:1-16; 16:1-4; 21:17-24; 22:17; 2 Kings 1:2-4, 16; 3; 9:7-10; 14:25; 19:6, 20, 32-37; 20:5, 16-18; 21:10-15; 22:16-20.
6. See Nicholson, *Exiles*, p. 138; Robert P. Carroll, *From Chaos to Covenant: Prophecy in the Books of Jeremiah* (New York: Crossroad Press, 1981).

CHAPTER NINE

Ezekiel

The theological themes in Ezekiel are similar to those in the books of Isaiah and Jeremiah, but they are treated distinctively. Cultic idolatry is a more prominent concern, and it provokes in the prophet an extraordinary moral outrage. Sin and repentance are treated as acts of the rational mind—not, as in Jeremiah, as profound movements of the heart. In various ways Ezekiel displays the mind and sensibilities of a priest. Ritual holiness clearly meant a great deal to him. His plan for the future great society (Ezek 40–48) places a temple at the center, with a sacred precinct—a kind of protective moat—around it.

The expression of hope in this treatise is as cerebral as Ezekiel's theory of sin and redemption. Nevertheless, for all its eccentricity, his words contained constructive counsel for his contemporaries. Although some of that counsel sounds strange to modern ears, it is a significant part of the prophetic legacy, and it enjoys a prominent place in the biblical canon. As a study in priestly piety and the psychological effects of exile, the figure of Ezekiel is full of interest, from his lengthy, graphic visions and his episodes of catatonia to his ambivalent relations with the elders of Judah. The book of Ezekiel does not command the same attention in religious usage today as do other prophetic books; however, it represents an important strand in Israelite-Jewish piety. Elsewhere, this strand is represented most fully in the priestly stratum of the Pentateuch. Ezekiel is generally thought to have exerted a strong influence on this tradition and, through it, on all subsequent Judaism.

The world of Ezekiel was completely different from the world of earlier prophets. It was, of course, the world of exile. We need only mention the word to evoke the image of a strange new setting. Although the Bible records few details of the life of the Judean exiles, it is not difficult to imagine it. The most obvious changes from life in Judah were geographic, social, and economic, and we should not minimize the significance of these changes for the history of Judaism. But as far as our understanding of the setting of Ezekiel is concerned, the greatest difference between the world of exile and the world of preexilic prophecy was not a matter of material circumstance or location, nor even of living by coercion in an alien land. For the prophet, the greatest difference between a Judean and an exilic setting was the radical change in the political situation of the exiles. Previous prophets had spoken to kings, priests, merchants, judges, and landowners—in short, the leaders of an established nation. Those leaders possessed the political power and economic resources necessary to affect the course of national policy and the social conditions in which the Judean people lived. By contrast, the exiles addressed by Ezekiel had neither property nor political power. They were virtually helpless to affect their own lives politically and economically, let alone the lives of others.

In Judah before the fall, prophets spoke in public, particularly in the temple compound (Amos 7; Jer 7), or they accosted rulers directly, in person (Isa 7) or in writing (Jer 36). Instead, Exekiel was visited in his home by the elders of Judah (Ezek 8:1; 14:1). Consultations of this sort may have occurred in Israel before the exile, but none is mentioned in the Latter Prophets. It is only in the Deuteronomic History that such occasions are recalled (e.g., 2 Kings 5:8-19; 22:14-20), and these recollections may be colored by the experience of exilic redactors.

The changed relationship between prophet and audience is reflected in Ezekiel's form of communication. Preexilic prophecy consisted almost entirely of short, poetic oracles developed out of direct, oral confrontation with religious and political leaders. Oracles of this kind are almost entirely lacking in the book of Ezekiel; instead, there are expansive prose discourses, allegories, and visionary narratives. The closest literary relations of the writings in this book are the prose discourses in the book of Jeremiah. The similarities between the two probably are not accidental, but reflect the same kind of social setting. Like the prose book of Ezekiel, the prose of Jeremiah also was composed for an exilic audience.

Although there are marked similarities between the prose writings in these two books, there is a great difference in the overall composition of the two. In Jeremiah, the prose constitutes roughly half the book and is interspersed with large groups of oracles in traditional poetic form. The book of Ezekiel, on the other hand, is almost entirely prose (except for the oracles on foreign nations, which are a special problem both here and in Jeremiah). There is no collection of poetic oracles concerning Judah and Jerusalem, as there is in Jeremiah. A few scholarly attempts have been made to distinguish a nucleus of poetic sayings in the midst of the prose, but these attempts have failed to convince other scholars. The manifest unity of thought and literary style in the book is a formidable obstacle to that hypothesis. However small or large the contribution of Ezekiel himself may have been to the writing of the book, as we have it, the book is a prose composition.

In the case of Jeremiah, we viewed the prophet as working in essentially the same social situation as his predecessors and employing the same oracular forms; and we attributed the prose portions of the book to anonymous writers of the exilic period. In the case of Ezekiel, we must view the prophet as working in a radically changed social situation and developing new literary forms appropriate to this new situation. The redactors of his book employed the same style as Ezekiel himself. Indeed, their work consisted largely of expanding his narratives and discourses. Therefore, it is much more difficult to distinguish the various strata in the book of Ezekiel than in that of Jeremiah. An interpreter of Ezekiel must deal with the message of the book largely in its canonical form. Consequently, it is understood when we refer to Ezekiel, that we mean the *picture of* Ezekiel presented in the book—a picture that is partly the work of redactors (May, 45-51)—so we cannot be sure how accurate a portrait this is. Nevertheless, it is possible to discuss the theology of the book without being sure of its writers.

On an abstract level, the message of Ezekiel resembles that of other prophets. He condemns the Judean people and their leaders for religious idolatry and moral corruption, and prophesies national destruction as YHWH's punishment for their wickedness. However, on a more concrete level, his message is distinctive, and so is his rhetorical style. Even after only a casual acquaintance with the biblical writings, one can open the book of Ezekiel to any page, from the opening vision of the glory of YHWH to the final plan for a new Jerusalem, and know at once that it is the book of Ezekiel and not any other. By contrast, one must be intimately familiar with the oracles of the preexilic prophets to be able to distinguish them readily one from another. This unity of style is matched by a unity of theme. The dominant theme of Ezekiel's first twenty-four chapters is the wrath of YHWH, poured out relentlessly against the people of Judah. The book is more unitary in this regard than any other prophetic book. Here, more than anywhere else, it is necessary to immerse oneself in the text in order to capture its mood and character.

DIVINE RAGE

Prophetic speech is intemperate. Evoked by moral passion, it runs to excess, and nowhere is that excess more evident than in Ezekiel's picture of the wrath of YHWH against the wicked Judeans. No term except "divine rage" is adequate. Consider the following examples:

> My anger shall spend itself, and I will vent my fury on them and satisfy myself; and they shall know that I, YHWH, have spoken in my jealousy, when I spend my fury on them . . . . You shall be . . . a warning and a horror to the nations . . . when I loose against you my deadly arrows of famine, arrows for destruction, which I will let loose to destroy you, and when I bring more and more famine upon you, and break your staff of bread. I will send famine and wild animals against you, and they will rob you of your children; pestilence and bloodshed shall pass through you; and I will bring the sword upon you. I, YHWH, have spoken. (5:13-17 JMW)

> You shall know that I am YHWH, when their corpses lie among their idols all around their altars on every high hill. (6:13 JMW)

> My eye will not spare; I will not pity . . . .
> Then you will know that I am YHWH, the Slayer! (7:9 JMW)

> Cut down old men, young men and young women, little children and women . . . fill the courts with the slain! (9:6-7)

This is divine rage, and it permeates Ezekiel 1–24. What can we make of it theologically? This question is of some importance, because such an unqualified assertion of divine wrath stands in tension, to say the least, with innumerable assertions of divine mercy, both in the prophetic books and elsewhere in the Hebrew Bible. Is it an aberration in the prophetic witness, the work of an eccentric? Or is the excess merely rhetorical?

As attractive as the psychological and rhetorical approaches to these writings may be, they are speculative. Perhaps Ezekiel was strange or neurotic, but there is no way to be sure. Perhaps his excess was intended as a rhetorical or pedagogical device, but again, we cannot be sure. The book comes to us as a serious treatise on the way of YHWH with Israel, and that is how we must deal with it.

In my judgment, Ezekiel's relentless reiteration of divine rage is the dark side of his retributive theology. As I shall show later, an idealistic understanding of human behavior informs his work. It is taken for granted that people know the meaning of righteousness and holiness and that they can conform to these standards if they choose. The book conveys no sense of the ambiguity of life, the inevitable conflict of values in human relations, or the nonrational factors in human behavior. The writer's concept of sin is superficial. It takes no account of the will's bondage to the deep forces of the psyche, forces the rational mind cannot eradicate or control.

This rationalistic idealism can produce positive results in some settings; it is the basic philosophy of the elementary school, the capitalistic marketplace, and the athletic field. But the perfectionism that underlies this philosophy is ultimately cruel, especially to the ungifted or unfortunate. When it is sanctioned by theology, it becomes heartless and unforgiving. It is not surprising, therefore, that Ezekiel's idealism is accompanied by an acute sense of divine rage.

In Ezekiel's eyes, the captivity of Judah and the destruction of Jerusalem were proof of the nation's abject failure and manifest demonstrations of the wrath of God. Ezekiel was not the only one to interpret these events in essentially this way; all the canonical prophets did so. However, Ezekiel's perception of the state of affairs in Judah was extreme. Commentators generally assume that his picture of cultic abominations practiced in the temple of Jerusalem is an objective picture of the activities that actually took place there. However, this assumption is questionable. Ezekiel's picture of the cult (Ezek 8) is so bizarre that it appears distorted by his outrage. Certainly his characterization of the history of Israel and Judah as an era of unrelieved idolatry, lust, and wickedness (Ezek 16; 20) has little relation to historical fact. This account is deeply colored by moral indignation, and so is his description of Judean ritual. However, his one-sided interpretation of Israel's history and his unqualified assertion of divine wrath fit perfectly with the rationalistic understanding of guilt and innocence that permeates the book. These features are all of a piece theologically.

In Ezekiel, the logic of God's wrath is quite simple, at least on the surface, and it does not lend itself to protracted theological discussion. Nevertheless, since the theme of wrath is so prominent, it demands attention at the beginning of our discussion and will continue to come up in various ways.

But here I want to expand on Ezekiel's interpretation of the history of Israel, which he reviews in three major texts. Chapter 16 is a long allegorical narrative about Jerusalem as the compulsively adulterous wife of YHWH. Omitting verses 53-63, which promise the eventual restoration of the city, that review extends over fifty-two verses, and the other two texts are nearly as long. All together, the three narratives fill ten pages of the Stuttgart edition of the Hebrew Bible! The second text is 20:1-32, which is also supplemented by a promise of restoration (vss 33-44). Departing from the allegorical mode, this text makes a straightforward evaluation of the history of Israel, from the time of the exodus to Ezekiel's time. Finally, in 23:1-49, he allegorizes the history of Jerusalem again, this time comparing the city to Samaria, the sister city. All three texts are addressed to the same readers, though the subject of the narrative shifts from the city to the nation, and then back to the city.

The message of these texts is clear, and it is very simple. Throughout their history, YHWH lavished blessings upon the people of Israel and showed unflagging compassion and forbearance toward them; but they responded, from the first moment to the last, with unrelieved ingratitude, infidelity, and iniquity. Their wickedness was absolute and unqualified. There was nothing at all in their entire history that deserved approbation or mitigated the prophet's condemnation. Ezekiel's account thus differs dramatically from that of the Torah and the Former Prophets. That difference is especially noticeable when one compares his evaluation of Jerusalem and Samaria with the evaluation in the books of Kings. The writers of Kings were very critical of Jerusalem and its monarchs, but they praised the reformers Asa, Hezekiah, and Josiah. By contrast, they utterly condemned all the kings of Samaria. But Ezekiel considered Jerusalem even worse than Samaria. We cannot accept the books of Kings uncritically as the norm for judging Ezekiel's view, since these books too are theologically biased. Yet their account of the history of Israel and Judah is much more convincing than Ezekiel's, and they enable us to see the great exaggeration of Ezekiel's bias.

Summarizing the message of these three chapters of Ezekiel in this way robs them of their impact. Heard in their entirety when they are read aloud, as they would have been in ancient times, they have an enormous rhetorical effect. Particularly in the allegories, the hearer is carried along in rapt attention, mesmerized by the cadences of the story. The single moral is drummed into one's ears again and again and again. There is no subtlety here, only one obvious point—made, repeated, and made again. This is not ordinary historical or theological discourse, but didactic rhetoric. Its aim is to create an emotional effect. It rivets the attention and provokes response and reflection. Its effect would be blunted if the narratives were balanced in their historical assessments or theological assertions; therefore, we should not criticize them too severely. Nevertheless, since they are canonical texts, we have the responsibility of measuring their assertions—especially their theological assertions—against other witnesses in the Bible.

THE CRISIS OF THE ABSENCE OF YHWH'S GLORY

As perceived by Ezekiel, the Judean crisis of 598–587 had many dimensions. Three of those dimensions—the crisis of the absence of YHWH's glory, the crisis of moral responsibility, and the crisis of leadership—were particlarly acute. I will treat each of these separately.

Ezekiel was a priest (1:3) for whom the real presence of YHWH in the service of the altar would have been a matter of deep conviction—or rather, of intense personal experience. His life was shaped by regard for the holy—the vigilant separation of the holy from the profane, the clean from the unclean. The objectivity of these qualities, in act and being, as they were perceived and felt by an ancient Israelite priest who lived most of his life in the sanctuary, is not easy for us to appreciate. It requires an effort of sympathetic imagination to understand Ezekiel's experience of the presence and the absence of YHWH's glory.

I should note here that it is precisely as *YHWH* that Ezekiel speaks of God. The name *YHWH* is used 435 times in the book, while *'elohim,* the common Semitic designation of deity ("God" in the English versions), is used only 36 times. When *'elohim* does occur, it is almost always qualified as "YHWH their elohim" or "elohim of Israel." Elsewhere in the Hebrew Bible, *YHWH* occurs almost three times as often as *'elohim.* So it can readily be seen that the ratio of twelve to one in Ezekiel is remarkable, even among the Latter Prophets. Thus Ezekiel is supremely the prophet of YHWH; it is by this covenantal name alone that God is known and that God's word is proclaimed. Though the reader may tire of the repetition of the name *YHWH,* it is used here to reflect the usage of the book itself.

The most important indications of Ezekiel's understanding of YHWH's presence are contained in the accounts of his visions (1:1–3:15; 3:16–7:17; 8:1–11:25). These recall, first of all, experiences of the presence of YHWH while Ezekiel was among the exiles in Babylon. But the accounts also provide indirect evidence of his understanding of the presence of YHWH while he still served as a priest at the altar of YHWH in Israel, as he must have understood it before his deportation.

In the third vision (8:1–11:25), the prophet sees himself being carried to the temple in Jerusalem, where a truly amazing drama takes place. I cannot enter here into the debate over the location of Ezekiel's ministry that has been provoked by his allusions to Jerusalem, especially the allusions in this vision. I must be content to say simply that I see no reason to conclude that any of the events described in this vision, including the death of Pelatiah (11:13), actually took place—in Jerusalem or anywhere else. As far as we know, they existed only in the vision, and there is no reason to suppose either that Ezekiel witnessed these events in person or that he was clairvoyant. Both assumptions are gratuitous. Despite minor inconsistencies and duplications in the accounts of the visions, they are explained most readily as what they appear to be—simply visions. The reports convey a message to the writer's audience, but they give us no information about actual events in Jerusalem.

To return to Ezekiel's sense of the presence of YHWH, we observe his deep regard for the sanctity of the temple in this great third vision. It is shown in the horror experienced by the seer at the abominations committed by the idolaters (8:6-18), but even more in the ferocity of the treatment meted out to them by the six executioners (9:1ff.): "Smite! . . . Show no pity! . . . Slay!" (9:5f.). Such rage is possible only in one incensed by the profanation of what he holds truly sacred. Only because Ezekiel believed that the very glory of YHWH, the power that sustains the whole earth (Isa 6:3), was accessible to faithful worshipers in the lawful ritual of the sanctuary, could he become so enraged at the thought of Israel's idolatry. To be sure, the wrath described in the vision is YHWH's, but the vision itself is an expression of the seer's own deepest feelings. This is true of all dreams and visions. It is not surprising, of course, that a priest should believe in the real presence of YHWH in the ritual of the sanctuary. Ezekiel's vision merely confirms what we would expect of him.

According to the vision, Israel's cult was totally idolatrous, so the glory of YHWH abandoned the temple (11:22f.). The vision is wonderfully anthropomorphic. The glory, radiating above the chariot-throne like an incandescent aura, is lifted by the attendant cherubim and taken away through the east gate of the temple. This was the same gate through which it would eventually return, according to the plan of restoration that concludes the book (43:1ff.).

Ezekiel's third vision is dated in the sixth year of exile (8:1)—that is, 592–591—and the question generally asked about the idolatries it describes is whether they were reflections of practices actually conducted in the temple of Jerusalem at that time, during the reign of Zedekiah (597–587). It is possible that they were, although there is no reason to think the practices of Zedekiah's time differed substantially from those of Jehoiakim's (609–598), when Ezekiel was still in Jerusalem. Josiah's cultic reform (621) perished with him in 609, and the gates were open to all sorts of alien rites from that time forward. It is best not to try to relate the details of Ezekiel's vision to practices of a specific time, but rather to take the vision as his evaluation of Judean worship generally. It is a caricature, to be sure, but so are Ezekiel's sketches of Israel's history (chaps 16, 20, 23). It was clearly his habit to write in this way.

The point of the vision is that the life-giving, sanctifying power of YHWH was no longer accessible to Israel in worship. Worship had become a deadly affair. Was YHWH's glory then no longer accessible to Israel at all? The answer is a qualified no, in that it continued to be known to the exiles only through the visions of Ezekiel. The prophet-seer himself was the sole channel of the glory during the interval of the exile. This is not to say that Israel would have no interaction with YHWH during the interval. Indeed, Israel would experience the wrath of YHWH sorely, but the glory—the enlivening, fulfilling power of YHWH—would be effectively denied. It is significant that the glory of YHWH is never mentioned in Ezekiel outside the visions, while it is the central theme of the visionary reports themselves (1:28; 3:12-13; 8:4; 9:3; 10:4, 18-19; 11:22-23; cf. 43:2, 4-5; 44:4).

If the glory of YHWH had withdrawn from the apostate community of Israel during the age of wrath, its return would mark the decisive event in the age of restoration (43:1-9). By coming back to the sanctuary, it would legitimize the public worship of YHWH, making it effective once again. This, at least, is the causal relationship suggested in the vision. In reality, however, the opposite was the case. Just as the false worship of the preexilic sanctuary had effectively driven the glory away, so in the postexilic sanctuary, a purified worship would bring it back into the life of Israel. What the glory represents here is not the presence of YHWH in the world, but the moral power of the public worship of YHWH. The whole canonical prophetic witness presupposes that YHWH is present everywhere, at all times, and in all events. However, the behavior of the religious community does not always reflect a proper understanding of this presence, nor the conditions of life it imposes upon the faithful. An idolatrous, self-seeking, materialistic, or magical cult merely reinforces the socially destructive impulses of human beings, and thus also becomes self-destructive for the worshipers. It is in this sense that the glory of YHWH "departs" from such worship.

What sort of worship is morally and socially creative? Or, put another way, what conditions enable the glory to abide in the midst of the community? Surely one indispensable condition of morally effective worship is continual prophetic criticism. Unless the prophets discern and give voice to the probing, judging word of YHWH, ritual can sink quickly into self-magnifying magic. At least, this is the testimony of the prophets.

I have said that the glory of YHWH was known to Israel during the age of wrath only in a limited way—that is, through the visions of Ezekiel. It was his conviction that the sanctifying presence of YHWH, imagined as incandescent glory, was experienced primarily in the ritual of the sanctuary, so that until a new and purified sanctuary could be created in days to come, the Israel of the exile must endure without such experience. This was the priest speaking. Yet the fundamental point suggested by his teaching—that regular, corporate worship is an indispensable element in the life of the people of YHWH—was the common tenet of postexilic Judaism, and certainly was not denied by the other prophets, before or after the exile. Whether proper worship required the sacrificial system or the temple of Jerusalem was a matter for debate, but the necessity of corporate worship was not. The idea of a purely private piety is alien to the Hebrew Bible.

If the glory of YHWH was removed from Israel during an age without worship, the word of YHWH was not. Ezekiel saw to that. His oracular discourses were a saving link between the scattered remnants of Israel and their God. It was this witness, and that of other prophets and psalmists, that kept Israel alive in an age of transition and inspired the creation of new institutional forms in the Persian era.

The Hebrew Bible tells us very little about the transmission of these writings, or of the relationship of the writers to their audience. Jeremiah 36 provides most of the relevant information about the literary process, and it presupposes a preexilic, not an exilic situation. However, we are given a few glimpses into the prophet/audience relationship in the book of Ezekiel, and what we see there confirms the importance of the prophetic word for keeping Israel in being during the exile.

Twice we are shown the elders of the exiles consulting the prophet in order to secure an oracle of YHWH, presumably on a matter of religious importance (14:1-11; 20:1-4). Since the vision described in chapters 8–11 also occurred in the presence of elders (8:1), it seems likely that they were inquiring of YHWH through the prophet on that occasion also. The events reported in 8:1ff. and 20:1ff. are dated. They occurred about a year apart (592 and 591, respectively), so we infer that periodic consultation took place between the leaders of the people and the prophet.

Both times when the elders made specific inquiry of Ezekiel, he refused to give the oracle they requested (14:4-5; 20:3). In his mind, they were idolaters, considered unfit to receive the word of YHWH. In spite of this, he did deliver an oracle to them, though naturally it was an oracle of denunciation and doom. Therefore, his declaration that any prophet who spoke a word to idolators would be destroyed along with them (14:9) could refer only to a prophet who encouraged them in their idolatry, not just any prophet.

The elders obviously did not believe their behavior was abominable, since they were making a deliberate effort to learn YHWH's word. By seeking YHWH, they were taking seriously YHWH's power to bless, and they would have had to be oblivious to the whole prophetic tradition to have thought YHWH's blessing available without regard to YHWH's righteous will. So Ezekiel's condemnation was another rhetorical exaggeration. His condescension to deliver an oracle is a surer clue to his regard for them, and for their potential as bearers of the Yahwistic tradition, than was his condemnation.

The prophetic witness, for weal or woe, was the exiles' primary link with their past in a situation devoid of all other religious forms. Jews of a later age had their scrolls of the Torah and Prophets, but those of Ezekiel's time did not. The solitary prophet was the only bearer of tradition among the scattered groups of exiles.

The famous vision of the valley full of bones (Ezek 37) is a memorable image of the power of prophetic proclamation. The bones are given flesh and brought to life by prophesying over them (37:4ff.). The spirit of YHWH is the ultimate agent of life (37:14), but the action of the spirit is inseparable from the prophesying. The word gives life. In the vision of the bones, the enlivening word is a word of reconstruction and hope, but that word does not need to be affirmative. Prophetic criticism is also life-giving, for it is corrective and disciplinary, and can warn against self-destruction. Even Ezekiel's denunciations were sustaining for those with ears to hear.

THE CRISIS OF MORAL RESPONSIBLITY

Israel's survival as a religious community after 587 depended upon the moral purpose of the people. Other factors were involved, but without the people's determination to forge a future for themselves, none was possible. Individually, many could have survived, of course, but the continuation of Israel, the community of the covenant, could not occur—not without a persistent, corporate effort. Two serious hindrances to this effort were preoccupation with past failure and morbid guilt. These sentiments are expressed well in two sayings quoted in Ezekiel:

> The parents have eaten sour grapes,
> and the children's teeth are set on edge. (18:2)
>
> Our transgressions and our sins weigh upon us,
> and we waste away because of them;
> how then can we live? (33:10).

These sayings explain the plight of the exiles in different ways. The second accounts for it in terms of the speakers' own sin, while the first, which reflects the ancient doctrine of collective retribution (Exod 20:5; 34:7; etc.), blames their plight on former generations. Both ideas could be morally debilitating. In the long discourses that accompany these quotations, the prophet denies the validity of both claims and affirms the direct responsibility of all persons for their own life and destiny (18:1-32; 33:10-20). This astonishing affirmation, which flies squarely in the face of so much human experience, must be understood as a stimulus to hope and action, not as an empirical account of human existence. It is prophetic exhortation, not sociological analysis. A closer look at these and several other related passages can begin with 18:1-32.

There was much truth in the popular adage on which the text for Ezekiel's discourse on individual retribution was based. Vast quantities of "sour grapes" had been consumed by the people of Judah, and especially by their leaders, during the century before the Babylonian conquest, and there was no doubt that the present generation suffered the aftertaste. Politically, cultically, socially, the causes of the debacle of 597 could be found—substantially if not exclusively—in Judean policies of the seventh century. This point was an important part of the Deuteronomists' interpretation of the fall of Judah (2 Kings 23:26f.), but the inference the exiles drew from this observation was that they were wholly rejected by YHWH as a consequence of their ancestors' failure. Their use of the proverb implied that they were not responsible for the circumstances of their lives. Ezekiel's treatise disputes both these claims.

" 'All persons are mine,' says the Lord YHWH" (18:3f.),[1] and the positive corollary of this fundamental article of the writer's faith is that no person or generation is cast off by YHWH because of the sins of forebears and, further, that no person or generation is absolved from moral accountability because of the virtues of forebears. All generations and individuals have the opportunity and the responsibility to shape their own destiny *in the sight of God.* This is a statement of religious belief, not a scientific calculus.

Furthermore, every person's accountability to God is renewed every day, and so is the moral freedom that makes it possible. A record of previous moral failure does not prevent one from repenting and achieving rectitude (18:21-23). The past can be entirely forgiven, and the future is truly open. By the same token, people cannot rest on their laurels; former achievements cannot compensate for present failings, which are judged solely on their merits (18:24). Thus whether one "lives" or "dies" in each moment depends upon the quality of one's behavior in that moment.

Several things should be said about this treatise, which is in the form of a parable about a father, son, and grandson. I have mentioned that it fails to take into account the fact that human acts have lingering effects at many levels of life; the consequences of some acts persist for generations. Moreover, attitudes become hardened and policies institutionalized. In these and other ways, freedom is limited—even the freedom of the will is restricted by conditioning and habit—and some awareness of these facts of life is suggested in the proverb cited by the prophet. Doubtless he was as discerning as his audience. However, his single concern was to reawaken the peoples' sensibility to the measure of freedom and responsibility that was theirs—not only in that moment, but in every moment of their lives.

The consequences of good and evil behavior, according to Ezekiel, are "life" and "death." It is clear that he does not mean physical life and death, for if the wicked can turn from their wickedness, which results in "death," and still live, then they cannot have died physically. Ezekiel does not explain exactly what he means, so we must assume that he refers to the qualities of human experience: peace, joy, satisfaction, harmony with others, and so forth, on the one hand, and their opposites, on the other. In any case, there is no mention of extraneous reward or punishment: health or sickness, wealth or poverty, power or weakness. The implication is that the righteous life is self-authenticating—it *is* life.

I have related Ezekiel's parable both to generations and to individuals. Most modern interpretation of the passage concentrates on the idea of individual responsibility, which is thought to be the point of the passage and judged to be one of Ezekiel's chief contributions to the development of religious thought. However, P. M. Joyce challenges this interpretation, asserting that the writer's concern was not the moral independence of individuals, but the moral independence of a generation.[2] Joyce writes, "I believe that it is really not the '*unit* of responsibility' which is the author's concern at all, but rather the urgent need for his audience to accept responsibility as such." And again, "The question of individual responsibility is really not an issue in the book. It may occasionally be found, along with other elements, but it is not being set forth as something new. Indeed, it seems to me that the overwhelming emphasis in Ezekiel 1–37 (and in the rest of the book, too) is rather on the *People* of God as the unit which Yahweh saves."[3]

I agree with Joyce's judgment in large part, yet I wonder whether he has not overstated the case somewhat. Surely he is right about the author's emphasis, and therefore he is right to criticize the prevailing view of the passage. Nevertheless, it seems to me that more can be said about the individual as the moral unit in Ezekiel 18 than Joyce has allowed. To be sure, from this parable, the author wants the audience to learn that if they wish to live before YHWH in their generation, they must take responsibility for their lives and act righteously; and if they do act righteously, they will indeed live before YHWH. But the parable he tells to teach this lesson involves three individuals, and therefore it is reasonable to ask whether the parable may not apply to individuals as well as to generations. It seems to me that it does.

There is a parallel in the commandments of the Torah, which are addressed to Israel as a community and to each individual in the community. This is reflected in the formulation of the commandments, which is sometimes in the singular and sometimes in the plural. It seems to me the same thing is true of Ezekiel's parable. The probability is even greater if the language of the parable was taken from the traditional entrance liturgy of the sanctuary, as is now commonly held by commentators. The decision for "life" or "death," meaning admission to or exclusion from the ritual activities of the community, is rendered by the priest and based upon a person's "righteousness." The unit of responsibility in such cases is clearly the individual person. The author of Ezekiel 18 was using this tradition to teach a lesson to all the Jews of his generation, and they could not have avoided applying it to each individual as well as to the group as a whole. It applies to both simultaneously, just as do the commandments of the Torah.

The two statements which conclude our text have important theological implications: "Cast away from you all the transgression that you have committed against me, and get yourselves a new heart and a new spirit," and "I have no pleasure in the death of anyone, says the Lord God. Turn, then, and live" (18:31-32).

How strange the exhortation to get a new heart sounds to a modern reader. We have learned to regard the psyche as the master of the will, not its servant; so to our mind, it would not be easy to acquire a new heart by an act of will. At the very least, it would require psychotherapy. How shall we interpret Ezekiel's exhortation?

First, we must remember that *heart* in Hebrew (*lebab* or *leb*) is not thought of as the seat of the emotions. More often than not, it means *mind*, frequently in the sense of the will or moral intention. Much less often it denotes the emotions. In the Hebrew Bible, the emotions are located lower in the viscera. *Spirit* (*ruah*), conjoined here with *heart*, ordinarily has more to do with psychic energy or disposition than with mental processes, but here, as in other postexilic writings, it is synonymous with "heart."[4]

The point is not that these words denote intellect or will to the exclusion of feeling or temperament, for the various facets of human consciousness were not as clearly distinguished by the biblical writers as we distinguish them, but that they denote aspects of human activity which are subject to self-control, however imperfectly. A good parallel to Ezekiel's admonition occurs in Paul's letter to the Romans: "Do not be conformed to this world, but be transformed by the renewal of your mind, that you may prove what is the will of God, what is good and acceptable and perfect" (Rom 12:2).

The whole discourse in Ezekiel 18 is directed to one end—to counteract defeatism and self-pity, and inspire determination. Many factors in their situation affected the form and quality of their corporate life, but without the determination to take responsibility for their own lives, there could be no significant corporate life. Consequently, the exiles' will was a decisive factor in their situation.

The second assertion singled out for comment states that YHWH takes no pleasure in the death of anyone, even the wicked (18:23). The book of Ezekiel is full of moral outrage and vengeance, and the affirmations in chapter 18 at first seem inconsistent, but they are not. We must not be misled by the extreme *mood* of the denunciations. The logic of chapter 18 is consistent with the logic of the oracles of doom. The exiles already had received any punishment due them for their idolatry, and for their ancestors' idolatry, in the bargain. Their existence was a living death. Probably some had not acknowledged the finality of the judgment upon them and continued to hope for a return to Judah (cf. Jer 29); for them, the full force of the blow was not yet felt. Yet for most of them, the judgment was complete, and the decision about whether to "live" was the thing that mattered most. That, and the assurance, without which a positive decision could hardly be made, that God did not desire the death of the wicked, but that they turn and live. "Behold, all persons are mine . . . . The righteous shall surely live" (18:4-9)—this is the theological foundation of the prophet's appeal for moral commitment.

The saying quoted in 33:10 is quite different from that in 18:2. In 18:2, the speakers blame their ancestors for their predicament; in 33:10, they blame themselves. Seeing the dead end they have come to, they declare, "We are wasting away [literally, rotting away] because of our transgressions and our sins." This puts the problem graphically and represents a certain ethical advance over the other saying. Although it is debatable whether the last Judean generation under the monarchy was more responsible for the fall of the nation than were the preceding ones, this acknowledgment of responsibility was a positive sign. It was the precondition of a new commitment, not the commitment itself. Indeed, as the quotation makes clear, the speakers were paralyzed by their feelings of guilt and futility. Therefore the prophet's task was to cure their paralysis without denying their guilt.

The rebuttal in this chapter is the same as that in chapter 18: God judges present behavior on its own merits, not on the basis of past action. There is no carry-over, of either punishment or reward. Rather, the future is entirely open. If you fail to live in the coming days, you have only yourselves to blame, because God does not desire the death of the wicked, but only that they turn and live. Like Ezekiel 18, this passage must not be judged as a psychosocial analysis of human existence, but as a plea. There is enough truth in it to warrant the appeal, though perhaps not quite enough to justify the claim. But in the circumstances, it was only the appeal that mattered.

The ethical theory presented in these texts is often called rationalistic, and in a way it is. But it is more priestly pragmatism than speculative rationalism. To describe it as priestly is not to deny that Ezekiel was a true prophet, for he surely was that. However, his denial of the old idea of corporate guilt in favor of individual retribution goes beyond anything recorded in the other prophetic books, and it has a close affinity to the understanding of guilt and atonement presupposed by the Priestly Code of the Pentateuch. The major premise of the Pentateuchal system of sin and guilt offerings is that the stain of former transgressions can be eradicated. By YHWH's own institution, a means is provided for removing guilt, forgetting the past, and beginning again. Forgiveness is actually granted, the life-giving relation to YHWH actually restored.

The Hebrew sacrificial system appears mechanical to modern eyes, and it is not my purpose to defend it, as such. I am concerned only with the underlying conviction that YHWH willed moral restitution, rather than destruction for the sinner, and was prepared to reestablish fellowship with the penitent. There were limits, according to the priestly tradition; some crimes (murder, for example) were capital offenses, for which ritual atonement could not be made, and in this sense, they were unforgivable. But again, here we are not interested in a detailed comparison of Ezekiel's thought with that of the priestly law. Obviously there were many differences, yet the two were alike in their basic theological assumptions.

Their similarity can be seen clearly in the concluding section of the Holiness Code (Lev 19–26). The Holiness Code is usually dated about the time of Ezekiel, and is often regarded as the middle term between Ezekiel 40–48 and the later Priestly Code (Exod 25–31, etc.). There is a remarkable affinity between Leviticus 26:39-45 and the two texts in Ezekiel which we have been considering. Leviticus 26:39 concludes a long litany of impenitence which occupies the entire chapter up to this point. It describes the response Israel could expect from YHWH, should the people become unfaithful in the course of time. The picture it paints of natural and social punishment is what we would expect to find here. What is surprising about this text is its description of YHWH's patience. Each punishment is presented as a divine discipline, meant to produce contrition and obedience. Round after round of such punishments is rehearsed, and only at the end of a long catalog of human refusals and divine frustrations, is the actual destruction of the nation mentioned (Lev 26:27-39). Then the litany closes with a statement reminiscent of Ezekiel 33:10 and 18:2:

> And those of you who are left shall waste away in the land of your enemies, because of their iniquities; and because of the iniquities of their ancestors, they shall waste away like them. (Lev 26:39 JMW)

However, this is not the last word. Just as in Ezekiel, the extremity of the divine wrath does not preclude the possibility of forgiveness:

> But if they confess their iniquity and the iniquity of their ancestors . . . I will remember my covenant with Jacob. . . . The land shall lie deserted by them . . . but, when they are in the land of their enemies . . . I will remember in their favor the covenant with their ancestors . . . to be their God. I am the LORD.
>
> (Lev 26:40-45)

Unlike the two passages in Ezekiel, this chapter of Leviticus leaves the final exhortation unspoken and concentrates instead on YHWH's intention. It is this intention, YHWH's eternal will to be God for the people of the covenant, that is the very ground of Ezekiel's ardent appeal. The two writings could not be closer in their basic theological affirmation. Furthermore, neither presupposes the existence of the Jerusalem temple or the sacrificial system as an essential factor in restoring the divine/human relationship. In this respect, they are akin to Jeremiah 29.

My point is not to suggest a dichotomy between the priestly and prophetic traditions, but to observe the nuances of each. Ezekiel exhibits a straightforward practicality, a kind of common-sense rationalism which may appropriately be called priestly, while Jeremiah displays a deep awareness of the bondage of the human will, which does not yield readily to moral admonition. Isaiah 6:9-13 shows the same awareness. I hestiate to call this awareness prophetic, because it is evident in some nonprophetic writings—Psalm 51, for example. Perhaps it is better not to label it at all.

One corollary of Ezekiel's doctrine of strict retribution is the rejection of the idea of vicarious atonement. The famous reply of YHWH to Abraham, that YHWH would spare the wicked city of Sodom for the sake of only ten righteous citizens (Gen 18:32), finds its antithesis in Ezekiel's anecdote of the three heroes of faith. Ezekiel declares that not even men of legendary virtue—Noah, Daniel, and Job—could induce YHWH to reduce the punishment of an evil country (14:12-20). There is no transfer of merit from one person to another, either from parent to child or from neighbor to neighbor. Consequently, there can be no transfer of reward. No one can save others from their just deserts. Once again, the prophet's pronouncement reflects an incomplete account of the facts of life. However, as a word for dispirited exiles, it has its value: Let no one rely on someone else's virtue in time of trial!

An odd note has been added to the anecdote of the three heroes (14:21-23): If by chance a few survivors should escape Jerusalem's destruction and come to the exiles, this would serve the purpose of "comforting" (the word used in Isa 40:1) the exiles by letting them know that the city deserved what it got. Strange comfort. Some commentators think this note redactional, and they may be right.[5] However, it is fully in the spirit of Ezekiel, even if it strains the logic of the anecdote. Here again is the lovelessness of the absolute idealist, to use H. Richard Niebuhr's phrase.

No one can save others from their just deserts by vicarious atonement. However, one can warn others of the consequences of their sin, and thus perhaps provoke them to amend their lives and receive YHWH's approbation. It was as exhorter that Ezekiel understood his own responsibility (33:1-9; 3:16-21). The calculus used to gauge the worth of the exhorter is exactly the same as that used to gauge the worth of the audience—a simple accounting of deeds performed, without regard for complicating circumstances or the dynamics of interpersonal behavior.

Two types of warning are suggested. In one type, the prophet sees a disaster coming ("the sword," 33:1ff.) and issues a warning. The tacit assumption is that people should examine their own lives and decide whether to repent before it is too late. In the other type, the prophet observes people's wickedness and warns that it will eventually bring punishment (33:7-9; 3:17-19). In either case, if the prophet fails to do his duty, he is held responsible for the death of those who fall, though it is not said what will happen to him as a result. I infer that he will "die," since when he does fulfill his responsibility, he will "save his own life" (33:9; 3:19). The prophet must warn the righteous to hold fast and the wicked to repent (3:19-20), but he is judged only on his own performance of this duty (3:21); he does not share the fate of his audience because of any transmitted guilt or virtue.

There is a consistent logic, with considerable appeal, in all the passages we have been considering. It affirms the worth of good deeds, regardless of the doer's legacy or past performance. In a situation like the early exile, Ezekiel's ethic made sense pragmatically, despite its failure to give an adequate account of the human situation or the love of God. In other situations, it could have crippling effects.

I want to mention one final feature of these texts, and that is the standard by which righteousness and wickedness are to be judged. Of the many aspects of traditional Israelite *torah* to which the prophet might have appealed, the ones he chose are noteworthy. Ezekiel 18:6-8 is the crucial passage, since 33:15 is only an abbreviated allusion to the longer catalog in chapter 18. Most of the acts mentioned involve interpersonal relations: The acts affirmed are feeding the hungry, clothing the naked, and restoring pledges on time; idolatry, adultery, oppression, robbery, usury, and extortion are repudiated (vs 18). Ezekiel's priestly viewpoint is shown when he lists the morally inconsequential act of intercourse during menstruation alongside adultery, as an offense. There are also some allusions too vague for us to decipher (e.g., "eating on the hills," vs 6). All in all, though, this statement is impressive. The personal and moral well-being of persons is the principal concern, framed in positive as well as negative terms. This concern is linked to the prohibition of idolatry, which is fundamental to biblical religion in all ages, and to the broad injunction to obey God's laws, which, though vague, is a useful conclusion when addressing an audience acquainted with the torah tradition.

A similar, but somewhat longer list of acts, all negative in this case, is contained in 22:1-12. The same themes are present here, but the variations are more numerous. This judgment of the "bloody city," Jerusalem (22:1-31), includes Ezekiel's fullest catalog of moral crimes, as well as his fullest indictment of the officials of the nation (22:23-31). It is to this subject that we now turn.

THE CRISIS OF LEADERSHIP

Prophesying, like preaching, lends itself to generalization and oversimplification. Indictments become sweeping, grandly imprecise historical resumes. Whole eras can be characterized in a few vague terms and whole communities condemned in a single phrase. Nowhere in the prophetic literature is this tendency carried further than in Ezekiel. Perhaps because he lived in exile, where old institutions no longer prevailed and old officials no longer ruled, it was easy to generalize about a remote situation that was rapidly receding into the past. In any case, Ezekiel's charges against Israel's leaders are much less specific than are those of the earlier prophets.

His most important treatments of the *kings* of Judah are the parable of the vultures (or eagles) in 17:1-21 and the lament over the young lions in 19:1-9. In these texts, as elsewhere, he uses parable to good effect. The second poem is not a direct criticism of the kings, but a retrospective comment on their fate. The two lions, trapped and caged as soon as they become competent hunters, are usually identified as Jehoahaz and Jehoiachin, who were dethroned and deported—the first by Necho of Egypt in 609, the second by Nebuchadrezzar of Babylon in 598. It is possible that the poet's description of them as man-eaters (19:3, 6) is an allusion to their deeds, but this is unlikely, since neither reigned more than a few months, not long enough to do much of anything. So it must be simply a poetic touch to a parable about lions, or else a general allusion to the power of kings. Thus, the point of the poem is not to condemn the two kings for their policies, but to depict the sad plight of the lioness, Judah, bereft of her young lions. There is no mention, here or elsewhere, of Jehoiakim, who reigned during the whole decade between Jehoahaz and Jehoiachin, and who truly was culpable, from a prophetic viewpoint. If one were cataloging royal crimes, Jehoiakim could hardly be omitted. The poet's silence confirms the conclusion that 19:1-9 is a simple lament, not a veiled criticism.

In the parable of the vultures (17:1-21), Jehoiachin's deportation to Babylon is recalled again, and this time there is severe criticism of the policy of Zedekiah, his successor. Zedekiah conspired with Egypt, thus breaking his treaty with Nebuchadrezzar, which was both a breach of covenant and a futile political move. In the prophet's view, the Judean's will toward self-determination was self-destructive. This was an age of great empires, and the futile attempt by the petty kings of Judah to compete in the struggle for sovereignty, even over so small a territory as Judah, was interpreted by Ezekiel, as by Jeremiah before him, as opposition to God's will. Although it may have been right in principle, it was unattainable in fact, and persistence in a doomed cause appeared evil in the prophet's eyes, since it jeopardized the lives and property of thousands of families. Therefore we can appreciate Ezekiel's charge: "The princes of Israel in [Jerusalem], everyone according to his power, have been bent on shedding blood" (22:6).

The parable of the vine (19:10-14) points to the underlying cause of the kings' failure—pride. This root of evil is universal, but the institution of absolute monarchy is a particularly fertile soil in which to grow.

It is a strange feature of Ezekiel's discussion of the kings of Judah that he rarely uses the term *king* (*melek*). Apart from 17:12-21 (an interpretation of the parable of the vultures), where the word is used three times, it occurs only once in the primary stratum of the book (7:27), and not even there in the LXX. On the other hand, *prince* (*nasi*) is used several times (12:12; 19:1; 21:25 [Heb 30]; 22:6, 25 [LXX], 27 [*sar*]). Was the title *king* offensive to the prophet? Did he share the old antimonarchical view, that YHWH alone was king (Jud 8:23)? It is possible that he did, though he never uses the title for YHWH. The redactors also avoided the term. In their blueprint for the future theocracy (Ezek 40–48), the title of the ruler is *prince*, not *king*. Furthermore, that person's power is severely limited: his role is merely ceremonial (44:3; 45:7, 22; 46:2, 4, 12, 17, 18, 21). Clearly then, kings and kingship played no significant part in the thought of Ezekiel or of his followers.

In the last specific denunciation of Judah's leaders in the book, *princes* are ranged alongside *priests* and *prophets* (22:23-31; the alliteration is not present in the Hebrew). The charge against the princes (vss 25 and 27) is much the same as that in the texts cited above[6]—wasting human and material resources. Less compelling to our minds is the priests' alleged disregard of sabbath regulations and distinctions of clean and unclean, holy and profane (vs 26). The prophets are denounced for deluding the people (vs 28). This accusation, explained in 13:10, states that the prophets have comforted the people with the promise of *shalom*, peace and prosperity, in a time of imminent disaster. Instead, they should have been warning the nation and advising a change of course (13:2-7); or, as Ezekiel put it so vividly, they should have "gone up into the breaches . . . so that [the house of Israel] might stand in battle on the day of the LORD" (13:5, cf. 22:30). In short, the prophets had failed as watchmen of the people (3:16-21; 33:1-20); as a result, the people's blood was on their hands.

These few passages constitute Ezekiel's full indictment of the leaders of Judah. It is a slender list, when compared with Jeremiah's, for example; but this difference probably is due to the difference in the settings of the two prophets. Jeremiah's career was spent in direct dialogue with the royal and priestly houses of Judah; Ezekiel's was spent in exile, so his attention was focused on other things.

Ezekiel's reflections on leadership were not confined to the failure of contemporary Judean rulers, but included the theological foundations of authentic leadership. The primary text on this theme is the parable of the shepherds in chapter 34.

SHEPHERDS AND THE GOOD SHEPHERD

Rulers and gods have been called shepherds in many cultures, including those of the ancient Near East. The image is appropriate because it combines the qualities of sovereignty and intimacy. The religious metaphor is a natural one in pastoral societies, since people imagine the divine in terms of their own experience. It came to be one of the most important funerary images in Judaism and Christianity, though this usage presupposed the development of belief in an afterlife, evidence of which is rare in the Hebrew Bible. As an image of human and divine leadership in life it is used effectively in Ezekiel 34. A careful reading of this chapter alongside John 10:1-18 will show how this text influenced early Christian piety.

The chapter begins with a remarkable statement concerning the duties of kings (34:2-4), including strengthening and healing the sick, binding up the crippled, and restoring the lost. This list is clearly not based on a minimalist understanding of the role of government as the protector of peace and preserver of order, but on an understanding of government as a constructive agent of social welfare and reliever of human misery. The king—not merely the priest or physician—is conceived of as "pastor" to the sick and the lost. How modern this ideal of government seems.

According to the prophet, it was the failure of Israel's rulers to be true shepherds in this sense that caused the scattering of their flock (34:5-6). This is an important text because it explains the exile as being the result of a false social and political orientation of the nation, not, as is explained elsewhere, the result of cultic idolatry. Instead of using their power for the benefit of the people, the rulers fed themselves (vs 2). This accusation echoes Samuel's famous speech which decries kingship on the grounds that it is self-serving and exploitative (1 Sam 8:10-18). Since Israel's shepherds consumed their flock rather than preserving it, Ezekiel declared that in the future, YHWH himself would do the shepherding (34:10-16).

Ezekiel's parable of the good shepherd is one of many texts in the Hebrew Bible which disprove the idea, still widespread in churches today, that Jesus was the first to affirm the outgoing, redemptive love of God. From the Pentateuch to the Psalms, there is abundant evidence to the contrary. Ezekiel's parable of the good shepherd is the direct antecedent of the Lukan parables of the lost sheep, the lost coin, and the prodigal son. The truth is that New Testament teaching builds upon the Hebrew Bible in this respect, as in many, many others. In Ezekiel 34, YHWH not only accepts the straying sheep back into the fold but goes out in search of them and leads them back. To be sure, the specific human problems Ezekiel had in mind were different from those in the mind of the evangelists, but the understanding of God implied in their parables is essentially the same.

Ezekiel's parable is silent as to the form of political organization of the new Israel under God's "shepherding." The text protests against monarchy as it was in the preexilic era, but it gives no hint of a possible alternative. The notion of *direct* divine rule is expressed elsewhere in the Hebrew Bible, as well as here (34:15). Gideon's repudiation of kingship ("I will not rule over you, and my son will not rule over you; the LORD will rule over you," Judg 8:23) is the best example. This assertion at first appears disingenuous or naive, because every social group, in order to exist, must have structure, role differentiation, and a hierarchy of authority. The alternative is anarchy and chaos. However, on closer examination, Gideon's protest is simply an endorsement of the status quo. It is not a protest against all human government, but only against the monarchy. By

"God's" ruling, it refers to the old political institutions; this is not anarchic, merely conservative. The status quo in the time of the judges was a combination of rule by male elders within clans and villages, and charismatic intertribal leadership. For the conservatives of Gideon's time (or the time of the Deuteronomic historian), this was "YHWH's" rule because it was the old accepted way, hallowed by tradition and sanctioned by cultic practice. However, it was just as human as monarchy or any other form of government.

Ezekiel 34:10-16 was written when Israel had no independent governing institutions, so it could not have been merely an endorsement of the status quo. It is uncertain whether it represents a rejection of the principle of monarchy or only a rejection of the particular kings of Judah. The next section of the book, 34:17-31, which may be from another hand or a later time, endorses a revival of the Davidic royal line (vss 23-24), though this endorsement is perfunctory. There is, however, an explicit endorsement of the idea of a Davidic restoration in Ezekiel 37:24-28. This text is one of the latest serious expressions of Davidic messianism in the prophetic books. For the most part, the writers of Ezekiel, like the prophets generally, confined themselves to criticism of familiar institutions and did not make practical proposals for political reconstruction. The design of the new Israel in Ezekiel 40–48 may appear to be such a proposal, but it really is an artist's conception of the country, resettled by the tribes of Israel in an artificial pattern. It is idealized and impracticable.

AUTHORIZATION OF EZEKIEL AS THE PROPHET OF YHWH

An essential element in the relations between YHWH and Israel is prophecy, for without it, YHWH is not truly known or acknowledged. Three groups of texts in the book of Ezekiel deal directly with the nature and purpose of this vital link in the divine/human relationship. The first group, 1:1–3:21, comes at the beginning of the collection of prophecies of doom for Israel (chaps 4–24); the second group, 13:1–14:23, comes toward the middle of this collection; and we find the third group, 33:1-35, at the beginning of the collection of prophecies of restoration for Israel (33–48).

The placement of the first and third groups of texts on the prophetic office is strategic, since each group comes at the beginning of one of the two great collections of Israel oracles. Each group is highlighted by an announcement that the prophet is the *watchman of Israel* (3:16-21; 33:1-9), which thus serves as a preface to both collections. This is a feature of the final redaction of the book, and this redaction, like that of the books of Isaiah and Jeremiah, is characterized by a tripartite arrangement—oracles of doom for Israel, oracles of doom for foreign nations, and oracles of restoration for Israel. As I said in the chapter on Isaiah, there is an important message in the arrangement itself. However, it is a message from the final redactors of the prophetic canon and does not necessarily reflect the original intentions of Isaiah, Jeremiah, and Ezekiel.

Be that as it may, the substance of the texts on the prophetic office in Ezekiel seems to belong to the primary stratum of the book. Taken together, these three groups of texts have three principal themes: The first is the authorization of Ezekiel as the prophet of YHWH; the second is the definition of the nature and limits of the prophet's responsibility; and the third is the condemnation of false prophets.

Visions of YHWH are important in the prophetic tradition, as we have seen in the case of Isaiah and Jeremiah, and the visions of Ezekiel are the supreme examples. If Zimmerli and other commentators are correct, the reports of Ezekiel's visions have undergone substantial expansion in the course of their literary history. Consequently, we cannot be sure how much of what is written reflects Ezekiel's actual experiences, although there is no point in doubting that Ezekiel had experiences like these. In a society that expected visions as a mark of prophetic authority, they certainly occurred. The important question is not how probable the experiences were historically, but how relevant they were theologically. A vision might have been an indispensable mark of a prophet in Israel, but a vision did not, by itself, authenticate a prophet as a true prophet of YHWH, because a vision could lie (1 Kings 22; Ezek 13:9). The validity of prophecy lay in the validity of the message, not in the nature of the psychological events that evoked or accompanied the formulation of the message. Ezekiel's prophetic visions are by far the most impressive of all those reported in the Hebrew Bible, and therefore hold considerable literary and psychological interest. However, the content of Ezekiel's prophetic message is not essentially different from that of other prophets.

Visions, like dreams, occur at a deep level of the mind, far from waking consciousness. Of all mental states, they are the least subject to rational control. It is ironic, therefore, that Ezekiel, the most rationalistic of the great prophets of Israel, should have been authorized as a prophet by the most extensive, colorful, and nonrational experiences.

The purpose of Ezekiel's authorization was to give warning to Israel of impending divine punishment, so the people would know that a prophet of YHWH had been among them (2:3-5), and they would have the opportunity to take appropriate action in the face of YHWH's impending judgment (3:16-21). The prophet's responsibility was strictly limited to announcing the danger. No matter what happened to the people as a result of their response, the prophet would "save his life" if he fulfilled his duty.

This statement of the relationship between prophet and people is consistent with the analysis of moral responsibility in Ezekiel 18, being just as rationalistic and mechanical. There are no complexities or ambiguities, and there is no empathy, no genuinely human interaction between the warner and the audience. Certainly there is no sense of personal interdependence or shared destiny. The prophet might as well be a complete stranger to them; he is in effect a disembodied voice. How different was Ezekiel's perception from that of Jeremiah!

The warner, in his turn, is treated with the same kind of mechanical justice that is meted out to the people. If he does his duty he will save his life, whether or not the people save theirs. If he fails to do his duty to warn them, and they perish as a result, their "blood" will be "required at his hand"—that is, he must bear the penalty for a capital crime. It is all so clear and simple, but at the same time, cold and impersonal. Nothing is shared at any level of human experience except common vulnerability under a mechanical system of divine justice. The prophet is neither pastor nor teacher. He makes no intercession to YHWH on the people's behalf, and he ignores their needs and sufferings. He is merely a warner of approaching danger.

The understanding of the prophet's relation to the people which informs these texts is evident once again in 14:1-11, but here the moral isolation of prophet from people is even more complete. It is virtual alienation. When the story begins and we are told that certain elders of Israel went to visit Ezekiel in his house, we expect to hear of some positive human exchange between them—some sign or act of friendship or some hint about their common life in Babylon. But we are completely disappointed. Ezekiel simply repudiates the elders as unworthy of his counsel. The message is harsh but clear: If those who seek a word of YHWH from the prophet are unrighteous, the prophet must turn his back on them. If he answers them, he will be punished as severely as they. There is no word of YHWH for such godless people, but only rejection. This account is not a story about real people, but a dramatization of religious theory. The figures never touch one another as human beings, because their humanity is not a factor. They are mere markers in a theological game.

This text implies a high doctrine of the word of YHWH, for it presupposes that the word is too precious, too sacred to be squandered or profaned by association with idolators. At the same time, the redemptive power of the word is implicitly denied, for who more than idolators could be helped by the word of truth about God? Yet here it is part of their punishment to deny it to wicked people. Of course, they are Israelites, who, according to Ezekiel, have long abused the privilege of hearing the word of YHWH. Therefore, here he is declaring a denial of the word, not so much to the wicked generally as to the Israelites in his own time.

Ezekiel makes short shrift of other prophets who, in his judgment, "prophesy out of their own imagination" (13:17). To him, they are mere diviners and magicians who sell things to inquirers for "handfuls of barley and pieces of bread" (vs 19). These practicioners are alleged to have "disheartened the righteous" and "encouraged the wicked"(vs 22), but this charge could mean many things. There is no way to tell what they actually were doing or saying to the people. It could have been almost anything, considering that the one who condemned them also refused to answer the "idolatrous" elders who came to his house, except to tell them that the very act of inquiry was sufficient grounds for condemnation (14:6-11). Any other answer given by other prophets presumably would have been grounds for those prophets' condemnation, too. If the true prophet of YHWH is only a watchman, warning people of approaching punishment, anyone who does not do this is, by definition, a false prophet. In the circumstances of exile in the sixth century, there was value in this concept of the nature of prophecy, but it was a very narrow concept.

EZEKIEL'S PROPHETIC SIGNS

Ezekiel 4:1–5:12 reports a series of prophetic signs acted out by the prophet. These portend the final siege of Jerusalem, the fall of the city, and the scattering of the Judean exiles. This message is expounded at length in subsequent chapters of the book, so the point of the signs is not unique. However, the account provides a dramatic transition from the account of Ezekiel's inaugural vision (1–3) to the discourses that follow.

Ezekiel's signs are bizarre, like so many other prophetic signs. Since there is no mention of an audience, some commentators have wondered whether they were magical in intent. Once again, as in the case of the visions, I see no reason to suppose that the actions described ever took place. The account is purely literary, a simple narrative that makes a vivid point in a memorable way. The meaning of the signs is clear, because it is clearly explained; thus Ezekiel's signs are essentially the same in form and function as the signs of Isaiah and Jeremiah (see the discussion of prophetic signs in chapter 3).

THE FUTURE OF ISRAEL

The promise of Israel's restoration is set forth in the last vision of Ezekiel, chapters 40–48, and in several other passages, some inserted in the collection of doom oracles (11:14-21; 16:53-63; 17:22-24; 20:33-44), some gathered together in chapters 34–39.

The fundamental theological premise underlying the promise of restoration is clearly stated in chapters 18 and 33:10-16—that the righteous and the wicked who renounce their wickedness will have life before YHWH. In principle, therefore, nothing is inconsistent in the idea that a future restoration will follow the punishment of Israel. The prophecy of salvation is thus logically rooted in the idea of retribution. This is only one of its roots, however; the other, as we shall see, is the idea of grace.

A serial reading of the texts I have listed above, excluding 40–48, yields a picture of Israel's restoration that can be described in a few words. All the texts do not say exactly the same thing, but neither do they contradict one another. Materially, the restoration will take place in the land of Israel, into which all living exiles of Israel and Judah will be gathered. The sanctuary of YHWH will be restored, and the whole land will be purged of idolatry. The populace will flourish, and the fruit of the land will be abundant. Oppressors, both Israelite

Eleanor —

Please bring the main dish for 6 people Saturday at 6^{00} P.M.

Thanks,

Jim

and foreign, will be destroyed, a new Davidic king will be installed as the ruler of a united people, and permanent peace will be secured. Even the weapons of war will be burned (39:9-10).

This is the full account of the external circumstances of the new Israel. There is nothing distinctive; it is the standard picture of restoration, reflected in many places in the prophetic canon. But Ezekiel's picture is distinctive in the way the *purpose* of the restoration is proclaimed.

The purpose of Israel's restoration is twofold: to vindicate YHWH's name; and to fulfill YHWH's intention for Israel. Vindication of the name and honor of YHWH is the underlying motive of all YHWH's acts, from the destruction of Judah and its cultic establishment, through the events of the exilic age, to the age of restoration. Here as everywhere, Ezekiel is the prophet of YHWH's holy name. Just as the essence of unrighteousness and idolatry is profanation of the name, so the essence of faith and obedience is sanctification of the name. The events of history, both in Israel and in other nations, are understood ultimately as either denial or acknowledgment of the holiness and power of YHWH. In the time to come, acknowledgment of YHWH, which is the source and goal of life, will mean, for Israel, confession of former wickedness and recognition of the justice of YHWH's punishment. For the other nations, it will mean recognition of Israel's fall and exile as a sign of YHWH's justice, but also the recognition of Israel's reestablishment as a sign of YHWH's grace.

The second purpose of Israel's restoration is to achieve a true relationship between Israel and YHWH—one marked by proper worship and obedience. However, this will come about only when YHWH replaces the stony heart of Israel with a heart of flesh—in other words, when an unwilling mind is replaced by a willing mind, one whose disposition is to serve YHWH. How this will come about is not explained, but it is implied that it will not be the result of ordinary human action. The routine ways of religious instruction or cultic observance will not suffice. Something extraordinary will be necessary, so extraordinary that it will be perceived as a special act of God, not merely a human decision. Of course human decision will be involved, since what is to occur will be precisely a result of the human will, a will in obedience to the way of YHWH. But the source and occasion of this new obedience, this transformation of the believer's life from the inside out, will be recognized as the work of YHWH.

Nothing is said about social justice in the restored community, except that the new "shepherd" will not oppress the "sheep" as the old shepherds did (chap 34). This silence concerning social justice in the new Israel may seem surprising, in the light of prophetic teaching generally, but it is not really surprising in the book of Ezekiel, where social justice is not a major theme. While one could draw out the social implications of the numerous statements about Israel's iniquity, these have to do primarily with cultic idolatry and the disposition to iniquity. Social relations are not the focus of concern.

THE VISION OF ISRAEL RESTORED

Most readers are bored by Ezekiel 40–48, finding little of theological interest. The meticulously detailed description of the temple in the first three chapters admittedly demands patience, but once past this point, the text contains a number of theologically significant features. Even the catalog of temple measurements has more theological significance than at first may appear.

Placement of the temple measurements at the beginning of the vision determines the primacy of the temple in the society the writer imagines. This of course refers to acts of worship, but it also refers to the temple and its compound as an architectural reality. The physical structure itself is central, a place to be filled with the glory of YHWH (43:1-5; 44:4-9); thus it will embody the self-manifestation of God. Its centrality in the life of Israel will be marked by its placement at the geographic center of the new nation, with the territorial allotments to the priests, the prince, and the tribes of Israel placed around it in perfect symmetry. Not only will the temple and its rituals have a central function in the life of the new Israel, the temple will *be* the center of Israel in every way. Form and function will be one. The material embodiment of the idea will be complete.

When the seer sees the glory of YHWH enter the new temple, he hears a voice speaking from inside the temple (43:6). It tells him to describe the temple to the house of Israel "so they may be ashamed of their iniquities" (vs 10). What a strange thing to say—that the description of the temple is intended to produce a feeling of shame, a material edifice to effect a moral response. But this is not the end of the command. It goes on to say that if the people are ashamed, then the seer is to depict the temple and report its ordinances for them to see and understand. Here the condition of being ashamed produces the ability to see the plan of the temple. This is the reverse of the first statement. Apparently, then, the writer meant to suggest that a reciprocal effect was produced between moral contrition and the portrayal of the temple. The inclination of the modern reader is to interpret the portrayal of the temple not as the decisive thing, but as a symbol of something else, such as the worship of YHWH, but this may be wrong. Perhaps it is not the portrayal, but the very *portrait* that counts. Jon Levenson has argued as much, and he may be correct.[7] In our experience, we moderns separate the ethical from the esthetic, the moral from the physical, but Ezekiel apparently did not.

Chapter 44 moves quickly through five features of the visionary establishment: the place of the prince in the temple, the exclusion of foreigners, the demotion of the Levites, the elevation of the Zadokite priests, and the economic support of the priests.

The prince, presumably understood as the political head of the restored community, but whose political functions are not defined, is provided with a private entrance to the temple—the east gate (44:1-3). No one else may use it. In the absence of any reference to his political responsibilies, this text is commonly taken to suggest that the prince's role was meant to be purely ceremonial. However, political responsibilities are not assigned to anyone else in this vision. The text is silent about who is to govern.

The use of the title *prince* instead of *king* is frequently interpreted as a rejection of the preexilic institution of monarchy, but this inference is problematic, as Levenson's lengthy discussion shows.[8] In short, Ezekiel 40–48 really provides no substantive proposal concerning the role of civil government, or of civil leaders, as instruments of divine rule in the new Israel.

Foreigners, the "uncircumsized in heart and flesh" (vs 9), including those living in the midst of Israel, are excluded from the temple (44:4-9). Is this a purely religious definition without ethnic implications—that is, does "foreigner" mean nothing more than "uncircumcized" here? Or does it presuppose that the foreigner, being ethnically different, is disqualified on this ground as well? Is the ground of exclusion a matter of blood lineage as well as ritual consecration? If so, this understanding of the membership of the core religious community is restricted indeed, and it stands in radical tension with the much wider view expressed elsewhere in the prophetic canon, notably Isaiah 56:1-8. It corresponds, on the other hand, with the understanding exhibited in the expulsion of foreign wives from the postexilic Judean community (Neh 10:28-30; 13:3, 23-30; Ezra 9:1–10:44).

The ministry of the altar is given exclusively to priests of the Judean house of Zadok, on the ground that they—by implication, that they alone of all the priests—remained faithful to YHWH (44:15-27). All other "Levites" are demoted to the status of custodians of the temple (44:10-14). The inference is unavoidable that the writer of the visionary tract was a Zadokite and that his evaluations amount to special pleading.

The final items in Ezekiel 44 are the prescription of offerings to support the priests and the prohibition of their private ownership of land (vss 28-31; land is provided around the temple for their common residency, alongside the remaining Levites, 45:1-5). Thus it introduces the subject of land allocation, which is continued in 45:1-9 and 48:1-29. Despite this rather low-key catalog, there are some significant ethical implications in what is said.

The twelve secular tribes of Israel are given equal portions of land, assigned arbitrarily in a neat symmetrical pattern: three each on the four sides of the large central compound.[9] Both the equal size of the portions and the arbitrary nature of their placement are ethically significant. This is obvious in the size of the allotments, but not quite so obvious in their arbitrary placement. Actually, this placement eliminates all hereditary property rights, which were the principal basis of wealth in the old Israel. Every tribe begins afresh in the new Israel, with equal property, and therefore equal wealth.

There is also a major restriction on the property rights of the prince. Although he is given a huge parcel of land (45:7), he cannot acquire any of the land allotted to others (45:8), and he cannot give any of the land allotted to him to his servants as a permanent possession (46:17). He can only permit them to enjoy a life tenancy. These restrictions preclude practices that are nearly universal in monarchies. Kings amass land by all sorts of means, and they pay their supporters and armies with it. The prince in the new Israel of Ezekiel 40–48 would not be allowed to do this. On the other hand, to ensure that this restriction would work, the prince, like the priests, was to have income from the people's offerings (45:16-17). The ethical concern underlying all these provisions was that the prince would not oppress the people by dispossessing them of their land (46:18).

One last provision of the allotment of land deserves special notice: An area of about ten square miles near the holy district is designated as public land (45:6). It shall belong to "the city," the "whole house of Israel." Nothing is said about how it is to be used. Here, as elsewhere in Ezekiel 40–48, the details of use and function are omitted from the plan; only the fundamental idea is presented. This idea of public lands which cannot be sold for private use is one of the most important in the history of civilization. It is not unique in the book of Ezekiel, of course, but it is nevertheless an important element of this vision of the city of God.

Another idea, which occupies a more prominent place in the vision, is the mythic idea of a restored paradise (47:1-12). The seer is shown a picture of a stream of pure water, rising from the east side of the temple compound and flowing down the holy mountain to the Dead Sea. This sacred stream turns the land into a lush garden and the Dead Sea itself into a reservoir of sweet water. The parallel to Second Isaiah's promise of a desert made into a garden is obvious, though Ezekiel's vision differs from Second Isaiah's in linking the purifying, fructifying waters to the sanctuary and the holy mountain of YHWH. The affinity to the idea of a primordial river in the Garden of Eden (Gen 2:10) is also evident.10 This is a vivid way to affirm God's will to bless Israel materially as well as spiritually. The transformation of a semiarid, mountainous land into a garden is something only God can do, so the restoration of Israel is an act of pure grace, completely without human agency. And this is true not only of Israel's material restoration, but also of its spiritual restoration. The glory of YHWH returns to the temple unaided by human action (43:1-5). The transcendent freedom of God is thus doubly affirmed. This affirmation is consistent with what is said about God's freedom in the rest of the book. Therefore, whether or not the two parts of the book were the work of different authors, their theological understanding was essentially the same.

ORACLES ON FOREIGN NATIONS

The collection of oracles on foreign nations in Ezekiel 25–32 neatly separates the oracles of judgment against Israel (1–24) from the oracles of salvation for

Israel (33–48). Like Isaiah 13–23 and Jeremiah 46–51, this is an artificial, redactional arrangement, and also like the other groups, these in Ezekiel are of unknown authorship. They are written in the style of Ezekiel and use his characteristic phrases, but much of the material seems derivative and adds nothing to our knowledge of the theology of the Latter Prophets. The section on Tyre is quite interesting as a historical commentary on commerce in the late biblical period, and it contains some well-phrased reflections on the arrogance of wealth. The section on Egypt, the longest in this collection (29:1–32:32), contains the famous picture of the shades of uncircumcized kings in Sheol (32:17-32). The writer was incensed over the role played by Egypt in the fall of Judah, its leadership of the anti-Babylonian conspiracy into which the last kings were drawn (note, e.g., 29:13-16). This seems to have been the motivation for this lengthy treatise.

CONCLUSION

Among the so-called major prophets—Isaiah, Jeremiah, and Ezekiel—Ezekiel is unique in his representation of the priestly tradition. While it would be incorrect to separate priestly and prophetic interests radically, the emphases of the two were surely different. Thus, though the temple of Jerusalem has the dominant place in Ezekiel's vision of the future, it has a much smaller place in Second Isaiah's. While the life-giving, redemptive word of YHWH was Second Isaiah's major theme, from beginning (40:1-8) to end (55:10-11), Ezekiel was preoccupied with ritual holiness. It has been common in scholarly study of the prophets to trace the prophetic line, with its ethical interests, from the eighth-century prophets through Jeremiah, Zephaniah, and Habakkuk to Second Isaiah and Jonah, and the priestly line, with its ritual interests, from Ezekiel to Joel, Haggai, and Malachi. This scheme is an oversimplification, but it contains some truth. Certainly, Ezekiel occupies the premier place among the defenders of YHWH's glory in the midst of the cultic community of Israel

SELECT BIBLIOGRAPHY

Blenkinsopp, Joseph. *Ezekiel.* Interpretation. Louisville: Westminster/John Knox Press, 1990.

Brownlee, William H. *Ezekiel 1–19.* Word Biblical Commentary. Waco, Tex.: Word Books, 1986.

David, Ellen F. *Swallowing the Scroll: Textuality and the Dynamics of Discourse in Ezekiel's Prophecy. JSOT*Sup 78. Sheffield: JSOT, 1989.

Eichrodt, Walther. *Ezekiel.* Philadelphia: Westminster Press, 1970.

Gowan, Donald E. *Ezekiel.* Atlanta: John Knox Press, 1985.

Greenberg, Moshe. *Ezekiel 1–20.* Anchor Bible. Garden City, N.Y.: Doubleday, 1983.

Hals, Ronald M. *Ezekiel.* Forms of the Old Testament Literature. Grand Rapids: Eerdmans, 1989.

Interpretation 38 (April 1984).

Joyce, Paul M. *Divine Initiative and Human Response in Ezekiel. JSOT*Sup 51. Sheffield: JSOT, 1989.

Levenson, Jon D. *The Theology of the Program of Restoration of Ezekiel 40–48.* Harvard Semitic Monographs 10. Missoula, Mont.: Scholars Press, 1976.

Lust, Johan, ed. *Ezekiel and His Book.* BETL LXXIV. Leuven: University Press, 1986.

May, Herbert G. "The Book of Ezekiel." *The Interpreter's Bible.* Vol. 6. Nashville: Abingdon Press, 1956.

Robinson, H. Wheeler. *Two Hebrew Prophets: Studies in Hosea and Ezekiel.* London: Lutterworth, 1948.

Wevers, John W. *Ezekiel.* New Century Bible Commentary. Grand Rapids: Eerdmans, 1969.

Zimmerli, Walther. *Ezekiel.* 2 vols. Hermeneia. Philadelphia: Fortress Press, 1979, 1983.

______. *I Am Yahweh.* Atlanta: John Knox Press, 1982.

______. "The Message of the Prophet Ezekiel." *Interpretation* 23 (1969): 131-57.

NOTES

1. NRSV, "All lives are mine."
2. "Individual Responsibility in Ezekiel 18?" (Studia Biblica, 1978), *JSOT*Sup 11 (Sheffield: JSOT, 1979), pp. 185-96; and "Ezekiel and Individual Responsibility," *Ezekiel and His Book*, ed. J. Lust, pp. 317-21.
3. Studia Biblica, 1978, pp. 187, 195.
4. See BDB, pp. 523-25, 925-26.
5. E.g., May.
6. Reading *princes* in vs 25 with LXX, RSV, NEB, etc.
7. Jon D. Levenson, *The Theology of the Program of Restoration of Ezekiel 40–48.*
8. Ibid., pp. 55-107.
9. Manasseh and Ephraim, the sons of Joseph, replace Joseph and the unpropertied Levi in the list.
10. See Levenson, pp. 25-36, for a detailed discussion.

CHAPTER TEN

Amos

Amos, Hosea, Isaiah, and Micah were the great eighth-century prophets. The first two prophesied in the kingdom of Israel; the last two, in the kingdom of Judah. The origins of Hosea and Isaiah are unknown, though interpreters of the Bible have assumed they were Israelite and Judean, respectively, because they prophesied in those regions. But Amos, from Tekoa in Judah, prophesied in Israel, so the assumption is tenuous. Micah, on the other hand, from Moresheth in Judah, prophesied in Judah. The two kingdoms were small and closely connected in many ways, so the border between them was artificial. This was certainly true in the eyes of the prophets.

These four prophets invite comparison, not only because they were contemporaries, but because their extant writings are similar in size and content. Most of their oracles are oracles of judgment, and they emphasize similar themes: religious apostasy, cultic idolatry, political folly, and social injustice. There is no corresponding similarity, however, on the theme of salvation. Amos and Micah did not prophesy salvation. It was the redactors who supplied words of salvation for both books, though they did so unequally (Amos 9:8*b*-15; Mic 4–7). On the other hand, substantial oracles of salvation can be attributed to Hosea and Isaiah. The eighth-century prophets are thought of primarily as advocates of social justice and critics of the status quo. This is understandable, for although their message contains more than social criticism, that is a prominent part of it, especially the message of Amos and Micah.

GOD'S JUSTICE FOR THE NATIONS

Following an unusually brief editorial superscription (1:1) and an equally brief, and possibly editorial, introductory word about the thundering voice of God (1:2), the first section of Amos establishes an international perspective. This is the only prophetic book that begins with oracles against foreign nations (except of course Obadiah and Nahum, which consist entirely of such oracles). The big groups of similar oracles are embedded in the books of Isaiah, Jeremiah, and Ezekiel, where they stand in virtual isolation from the oracles concerning Israel and Judah. But here in Amos, the book begins with a substantial group of oracles on foreign nations, and they are fully integrated with oracles that concern Israel and Judah. This is perhaps the most memorable group of oracles on foreign nations in the Hebrew Bible—not only for the reason just stated, but because of the superb literary form.

The Tyre, Edom, and Judah oracles have a form slightly different from that of the Damascus, Philistia, Ammon, and Moab oracles, and on this and other grounds, sometimes are judged secondary additions. This judgment may be right, but the three oracles are not casual intrusions. All three have the same form and are placed so as to create an integrated composition.[1] Furthermore, the point of the Tyre and Edom oracles is the same as that of the others. Therefore, as far as the message is concerned, it does not matter whether these two oracles are attributed to Amos or to a redactor. Taking them into consideration, as one must in the end, simply widens the geopolitical horizon of the composition. It does not alter its message.

The Judah oracle is a different matter. The point of this oracle is not the same as the others. It charges Judah with general religious laxity, while the others charge the nations with specific crimes against other nations. Also, this is the only oracle in the book that mentions Judah. Elsewhere, the prophet speaks of Israel as a single people of YHWH, so this separate mention of Judah seems to be redactional. All in all, then, while this oracle is formally integral to the composition, it is somewhat disturbing to the prophetic intention of the rest of the book.

Damascus, Philistia, Tyre, Edom, Ammon, and Moab are condemned for violent crimes against other peoples, and all six are threatened with corresponding violence at the hands of others. The prophet's assertion is that God holds these nations accountable for their wicked treatment of one another, and punishes them with a punishment that corresponds to the crime. We assume Amos addressed this message to the rulers of Israel. They would have been encouraged by his rebuke of rival nations but disquieted by his rebuke of Israel. Encouragement of a nation against other nations was common in ancient religions, as in religions of other times, but rebuke of a nation from within was uncommon. In fact, no extant religious texts outside the Bible contain this kind of prophetic criticism. Amos's assertion is threefold: God holds both Israel and the nations accountable for their mistreatment of other human beings; God punishes this mistreatment in kind; and God punishes it within the process of history. These ideas have been discussed in earlier chapters, and that discussion does not need to be repeated here. However, it is only fair to remind ourselves that Amos's oracles are the earliest ones of all and that none are more effective than his.

It is easy enough to challenge Amos's assertion that nations are proportionately punished for their crimes against one another. This is clearly an oversimplification, yet we need not be put off by it, for Amos was a prophet, not a historian. It is not the precision of his historical analysis that is important here, but the power of his ethical witness. With one masterful stroke, he puts politics and human relations squarely within the realm of theology, and he puts religion squarely in the realm of politics and human relations.

The Israel oracle does not charge the nation with crimes against other peoples, as the other oracles do, but with crimes against fellow Israelites. The details are not so important for our present purposes, since the list of offenses may be taken as representative, rather than comprehensive. As far as we can tell (the exact meaning of 2:7 is uncertain) all the accusations involve oppression and exploitation of poor, weak, defenseless people. Therefore, the ones accused must have been relatively prosperous, strong, and securely placed. Amos was not content merely to condemn these offenses as morally wrong; he prophesied divine punishment for them. The punishment was to take the form of military conquest (2:13-16), the same punishment he prophesied for the other nations.

What Amos's oracles against the foreign nations assert is that violence in international relations is reciprocal. It is difficult to argue with this assertion, even though the relation of cause and effect is not always as precise as Amos seems to suggest. The corresponding oracle on Israel asserts something different—namely, that oppression and injustice within a nation lead to its destruction; specifically, in the case of the kingdom of Israel, that oppression of the poor would be punished by military subjugation by a foreign power. One could easily dispute this assertion as a simple statement of historical cause and effect, but to do so probably would be to miss Amos's real point: That oppression of the weak is defiance of the will of God and a violation of the true spirit of the people of God. It is destructive of the fabric of Israelite society, and therefore jeopardizes the nation's integrity and its survival. Understood in this way, it is clear that Amos's oracle proclaims one of the central ethical ideas of the prophetic canon—indeed, of the whole Bible.

AMOS'S CALL AND CONFRONTATION WITH AMAZIAH

The account of Amos's call is one sentence long: "YHWH took me from following the flock, and YHWH said to me, 'Go, prophesy to my people Israel' " (7:15). How different from the calls of Isaiah, Jeremiah, and especially Ezekiel. It does not stand apart as a self-contained narrative—it is much too short for that—but is part of the narrative of a confrontation between Amos and Amaziah, the chief priest of the royal sanctuary in Bethel (7:10-17). The placement of this narrative in the middle of a series of vision narratives (7:1-9; 8:1-3) has led many readers to conclude that the visions constituted Amos's call. However, that is certainly not stated. It is more likely that the confrontation narrative was placed where it is simply because of the close similarity of 7:11 ("Jeroboam shall die by the sword") to 7:9 ("I will rise against the house of Jeroboam with the sword"). In any event, we are told nothing directly about the call experience itself. Amos's report ("YHWH took me . . . and said, 'Go, prophesy.' ") thus resembles Hosea's ("YHWH said, 'Go, take a wife' " [1:2]). What the prophet felt or imagined—or "saw"—was not reported. What really mattered was discernment of the call and obedient response.

The confrontation with Amaziah shows how important was Amos's prophesying in the eyes of Israel's leaders. It was tantamount to political conspiracy (7:10); therefore, the priest called for royal support and expelled the prophet from Bethel. We don't know what Amos did in response. Commentators have puzzled for years over whether the dialogue between Amaziah and Amos involves the charge and denial of Amos's professionalism, but this question cannot be answered conclusively on the basis of the existing report. It is clear that the dispute involved whether Amos ought to prophesy in Bethel. Amos believed his commission obligated him to do so. But Amaziah had the authority to prevent him. In the face of what he took as a usurpation of God's authority, Amos condemned the priest and prophesied his death as a punishment from God (7:16-17).

The idea that a prophet should prophesy his opponent's death may seem immoral to us. However, Amos was saying, in effect, that Amaziah, trying to silence the prophecy of national disaster, would himself perish in that disaster. This idea is different from the idea that a prophet could strike someone dead with a word, as in the story of Jeremiah and Hananiah (Jer 28:15-17). That is magic, but Amos's prophecy was not. Amos's reply presupposed that his prophecy of disaster offered Amaziah the opportunity of a free response. Amaziah's personal destiny would be determined by the kind of response he made. He could continue doing what he was doing and thus contribute to the nation's fall, or he could do something constructive and help to avert it. If he did the second, he might live, but if he did the first, he would die with the rest of the nation. On closer inspection, then, Amos's prophecy concerning Amaziah's future makes sense both morally and practically.

SOCIAL JUSTICE

Amos's evaluation of the state of social justice in Israel is stated most vividly in four well-known texts:

> Hear this word, you cows of Bashan!
>   who are on Mount Samaria,
> who oppress the poor, who crush the needy,
>   who say to their husbands, "Bring something to drink." (4:1)

> They hate the one who reproves in the gate,
>   and they abhor the one who speaks the truth.
> Therefore because you trample on the poor,
>   and take from them levies of grain . . .
> you who afflict the righteous, who take a bribe,
>   and push aside the needy in the gate . . . . (5:10-13)
>
> Alas for those who are at ease in Zion,
>   and for those who feel secure on Mount Samaria! (6:1)
>
> Hear this, you that trample on the needy,
>   and bring to ruin the poor of the land . . .
> buying the poor for silver
>   and the needy for a pair of sandals. (8:4-6)

These oracles have stung the conscience of millions and inspired their zeal for social justice. The power of Amos's words has not diminished in recent times, but has increased, thanks in part to liberation theology and other movements of social reform. Contemporary advocates of reform find a strong resource in the prophetic witness. There is a fundamental rightness in this. It is entirely legitimate to appeal to the spirit of the Hebrew prophets in support of the continuing quest for social justice.

It is much less clear, however, whether support for particular ideas of reform is to be found here. The oracles are too brief, and the categories they employ are too general. They tell us little or nothing about the social or economic circumstances of the perpetrators or of the victims of injustice, or even the particular acts the prophets decried. The audience usually is addressed in the second person, so we cannot even be sure who it is.

What we learn from Amos's oracles is that poor and powerless people in Israel were being cheated, exploited, and denied justice in the courts by people wealthier and more powerful than they—people ridiculed by the prophet for their self-indulgent greed and self-serving religiosity. We also learn that such behavior was denounced as a violation of the will of God. These are extremely important ethical assertions, though they do not constitute an analysis of the socioeconomic order or a program of social reform.

The prophets are a wonderful resource for ethical ideals and general social criticism, but they do not provide the practical resources for the highly complex task of analyzing the social and economic order of modern nations, let alone any strategies for solving concrete social and economic problems in the modern world, including the problem of poverty. Whatever practical remedies of the social injustices existing in ancient Israel may be implied by the prophetic oracles would be more applicable to small, agrarian nations than to large, industrialized nations or huge communities of such nations. Nevertheless, the moral principles contained in these oracles are surely relevant to the life and witness of the people of God today.

THE PROVIDENCE OF GOD

Like all the prophets of Israel, Amos believed that the historic destiny of the people was shaped by the providence of God—that is, divine acts of blessing and judgment. Many modern theologians are bothered by the prophets' anthropomorphic interpretation of providence. They prefer to speak of a moral order in human history rather than a God who acts. The notion of a moral order immanent in history is not incompatible with belief in a transcendent God, and I suspect that the prophets might have found it compatible with their own understanding. The most important question raised by the prophetic oracles of judgment is not how God acts but whether there are lasting social consequences of human behavior.

The next text I want to consider is 9:7-8:

> Are you not like the Ethiopians to me,
> O people of Israel? says the LORD.
> Did I not bring up Israel from the land of Egypt,
> and the Philistines from Caphtor, and the Arameans from Kir?
> The eyes of the Lord GOD are upon the sinful kingdom,
> and I will destroy it from the face of the earth.

The assertion that Israel has the same status in the eyes of YHWH as other nations is similar to the message of 1:3–2:16, which we discussed above, but there is a difference. The point of 1:3–2:16 is that God punishes the nations equally for their political crimes. The point of 9:7 is that God guides the nations equally in their historic migrations. So the working of providence is negative in the first case and positive in the second, but it is universal in both.

The prophet goes on to say that Israel, a sinful kingdom, will be destroyed by YHWH. There is no explicit connection between this assertion and the prior assertion that Israel has the same status in YHWH's eyes as other nations, so we can only infer what connection may have been intended. It appears to be that, since Israel has the same status before YHWH as other nations, Israel should not expect to be exempted from the ordinary working of divine justice.

The theme of 9:7-8 is found again in 3:1-2, though with a variation:

> Hear this word that the LORD has spoken against you, O people of Israel, against the whole family which I brought up out of the land of Egypt:
>
> You only have I known
> of all the families of the earth;
> therefore I will punish you
> for all your iniquities.

The threat of YHWH's punishment of Israel is the same here as in 9:7-8, but the premises of the two seem at first to contradict each other. Thus Amos 9:7 assumes that Israel is just like the other nations, while 3:2 assumes that it is unlike them.

However, the contradiction disappears on closer inspection. Israel is like other nations, according to 9:7, with regard to God's guidance of their migrations, but unlike other nations, according to 3:2, in being "known" by YHWH in a unique way. The terms of the two comparisons are different, so there is no contradiction between them. Still, it is curious that in 9:7-8 a prophecy of Israel's punishment is linked to a likeness between Israel and other nations, while in 3:1-2, a similar prophecy is linked to a difference between them. The outcome is the same in both, but the justification for it is different.

To be "known" by YHWH, as Israel was known, meant to participate in the covenantal relationship, a relationship of faith, moral commitment, and knowledge of God. There were many benefits of the covenant relation for Israel, but Amos denied that these included immunity from judgment. The Israelites must have taken such immunity for granted, but Amos challenged their presumption.

Another passage to consider in this context is 4:6-12, part of a longer composition, 4:4-13, which I will discuss later. This middle portion describes a new dimension of divine providence that is not mentioned in the two previous texts. This dimension is remedial discipline. The prophet recites a series of five divine acts meant to provoke Israel to repentance (4:4). All five were social calamities (vss 6, 7, 9, 10, 11); these calamities were grievous, but none was fatal to the nation as a whole. After each act, Israel failed to respond in the appropriate way (vss 6, 8, 10, 11), and as a result, YHWH determined to perform a final act of judgment that would be devastating to the whole nation (vs 12).

It is not completely clear what this act was to be, though it appears to be the overthrowing of the entire nation, in the same way a part of it was overthrown in the previous calamity—that is, in the manner of Sodom and Gomorrah. Thus verse 11 speaks of part of the nation, while verse 12 alludes to the overthrow of the whole nation.

Natural events, especially extraordinary ones, were universally interpreted in the ancient world as acts of the gods. This was true in Israel, too, except that in Israel, orthodox Yahwists believed there was only one divine actor. Not all calamities were interpreted as punishments for sin, though many were. Other explanations were possible, but all involved the divine will. In the present text Amos describes a divine purpose that is educational, even though it employs painful means. This litany of calamities recalls the story of the Egyptian plagues (Exod 7–11). Even the number of calamities (five) echoes the number in the Exodus narrative (twice five), and it is conceivable that the plague tradition influenced Amos's litany, directly or indirectly. The outcome of both stories is the overwhelming destruction of an incorrigible nation.

There is no denying the awful finality of Amos's prophecy, yet for the faithful people of God, the fundamental point of his litany of divine discipline was positive. It represented God as a teacher, or parent, patiently summoning the people to a life of obedience.

Amos 9:7-8 and 3:1-2 speak about the providence of God in historical events, while 4:6-12 speaks about the providence of God in natural events. Yet this distinction, which we make routinely, was not made in ancient Israel. The very concept of "history" and "nature" originated long after the Hebrew prophets, and in another culture. The biblical writers viewed the world as one realm, all of which was sustained by God's power and governed by God's will. Therefore Amos could speak equally of an escape from slavery and of a shortage of rain as manifestations of God's purpose.

The biblical writers also perceived the relation of human beings to the rest of the created world in a more unitary way than we do. The dualism of mind and matter that has characterized much of Western thought for two thousand years was unknown to the ancient Israelites. This does not mean that we can perceive the world as the Israelites did or that we ought to interpret events just as they did. What it means is that in order to appropriate the biblical witness of faith without distorting it, we must rethink the dualism that affects our thought and our behavior.

Another passage in Amos deals with a series of divine acts similar to those in chapter 4. This passage is 7:1–8:3, the account of Amos's visions. It frames the report of his confrontation with Amaziah (7:10-17). The events in the visions are purely visionary—that is, they occur only in Amos's imagination, not in Israel's life. They are like the imaginary events in the parables of Jesus, which were invented in order to make a point. The truth of the lesson has nothing to do with the historical actuality of the events in the story. This seems to me to be the case in the story of Amos's "visions," and perhaps also in the litany in 4:6-12.

Both 7:1–8:3 and 4:6-12 concern a series of acts that disclose a dimension of God's will for Israel. The lesson of the visions is that YHWH's patience with an intractable people, who are likened to Jacob as a small boy, is not endless, but will eventually yield to punishment. The lesson is taught by means of four visions, each more ominous than the last, in which Israel is threatened by YHWH's judgment. The prophet twice intercedes for Israel, appealing to YHWH's compassion for "little Jacob," and each time God relents, but at last the irrevocable judgment falls.

WORSHIP

The prophets' critique of Israel's worship is devastating. Amos 5:21-24 is a good example. Speaking for YHWH, Amos declares:

> I hate, I despise your festivals,
>   and I take no delight in your solemn assemblies.
> Even though you offer me your burnt offerings and grain offerings,
>   I will not accept them,

> and the offerings of well-being of your fatted animals
> I will not look upon.
> Take away from me the noise of your songs;
> I will not listen to the melody of your harps.
> But let justice roll down like waters,
> and righteousness like an ever-flowing stream.

Not only are animal sacrifices repudiated, but so are songs and solemn assemblies! This strikes at the heart of ritual worship. Many interpreters of Amos have softened the blow by saying that what Amos rejected was not worship, as such, but worship without social justice. However, the arguments presented are not convincing. The best argument is that a community without religious ritual was inconceivable to anyone in ancient Israel, but the problem with this is that Amos did not expect the community of Israel to last. Consequently, there is no reason to doubt the plain sense of his rejection of Israel's worship, for it would not last either. Had Amos prophesied the future restoration of Israel, as Hosea did, he, like Hosea, would have assumed that the people would worship YHWH (Hos 3:5; 14:2). But Amos did not prophesy such a restoration; therefore, the question of the legitimacy of worship in the life of an obedient community is irrelevant to the oracles of Amos.

Although Amos repudiated Israel's worship, he was not unaffected by the liturgical tradition. We have already noted some of the influences of these traditions on other prophetic writings, notably Second Isaiah, Jeremiah, and Ezekiel. The book of Amos shows similar influence, especially at three points: The first is the use of portions of a hymn in a series of oracles against the sanctuaries of Israel (4:13; 5:8; 9:5-6); the second is the imitation of a cultic litany in the oracle on divine discipline (4:4-13); and the third is the use of the pattern of a ritual curse of enemies in the oracles against the nations (1:3–2:6).

This evidence of cultic influence on the forms of Amos's proclamation does not dull the force of his attack on the sanctuaries of Israel. However much he may have owed to liturgical traditions, and even to current ritual practices, Amos still could have believed that these practices would be abolished in the day of God's wrath, together with the sanctuaries that housed them. Nevertheless, his use of liturgical forms is testimony at least to the rhetorical value of these forms.

THE DAY OF YHWH

Amos held out no hope for the kingdom of Israel:

> "The end has come upon my people Israel;
> I will never again pass them by.
> The songs of the temple shall become wailings in that day,"
> says the Lord God;
> "the dead bodies shall be many,
> cast out in every place. Be silent!" (8:2-3)

The logic of Amos's prophecy of the end of Israel is the same as that of his prophecy of the end of Damascus, Philistia, Tyre, Edom, Ammon, and Moab (1:3–2:3). Each kingdom had brutalized innocent people, so each would be brutalized itself by conquerors. This was the logic of retributive justice, enforced by the sovereign will of God. The only difference between Israel and the other powers was that the others had acted against foreign peoples, while the powerful in Israel had acted against their own people. Clearly, Amos did not recognize this as a real difference in the eyes of God. The moral implication is clear: It is the humanity of people that matters, not their nationality.

The end of Israel is prophesied consistently throughout the book. The only exception is a small one, and restricted to a few: "the remnant of Joseph" (5:15). The poetry is not expansive in this text—or anywhere else for that matter—so we cannot tell exactly what Amos had in mind. What the passage seems to be saying is that those who act justly may find grace, even in the time of calamity. However, it is not explained why only the tribe of Joseph is mentioned. The traditional tribal territories of the Joseph tribe—Ephraim and Manasseh—were the central ones in the northern kingdom of Israel, and its capital, Samaria, was on the border between them. This may account for the allusion to Joseph here and in 5:6. Hosea frequently made Ephraim, as the central tribe in the kingdom, the subject of his oracles. Amos's usage may be similar.

In any case, it is the prophetic point of this text that is most important. How should faithful people behave in view of the impending conquest of the kingdom? Amos's answer is that they should "hate evil and love good, and establish justice in the gate" (5:15). In other words, they should behave the same way in a time of crisis as at any other time, in accordance with the righteous demands of YHWH. What would become of them then? Not surprisingly, the answer to this is less clear, for who could say what would become of them? What happens to conquered people? The most the prophet reasonably could say was what he actually said: "It may be that YHWH, the God of hosts, will be gracious to the remnant of Joseph." As far as the kingdom itself was concerned—the cities, sanctuaries, and ruling class—the only realistic expectation was woeful.

> Alas for you who desire the day of the Lord!
>   Why do you want the day of the Lord?
> It is darkness, not light;
>   as if someone fled from a lion,
>   and was met by a bear;
> or went into the house and rested a hand against the wall,
>   and was bitten by a snake.
> Is not the day of the Lord darkness, not light,
>   and gloom with no brightness in it?

Who in Israel would not have wanted to see the day of YHWH, a day of victory over the enemies of YHWH, and therefore, they assumed, over the enemies of Israel? Only a radical like Amos would have distinguished YHWH's victory from

Israel's victory, for only a radical like Amos would have numbered Israel among the enemies of YHWH. And only a prophet would have spoken in such an uncompromising way. There is no qualification of the indictment or the punishment. This is prophecy, not history or theology. History requires a more balanced account of a nation's story, and theology requires a more nuanced account of the ways of God. Yet Amos's oracle is certainly a model of prophetic rhetoric.

One sometimes-missed feature of Amos's prophecy of the end is associated with the doxological fragments in 4:13; 5:8-9; and 9:5-6. Most commentators treat these fragments as later additions and therefore do not attempt to relate them organically to their context. The fragments do have such a relation, however, and it is worth noting. It is possible that the fragments were incorporated secondarily, to be sure, but if so, a new rhetorical effect has been created by this expansion of the earlier text. On the other hand, it is possible that they were there from the beginning. The fragments are pieces of a hymn that celebrates YHWH's sovereignty over the skies, the seas, and the earth. Since such "creation theology" used to be considered postexilic, the hymnic fragments in Amos were thought to be late. However, creation theology existed throughout Israel's cultural environment for centuries before the Hebrew Bible was written, and it is very likely that many biblical creation texts are preexilic. Accordingly, I see no reason to single out the doxological fragments in Amos as secondary, simply on the a priori assumption that material like this is late.

The doxologies, as they are usually called, are strategically placed in order to highlight a series of oracles against the sanctuaries of Israel. If the doxologies are cultic in origin, as is likely, their incorporation into these oracles is suitably ironic. The first oracle (4:4-13) includes the litany of divine discipline, which I have discussed. It begins satirically with an invitation: "Come to Bethel and transgress; to Gilgal, and multiply transgression." It reaches a climax in a prophecy of Israel's final, fatal meeting with God (vs 12). And it closes with a hymnic declaration of who God is. This is no local, national deity, but the One who forms mountains, inspires human thought, and controls light and darkness (vs 13). The meaning is evident: It is the unbounded scope of YHWH's sovereignty that makes it possible for YHWH to punish the nations (1:3–2:16).

The second doxology (5:8-9) also occurs in an oracle (5:1-9) concerning the sanctuaries of Bethel and Gilgal, though this time Beersheba is added. Several themes from the first doxology are repeated here, and others are added. The most significant new element is the ominous last line: "Who makes destruction flash forth against the strong, so that destruction comes upon the fortress." This heavy theme is only dimly anticipated by the line "who makes the morning darkness" in the first doxology. Thus a kind of crescendo develops through the first two oracles and reaches a climax in the third (9:1-6). Here there is a shattering picture of the destruction of the national cultus and the desperate flight of the worshipers, who are searched out by YHWH, wherever they try to flee, and slain.

> The Lord, God of hosts,
> he who touches the earth and it melts,
>   and all who live in it mourn,
> and all of it rises like the Nile,
>   and sinks again, like the Nile of Egypt;
> who builds his upper chambers in the heavens,
>   and founds his vault upon the earth;
> who calls for the waters of the sea,
>   and pours them out upon the surface of the earth—
> the Lord is his name.

Amos foresaw no future for Israel after the destruction of the kingdom, although Hosea, his contemporary, did. In retrospect, we can say that Amos was right, for the kingdom of Israel was destroyed. We do not know to what extent the people of the kingdom and their descendants shared in the future of the people of YHWH. We assume that some of them did, first in the kingdom of Judah, during the remaining 135 years of its history, and then in the Jewish communities established in exile. However, the records are silent about this. So Amos's foresight may have been more clear than Hosea's. But Hosea's theological insight was more broad than Amos's. Hosea's prophecy of the restoration of Israel was correct—not because he predicted its concrete form, for he did not, but because his understanding of God's love proved true for thousands of faithful people. However, his estimate of the existing kingdom of Israel was essentially the same as Amos's, as was the theological understanding on which it was based.

AMOS 9:8*b*, 11-15

The ending of the book is almost universally regarded by critical scholars as redactional. Verse 8*b* reverses the prophecy contained in 9-10, and 11-15 presupposes the fall of Judah (587 BCE), which occurred long after Amos's time. Those concerned with defending the unity of authorship of the whole book of Amos do not interpret the fallen booth of David as the destruction of the kingdom of Judah in 587 BCE, but as the division of the Davidic-Solomonic kingdom in 922, or some other comparable event; they argue that Amos, being a Judean himself, could have embraced the Davidic monarchical ideal, as well as the Jerusalemite Zion theology. This thesis is possible, a priori, but the trouble is that neither the Davidic kingship nor Zion-Jerusalem is ever mentioned in the oracles of judgment as factors in the accusations. The only mention of Zion-Jerusalem in the book is in the brief, self-contained statement in 1:2, which serves as an introduction to the collection as a whole, and certainly appears to be editorial. Thus, at the beginning (1:2) and at the end (9:8*b*-15), the Judean editor has framed Amos's oracles of doom (1:3–9:8*a*) with words expressive of a Judean perspective.

The idea that the Davidic monarchy would be restored "as in the days of old" (vs 11) is found also in Jeremiah 33:7, but nowhere else in the exilic or postexilic prophetic writings. This specific hope faded as time passed, and more realistic hopes took its place—for example, Zechariah's proposal of a diarchy consisting of a civil and a cultic leader (Zech 4:11-14). Nevertheless, the trust in God's redemptive purpose which underlies Amos's prophecy is expressed in many ways throughout the prophetic corpus; it is at the heart of the prophetic witness. This oracle of Davidic restoration lacks, however, any sense of the moral condition of renewal which otherwise permeates the prophetic witness. Thus, for example, in the promises of restoration in Hosea 2, 3, 11, and 14, God's demand of faithful response is expressed alongside the promise of God's grace. These promises are therefore entirely consistent theologically with the oracles of denunciation and punishment in the book of Hosea. But the hopeful ending in Amos 9:11-15 contains no hint of the moral earnestness of the prophet Amos. Therefore, it seems highly unlikely that it was written by him.

Of all the oracles contained in the books of the prophets, only those of Amos and Hosea are known to have been addressed to the northern kingdom of Israel. These two books complement each other, in the sense that Amos emphasizes social acts and relationships—particularly social injustice—while Hosea emphasizes the inner sources of behavior—that is, the knowledge of God, or faith. Both are classic examples of prophetic proclamation, and two of the most important literary monuments of the kingdom of Israel. These books should be studied together; therefore, it is to Hosea that we turn next.

SELECT BIBLIOGRAPHY

Andersen, Francis I., and David Noel Freedman. *Amos.* Anchor Bible. Garden City, N.Y.: Doubleday, 1989.

Barstad, Hans M. *The Religious Polemics of Amos.* *VT*Sup 34. Leiden: E. J. Brill, 1984.

Boyle, M. O'R. "The Covenant Lawsuit of the Prophet Amos: III 1–IV 13." *VT* 21 (1971): 338-62.

Coote, Robert B. *Amos Among the Prophets: Composition and Theology.* Philadelphia: Fortress Press, 1981.

Crenshaw, James L. *Hymnic Affirmations of Divine Justice: The Doxologies of Amos and Related Texts in the Old Testament.* SBLDS 24. Missoula, Mont.: Scholars Press, 1975.

Cripps, Richard S. *A Critical and Exegetical Commentary on the Book of Amos.* 2nd ed. London: SPCK, 1955.

Hammershaimb, Erling. *The Book of Amos: A Commentary.* Oxford: Basil Blackwell, 1970.

Hayes, John H. *Amos: The Eighth-century Prophet.* Nashville: Abingdon Press, 1989.

Limburg, James. *Hosea-Micah.* Interpretation. Atlanta: John Knox Press, 1988.

Martin-Achard, R. *God's People in Crisis: A Commentary on the Book of Amos.* International Theological Commentary. Grand Rapids: Eerdmans, 1984.

Mays, James L. *Amos.* Philadelphia: Westminster Press, 1969.

Review and Expositor 64/4 (1966).

Soggin, J. Alberto. *The Prophet Amos.* London: SCM Press, 1987.

Southwestern Journal of Theology 9/1 (1966).

Stuart, Douglas. *Hosea-Jonah.* Word Biblical Commentary. Waco, Tex.: Word Books, 1987.

Tucker, Gene M. "The Law in the Eighth-century Prophets." *Canon, Theology, and Old Testament Interpretation*, ed. Gene M. Tucker et al. Philadelphia: Fortress Press, 1988.

Ward, James M. *Amos and Isaiah.* Nashville: Abingdon Press, 1969.

______. *Amos and Hosea.* Atlanta: John Knox Press, 1981.

Wolff, Hans Walter. *Amos the Prophet: The Man and His Background.* Philadelphia: Fortress Press, 1973.

______. *Joel and Amos.* Hermeneia. Philadelphia: Fortress Press, 1977.

NOTES

1. See Ward, *Amos and Isaiah*, pp. 94-99.

CHAPTER ELEVEN

Hosea

Theologically, the book of Hosea is the most important of the Twelve Prophets. In breadth of thematic substance and depth of insight, it is unequaled in this collection. It stands with the two Isaiahs and Jeremiah at the pinnacle of prophetic thought. And since it is the only extant book by a northern Israelite prophet, it is doubly important.

Like the other preexilic prophetic books, the book of Hosea contains a searching moral critique of the Israelite community, especially of the ruling class and the cultic leadership. In Hosea, however, this critique is given a fuller theological foundation than in some of the other books, and it is balanced by a fuller constructive proclamation. Another distinctive feature of Hosea's work is that it makes extensive use of the historical traditions of Israel, particularly those reflected in the narratives of the Pentateuch. Finally, the literary imagination is unusually rich. Vivid images and metaphors abound, increasing the rhetorical force of the poetry. Most notable are the famous allegories of Israel as the wife and child of YHWH (Hos 2; 11).

THE PATTERN OF ISRAEL'S HISTORY

Interpretation of Israel's history is the foundation of Hosea's message; no other prophet made more sustained use of the historical traditions. For him, the story of YHWH's deliverance of the ancestors of Israel was the source of the knowledge of God, and it also served as the model for the continuing story of YHWH's relations with Israel. In Hosea, the story of the past is the paradigm of the future.

The traditions recalled—the deliverance of Israel from Egypt, the guidance in the wilderness, the gift of the land—these were the main stages in the journey from Egypt to Canaan that made possible the formation of Israel as the people of YHWH. In Hosea's thought, these saving acts of God provided the key to Israel's understanding of the promises and demands of God, who was known by what had been done on Israel's behalf in the formative events of history.

Hosea focused on the latter half of the Pentateuchal narrative as we know it—the Exodus, wilderness, and settlement traditions. The first half of the narrative is used very little: Creation traditions are not used at all, and patriarchal traditions are used only in chapter 12. Further, even though the deliverance from Egypt and guidance in the wilderness are important themes, Sinai, so closely associated with them in the Pentateuch, is never mentioned. There are references to the covenant with YHWH (6:7; 8:1), *torah* (4:6; 8:1, 12), and the new covenant (2:18), but none to Sinai.

The theological foundation of Hosea's proclamation is his interpretation of the historic acts of God. However, these acts are not the explicit theme of the majority of his oracles, most of which deal with Israel's response to God's acts, rather than the acts themselves. According to Hosea, Israel's historic response to God's deliverance from Egypt, guidance in the wilderness, and gift of the land was to forget the giver and abuse the gifts. Ungrateful and unfaithful, Israel squandered the opportunity to become the true people of YHWH. The dominant theme of Hosea's oracles is Israel's infidelity as manifested in various aspects of life. The result of this infidelity, in Hosea's view, would be surrender of the divine gifts: Israel would be destroyed as a nation and exiled from the land.

This is a familiar message in preexilic prophecy. But Hosea did not stop with the proclamation of divine judgment, as some prophets did. In Hosea's view, the exile from the land of promise was to serve a double purpose; it would be a well-deserved punishment for Israel's apostasy, to be sure, but it would be more than that. Ultimately, God would deal redemptively with Israel in exile, not merely retributively. Consequently, the exile would not be the last chapter in the story, but the prelude to a new beginning. This new chapter in Israel's story could be imagined as a recapitulation of the original story of salvation. Once again, YHWH would bring Israel out of "Egypt," guide the people through "the wilderness," and resettle them in the land, this time as a faithful people. Thus there would be a second Exodus and a second settlement in the land of promise. Future blessing would replace the present curse. The moral condition upon which this renewal depended was true repentance and knowledge of God; a chastened people would learn the lesson of divine discipline. The future would not be a mere repetition of the past, even though hope for the future was expressed in the symbols of the past.

PARABLES OF YHWH AND ISRAEL

Hosea's interpretation of Israel's history, the implicit basis of all his oracles, is presented in chapters 1–3, 11, and, in somewhat looser form, 12–14. The entire story of Israel and YHWH is told in two texts, both constructed around metaphors of the divine/human relationship; I will refer to them as parables. The first is the parable of Israel, the wife of YHWH (2); and the second is the parable of Israel, the child of YHWH (11). In both, the chronological sequence of past, present, future is followed, and the same pattern appears again in 12–14, where 12 deals with the past, 13 with the present, and 14 with the future. Study of these texts, especially the parabolic poems in 2 and 11, provides the basis for interpreting the other oracles in the book.

"When Israel was a child I loved him, and out of Egypt I called my son" (11:1 RSV), the most famous line in the book of Hosea, begins the parable of Israel as the wayward child of God, a story told in essential outline and chronological order. It is a story of two cycles of history, each beginning with a deliverance "out of Egypt"; thus the first exodus is the archetype of the future salvation. Between the first and the second exodus there is the period of filial disobedience, followed by the period of divine discipline. The disobedience is described only briefly in this poem, characterized as idolatry—the baalization of Israel's worship (11:2). Elsewhere in the book changes are rung on this and related themes. The divine discipline of the child takes the form of military conquest and exile (vss 5-6), which is punitive, but ultimately redemptive. Although punishment of an incorrigible child might have been the end of the story, YHWH's love transcends retributive human standards of justice and requires an act of redemption (11:8-9).

> How can I give you up, Ephraim?
>   How can I hand you over, O Israel? . . . .
> My heart recoils within me;
>   my compassion grows warm and tender.
> I will not execute my fierce anger;
>   I will not again destroy Ephraim;
> for I am God and no mortal,
>   the Holy One in your midst,
>   and I will not come in wrath.

As a consequence of this abiding love, the end of the story is the restoration of the chastened child (vss 10-11).

The other parable of YHWH and Israel (chap 2) tells essentially the same story, though in greater detail, and uses the metaphor of marriage as the symbol of the divine/human relationship. This time the tale begins in the present and refers to the past at a later point (2:8, 15); it concludes in the same way as the parable of the child, with the promise of a future restoration of Israel (vss 16-23). Once again the exodus from Egypt is the archetypal event of redemption (vs 15), and here it is linked to the memory of divine guidance in the wilderness (vs 14). The most important tradition in this poem is the settlement in the blessed land of "grain, wine and oil." This was the sustaining gift of YHWH, the "husband" of Israel, to his bride (vs 8), which would be revoked as punishment for infidelity (vs 9 et passim), but would eventually be restored when the marriage was renewed (vss 21-22). In this story the parable is sustained entirely on a parabolic plane; thus, unlike chapter 11, it does not mention military conquest or political exile concretely, but only implies them symbolically. Yet the two stories are consistent in their representation of the history of Israel; the same understanding of the past undergirds both, and they project the same picture of the future. It is this interpretation of Israel's history that informs and unifies the entire book of Hosea.

One other section, chapters 12–14, the concluding section of the book, is structured in a similar fashion to the historical allegories, though without explicit use of the exodus/wilderness/settlement typology. Chapter 12 deals with the unrighteousness of Israel as represented by the ancestor Jacob. Although this unrighteousness is shown to have persisted into the present, its ancient beginning in the behavior of Jacob is stressed. Chapter 13 describes the consequences of this behavior—the coming devastation of Israel; but chapter 14, echoing the promises in chapters 2 and 11, prophesies the eventual restoration of the people of God. Thus once again, a comprehensive view of Israel's history can be seen to control Hosea's proclamation.

HOSEA'S SYMBOLIC ACTS

The book of Hosea begins with an account of Hosea's symbolic marriage to a whorish woman. This act, and the others that follow from it, should be interpreted as expressions of Hosea's historical understanding. Although psychologizing inferences have often been drawn from the report of the marriage and made the foundation for intepreting Hosea's message, we are on surer ground if we proceed in the opposite direction. Accordingly, having sketched the theological framework of Hosea's message, we are prepared to discuss the acts which expressed it symbolically.

The prophets performed many strange acts as part of their service to the word of God. There are prime examples of those acts in Isaiah, Jeremiah, and Ezekiel, as we have seen, but none was stranger than the acts of Hosea. There were five, and they all revolved around his marriage to Gomer bath Diblaim, a "wife of whoredom." He married her to symbolize YHWH's "marriage" to whorish Israel (1:2-3). Then he had three children with her and gave them symbolic names (1:4-9). Finally, he ransomed a woman, who is unnamed but may have been Gomer, as a symbol of YHWH's redemptive love for Israel (3:1-5).

The accounts of these acts in chapters 1 and 3 enclose the parable of Israel's history in chapter 2, where YHWH and Israel are called "husband" and "wife," and the people of Israel are depicted as the children of that marriage. The close literary relationship of the accounts of Hosea's symbolic acts (chaps 1; 3) to the parable of YHWH and Israel (chap 2) has led many interpreters to fuse the two into a continuous double-decker story of two marriages—Hosea's to Gomer and YHWH's to Israel. This inference could be correct. The Greek translator of the book of Hosea seems to have drawn that inference in ancient times, for he changed the Hebrew plurals in 2:1 ("Say to your *sisters*, 'My People,' and to your *brothers*, 'Pitied'") to singulars, thus permitting the double allusion to the people of Israel and the children of Hosea and Gomer.

However, the Hebrew text of chapter 2 gives no clear indication that it is about Hosea, Gomer, and their children. The symbolic names of the children are alluded to in 2:21-23, to be sure, but this promise, like the one in 1:10–2:1, is addressed to Israel. The point is that, in the future, the punishments of God, which had been signaled by the names of Hosea's children, will have been completed, and a relationship of blessing between YHWH and Israel will be restored. Taken by itself, chapter 2 is explicitly about YHWH and Israel. It seems to me that chapter 2 does not provide a definite link between chapters 1 and 3 in the story of Hosea's relations with Gomer. Moreover, we are not really sure of the identity of the woman in chapter 3. If she was not Gomer, as she may not have been, then we know nothing about any prior relationship between her and Hosea, and we obviously cannot draw any theological inferences from it. Nevertheless, we are not left in any doubt about the meaning of the act, for it is explained in the account. But we cannot get behind the account to discover whether the act had some other "original" meaning, when and if it was actually performed. Whatever the prophet's original intention may have been, the message conveyed to the reader is the message stated in the text itself. And this is true of the symbolic acts of other prophets, as well as those of Hosea.

Hosea married Gomer bath Diblaim, a "woman of whoredom," to fulfill his prophetic commission—to symbolize YHWH's "marriage" to a people "of whoredom." Whether Gomer was a sacred or a secular prostitute, or merely the devotee of an idolatrous cult, is unknown. It is also unknown whether the marriage itself, apart from the written account of it, was perceived by others as a marriage to a "woman of whoredom." Like most other symbolic prophetic acts, this one probably conveyed no meaning without a stated explanation. This certainly was true of the names Hosea gave his children: Jezreel, Lo-ruhamah (Not Pitied), and Lo-ammi (Not My People). None of these is self-explanatory, but each is clearly explained in the prophet's report.

The first sign, Hosea's marriage to a whorish woman, is an indictment of the people of Israel for religious apostasy. The particulars are not given here, but are amply supplied in later oracles. The second sign, the name Jezreel, is both an indictment and a prophecy of punishment. The indictment is against the reigning dynasty of the northern Israelite kingdom, the house of Jehu, for an act of bloodshed in the valley of Jezreel. If the prophet was thinking of an event recorded in the canonical Bible, the best guess is that it was the slaughter of the royal house of Omri and Ahab by the usurper Jehu (2 Kings 9–10). So the destruction of the house of Jehu, prophesied in Hosea 1:4, would be a fitting punishment. The third sign, the name Lo-ruhamah, meaning Not Pitied, is explained as the announcement of the end of divine favor for the "house of Israel"—that is, the northern kingdom. The fourth sign, the name Lo-ammi, meaning Not My People, is the announcement of the end of the special relationship between the people of Israel and YHWH.

Thus the four sign narratives together form a kind of prophetic tract, containing both an indictment of Israel and an announcement of divine punishment. The scope of the punishment is expanded in the three signs—from the current dynasty to the kingdom, and then to the whole people. The substance of the indictment, though stated somewhat cryptically, is the same double charge that runs through the rest of the book—the charge of religious apostasy and political corruption. Thus, in a series of terse pronouncements embodied in memorable signs, the opening narrative provides a powerful introduction to the oracles in the remainder of the book.

RANSOMING AN ADULTEROUS WIFE

Hosea's final symbolic act is the ransoming of an adulterous woman (chap 3). She is not identified by name, though most interpreters conclude that she was Gomer, and in that case, the act obviously would have been far more significant. It would have been the reestablishment of a prior relationship, thus symbolizing YHWH's ongoing relationship with Israel. Nevertheless, even if the woman were not Gomer—a possibility that was perfectly legal in ancient Israel—the act would have conveyed the symbolic meaning intended by Hosea and explained in the report. It is this meaning we must take into account, not some other.

The woman was an adulteress, the lover of a paramour (literally, "friend"). She may have been a slave and thus a concubine, since Hosea was required to pay ransom for her. Having thus secured the right to take her as his wife or concubine, he subjected her to a period of testing, to see whether she could behave without prostituting herself. Meanwhile, he would wait for her. If she proved chaste—this is the clear implication, though it is not stated—she would be given the status for which she had been ransomed. All this was symbolic of the way YHWH intended to treat the "adulteress" Israel. Out of love, YHWH would act redemptively, but would subject the people to a time of discipline to test their fidelity. Afterward, the people would be given the status of a proper community, with the appropriate institutions of government and cultus.

This act of Hosea communicates the same message contained in the allegories of covenantal history (chaps 2; 11), a consistent message of divine redemption following a time of testing in the "wilderness," away from the blessings of land, government, and cultus. It is a redemption grounded in love, but a righteous love which demands righteousness and fidelity as the conditions of blessedness.

YHWH AS HUSBAND AND PARENT

The materials we have been discussing are based on two metaphors used in reference to God: the first is that of a husband (1–3); the second, that of a parent (11). Although these metaphors are used with great rhetorical effect in the book of Hosea, they have become problematic for many readers today and therefore call for further comment.

I have called the second metaphor that of a parent; however, most writers on the book of Hosea, and most readers, would call it the metaphor of a father. I have chosen "parent" because Hosea 11 does not actually refer to God as "father," and the neutral "parent" does justice to what is said, but avoids the masculine term so offensive to many today.

Hosea may have been thinking of YHWH as a father, since in the Hebrew Bible, God usually is spoken of in masculine terms. This is especially true when God is called YHWH, for YHWH traditionally was the ruling warrior god of a patriarchal society. Only occasionally do the biblical writers use feminine images for God, and almost always those images are associated with childbirth and childrearing—that is, metaphors of creation. Since this is the case elsewhere (e.g., Isa 49:14-15), it could be the case here in Hosea 11 as well, because everything said in this passage about nurturing could apply equally well to either a father or a mother. However, the husband metaphor in Hosea 1–3 is a different matter. Israel is clearly imagined as the "wife" of God in these chapters, and this necessarily makes God a "husband."

Exegetically, we can do nothing about this masculine language for God. It is simply there—clear, explicit, and unyielding. We cannot neutralize "husband" to "spouse," because there is a "wife" in the picture. We could neutralize the masculine language in 11:1—for example, "When Israel was young I loved them, and out of Egypt I called my children." But there is no corresponding way to neutralize the masculine language in Hosea 1–3.

Actually, this language is doubly offensive. It uses a male metaphor for God and describes Israel as an adulterous wife. And not just a wife, which in the biblical mentality was a subordinate role, but an adulterous wife and a prostitute. The text supports the sterotype of the wicked woman, temptress and seducer of the "man of God," a woman unfit to be wife and mother except by the extraordinary grace and discipline of her husband. Such language is unacceptable in theological discourse today. Unfortunately, few metaphors available today can suggest as many aspects of the divine/human relationship as the marriage metaphor did in ancient Israel. God's relation to human beings is intimately personal, comprehensive, and enduring, and all these qualities were suggested by the metaphor of marriage. It also suggested the quality of sovereignty, inherent in God's relation to human beings, since husbands were legally sovereign in Israel, and it is this very understanding of marriage as a relationship of subordination for women that has made the metaphor unusable today.

What metaphors can we use instead? That of parent is still useful, for despite all the actual failures of parents in modern society, the parent/child relationship is still understood normatively to be intimately personal, comprehensive, and enduring. It involves a certain parental sovereignty, at least in the early years of childhood, and in addition, it is generative. But there are no other fully appropriate or comprehensive single metaphors. "Friend" is useful, and has biblical precedents (e.g., Isa 41:8; Jer 3:4), but must be qualified, because friendship generally involves equal or similar status, and God is not our equal. "Lord" is masculine and not very intimate; "Judge" is not intimate, comprehensive, or enduring.

However, it is possible to use clusters of metaphors which, together, can suggest aspects of the divine/human relationship and, at the same time, keep clear in the user's mind that these are simply metaphors, not univocal designations of deity. By changing the metaphors frequently and using them in combinations, the advantages of metaphorical discourse about God can be gained without most of the liabilities. It must always be remembered, of course, in using metaphors theologically, that a metaphor does not define the referent, but merely suggests in a vivid way a quality of the referent. Thus, when Carl Sandburg wrote that "the fog comes on little cat feet," he was not confusing fog and cats, but characterizing the quiet, almost unobserved formation of fog. Similarly, God is not any of the things denoted by the metaphors we use theologically, which merely suggest, by comparison, certain qualities of the divine/human relationship. Therefore, they should not be absolutized.

WORSHIP AS RESOURCE AND STUMBLING BLOCK

Religious ritual permeated life in Israel, as in all ancient societies. So it is not surprising to find that ritual is the most prominent theme in the prophetic literature. The prevailing ritual practice and ideology were the object of condemnation, and normative Yahwistic practice and ideology were the aim of exhortation. As always, words of condemnation outnumber words of exhortation, and these are found in almost every chapter of Hosea. Then in the last chapter, there is a switch to exhortation as a part of the final promise of restoration. First, let us look at the condemnation.

The theme of Hosea's criticism is stated at the beginning of the book: The land of Israel "commits great whoredom by forsaking the LORD" (1:2). By itself, this charge could mean several things, but it becomes evident in the following parable of Israel's history that it refers mainly to cultic idolatry. Israel, the "wife" of YHWH, has become an adulterer (2:2) with "lovers," whom she mistakenly believes to be her source of well-being (vs 5). These lovers are fertility gods of the indigenous Canaanite religion, headed by the rain god Baal (vs 13). However, the people may not actually have abandoned the cult of YHWH in a simple exchange for the cult of Baal; it is more likely that they baalized the YHWH cult. This is suggested by the assertion in 2:16 that in the future, Israel would no longer call YHWH "my baal." Apparently Israel had been doing so in the past, with a resulting confusion of identities. Yet Israel also frequented the shrines of the fertility gods, including the Baal of Peor (9:10), and the grain god Dagon (9:1-2); the ubiquitous worship "on the high places" probably was devoted to such gods (4:13; 10:8; 12:11).

In Hosea's discourse in chapter 12 on the relation between past and present sin, he speaks of Israel straying with El and being devoted to "holy ones" (11:12)—probably El, the high god of the Canaanite pantheon, and the lesser deities that populated Canaanite religion. In this case, El may have been the persona of the god worshiped at Beth-El (12:4: "[El] Beth-El will find us, and there he will speak with us," meaning the El of Beth-El). Here, as elsewhere in this chapter, Hosea interprets Jacob's behavior critically.

It is difficult to get a picture of the psychological, moral, and social effects of Baal worship from the prophets' accusations. They seldom spell out these effects, but merely point to the most obvious marks of the cultic practice itself. Some of these marks—offering raisin cakes (3:1) and divining the future (4:11)—seem bizarre to us, but they do not necessarily have pathological social effects. Flagellation (7:14) may be pathological, but the effects are primarily individual rather than communal.

Prostitution (4:10, 13-14), on the other hand, has baneful social consequences, which are worsened by the endorsement of the religious establishment. The use of plastic images of God (8:5-6; 10:5; 13:2), a violation of the Second Commandment, has more subtle consequences, though these are doubtless real in the long run. Priestly profiteering in sin offerings (4:8; cf. 8:11, 13), resembling the medieval sale of indulgences, was less a cultic sin of the worshipers than a moral sin of the priests. Finally, sheer excess and superficiality of ritual seem to be the butt of some of Hosea's criticisms (3:4; 6:6; 10:1-2,8; 12:11).

When it came to the cultic institution of the future, Hosea did not have much to say, but he did affirm a place for it in the covenant community. It is unlikely that he could have done otherwise, for a cultless society was probably inconceivable in ancient times. The only question was what kind of cult it would be.

In the account of the ransoming of the adulterous woman (chap 3), Hosea seems to take it for granted that the use of sacrifice, pillar, ephod, and teraphim would be suspended during the intervening time of chastening, but would be restored in the time of renewal. Strangely, however, in the great parable of chapter 2, he says nothing about a future cultic establishment. He says only that Israel will not call YHWH "my baal" in the future (2:16). It is only in the last oracle of the book that we find anything substantive about Israel's worship of YHWH in the time of restoration. The crucial words are in 14:2:

> Return, O Israel, to the LORD your God,
> for you have stumbled because of your iniquity.
> Take [only] words with you
> and return to the LORD;
> say to him,
> "Take away all guilt;

> accept that which is good,
> and we will offer
> the fruit of our lips."

I take this injunction to mean that the proper worship of God is entirely verbal, involving none of the usual material features of the sacrifical cultus. This point is clearer in the MT than in the English versions. It reads: "And we will offer the *bulls* of our lips." If this is the correct text, it seems to be a deliberate play on the contrast between the flesh-and-blood bulls of the old cultus and the metaphorical "bulls" of the future cultus, which would be purely verbal offerings—words of praise, prayer, confession, and exhortation. The English versions prefer to follow the LXX in reading "fruit (*pry*) of our lips," instead of "bulls (*prym*) of our lips." The point is the same either way, but it is much more graphic in the Hebrew.

Hosea's preference for psalms over sacrifices as a fitting offering to God naturally strikes a positive chord in the hearts of modern readers. Whether or not Hosea was fully aware of the implications of his words, they imply a nonsacrificial, verbal form of worship, and although such a form was developed in the synagogue much later, Hosea's prophecy adumbrated that development in the eighth century. These few words about the creative possibilities of worship are a slender theoretical foundation for authentic liturgical practice, but they occupy a prominent place in the climactic prophecy of the book of Hosea, and therefore signify more than their number alone might suggest. Thus there can be no doubt that Hosea acknowledged corporate worship, not only as a potential stumbling block to faith, but also as a resource for it.

We are now prepared to consider Hosea's most famous word about worship:

> Therefore I have hewn them by the prophets,
> I have killed them by the words of my mouth,
> and my judgment goes forth as the light.
> For I desire steadfast love and not sacrifice,
> the knowledge of God rather than burnt offerings. (6:5-6)

Here, in the opinion of a long line of interpreters, moral obedience to God is affirmed, and ritual performance (or at least, ritual performance divorced from moral obedience) is rejected. This interpretation is not wrong, but there is more to be said about this passage, particularly in the light of the affirmation of ritual contained in Hosea 14.

Hosea 6:5-6 specifically rejects Israel's historic sacrificial system as a means of interaction with God. This is not a rejection of all ritual, although it is probably legitimate to take it as a rejection of ritual worship not accompanied by commitment to righteousness and social justice.

Hosea 4 contains another noteworthy criticism of the Israelite cultus. Here he assigns heavier blame to the priests than to the people for the baalization and venalization of worship:

> Yet let no one contend,
>   and let none accuse,
>   for with you is my contention, O priest.
> You shall stumble by day;
>   the prophet also shall stumble with you by night;
> and I will destroy your [people].[1]
>
> My people are destroyed for lack of knowledge;
>   because you have rejected knowledge,
>   I reject you from being a priest to me.
> And since you have forgotten the (*torah*) of your God,
> I also will forget your children.
>
> The more they increased,
>   the more they sinned against me;
>   they changed their glory into shame.
> They feed on the sin of my people,
>   they are greedy for their iniquity.
> And it shall be like people like priest. (4:4-9)

I will say more later about Hosea's idea of the knowledge of God and its function in the life of faith. Here it is pertinent to note that it is to the priests that he attributes the responsibility for inculcating this knowledge. He is not referring to knowledge of the rules of ritual, the myriad laws that regulate activities in the sanctuaries; the only allusion to such activities in this passage is a denunciation (vs 8). The knowledge meant here is theological knowledge, the knowledge of God, the faith transmitted from generation to generation by parents, elders, and religious leaders in the community—especially by religious leaders.

Theirs was the special duty of transmitting *torah*, teaching. The moral strength and inner integrity of the people were built on this teaching, as appropriated and transformed into personal knowledge. To fail in this task of instruction was to fail as a priest, and thus contribute to the destruction of the community from the inside. In the end, both people and priest would share in that destruction, just as they shared in the guilt.

THE BURDEN OF KINGS

The two great issues in Hosea's proclamation are religion and politics. Accordingly, the chief targets of his prophetic assault are priests and kings. This assault is not balanced by a full, constructive proposal for Israel's religious and political institutions. The only good word about kingship in the book of Hosea is the promise of eventual restoration of Davidic rule in 3:5, and this word, in my judgment, is part of the Judean redaction. Hosea's own view was that the monarchy had been corrupt and godless from the days of its establishment in Gibeah (9:9; 10:9). Perverse in root and branch, nothing good could be expected from it.

> They made kings, but not through me;
> they set up princes, but without my knowledge. (8:4)

This key verse in Hosea's major indictment of the Israelite kings could refer to the whole history of the monarchy, as 9:9 and 10:9 suggest, or it could refer to the reigning kings of Hosea's time. A third possibility is that, like 1:4-5, it refers to the dynasty of Jehu.

Whatever the merits of monarchy may have been, the behavior of Israel's kings in Hosea's time was deplorable. The last two decades of the northern Israelite monarchy were filled with deeds of political assassination and military savagery (2 Kings 15:8-31; 17:1-6). They were also marked by a short-sighted, vacillating foreign policy which undermined stability and kept Israel embroiled in war. The last years of the kingdom of Samaria seemed a tempest of self-destruction. Small wonder that all Hosea's oracles on the kingship are scathing (1:4; 5:1-7; 5:8-15; 7:3-7; 8:1-14; 10:34). The negative account of the kingdom of Israel in 2 Kings is echoed in the words of Hosea.

Hosea tells us very little about specific events in his time. The only one we can identify in his oracles is the Syro-Ephraimite war of 735–734 (5:8-15; cf. 2 Kings 15:37; 16:5; Isa 7:1), and even this is disputed. But the specific identification is not important for our present purposes. It is Hosea's description of the fraternal strife between Israel (Ephraim) and Judah that is important. By common tradition and religion, the two peoples were one, but they were divided by royal politics. Some of the effects of the division are detailed in this oracle, but the real cause of the conflict, which recurred from generation to generation, was the rivalry between the kings of Samaria and Jerusalem. As a defender of covenantal integrity, Hosea denounced both kingdoms. Obviously, the monarchy, founded as a means to maintain the integrity and independence of the covenant community against the assaults of the Philistines and others, had ceased to serve this purpose. It was no longer accountable to the people of YHWH, and it subverted the basic social values of Yahwism. Hosea was convinced that the Israelite monarchy would soon be suspended, if not abolished:

> Though they hire (allies) among the nations,
> I will soon gather them up;
> And they will dispense for a little while,
> with the burden of kings and princes. (8:10 JMW)

In prophetic perspective, the purpose of the monarchy was to serve the people of God and the covenantal goals of justice and righteousness. In actual practice, it was impossible for the kings of Israel to avoid subverting this purpose. Perennially engaged in international commerce and politics, they inevitably adopted international standards of value. They became indistinguishable from the kings of other nations, and they lost their distinctive vocation as servants of YHWH. Means and ends were reversed, and YHWH and the people came to be thought of as servants of the kings.

It is not clear whether Hosea expected the restoration of the monarchy after its destruction. As I said, the allusion in 3:5 to the people's return to "David their king" may be the comment of the later Judean redactor. On the other hand, the prophecy in 1:11 of the reunification of the covenantal people under "one head" is probably Hosea's. But this promise is not specifically monarchical; "one head" could mean a figure like Moses or Samuel, as well as a king. The concluding prophecy in the book does not mention the kingship. This silence says much about Hosea's estimate of the role of the kingship in the life of the people.

THE DYNAMICS OF FAITH

Among Hosea's contributions to the biblical witness, two stand out as most significant. The first is his prophecy of redemption, using the paradigm drawn from Israel's history (exodus, wilderness, and settlement); the second is his witness to the dynamics of faith and infidelity. It is this witness, above all, that distinguishes his oracles from the other prophetic oracles of denunciation. Hosea understood the psychology of sin and obedience, and his understanding deeply informs his oracles.

Scholarly interest in the psychological dimension of Hosea's work has centered on the psychology of his marriage. Naturally, this is an appealing approach; it humanizes the ancient prophet and forges a strong emotional tie with his audience today. It preaches well, too. However, in recent years commentators have called this approach into question as a romanticizing of the book. It errs in speculating about the possible psychological origin of Hosea's ideas. It is extremely difficult to trace a person's ideas to their origins, even when much is known about the person, and too little is known about Hosea even to hazard a guess. Nevertheless, his insights into the working of the human will are presented in the text, and it is not necessary to know the origin of those insights to appreciate them.

Hosea 2 and 3 say quite a lot about the psychology of faith and unfaith, though they say it concisely. Chapter 2 is a study in the dynamics of infidelity, while chapter 3 is a study in moral discipline. The parable of the faithless wife is a story of calculating self-interest. Her relations with her husband and her lovers are utilitarian, materialistic, and selfish. The interests of the husband mean nothing to her. There is no hint of mutuality or self-transcendence. She pursues lovers lustfully, hoping she can get more from them than she receives from her husband (2:5), and when her way is blocked, she hurries back to him in desperation (2:7).

This is a parable, of course, but at the same time, it is a true-to-life sketch of a certain type of person whose motives are material and sensual, and whose moral sensitivity is nil.

As a remedy for this sort of religion, Hosea prescribes deprivation, a time "in the wilderness" (2:9-14). In this way, he hopes the original purpose of Israel's religion can be recovered. That purpose was not to produce material goods or sensual satisfaction, which are given in nature as a free gift from God (2:8), but to produce righteousness, justice, steadfast love, and mercy (2:19), which constitute faithfulness and reflect a true knowledge of God (vs 20).

This is a compact presentation of the fundamentals of prophetic Yahwism. The simplicity of the story veils its profundity and its applicability to a wide range of religious and social experiences. It is retold symbolically in the acted sign of the ransomed wife in Hosea 3, where YHWH commands Hosea:

> Go, love a woman who has a lover and is an adulteress, just as the LORD loves the people of Israel, although they turn to other gods and love raisin cakes.

So Hosea ransoms the wanton woman as an act of love. Then, as a disciplinary experience and test of her chastity, he subjects her to a trial marriage which is not consummated. The goal of these actions, which symbolize YHWH's actions toward Israel but are nevertheless real in Hosea's life, is marital fidelity. The basic message of Hosea 3 is that faithfulness grows from love and discipline. Together with the parable in Hosea 2, it tells a comprehensible and memorable tale of true and false marriage, and true and false religion.

INWARD DISPOSITION AND OUTWARD ACT

The relation between inward disposition and outward act, which is dramatized in Hosea 1–3, is restated in nonsymbolic terms in 4:1-4 and echoed repeatedly in the following chapters. Thus, 4:1-4 serves as the connecting link between the symbolic narratives in 1–3 and the collected oracles in 4–14. According to 4:1-4, there was no faithfulness, steadfast love, or knowledge of God in Israel, and therefore the land was filled with evil—cursing, perjury, robbery, adultery, and murder. In the following chapters, Hosea describes the consequences of Israel's emptiness in various spheres of the nation's life.

Inward disposition and outward act are not related as simple cause and effect: the relation is reciprocal. The will determines behavior, but behavior creates habits of the heart and thus molds the will. Hosea could say that Israel's *deeds* encompassed the people (7:2) and kept them from returning to YHWH (5:4). Deeds can shape motives and affections until the will is captive. Hosea also made the more obvious point that Israel was ruled by its spirit, which he called whorish (4:11; 5:4; 10:2).

Habituated to sin and blinded by guilt, the people had become deaf to correction by the prophet, and they ridiculed his words as the ravings of a maniac (9:7*b*-9). Israel's habit of willfulness was inveterate; it had originated in the ancestor Jacob and was transmitted naturally to his descendants. This is the point of Hosea 12. The text is obscure in many details, but its purpose is to draw parallels between the behavior of the patriarch, the "seed," and that of the present generation of Israel, the "tree." Jacob's faults were deceit, lying, treachery, idolatry with the native gods ("holy ones" [*'elim*], 11:12; 12:1, 4), and self-aggrandizement (vss 3-4). Israel/Ephraim's faults are illicit alliances (12:1), commercial dishonesty (vs 7), fraudulent oath-taking (vs 11), and rejection of prophetic heritage and counsel (vss 10-14). These accusations are typical of prophecy, but the main point of this chapter is distinctively Hosean. Since Israel's malady is radical, the cure must be radical, and the cure propounded in this chapter (vss 2, 5-6, 9, 11*b*, 14) is radical indeed. Alone, it looks less like a cure than a lethal dosage. However, in the larger picture of the future presented in the book as a whole, it can be understood as a real, though painful, cure. It is nothing less than a new beginning as a people, after a disciplinary return to the austere life of the wilderness (vss 6, 9).

Hosea's thesis concerning the moral history of Israel is stated metaphorically in another text. The nation has "plowed wickedness, reaped injustice and eaten the fruit of lies" (10:13). The immediate setting of this summary assertion is an indictment of the nation's militarism, but it applies to other aspects of life as well. In contrast to Israel's actual behavior, the goal of covenantal righteousness is to "sow justice (*mishpat*)" so that the nation may "reap the fruit of loyalty (*hesed*)" (10:12). Thus the prophet draws a sharp contrast between the real Israel and the ideal.

At times, Hosea's strictures seem one-sided and exaggerated. They fail to take into account the complexity and moral ambiguity of Israel's life. However, there are some indications that he recognized this ambiguity. He does mention Israel's "divided heart" (10:2). This seems more nuanced than "whorish spirit." He calls Israel "a cake not turned"—a half-baked, or a mixed dough (7:8-10). Images like these suggest a mixture of good and evil in Israel's life, yet still retain the sharp edge of prophetic criticism.

KNOWLEDGE, LOVE, AND OBEDIENCE

The purpose of God in the life of Israel was to create a community of *sedeq* (righteousness), *mishpat* (justice), *hesed* (steadfast love), and *da'ath 'elohim* (knowledge of God). These are the key words in Hosea's message; together, they denote faithful obedience, or obedient faith. The absence of such faith in Israel, in Hosea's judgment, was the root cause of the social and political chaos he saw around him. Without the knowledge and love of God, there was no creative center, no source of morality. In a word, without the knowledge of God,

Israel was destroyed as a people (4:6). This was the negative reality: Without knowing God, the nation died.

The possibility always existed, of course, that by coming to know God, the nation could live:

> Come, let us return to the LORD;
> for it is he who has torn, and he will heal us;
> he has struck down, and he will bind us up.
> After two days he will revive us;
> on the third day he will raise us up,
> that we may live before him.
> Let us know, let us press on to know the LORD. (6:1-3)

This confession of confidence in the healing power of God expresses a valid understanding of the relation of faith and life, religious knowledge and human existence. But the problem with this confession, for which the confessors are condemned by the prophet (6:4-6), is that the words are not matched by constancy of devotion to God. The people's faithfulness is utilitarian, self-interested, ephemeral: It comes and goes with the sacrifices offered in the sanctuaries and does not endure. The key to enduring devotion was verbalized in the confession, but neglected in life. To learn to know YHWH truly, and thus to learn true devotion (*hesed*), required living in YHWH's presence. But the people thought this meant worshiping in the sanctuaries, while the prophet thought it meant living all of life covenantally. Thus knowledge of God and faithful obedience were interdependent; they grew together or not at all. Lacking both, the mind of the people was closed. There was no point of entry for knowledge to begin or for obedience to grow. For Hosea, a beginning was possible only after the destruction of the existing kingdom and the existing cultus. Then genuine growth of knowledge and obedience might occur:

> I will make for you a covenant in that day . . . . And I will take you for my wife forever; I will take you for my wife in righteousness and in justice, in steadfast love, and in mercy. I will take you for my wife in faithfulness; and you shall know the LORD. (2:18-20)

Hosea trusted in the grace of God to make this relationship of faithful obedience possible. The question in his mind was whether the people would respond. But even on this question, Hosea was hopeful.

CONCLUSION

Amos was the earliest of the Twelve Prophets, yet despite the generally chronological ordering of these books, Hosea was placed first in this collection. The reasons this was done are lost to history, but the theological appropriateness of the decision is clear. No other book in this group equals Hosea in the depth and range of its theological insights. The Twelve are commonly called the minor prophets. This practice is misleading, especially in this case, for there is nothing minor about the message of the book of Hosea. "Smaller," as Germans call these prophets, is a more accurate term. Hosea is a smaller book than Isaiah or Jeremiah, though it contains a message of similar importance.

Like the other eighth-century prophets, Hosea criticized the Israelite community, and especially its leaders, for social injustice, cultic idolatry, and political folly. But more fully than any other prophet, he diagnosed the moral and spiritual sources of these aberrations, placing them more deliberately in the context of Israel's religious history. His probing of the meaning of faith, understood as both knowledge of God and obedience to God, was unmatched until Jeremiah, who, significantly, seems to have been well acquainted with Hosea's work. Hosea's oracles contain many obscurities, possibly because they were written in an Ephraimite dialect, rather than the standard dialect of the Hebrew Bible. Nevertheless, the message of the book is sufficiently clear to make it accessible as one of the strongest components of the prophetic witness of faith.

SELECT BIBLIOGRAPHY

Andersen, Francis I., and David Noel Freedman. *Hosea.* Anchor Bible. Garden City, N.Y.: Doubleday, 1980.

Beeby, H. D. *Grace Abounding: A Commentary on the Book of Hosea.* International Theological Commentary. Grand Rapids: Eerdmans, 1989.

Buss, Martin J. *The Prophetic Word of Hosea: A Morphological Study.* BZAW 111. Berlin: Alfred Töpelmann, 1969.

Eichrodt, Walther. "The Holy One in Your Midst: The Theology of Hosea." *Interpretation* 15 (1961): 259-73.

Emmerson, Grace I. *Hosea: An Israelite Prophet in Judean Perspective. JSOT*Sup 28. Sheffield: JSOT, 1984.

Janzen, J. Gerald. "Metaphor and Reality in Hosea 11." *Semeia* 24 (1982): 7-44.

Limburg, James. *Hosea-Micah.* Interpretation. Atlanta: John Knox Press, 1988.

Mays, James L. *Hosea.* Philadelphia: Westminster Press, 1969.

Review and Expositor 4/4 (1975).

Ritschl, Dietrich. "God's Conversion: An Exposition of Hosea 11." *Interpretation* 15 (1961): 286-303.

Robinson, H. Wheeler. *Two Hebrew Prophets: Studies in Hosea and Ezekiel.* London: Lutterworth Press, 1948.

Southwestern Journal of Theology 18/1 (1975).

Stuart, Douglas. *Hosea-Jonah.* Word Biblical Commentary. Waco, Tex.: Word Books, 1987.

Ward, James M. *Hosea: A Theological Commentary.* New York: Harper & Row, 1969.

_____. *Amos and Hosea.* Atlanta: John Knox Press, 1981.

Weems, Renita J. "Gomer: Victim of Violence or Victim of Metaphor?" *Semeia* 47 (1989): 87-104.

Welch, Adam C. *Kings and Prophets of Israel.* London: Lutterworth Press, 1952.

Wolff, Hans Walter. "Guilt and Salvation: A Study of the Prophecy of Hosea." *Interpretation* 15 (1961): 274-85.

_____. *Hosea.* Hermeneia. Philadelphia: Fortress Press, 1965.

Yee, Gale A. *Composition and Tradition in the Book of Hosea: A Redactional Critical Investigation.* SBLDS 102. Atlanta: Scholars Press, 1987.

NOTES

1. Reading *'ameka* ("your people") for *'imeka* ("your mother").

CHAPTER TWELVE

Micah

The book of Micah resembles the book of Isaiah in form and theology, though on a much smaller scale. The first part of the book (Mic 1–3) contains the oracles of the prophet himself, who, like Isaiah, prophesied in Judah in the eighth century. These oracles, like most of Isaiah's (cf. Isa 1–11; 28–32), are oracles of judgment, which have been supplemented by two later groups. The first group, Micah 4–5 (like Isa 40–55), are prophecies of salvation, while the second, Micah 6–7 (like Isa 56–66), is a mixture of accusation, lamentation, and prophecy of salvation. Jerusalem/Zion figures prominently in both supplementary sections of Micah, as it does in Second and Third Isaiah. The anonymous prophecies in Micah 4–7 apparently were composed in the sixth and early fifth centuries, just as were those in Isaiah 40–66. Virtually all the supplementary material in both books is poetry (contrast the extensive prose additions to the book of Jeremiah). Isaiah 13–23 and 36–39 have no counterpart in Micah; however, the similarities between the two books are noteworthy, suggesting the possibility that the two may have been compiled in the same prophetic circle.

The resemblance of Micah to Isaiah is not only structural, but extends to the message as well. Naturally, the much larger book of Isaiah contains many themes not in Micah, but the themes of Micah are prominent in Isaiah, too. Their basic message is the same and can be summarized in the following broad terms: The historic fall of the kingdom of Judah is interpreted theologically as a divine punishment for the sins of the nation, and the eventual restoration of a religious community in Jerusalem is prophesied as an act of God's grace. Moreover, this story of the judgment and salvation of God's people becomes the paradigm of God's rule over all the nations of the world. This universal rule will be established in the future, and Jerusalem/Zion will play a central part in it.

The contribution of Isaiah and Micah themselves consists almost entirely of the denunciation of Judah's sin and the prophecy of God's punishment. The rest of the message is the work of others, although the supplements are not alien theologically to the message of Micah and Isaiah. Indeed, they are constructed on the same theological foundations. It is the historical perspective of the later writers that differs from that of the two prophets. The destruction of the kingdom of Judah and the city of Jerusalem, which Isaiah and Micah prophesied, had finally come to pass. This event and its aftermath changed the circumstances of the surviving Jewish community radically and evoked further reflections on the purpose of God in human history. As a result, the books of Isaiah and Micah were produced in their canonical form.

THE SIN OF THE HOUSE OF JUDAH

The popular view of the preexilic prophets as advocates of social justice is correct for Micah. His oracles consist of indictments of the leaders of Judah for offenses against powerless people and prophecies of God's judgment for these offenses. The list of offenses is small, but so is the number of oracles. Fields, houses, and clothing are seized (2:2, 8), women are driven from their homes and their children deprived of dignity (2:8), and justice is denied in courts corrupted by bribery (3:9-11). The rulers also are accused of "tearing the skin" off people (3:1-3), but it is impossible to tell whether that charge is literal or figurative. All these are charges of direct physical, economic, and judicial abuse. A lesser charge is made against the prophets—that they prophesy "peace" to those who pay them and "war" to those who do not (3:5). Concretely, *peace* probably means prosperity (*shalom* often has this connotation), and *war* means hardship. It is greed that all these offenses have in common, but all of them are social offenses, not cultic. Only once is a cultic offense—idolatry—mentioned (1:7).

In addition to these concrete accusations, Micah adds several others that are quite vague. Samaria is called "the sin of Jacob" (1:6-7) and Jerusalem "the sin of Judah" (1:5). If this means more than that the kingdoms' evils were concentrated in their capitals, the meaning is lost to us now. Further, Lachish is called "the beginning of sin to daughter Zion," filled with "the transgressions of Israel" (1:13). Lachish was one of the fortified cities between Jerusalem and the Philistine plain. We can guess that the "sin" was political, but this is only a guess. Some commentators, including James Mays, regard the statement about Samaria as part of the later expansion of the book. If this judgment is correct, Micah's own oracles concerned only Judah, not the northern kingdom of Israel. However, the theological content of his oracles is not affected, one way or the other.

So Micah's catalog of Judah's crimes is a slender one, as is the sheaf of his oracles. But it is enough to tell us what was important to him as a prophet of God. Social justice was the cause he espoused, and he did so with moral passion and rhetorical power.

The divine punishment prophesied for Judah's injustice was military conquest and exile (1:6, 15; 2:4, 12-13). Those who expropriated the property of others

(2:2) would see it parceled out to their captors (2:4-5), a perfect example of punishment that fits the crime. Micah said that in the end,

> Zion shall be plowed as a field;
> Jerusalem shall become a heap of ruins,
> and the mountain of the house a wooded height. (3:12)

Micah did not make many charges against the prominent people of the kingdom, and those were stated simply, without nuance or qualification. His message of doom was equally simple and direct.

THE EXPANDED MESSAGE OF THE BOOK

Micah's witness was subsumed into the witness of the expanded book. Chapters 4–5 are a logical sequel to 1–3. In this prophecy of a new age, God's judgment against the unjust rulers of Israel is extended to all nations, and Zion/Jerusalem is simultaneously exalted as the religious center of the world. The weak and afflicted are recognized as people of worth, and violent crime and oppression are abolished. These goals are merely affirmed as the intentions of divine rule, with no indication of the kinds of intermediate agency or material means that would be required to achieve them. This section of the book is postexilic in perspective, for it presupposes the fall of Jerusalem. However, there is no indication of the concrete social setting of the audience or the specific purpose of the writing. It is an affirmation of faith in God and in the continuity of God's dealings with the religious community of Israel; implicitly, it serves as an appeal for an appropriate moral response from Israel. However, it contains no further directive for the faithful.

The second supplementary section of the book, chapters 6–7, differs from chapters 4–5 in content, if not in date. Many scholars date it too in the postexilic period, and this seems right for the final form, though chapter 6 is relatively timeless and could be preexilic. At the same time, these chapters have greater affinity to chapters 1–3 than do chapters 4–5. Mays' characterization of this section is apt.[1] It is a dialogue between God and the community of believers about the state of their relationship. The dialogue begins in estrangement (6:1–7:6), turns on an affirmation of trust (7:7), and concludes in reconciliation (7:8-20). Oracles of judgment (6:9-16) and salvation (7:11-13) are integrated into the dialogue and provide thematic links to the oracles of judgment in chapters 1–3, on the one hand, and to the oracles of salvation in chapters 4–5, on the other. Thus chapters 6–7 serve as a unifying supplement to the rest of the book.

MICAH 4–5

The opening poem of this section (4:1-5) is the famous swords-into-plowshares prophecy, which appears also in Isaiah 2:2-4. The impression one receives from this, after reading Micah 1–3, is that the divine punishment prophesied in 1–3 is being reversed. Yet closer scrutiny reveals that this impression is superficial. Those criticized in the oracles of judgment are not the same people who are being addressed in the promises of salvation. These are the survivors of the fall of Judah and their heirs—the little people, the lame and afflicted (4:6-7)—not the mighty, unjust people repudiated earlier. So there is no contradiction between the threats of divine judgment and the promises of salvation. Indeed, far from reversing the moral criticism of the mighty in the oracles of judgment, the oracles of salvation contain a further, implicit repudiation. The new Zion described in the oracles of salvation would be a city of righteousness and peace, of obedience to *torah,* with no room for workers of evil. Thus, in effect, the promise of salvation in the supplement reinforces the moral strictures in the original oracles of Micah.

Not all salvation oracles in the books of the prophets are like this one. For example, the promise of the restoration of the Davidic monarchy in Amos 9:11-15 is a simple reversal of Amos's prophecy of doom; it has no ethical content and therefore is out of tune with the rest of the book of Amos. By contrast, Micah 4 matches Micah 1–3 in moral earnestness. Admittedly, there is no heavy stress on the themes that dominate chapters 1–3, but what is said is certainly consonant with those earlier oracles.

The theme of Micah 4–5 is not unified, but combines a medley of themes common in postexilic Judaism. The setting of a peaceable kingdom which frames the section (4:3; 5:10) contains inserts which depict military action against the enemies of Israel (4:13; 5:5-6). To reconcile these images, one might argue that military action was a necessary step to peace, but this may be too easy a harmonization. It is more likely that the conflicting images reflect the perennial religious debate over the legitimacy of war, which may have begun already in the postexilic period.

The reversal of fortunes for the people of God is the main theme of Micah 4–5. The suffering and humiliation of the present will pass away, "Jacob" will become "like a lion among the animals of the forest" (5:8), and the kingdom of Daughter Jerusalem will be restored. A new Davidic king will spring, like David himself, from humble stock in Bethlehem (5:2), but nevertheless will become "great to the ends of the earth" because he rules in the strength of YHWH (5:4). These sentiments, expressed in many exilic texts, must have been powerfully felt by subjugated Jews. Such sentiments inspired, among other things, the rebuilding of Jerusalem and its temple in the sixth century. However, the royalist sentiment expressed here was not satisfied by these achievements. It lingered on as a messianic hope, though it paled as the centuries passed and there was no opportunity to reestablish the Israelite monarchy. However, if *king* in this text is merely a symbol of political order, then the promise was realizable. New political institutions were developed in Jewish communities, within the limits determined by their subject status in foreign kingdoms, and the interdependence of political and religious institutions continued in Judaism as it had throughout the earlier history of Israel.

Perhaps the noblest sentiment expressed in these chapters is the promise of redemption for the lame and afflicted (4:6-7). In retribution theology, afflictions often were interpreted as God's punishment for sin, but there is no hint of this idea here. Those with afflictions are simply subjects of God's saving rule.

MICAH 6–7

In Micah 1–3 and 4–5, the style of address is prophetic speech to the people about their relation to God. In 6–7 the style changes to I-Thou speech, a direct dialogue between YHWH and the people. Commentators, understandably, have made the most of this change.

Mays, for example, identifies the subject of 6–7 as the direct, intimate relationship between God and Israel. However, the two chapters are not a seamless whole, but are made up of short poems of different literary genres, some prophetic and at least one liturgical (the lament in 7:1-7). Still, the redactor has produced a fairly coherent composition.

From the point of view of a prophet speaking for God, the substantive difference between third- and first-person address is sometimes small or none, even though there is a formal difference. Shifts between the two are common in the prophetic writings, and much of the time the substance of the point being made is not affected. However, shifts in person are much more significant when the point of view is that of the people. Then second-person address to God is not the same as third-person discourse *about* God. Speech addressed *to* God presupposes a personal relationship. This is true even when the relationship seems problematic, as it does in the complaint psalms of the psalter and the speeches of Job.

The human situation presupposed in Micah 6–7 is different from the one presupposed in the rest of the book, particularly in 1–3. In Micah's oracles the audience is remote, veiled, and silent. The people do not defend themselves or define themselves in any way. We know almost nothing about them—only a few hints of their identity and a few allegations about their behavior. However, in 6–7 the audience steps from the background and speaks. We still learn nothing about their identity, but we do learn something about their human condition and faith.

The writer, speaking for God, fashions a query in the form of a trial speech (6:1). It is introduced as a "controversy" (*rib*), but its tone is more perplexed than critical:

> O my people, what have I done to you?
>   In what have I wearied you? Answer me.
> For I brought you up from the land of Egypt,
>   and redeemed you from the house of slavery . . . .
> O my people, remember. (6:3-5)

These words are echoed in YHWH's question to the people of Judah in Jeremiah 2:5-6:

> What wrong did your ancestors find in me,
> that they went far from me,
> and went after worthless things and became
> worthless themselves?
> They did not say, "Where is the LORD,
> who brought us up from the land of Egypt."

The prophet is dismayed by the people's faithlessness. How is it possible for anyone to abandon the only true source of human well-being? It seems so senseless that it leaves the prophet dumbfounded. This is the burden of both these texts.

In Micah 6, the writer continues by asking about the proper service to God. In this well-known passage, the writer answers, "To do justice (*mishpat*), love kindness (*hesed*), and walk humbly with your God" (6:8). This is a simple but eloquent statement of the fundamental moral disposition of the faithful person, even though it says nothing about the specific content of justice, or of walking with God.

This list of what YHWH requires of faithful people omits any reference to ritual worship, but instead, is set in stark contrast to a list of ritual offerings which, by implication, are repudiated. The usual inference drawn from this contrast is that, to the writer, morality was everything and ritual nothing. Indeed, by putting child sacrifice at the climax of the list of ritual acts, the writer makes the entire subject of ritual seem repugnant. But the choice between justice and atrocious sacrifice is artificial. Stating it in this way is rhetorically startling, but the statement offers little practical moral guidance. It warns against the temptation to ritual extremism, but it says nothing about the relation of morality to ordinary ritual. It is an eloquent but limited affirmation.

The last half of chapter 6 is not as vague about moral issues, but it is not as grand as the first half, either. The subject is dishonesty in business—merchants who cheat (6:10-11). This may not be the stuff of great moral treatises, but it is an everyday reality, so it is not beneath the interest of a prophet. Lying and violence (vs 12) compound the offense, though no particulars are given. The punishment prophesied (6:13-16) is general devastion of the land, probably the result of military conquest. Since this passage is embedded in the late supplement to the book of Micah, it may be late also. In substance, however, this is ethics at a basic level. It is timeless.

A LAST LAMENT AND CONFESSION OF FAITH

Chapter 7 provides an effective ending to the book of Micah, in spite of several rough seams. A lamentation that deplores universal wickedness (7:1-6) ends in a bold expression of confidence in the eventual triumph of justice (7:7-10). Formally, this conclusion serves the same purpose as does the certainty of a hearing in the complaint psalms of the psalter. The certainty of a hearing is based on confidence in God's justice, whenever the psalmist believes his affliction is not deserved, or on confidence in God's mercy whenever the psalmist suspects that it is. In Micah 7, the speaker confesses his guilt (7:9) and ends the confession with an eloquent appeal to God's steadfast love and compassion (vss 19-20). At the same time, he expresses confidence in his eventual vindication before the enemy who has taunted him in his distress, a vindication that ends in a reversal of their fortunes and the destruction of the enemy (vss 8-10). So because of his guilt, the writer must count upon God's love, a love that "will cast all our sins into the depths of the sea" (7:19). On the other hand, it is God's justice that he invokes in the face of a taunting enemy.

As in chapter 6, in chapter 7 there is a close affinity to the oracles of Jeremiah. In chapter 6 it was the plaintive question as to whether the people had found any fault in YHWH (6:3; cf. Jer 2:5). Here it is the bitter complaint that there are no righteous ones left among the people of God (7:2). Jeremiah searched in vain through the streets of Jerusalem for a single person who "acts justly and seeks truth" (Jer 5:1-5), and found none. The writer of Micah 7 goes even further. He paints a picture of Judean society in which all trustworthiness has vanished, and even members of the same household are enemies (7:2-6). If this was meant as an objective picture of the state of affairs, it probably was written during the chaotic last decades of the monarchy (Jeremiah's time), or after the fall of Jerusalem.

This ending, the confession of faith in God, is unique among the prophetic books. Instead of the usual prophecy of the exaltation of Israel and the defeat of pagan nations, it emphasizes the deliverance of faithful individuals. It recalls not the glory of the Davidic monarchy, but the faithfulness of God as it was manifested to Abraham and Jacob. It is not political hegemony that matters here, but the integrity of people's relationship with God. The words are an act of praise, which is the foundation of biblical piety.

CONCLUSION

The book of Micah is best known for the dictum that what YHWH requires is justice, steadfast love, and humility (6:8). But this deservedly famous quotation is not the only line in this book worth remembering. Overshadowed by the great book named for Micah's contemporary, the book of Micah does not always receive the consideration it deserves; yet it treats similar issues with comparable effect. It is thus an admirable, though shorter, companion to the book of Isaiah.

SELECT BIBLIOGRAPHY

Alfaro, Juan I., O.S.B. *Justice and Loyalty: A Commentary on the Book of Micah.* International Theological Commentary. Grand Rapids: Eerdmans, 1989.

Allen, Leslie C. *Joel, Obadiah, Jonah, and Micah.* New International Commentary on the Old Testament. Grand Rapids: Eerdmans, 1976.

Hagstrom, David G. *The Coherence of the Book of Micah: A Literary Analysis.* SBLDS 89. Atlanta: Scholars Press, 1988.

Hillers, Delbert. *Micah.* Hermeneia. Philadelphia: Fortress Press, 1984.

Kapelrud, A. S. "Eschatology in the Book of Micah." *VT* 11 (1961): 392-405.

Limburg, James. *Hosea-Micah.* Interpretation. Atlanta: John Knox Press, 1988.

Mays, James L. *Micah.* Philadelphia: Westminster Press, 1976.

Smith, Ralph L. *Micah-Malachi.* Word Biblical Commentary. Waco, Tex.: Word Books, 1984.

Stansell, Gary. *Micah and Isaiah: A Form and Tradition Historical Comparison.* SBLDS 85. Atlanta: Scholars Press, 1988.

van der Woude, A. S. "Micah in Dispute with the Pseudo-Prophets." *VT* 19 (1969): 244-60.

Willis, John T. "The Structure of the Book of Micah." *Svensk exegetisk årsbok* 34 (1969): 5-42.

Wolff, Hans Walter. *Micah the Prophet.* Philadelphia: Fortress Press, 1978.

NOTES

1. Mays, *Micah.*

CHAPTER THIRTEEN

Joel, Obadiah, and Jonah

These three small books have little in common, except that all are included in the scroll of the Twelve Prophets. I will discuss them in the order they occur in the Bible, disregarding Amos and Micah, which have been treated separately.

JOEL

A locust plague and the day of YHWH are the themes of the book of Joel, and the question of the relation between the two themes has dominated scholarly discussion of the book. For more than half a century, the prevailing view was that of Bernhard Duhm, who attributed the portions of the book dealing with locusts to the prophet Joel, and the eschatological portions to a secondary writer. Duhm considered both portions postexilic; he dated the later, eschatological portion, in the Hellenistic era. The literary links between the two themes were entirely secondary, in Duhm's view—the work of the later hand. Other scholars thought his dating too low, but accepted the rest of his analysis.

Another view, which prevails today, believes the book to be essentially a unity, in that the locust plague is the historic occasion for the eschatological prophecy. Thus a present calamity gives rise to thought about a future divine judgment. In this view, the literary links between the two themes are integral parts of the original composition.

Despite the current agreement over the essential unity of the book, scholars are divided about its original social setting and purpose. Some base their view on the repeated summons to a solemn, public fast (1:14; 2:12, 15) and place the composition in a liturgical setting, inferring that the writer was a cultic functionary. In that reading, the purpose of the prophecy of the day of YHWH is to add depth and urgency to the exhortation to fast.[1] Other scholars, however, emphasize the allusions to other prophetic writings and view the book as a purely literary work, created by a writing prophet.[2] Wolff regards the writer as a critic of the postexilic cultic establishment, rather than a supporter; in this reading, the book is understood as an opposition tract, spreading the message that ritual repentance is superficial and ineffectual. Genuine moral transformation is required by God, and this can come about only by the action of the spirit of God, which can be expected in the day of YHWH.

It should be clear from this disagreement over the setting and purpose of the book that the evidence is ambiguous. Both hypotheses are worthy of consideration, but neither commands clear assent. Once again, we discover that when evidence for the original social setting and purpose of a literary work is entirely internal, it is virtually impossible to determine them objectively. Critics who employ newer social scientific methods have made no real advance over older critics in this regard. They have been more successful with historical narratives like the books of Kings, where the social role of the prophets is depicted. But with texts like Joel, the results are meager or nil, so the original social setting remains unknown.

THE DAY OF YHWH

The movement of thought in the book clearly moves from the economic calamity caused by the locusts to the universal threat of the day of YHWH. But the economic calamity is described as a present reality, while the day of YHWH is merely a prophetic idea. Therefore we must ask, What was the purpose of the prophecy of the day of YHWH?

Eschatological prophecies function to sanction moral decisions. Much of the time, the decisions desired by prophets involve some kind of social action. However, the content of the action can range from ordinary repentance of private sin to extraordinary reformation of social institutions. Thus the extent of wanted change can vary from modest amelioration of behavior to radical transformation of society. In either case, the prophetic threat of eschatological judgment provides a motive for the response. It makes actors of the audience. Occasionally, the result desired by the prophet involves only an inward attitude, with no outward action—for example, patience in the face of circumstances one cannot change. In such cases, the eschatological prophecy functions to encourage the faithful to wait and hope for a better day. This can be true even of eschatological threats of judgment, for such threats are, in principle, directed against wickedness, not righteousness. Therefore they provide implicit encouragement to the godly, whether or not they contain words to this effect.

When we consider the book of Joel in each of the theoretical settings described above, we see that the prophecy of the day of YHWH functions in the first (liturgical) setting to encourage a certain communal action, and in the second (literary) setting to encourage hopeful endurance. It is urgent in the first setting to encourage public assembly for fasting and lamentation, a turning to God in word, thought, and affection. The prophecy of the awful day of judgment makes clear the urgency of this turning. The prophet was really concerned with intensified worship of God, in appropriate form and with sincerity of heart, according to this interpretation.

However, if Joel was an outsider to the Judean religious establishment, a critic looking in, then his prophecy of the day of YHWH had a different purpose. In this case it would be the future that was all important, not the present, and the prophecy must then be seen as a genuine prophecy, not merely a goad to communal action. Contrition and commitment might have been expected from such a prophecy, to be sure, but its main purpose would have been to herald God's creation of a new society in the future. Those who endured the coming judgment would be possessed by God's spirit in the new society, and God's will would be known and obeyed by all. Therefore no prophet would be needed to call people to repentance (2:28-29).

According to this second reading of the book, the lamentation over the locust plague and the call to fasting served merely as preludes to the prophecy of the day of YHWH, the purpose of which was to encourage trust in God's promise for the future. According to the first reading, however, the prophecy of the day of YHWH was simply a way to stress the urgency of the need to assemble for lamentation and fasting, with the purpose of relieving the suffering of the community after the destruction of their crops. Which of these interpretations should we accept?

JOEL AND THE CULT

Whether or not Joel was a cultic prophet, there is undeniable emphasis on the cult in the book. It requires a subtle imagination to reach Wolff's conclusion that the writer stood over against the cultic establishment and expressed his own sentiments as an eschatological hope. Wolff infers that the author regarded "established worship . . . as something to be taken for granted and, in itself, unassailable," but nevertheless "merely temporary and transient, something that [would] be overtaken by new, final acts of God."[3] Perhaps so. But to my mind, the passion expressed in the call to worship in 1:14 and 2:15-17 does not imply such a matter-of-fact attitude toward worship. On the contrary, it suggests a keen sense of urgency. Furthermore, there is nothing in the picture of the day of YHWH to suggest that worship would be superseded in that day. It is prophecy, not cultus, that will be superfluous in the future. Everyone will possess the spirit of YHWH and, in effect, be a prophet, but that does not mean worship will be unnecessary. The eschatological prophecy concludes with language drawn directly from the temple tradition of Jerusalem (3:17-18, 21*b*). And though it says nothing directly about the form or content of worship, it clearly affirms that YHWH's sanctuary will be maintained.

In summary, the clearest and strongest note sounded in the book of Joel is the affirmation of worship as the key to the relationship between Israel and God. By contrast, not a word is said about social ethics or obedience to the moral laws of the covenant.

Joel's passion for worship is matched by his passion for the idea of retribution. Hatred of the enemies of YHWH and of Israel hangs like a pall around his words. The hope of divine judgment upon the godless peoples of the world expressed here is bitter and vindictive. The prophet longs for God's judgment upon the godless peoples of the world. There is no hint of compassion, no suggestion of redemptive possibilities; for all but Israel, the prospect of the day of YHWH is unrelieved darkness.

The writer assumes that the fundamental disposition of God toward Israel is redemptive, that YHWH wishes to bless Israel. He quotes the old creedal affirmation of YHWH's attitude (2:13), but he mentions only YHWH's compassion, not YHWH's punitive justice. In short, justice for the nations is retributive, but justice for Israel is redemptive.

Joel is a small book and its purpose is limited. It is a call to public lamentation and fasting, a liturgical turning to God in the midst of a dire communal crisis. We may assume that its excesses are the result of the writer's sense of urgency.

OBADIAH

The book of Obadiah is a single oracle of judgment against Edom. Since this oracle has been transmitted as a separate prophetic book, it receives proportionally more attention than similar oracles in other books. Commentators' reactions to Obadiah range from dismissing it as a crude display of nationalism, to appreciating it as a word of reassurance for the discouraged exiles. This oracle has a close affinity to Jeremiah 49; the presence of two versions of essentially the same oracle in the prophetic canon suggests to some commmentators that it may have been a liturgy known to both writers.

Obadiah is a good example of a type of oracle common in prophetic literature. It begins with a concrete historical subject (e.g., a nation, king, city) and ends with an abstract ethical subject (e.g., idolatry, tyranny, immorality). The conclusion is often styled as an eschatological prophecy. The prophecy of the day of YHWH in Joel and in Zephaniah are other examples of this type of writing.

The writer condemns Edom as a "looter" of Judah after the nation's fall to Babylon, accusing Edom of "murderous violence" against a helpless neighbor (vs 10) and of gloating over the crime (vs 12). The prophet issues a threat from YHWH that Edom will be punished in kind and annihilated. The punishment will occur in the day of YHWH (vs 15), which will come upon all nations except those that take refuge "on Mt. Zion" (vs 17). "Jacob" will dispossess Edom and recover all the territories of the ancient Davidic kingdom. Then at last, "dominion shall belong to YHWH" (vs 21).

Whether a Jacobean reconquest of Canaan and its neighboring lands would constitute the establishment of YHWH's rule was, of course, moot. It all depended upon one's definition of YHWH's rule. Taken one way, Obadiah's prophecy could be viewed as a rationalization of Israelite nationalism. Viewed sympathetically, on the other hand, it might be interpreted as a kind of shorthand allusion to the establishment of a righteous Yahwistic community.

In the context of this oracle, the day of YHWH might symbolize a future military conquest by Israelite forces. However, since no agency is mentioned, we probably should regard it as merely an abstract eschatological idea. Behind the prophecy of the day of YHWH lay the belief that all evil deeds, including those unrequited in the ordinary course of human affairs, eventually would be punished by God in the way they deserved.

Some of the ideas contained in the oracle of Obadiah can be found in other oracles against Edom in the Hebrew Bible. Jeremiah 49:7-22, the other version of Obadiah's oracle, is of course the closest parallel (cf. Jer 49:14-16 with Ob 1–4; Jer 49:9-10 with Ob 5–6). Obadiah's is the longer version. Jeremiah 49 lacks the prophecy of the day of YHWH, as well as the section that recounts Edom's criminal acts against Judah. Thus Obadiah's version seems to be an eschatological expansion of an older oracle.

Ezekiel 25:12-14 is another oracle against Edom—an assurance of YHWH's punishment of Edom's act of vengeance against Judah. There is no reference to the time, manner, or agency of punishment. Amos 1:11-12 is similar. It prophesies that the cities and palaces of Edom will be burned as fitting punishment for Edom's fury. This oracle is as vague as Ezekiel's; neither is particularly edifying, in the absence of any indication of its historical setting or purpose.

This attitude toward Edom can hardly be explained as simply a Jewish response to Edomite acts during the last years of the Judean kingdom (594–587), as is often done. For one thing, we actually know very little about such acts.[4] Furthermore, the bitterness expressed in this whole series of oracles is too deep to be explained in this way. In all the allusions to Edom in the Hebrew Bible, not one good word is written about this neighboring people.[5] Why?

My hunch is that a profound, mutual hostility between Judah and Edom—partly political and partly religious—had developed over a long period of time and eventually became irrational. It was the kind of hatred that often develops between closely related peoples: Protestant and Catholic Christians in Northern Ireland, rival groups of Muslim Arabs in the Middle East, Muslim and Christian Arabs in Lebanon, to cite only a few examples. Over a long period of time, national and religious rivalry combine with competition for land, and the result is deep hostility. Momentary offenses are not the cause of such hostility, but occasions to vent it. And so it must have been with Edom and Judah in biblical times.

Some critics think Obadiah's oracle is a liturgical text. However, no clear parallels to it appear among known liturgical texts, so to me the hypothesis seems unlikely. It is hard to imagine that during the period of the second temple, the

Judean religious community would have recited a text like this regularly in its worship. However, it is not difficult to imagine the possible connections between this text and the liturgical concerns of that community.

JONAH

The book of Jonah is unique among the books of the prophets. It is neither a collection of oracles nor a historical report, but a short story. It is fiction, not history. Indeed, it is fantastic fiction, filled with fabulous happenings, of which the actions of the great fish are merely the best known. The story is parabolic and, like many other parables, its meaning is ambiguous. It is a didactic story, with an open-ended lesson, and it is comic, full of irony and satire.

INTERPRETING JONAH

Critical scholars today agree that the book is fiction, but they do not agree on its main point. If we knew the historical setting in which it was written, we might be better able to determine that purpose. However, judgments about the historical setting of the book of Jonah are all based, as they cannot help being, on prior judgments concerning its purpose. The range of opinions is wide, so a review of some of the principal ones can serve as an introduction to a discussion of the book.

Virtually all interpretations of the theological purpose of the book of Jonah focus on the adversarial relationship between God and Jonah: God is the protagonist and Jonah the antagonist. Consequently, the message of the book is inferred from the commands and questions of God to Jonah and Jonah's responding words and actions. Jonah is generally understood to represent the Jewish community in the postexilic period, and the book is understood as an effort to counter some belief or attitude of that community.

The most common scholarly view is that it was meant to counter *an exclusive doctrine of election*. The message then is twofold: First, that the grace of God is available to Gentiles, even those like the feared and hated Assyrians; second, that pride in the special election of the Jewish people is self-righteous.

A second interpretation is that the book was intended to counter *a rigid doctrine of retribution*. The message in this view is that unmerited grace is the fundamental factor in the relation of God to all human beings, including Gentiles. An interesting, though perhaps overly subtle variation of this view, proposed by Ronald Clements, is that the writer was bothered by the rigid application of the doctrine of retribution—not to Gentiles, but to Jews. He wanted to encourage postexilic Jews, who might have been tempted to despair of God's grace, to trust in God's eternal promises. The implied point of the book is that if God's forgiveness is available to the most wicked people imaginable, then surely it is available to repentant Jews.[6]

The point is understood somewhat differently if the book is taken as a satire.[7] In this case its primary purpose is to hold a mirror up to theological smugness and puncture self-inflated piety. This interpretation is not fundamentally different from others, but it emphasizes the book's satirical mode. However, if this interpretation is correct, it does rule out any other that views Jonah's repentance in the belly of the fish as genuine. If the book is a satire, then Jonah's repentance is a sham.

In fact, not a few interpreters focus on Jonah's behavior, including his repentance, as a personal response to the call of God, rather than on the relation between God and the Gentiles. Understood in this way, the book becomes a charting of the dynamics of religious vocation. The most subtle presentation of this view is that of the Lacocques.[8] They analyze Jonah's story as an inner religious pilgrimage—a faith-journey—from an initial rejection of divine vocation and the authentic selfhood that accompanies it, to an eventual acceptance of divine vocation and the mature faith and self-realization that accompanies it. This is an impressive interpretation of Jonah's journey; however, it also founders if Jonah's repentance in chapter 2 is a sham.

Yet another view of the point of the book sees it as an answer to disillusionment over the nonfulfillment of the prophecies of salvation of Second Isaiah and others. In other words, it sees the purpose of Jonah as similar to that of Malachi and Third Isaiah. However, this view is based less on what is said in the book of Jonah than on what is inferred from other prophetic books.

The wide variety of interpretations makes one wonder whether the book *has* a main point. If the test of the book's intention is its effect upon its readers, then its intention must have been to provoke discussion, rather than make a particular point. There probably is truth in this conclusion; nevertheless, I think the book *does* have a main point.

THE PRIMARY THEOLOGICAL QUESTION

In my judgment, the primary theological question asked by the story of Jonah is whether, in the circumstances described, YHWH did well to take pity upon the people of Nineveh, rather than acting toward them out of anger, as Jonah did. Doubtless there are other points to the story, especially in the satirizing of Jonah, but none of those is the main point. However, in order to answer the question about whether YHWH did well in these circumstances, one must first ask: What is YHWH like? and Why did YHWH act in this way?

The answer to the first question—What is YHWH like?—is provided by the creedal formula cited by Jonah: "I knew that you are a gracious God and merciful, slow to anger, and abounding in steadfast love, and ready to relent from punishing" (4:2). The answer to the second question—Why did YHWH act as he did?—is suggested by YHWH's description of the Ninevites as "more than a hundred and twenty thousand persons who do not know their right hand from their left" (4:11). The Lord YHWH is a compassionate God, whose forgiving love, at least some of the time, leads to a suspension of the punishment for sin that would be required by a strict retributive justice. The reason YHWH "relents from evil" in the present case—that is, the reason God suspends punishment—is that the people of Nineveh are helpless. It is also true that the Ninevites, warned of impending punishment, have confessed belief in God, performed rituals of contrition, and repented of their wicked ways (3:5-10). However, these acts are not mentioned by YHWH as grounds for the suspension of punishment. If they are factors at all, they are less important than the people's helplessness.

Jonah is angered by YHWH's suspension of the punishment due the wicked Ninevites. While YHWH is slow to anger, Jonah is quick to do so, and when YHWH questions his anger, Jonah quotes part of an old Yahwistic creedal description of YHWH—the part about YHWH's compassion and willingness to forgive; but he omits the part about YHWH's justice.[9] Here is the complete affirmation as it appears in Numbers 14:18:

> The LORD is slow to anger
> and abounding in steadfast love,
> forgiving iniquity and transgression,
> but by no means clearing the guilty,
> visiting the iniquity of the parents upon the children,
> to the third and the fourth generation.

This version of the creed puts equal stress upon divine forgiveness and divine justice. Had Jonah remembered the second part of the traditional statement, he would have been able to give a cogent, affirmative reply to YHWH's question. But the writer did not permit Jonah this reply.

When we examine the different versions of this creed in the Pentateuch, it becomes evident that the relation of God's mercy to God's justice was recognized as a serious theological problem in Jewish circles, and not merely by the writer of Jonah. That tension between mercy and justice, unresolved in Exodus 34:6-7 and Numbers 14:18, is resolved in Exodus 20:5-6 and Deuteronomy 7:9. According to both these versions of the creed, YHWH's mercy is shown to *those who love YHWH and keep his commandments,* while YHWH's relentless justice is shown to *those who hate him.* In other words, those who are fundamentally God-fearing and obedient to God's commandments can expect divine forgiveness for their occasional wickedness, but those who are fundamentally Godless can expect nothing but strict, retributive justice. This was one possible solution to the vexing problem of God's mercy in relation to God's justice. The book of Jonah can be viewed as a narrative reflection on the problem posed by the old creedal formulation, which the writer has Jonah quote at the decisive moment in his dialogue with YHWH.

MERCY AND JUSTICE

What is the relation of God's mercy to God's justice? Exodus 34:6-7 and Numbers 14:18 imply that it is simply a matter of the sovereign freedom of God—that is, God's freedom to be merciful to whom God will be merciful and just to whom God will be just. However, Exodus 20:5-6 and Deuteronomy 7:9 have linked the divine decision to the moral character of the human beings involved. Those responsible for the change must have been bothered, as Jonah was, over the unconditional quality of God's mercy, as described in the older version of the creed, the version Jonah quotes. It is just this kind of mercy that YHWH shows the Ninevites in the story: God pities them simply because they are helpless.

The question of the relation between divine justice and divine mercy is also suggested, implicitly, in the psalm of thanksgiving which Jonah recites while he is in the stomach of the fish. In this psalm, both affliction and deliverance from affliction are recalled as acts of God, without any attempt to justify either on the basis of the psalmist's character. Both are accepted simply as free acts of God. Jonah recites this psalm, but he obviously does not share the psalmist's understanding of grace.

Jonah's response to YHWH's pardon of the Ninevites is crucial in determining the point of the story. The writer describes Jonah's response succinctly: "But this was very displeasing to Jonah, and he became angry" (4:1). Jonah is angry enough to wish he were dead, and he prays to YHWH to take his life. His reason for anger is that YHWH, true to the nature of YHWH, has "relented from punishing"[10] —that is, YHWH has changed the decision to destroy the wicked Ninevites and has allowed them to live. It is not clear whether Jonah is angry because YHWH has decided not to punish all wicked people, whoever they may be, or because YHWH has decided not to punish the Ninevites specifically. The majority of commentators infer that it is the latter reason, though a significant minority infer that it is the former. Both conclusions are inferences, since Jonah's statement will support either.

Jonah's display of anger over God's deliverance of the Ninevites is, of course, only the first of two such displays. When YHWH later kills the plant that shades Jonah from the blazing sun, Jonah again asks YHWH to kill him, thus exhibiting the same rage over divine action that he displayed before. But once again the precise reason for Jonah's anger is unstated. Is his anger for the plant's sake, or is it for his own sake, because he has been denied its shade? The response of YHWH to Jonah's anger puts the emphasis on the plant itself: "You pity the plant" (or, as the most recent English versions render it, "You cared about" [NJV]; "were concerned about" [NRSV, NJB]; "are sorry about" [REB]). Nevertheless, YHWH's response does not rule out the possibility that Jonah's pity for the plant, like his anger over Nineveh's deliverance, is basically self-centered.

The final speech of YHWH brings the story to a close and establishes the main point: YHWH's pity for the Ninevites is likened to Jonah's pity for the plant.

What is this pity? Is it merely a *feeling* of sympathy over the plight of something or someone, or is it the quality of an *act* on behalf of the other? None of the English translations noted above conveys the specific meaning of the Hebrew word. The verbal root (*chus*) denotes an "emotion of sympathy," the feeling of "shared suffering," but this sympathy is "antecedent to action," an emotion that "motivates and initiates action on behalf of the one pitied."[11] In the Bible, the word usually is used theologically. This usage reflects a development in the legal tradition, discernible primarily in Deuteronomy, in which the word comes to signify mitigation or, more often, renunciation of prescribed punishment in the legal system.[12] In the prophetic writings, especially Ezekiel, it refers to the neutralization of deserved punishment. Thus the frequent meaning of the word in the biblical texts is "total renunciation of what one is legally empowered to do, not a mitigation of a punishment."[13] In Jonah, YHWH's pity of Nineveh is both the emotion of sympathy and the renunciation of prescribed punishment. Jonah of course cannot act on the basis of his pity for the plant, because YHWH has killed it. The only thing Jonah can do is to express the depth of his pity by asking YHWH to kill him, too.

Jonah does not explain exactly why YHWH's renunciation of Nineveh's punishment angers him—whether it is because it is Nineveh or because the strict demand of justice has not been met. Is it Nineveh he hates, or God's forgiveness of the wicked? He doesn't say. But he surely hates God's forgiveness of Nineveh. In this case, Jonah, the prophet of God, preferred relentless justice to compassionate mercy. But God, in this case at least, chose mercy over simple justice. And readers are left to ponder whether it should not have been so.

The book of Jonah ends abruptly with this unanswered question. It would be neater if, after the final speech of God, the protaganist made an appropriate response, as Job does in similar circumstances. Such an ending would provide formal closure to the book, but it would also change the effect. So we must be content not to bring closure to this intriguing story, but to leave it open, with its probing, final question.

SELECT BIBLIOGRAPHY

Ahlström, G. W. *Joel and the Temple Cult of Jerusalem. VT*Sup 21. Leiden: E. J. Brill, 1971.

Allen, Leslie C. *Joel, Obadiah, Jonah, and Micah.* New International Commentary on the Old Testament. Grand Rapids: Eerdmans, 1976.

Clements, Ronald E. "The Purpose of the Book of Jonah." *VT*Sup 28 Leiden: E. J. Brill, 1975.

Fretheim, Terence. *The Message of Jonah: A Theological Commentary.* Minneapolis: Augsburg Press, 1977.

Hauser, Allan John. "Jonah: In Pursuit of the Dove." *JBL* 104 (1985): 21-37.

Holbert, John C. "Deliverance Belongs to Yahweh." *JSOT* 21 (1981): 59-81.

Lacocque, A., and Pierre-Emmanuel Lacocque. *The Jonah Complex.* Atlanta: John Knox Press, 1981.

Landes, George M. "The Kerugma of the Book of Jonah." *Interpretation* 21 (1967): 3-31.

Limburg, James. *Hosea-Micah.* Interpretation. Atlanta: John Knox Press, 1988.

Prinsloo, Willem S. *The Theology of the Book of Joel.* BZAW 163. Berlin/New York: Walter de Gruyter, 1985.

Stuart, Douglas. *Hosea-Jonah.* Word Biblical Commentary. Waco, Tex.: Word Books, 1987.

Wolff, Hans Walter. *Joel and Amos.* Hermeneia. Philadelphia: Fortress Press, 1977.

______. *Obadiah and Jonah.* Minneapolis: Augsburg Press, 1986.

NOTES

1. See, e.g., Otto Eissfeldt, *Introduction to the Old Testament* (New York: Harper & Row, 1965), pp. 393-94.
2. Wolff, *Joel and Amos,* pp. 10-12.
3. Ibid., p. 13.
4. See Bruce C. Cresson, "The Condemnation of Edom in Post-exilic Judaism," *The Use of the Old Testament in the New and Other Essays,* ed. James M. Efird (Durham, N.C.: Duke University Press, 1972), pp. 125-48.
5. Ibid., p. 142.
6. Clements, "The Purpose of the Book of Jonah."
7. Holbert, "Deliverance Belongs to Yahweh."
8. Lacocque, *The Jonah Complex.*
9. Cf. Exod 20:5-6 [Deut 5:9*b*-10]; 34:6-7; Num 14:18; Deut 7:9.
10. Cf. NJV: "renounced the punishment He had planned to bring upon them."
11. S. Wagner, *TDOT* IV: 272.
12. Ibid., p. 273.
13. Ibid., p. 277.

CHAPTER FOURTEEN

Nahum, Habakkuk, and Zephaniah

Nahum, Habakkuk, and Zephaniah are Judean writings of the late seventh century, all containing prophetic reflections on the justice of God in history. The major world event in that period was the collapse of the Assyrian Empire, ending a two-hundred-year hegemony in Syria-Palestine. Nahum viewed the fall of Assyria as the overdue death of a tyrant and had no difficulty interpreting it as an act of divine justice, a view shared by most ancient and modern commentators. However, what first appeared as simple justice, later appeared more complex. Habakkuk, who may have shared Nahum's assessment of Assyria, realized that justice was precarious, for he saw that the Chaldeans, who helped destroy Assyria and then became the dominant power in western Asia, were no different from the Assyrians they replaced. So Habakkuk wondered whether there was any fulfillment of God's justice through the agency of world powers, or any justice at all for the smaller populations of the world.

Zephaniah, writing at about the same time, began his prophecy with a vision of the day of Yahweh as a time of total annihilation for humankind. His vision is understandable, in light of the international politics of the time, but it forces us to ask, What purpose would be served by such a day of wrath? The prophet conceded that a repentant few might find shelter in that day (2:3), but this hardly answers the question for the great communities of people. The prophet offers the remnant of Israel the hope of plundering Moab and Ammon, in revenge for crimes against themselves, but again, we wonder what godly purpose this would serve.

NAHUM

In this group of contemporaneous prophetic writings, which contain many searching questions about the moral coherence of history and fewer satisfying answers, the book of Nahum seems quite comprehensible. A small vassal like

Judah, on the western fringe of the Assyrian Empire, had experienced Assyrian rule entirely as a victim, not a beneficiary. It was natural, therefore, for Judeans to despise Assyria and rejoice at its fall.

In the longer perspective of time, the prophet's assessment of Nineveh as a "city of bloodshed, utterly deceitful, full of booty" (3:1) appears incomplete. The characterization of Assyria as a wanton butcher of subject peoples, perpetuated in modern sermons and textbooks, takes no account of its positive contributions to the political and economic life of the ancient Near East. Assyria is usually compared unfavorably to the Persian and Roman Empires in this regard, but the comparison is not entirely fair when all the evidence is examined. An assessment like H.W.F. Saggs' in his recent book on the Assyrian Empire is more objective.[1] In addition to providing a balanced evaluation of the empire politically and economically, Saggs corrects the one-sided picture of Assyrian military atrocities that appears almost universally in biblical commentaries.

Resettlement of communities for political and economic reasons, a policy that helps to account for the biblical denunciation of Assyria, was indeed practiced, but it was a policy employed chiefly with intractable vassals. According to the epigraphic evidence, Assyrian armies perpetrated atrocities only in the most serious cases of armed rebellion, and never during the initial conquest of another people. Ordinarily, military prisoners were treated well—the guards were ordered to take care of them. And no random atrocities by Assyrian soldiers have been documented.[2] The military reliefs in Assyrian royal palaces which depict the savage might of the Assyrian armies—and confirm the biblical view of Assyria in the minds of most readers of the Bible—were official propaganda used as an instrument of diplomacy, a kind of psychological warfare. Such reliefs were placed only in the audience chambers where foreign diplomats were received! Elsewhere in the palaces, the reliefs depicted religious and artistic scenes such as those in the villas of the Roman aristocracy, which we view with such approval.

Of course, Nahum was not a disinterested historian making an objective evaluation, so we should not expect a similar picture of Assyria from him. He expressed the sentiments of the victims of imperial power, whose suffering was a reality, and he also interpreted Assyria's fall as the working out of a just providence. This view is entirely in accord with biblical understanding of history generally; it corresponds, in particular, with Isaiah's interpretation of Assyria's role in world affairs (Isa 10:5-15).

It is difficult to estimate the possible impact of Nahum's words on his Judean audience. On the one hand, all of them, from the peasantry to the royal court, could be expected to share his feelings toward Assyria. On the other hand, his assessment of the bitter results of Assyrian despotism might have given the rulers of Judah pause, causing them to reconsider the goals of their own leadership. After all, the prophetic assessment of the kingdoms of Israel and Judah was almost as negative as the assessment of Assyria. The danger was that Nahum's words would encourage Judean self-righteousness. We do not know who heard these words, but whatever effect they may have had on the minds of his contemporaries, the policies of the Judean rulers in the remaining years of the kingdom showed little influence of the moral insights of the prophets.

Today Nahum should certainly be read together with other prophetic texts, especially Jeremiah and Jonah, in order to keep it in perspective. The placement of Jonah ahead of Nahum in the scroll of the Twelve Prophets is particularly interesting. One wonders whether it was intentional on the part of the editors. Nahum can help a modern religious community understand the experience of the victims of despotic rule, but it also should spur them to reflect upon their own political and moral responsibilities, in a world where millions of people still suffer from various forms of oppression.

Nahum's oracle on the fall of Nineveh is introduced by the announcement of a herald:

> Look! On the mountains the feet of one
> who brings good tidings,
> who proclaims peace!
> Celebrate your festivals, O Judah,
> fulfill your vows,
> for never again shall the wicked invade you,
> they are utterly cut off. (1:15)

To "bring good tidings," or good news, is the same term used by Second Isaiah in his introductory poem (40:9), the term the Greek translator rendered "evangelize." This term came to have rich connotations in later biblical usage—not all of those uses political. Here in Nahum, however, as also in Second Isaiah, the salvation announced is mainly political. These prophets understood the whole of life, not merely the inwardly religious aspects of it, to be the realm of interaction between God and the human community. The providential character of events in the arena of international politics is underscored by the preface to Nahum's oracle, a liturgical recital of the attributes of YHWH (1:2-8). In this way, the particular historical event is interpreted as a manifestation of YHWH's enduring righteousness.

Poetically, the book of Nahum is one of the most vivid examples of the large group of oracles which concern foreign nations, some of which we have discussed in earlier chapters. Its literary quality may account in part for its preservation as a separate book in the prophetic canon.

HABAKKUK

When the apostle Paul quoted Habakkuk's dictum that "the righteous shall live by faith" (2:4 RSV; cf. Gal 3:11, Rom 1:17), he fixed Habakkuk's place in Christian usage for all time. Not that Habakkuk would have been forgotten otherwise, for its merits are many, but Paul focused attention on a particular element of the writing as an anticipation of the gospel, and thus shaped Christian understanding of the book.

Paul's use of Habakkuk was selective and interpretative: selective, since it involved a single clause; interpretative, since it rendered the Hebrew word *'emunah* (usually "faithfulness" or "trustworthiness") by the Greek word *pistis* (usually "faith"). Paul was not the first to do this, for he was quoting the LXX. So it was actually the LXX, refracted through the prism of Paul's theology, which determined the importance of Habakkuk for Christian readers. The clause Paul quoted is indeed important, though there is more to the book than this one clause.

Habakkuk's complaint to YHWH that "the wicked surround the righteous—therefore judgment comes forth perverted," which begins the book and sets its tone, is reminiscent of the complaints of Jeremiah. Like them, it is rare in the prophetic literature. It is unusual in that it gives us an interior glimpse into the prophet's mind, rather than merely expressing his message to Israel. In particular, Habakkuk's complaint expresses perplexity over the frustration of YHWH's justice in human affairs. So the theme of the book is theodicy, but Habakkuk's treatment of the theme is not entirely clear. He was distressed over God's failure to punish certain wicked nations, but we are not sure which ones he had in mind. This question has been the primary concern of modern commentators on Habakkuk.

Who are the wicked in 1:2-4, whose wickedness is unpunished? Who are the punishers in 1:5-11? Who are the other wicked in 1:12-17? And at whom are the woes in 2:5-20 directed? Scholarly literature is full of conflicting answers. According to one proposal, the answers to the four questions are Judah, Chaldea, Chaldea, and Chaldea, respectively. However, another proposal suggests Assyria, Chaldea, Assyria, and Assyria; yet another, Judah, Chaldea, Chaldea, and Assyria. But perhaps the major premise of this approach, that Habakkuk's oracles chronicle the interactions of particular nations in a particular period of time, is wrong. Scrutiny of the text shows that it has been stripped of most of its historical particularity. As it comes to us, the text poses its questions without identifying the actors in the drama, except the "Chaldeans" in 1:16. So it is best to deal with the text on its own terms.

The issue raised by the book is the question of theodicy, the discrepancy between God's justice as it is imagined and the actual injustices of history. Habakkuk was troubled because the nations entrusted with power failed to implement justice. The presupposition of Habakkuk's commentary, of course, was the belief that God rules human history. The prophet was convinced that there must be some correlation between the morality of nations and their fortunes. However, the facts of history did not confirm his conviction.

The case of the Chaldean, or Neo-Babylonian, empire is presented as the principal illustration of the theological problem (1:7). Chaldea is depicted as an actual nation, not a mere symbol, like the Nineveh of the book of Jonah. There is no compelling reason to doubt that the prophecy was composed during the Chaldean era, as most scholars suppose. However, the sequence of statements in the prophetic dialogue between Habakkuk and YHWH cannot be correlated convincingly with the known sequence of events in that era. It reflects the era in a general way, but not, as far as we can tell, in chronological detail.

On the theological level, the book is particularly probing in its questions. It describes the superiority of the wicked over the righteous in real life (1:2-4) and asks how a righteous God can tolerate such injustice (1:2, 13). How long must Habakkuk wait to see God's punishment of the wicked? The answer given him is simply to keep waiting; eventually the punishment will come (2:2-3). In the meantime, the righteous will live by their fidelity (2:4).

The Hebrew word in 2:4 is *'emunah,* meaning "faithfulness," or "fidelity," as in the quality of a person. *Faith,* in the sense of faith in God, is expressed in other ways, notably by the phrase "the fear of God." Habakkuk's assertion is another way to make the point made in Ezekiel 18—that the wicked person "dies" and the righteous person "lives." In living faithfully, the righteous have true life, but not as a reward. The translation of the NJV is wrong here, I think ("But the righteous man is rewarded with life for his fidelity"). Faithfulness is a self-authenticating mode of existence, whose reward is intrinsic; faithful living is the fruit of righteousness and is its own true reward. Indeed, Habakkuk's phrase can be translated, "The righteous shall live *in* fidelity." One of the implications of the prophet's assertion, when viewed in relation to his whole dialogue with YHWH, is that outward measures of divine favor are not primary; power and wealth are not reliable signs of the quality of one's relationship with God. The true measure of righteousness is fidelity.

The corollary of this assertion, stated in the parallel line, is that the unrighteous will be deprived or in jeopardy (vs 4*a*). The exact meaning of the Hebrew is uncertain. It is translated in various ways by the versions, some of which (including the RSV) emend the text. In my opinion, the NEB is the best translation. It reads, "The reckless will be unsure of himself." This translation involves no emendation and treats the two parts of the verse as a simple, antithetic parallelism. The word translated "reckless" in the NEB may also be translated "audacious" or "puffed up." It suggests arrogant pride. The NRSV is satisfactory, too: "Look at the proud! Their spirit is not right in them." The phrase the NEB renders "will be unsure of himself" is literally, "His *nephesh* will not be upright in him." The *nephesh* is the self as a living being, the personality, the person. The RSV translates it "soul" here, following the KJV. This translation is acceptable, as long as *soul* is understood to mean the real self, and not, dualistically, a mere part of the self. The point of the Hebrew sentence is that the puffed-up person will be an insecure, distorted person. This person is the opposite of the righteous person who lives in fidelity or, one might say, lives faithfully. The one is unstable, the other stable. The character of both will eventually become manifest in their behavior, with tangible results. But both are essentially self-authenticating—one destructively, the other redemptively.

THE ORACLES OF WOE

The woe oracles in Habakkuk 2:6-20 are variations on the two themes of 2:1-4; thus 2:1-4 serves as a prologue to this middle section of the book. The second theme to appear is the one just discussed. The first is the promise that the "vision" would surely come to pass, though it would be very slow in coming. The vision must be the vindication of God's justice, which would correct the moral chaos of Habakkuk's time and answer the prophet's questions. The vision is distinct from the affirmation—that the righteous will live in fidelity and the reckless in instability. The affirmation is true in the present, while the vision remains to be proved true in the future.

In their own way, the woe oracles make the same points made in 2:1-4. They illustrate the inherent instability of reckless living and its inner distortion. This is the negative half of the point made in 2:4. The woe oracles also describe the baneful results that such living will eventually produce, thus illustrating the point of 2:3—that wickedness ultimately will be punished. Unrighteous, godless behavior is intrinsically empty and distorted, and it ultimately comes to nought in the justice of God. This is the message of Habakkuk 2.

I said earlier that the crucial Hebrew word in Habakkuk 2:4*b* (*'emunah*) means "faithfulness" or "fidelity," rather than "faith," and that the Greek word which translates it in the LXX and in Paul (*pistis*), which usually means "faith," changes the meaning. It would be a mistake, however, to regard this change as a total transformation. The emphasis in Habakkuk's phrase, "The righteous will live in [or by] faithfulness," is on the character and behavior of the person, whereas the emphasis in the Pauline use of this phrase is on faith in the being and action of God. Yet these two dimensions of the divine/human relationship are inseparable in both prophetic and Pauline thought. Faithfulness, in Habakkuk's witness, involves faith in God.

Paul analyzed the origin and character of faith in a way the prophets never had: He affirmed the source of faith to be God's gracious action in Jesus Christ, and he characterized faith as a gift, rather than a meritorious human achievement. Such affirmations go beyond anything in the prophetic literature; indeed, they presuppose theological questions not even formulated before the Hellenistic era. Therefore it would be anachronistic to compare Paul's thought in this regard with that of the prophets. Paul undoubtedly changed the emphasis of Habakkuk, but his statement was essentially compatible with the prophet's.

Other assertions in Habakkuk would need to be discussed in a complete catalog of the book's ideas. Some are expressed distinctively, but most are essentially the same as ideas expressed elsewhere in the prophetic literature. Most distinctive in Habakkuk's thought is his affirmation of disinterested, self-authenticating piety as the measure of righteousness, especially in a time of political and social upheaval. The psalm of Habakkuk, added by the redactor, captures the prophet's meaning: When the times are morally out of joint and injustice goes unchecked, the faithful may still "rejoice in YHWH . . . the God of my salvation" (3:18), and wait. Habakkuk believed God's justice would eventually become manifest (2:2-3); and in the meantime, the righteous would live in fidelity.

ZEPHANIAH

If the editorial dating of Zephaniah's prophecy during the reign of Josiah is correct, then it is possible that Zephaniah was a supporter of Josiah's national reform. Similar emphases exist in Zephaniah's message and in Josiah's platform (2 Kings 22–23): YHWH's power to judge nations; YHWH's intention to restore Judean sovereignty over the territories ruled by David and Solomon; and YHWH's support of a purified Jerusalem at the center of a godly kingdom. However, Zephaniah's oracles are not linked specifically to Josiah's reform, and it is not likely that they were preserved for this reason. The oracles are relatively timeless and would have been preserved because of their continuing relevance for faith.

As a word for all times and places, Zephaniah is in basic accord with the message of other prophetic writings. Behind the impassioned prophecy of universal judgment, we can discern the frustration of a godly prophet during turbulent times—frustration over the widespread, undeserved affliction of humble, pious people, and frustration over the undeserved privilege of the powerful. Announcing the day of wrath for the wicked was a way to claim God's favor for the pious. Eventually, the prophet was saying, God's preference would be manifest—not only for those with eyes of faith, but for all to see.

"When will the powerful lose their privileged security against the common perils of life?"

"In the day of YHWH!"

"When will idolaters and unbelievers be punished for their wickedness?"

"In the day of YHWH!"

"When will the righteous remnant of God's people be vindicated?"

"In the day of YHWH!"

"When will Jerusalem be purified and given its promised role in God's rule of the nations?"

"In the day of YHWH!"

This is the burden of Zephaniah's prophecy. In the prophecy of the day of YHWH, we discern an idea uncommon in the prophetic literature—that of universal human depravity:

> I will make the wicked stumble.
> I will cut off humanity from upon the face of the earth,
> says the LORD. (1:3)

"Humanity" and "the wicked" are parallel here and appear synonymous. If all human beings are wicked, then the presumption is that God is justified in punishing all of them. In any case, the prophet threatens destruction for "the whole earth"; "all the inhabitants of the earth" will be annihilated in the day of YHWH (1:18). Is this rhetorical exaggeration or literal prediction? Is an allusion to Genesis 2:7 present in the pairing of *'adam* (humanity) and *'adamah* (ground) in 1:3; if so, is the coming day of YHWH understood as a reversal of creation?

What kind of response did the prophet expect from his audience? Personal repentance? Social action? Cultic renewal? How do people react to words like these? Over time, the repetition of prophecies of universal destruction can dull people's ears. Were Zephaniah's words arresting to his ancient hearers? Probably, and may have been preserved for this reason. However, taken out of the historical context that gave them force and appeal, they are less moving, though some of the images remain vivid—guests being consecrated for the sacrificial meal (1:7), lamps being lighted to search out the wicked (1:12)!

Suddenly, in the middle of the book, a strange shift occurs. Instead of announcing the annihilation of all human beings, as before, the prophet appeals to those who might repent in time to be rescued from destruction (2:1-3); then, even more strangely, he promises that the remnant of Judah will take possession of the territories of Philistia, Moab, and Ammon (2:4-10). And next he predicts that even the remotest nations will worship YHWH (2:11)! Perhaps this was Josiah's agenda. Later readers would have interpreted "Philistia," "Moab," and "Ammon" to symbolize nations of their own time. But regardless of the historical context, the appeal and promise in chapter 2 seem to undercut the universal threat in chapter 1. Chapter 1 speaks of worldwide destruction, but chapter 2 speaks of a much more mundane divine act. The prophecy of the day of YHWH should be interpreted figuratively, if it is to be seen as a morally relevant word and not a mere hyperbole. The point is not that a sudden, material destruction of all peoples will occur at some time in the future, but that every evil act conflicts with God's righteousness, and therefore will eventually be judged for what it is.

Zephaniah 3 is addressed to the "soiled, defiled, oppressing city," recalling Nahum's oracle to "the city of bloodshed, utterly deceitful, full of booty" (Nah 3:1). Nahum referred to Nineveh; Zephaniah referred to Jerusalem; Nahum signaled the total destruction of Nineveh, but Zephaniah promised the reform and renewal of Jerusalem. It is difficult to date this portion of the book. The concluding lines seem to presuppose the exile (esp. vs 20), but the fall of Jerusalem is not mentioned. A date between 598 and 587 would account for both the presupposition and the omission, but this is only one possibility. If verse 20 is an exilic expansion of the original oracle, as some commentators think, the rest of the chapter can be taken as a commentary on the religious situation in Jerusalem, either before the reform of Josiah or after his death. Let us sketch the main ideas of chapter 3:

3:1-5—The rebellious, defiled, oppressing city puts no trust in YHWH, and her officials, prophets, and priests violate the torah.
3:6-7—The godless city is heedless to warnings implied by the destruction of other cities and nations.
3:8—YHWH announces the approaching day of wrath against all nations.
3:9-10—The speech (and thus the mind) of the peoples will be purified, and they will bring offerings to YHWH from the remotest lands.
3:11-13—The proud leaders of the city will be removed, and only the humble pious will remain in Israel.
3:14-20—The city, Daughter Zion, is exhorted to sing YHWH's praise and promised that her reproach in the eyes of other peoples will be removed, her exiles gathered to her, and her fortunes restored.

Except for the final promise of the exiles' return, which presupposes the exile, the entire composition makes good sense either as a summons to Josiah's reformers (ca. 621) or as a summons to the survivors of the fall of Jerusalem (after 598). By a natural extension, it makes sense also in any subsequent historical setting in which there is reasonable hope of a better future for the city of Jerusalem. The moral conditions of a renewal are suggested, though only in the most general terms. Thus, Zephaniah's message accords well in principle with the longer, more substantial prophecies of the other preexilic prophets.

CONCLUSION

With these three books, we leave the period of transition at the close of the monarchical era in Israel. The series of crises that marked this period evoked a remarkable prophetic response, as we have seen in these books, and even more in the books of Jeremiah and Ezekiel. In the final books in the scroll of the Twelve Prophets which we consider in the next chapter, we will leap ahead a full century to a completely different historical setting, a different set of religious concerns, and a different message.

SELECT BIBLIOGRAPHY

Achtemeier, Elizabeth. *Nahum-Malachi.* Interpretation. Atlanta: John Knox Press, 1986.

Christensen, Duane L. "Zephaniah 2:4-15: A Theological Basis for Josiah's Program of Political Expansion." *CBQ* 46 (1984): 669-82.

Gowan, Donald E. *The Triumph of Faith in Habakkuk.* Atlanta: John Knox Press, 1976.

Haldar, A. *Studies in the Book of Nahum.* Uppsala: University Press, 1947.

Peckham, Brian. "The Vision of Habakkuk." *CBQ* 48 (1986): 617-36.

Smith, Ralph L. *Micah-Malachi.* Word Biblical Commentary. Waco, Tex.: Word Books, 1984.

NOTES

1. H. W. Saggs, *The Might That Was Assyria* (London: Sidgwick & Jackson, 1984).
2. Ibid., pp. 261-64.

CHAPTER FIFTEEN

Haggai, Zechariah, and Malachi

HAGGAI

Haggai's brief oracles contain a straightforward message: a summons to Judean Jews in the sixth-century BCE to rebuild the temple of Jerusalem, so that YHWH could be honored and the people blessed. The book is sometimes criticized as ritualistic, in comparison to other prophetic books, but this judgment is unfair. To judge it by its omissions is to miss the point. Haggai's theological rationale for building the temple may have been partly questionable—the belief that doing so would guarantee good crops—but the social and religious importance of his project was undeniable. The reestablishment in Jerusalem of public worship on a solid basis depended upon this project, and it was important also for the continuation of Yahwism. Judaism survived the destruction of the second temple in 70 CE, but without the temple, Judaism might not have lasted until that time.

And the Bible gives principal credit for the rebuilding of the temple to Haggai. If this acknowledgment is correct, his oracles, delivered in the space of a few months during the autumn of 520 BCE, represent one of the most important building proposals in history. The positive consequences for the history of religion were enormous. In short, the reconstitution of the religious community, with its ritual center in the temple of Jerusalem, was a fateful event in the history of Judaism.

Haggai gave two reasons for rebuilding the temple. First, the Judeans ought not to be living in "paneled houses" while they neglected the building of a proper place of worship (1:4). Apparently the people were not opposed to the idea in principle, but only to the timing of it (vs 2). This may explain why Haggai offered a second reason: The recent drought and meager harvest were due to the people's failure to rebuild the temple (1:5-6, 9-11). Haggai promised them better fortune, once it was completed (1:8; 2:9, 18)—and even that the wealth of nations would flow to the new temple, in appropriate recognition of YHWH's sovereignty (2:6-9).

Haggai also endorsed Zerubbabel ben Shealtiel as YHWH's "signet ring" and chosen one (2:23). Most commentators hear messianic overtones in this declaration, and this may be a correct interpretation, since Zerubbabel was a descendant of the Davidic kings. However, Haggai's endorsement is extremely cautious, and it does not imply much more than the religious authorization accorded to all political and cultic leaders, in Israel and the ancient world generally. If this is Davidic messianism, it is not a vigorous form of it.

ZECHARIAH 1–8

Zechariah 1–8, or First Zechariah, has the same historical setting as Haggai, and like Haggai, supports the reconstruction of the temple of Jerusalem during the governorship of Zerubbabel ben Shealtiel (ca. 520). It is longer than Haggai, and its message is more complex, in both its political and its religious aspects. The book has had little importance in modern Christian exposition of the Bible, and there are several reasons for this neglect: It is written in a bizarre, visionary form; it lacks fullsome treatment of the great themes of biblical faith; and its social concerns are somewhat parochial. Nevertheless, page for page, it is as interesting as some of the more popular prophetic writings. When it is read with the help of a perceptive commentary (see esp. Petersen), it proves to be an intriguing and significant text.

The pressing issue in Judah in Zechariah's time was the reestablishment of the Yahwistic community. Zechariah had quite a lot to say about this, though he said it so cryptically that his meaning is easily missed. The form of his writing draws attention to itself and away from the message. Zechariah must be read carefully to be appreciated fully.

AUTHENTICATING THE PROPHET

Authentication of the prophet as a messenger of God is the first issue to be considered. It is mentioned several times in the book (2:9, 11; 4:9; 6:15), and it is suggested implicitly by the visionary form used as the medium of communication.

Every claim to speak for God requires validation, and according to abundant biblical testimony, the demand for validation was common in ancient Israel. Therefore it is not surprising to find the theme in the writings of the prophets, since they, more than anyone else, claimed to speak for God. Four times in Zechariah 1–8, the prophet asserts that his claim will be validated when his prophecies are fulfilled in the future. Then, he says, his audience will know that YHWH has sent him (2:9, 11; 4:9; 6:15). Clearly, this authentication was important to him, and I therefore infer that he employed the vision as his primary form of communication in order to give authority to his words, though there probably were rhetorical reasons too, considering how vivid and memorable these visions were. Yet it seems unlikely that the choice of the visionary form was motivated by rhetorical considerations alone, nor can it be explained, as the visions of Ezekiel were, in relation to a call to prophecy. Zechariah's visions are like those of Amos (Amos 7–8), in that they do not describe the prophet's call to the prophetic office, as such, but serve as the vehicle for a particular message from YHWH to Israel. The difference is that the whole of Zechariah 1–8 is visionary, while the visions of Amos constitute only a small portion of the book. Whether Zechariah experienced actual visions is a question that cannot be answered, any more than for any other prophet. Most commentators assume that he did, but the only evidence is internal, and internal evidence, in this case, is ambiguous.

Regardless of the answer, visions alone cannot authenticate a prophet's word as a word of God. As the Israelite historians knew, visions can lie, even when the visionaries believe them to be true (1 Kings 22:22-23), so there needs to be some test of authenticity other than the mental process through which a communication is formed. Zechariah must have understood this, or he would not have appealed to future world events to confirm his status as a true messenger of God. In doing this, he appealed to the same test of prophecy used in Deuteronomy 18:21-22. While the test of historical confirmation was not sufficient in itself to determine who spoke truly for God, it was a necessary one in the judgment of Zechariah and the Deuteronomist, among others.

VINDICATING GOD'S JUSTICE

Zechariah was concerned not only with his confirmation as an authentic prophet of God, but with the vindication of God's justice; to put it another way, he was concerned with the validation of both the source and the content of his message. Thus, for example, in 2:6-13, he declared that the divine origin of his message would be confirmed when the despoilers of Israel were themselves despoiled. It was important not only for particular prophecies to be confirmed as words of YHWH, but for YHWH's righteous rule in human affairs to be demonstrated. If YHWH's treatment of Israel were just, as all the prophets asserted, then the other nations, which also were subject to the sovereignty of YHWH, must be treated justly too. In the case of nations that despoiled Israel, this meant they eventually would be punished. When that happened, the prophetic proclamation of YHWH's righteousness would be confirmed, and so would the prophet himself, as a messenger of YHWH.

The theme of YHWH's justice recurs several times in the book, each time in a different way. The first occurs in the very first words of the prophet:

> The LORD was very angry with your ancestors. Therefore, say to them, Thus says the LORD of hosts: Return to me, says the LORD of hosts, and I will return to you, says the LORD of hosts. Do not be like your ancestors, to whom the former prophets proclaimed, "Thus says the LORD of hosts, Return from your evil ways and from your evil deeds." But they did not hear or heed me, says the LORD.

Zechariah's word to his contemporaries was short and simple: "Return to me, says the LORD of hosts and I will return to you." This word is enclosed in a brief commentary on the history of Israel's relationship with YHWH: Because the ancestors were incorrigible in their wickedness, they provoked YHWH's fierce anger. This is the traditional prophetic proclamation of God's retributive justice, and Zechariah's word to his audience follows naturally from that commentary: If they will turn to YHWH (turn away from evil), then YHWH will turn to them (treat them favorably).

This promise sounds at first like a simple quid pro quo. However, no extraneous benefits of the relationship are offered—only the personal relationship itself. In other words, the promise is essentially the same as the central promise of the Bible.

A second variation on the theme of YHWH's justice is introduced in Zechariah's first vision, with the complaint that Jerusalem is unconsoled while the other nations are at peace (1:11). The complaint is elaborated by recalling that the nations have compounded the injury to the city (vs 15). However, this idea is not completed until the second vision—the vision of the four horns—where it is promised that the nations which despoiled Judah will be despoiled (1:18-21; MT 2:1-4). Thus justice will finally be done. This is the last word in the visions about the punishment of the nations.

The theme that dominates the remainder of the visions is "the consolation of Judah." This consolation is to come through the reestablishment of the city, the cultic community, and the leadership of Jerusalem. These things evidently mattered much more to Zechariah than the punishment of the other nations.

In the oracle that intevenes between the third and fourth visions (2:6-13; MT 2:10-17), the theme of the judgment of the nations appears once more, this time with greater emphasis. Many commentators consider this oracle secondary, though recently Baruch Halpern has defended its place in the book on liturgical grounds. Citing Mesopotamian parallels, he argues that the book, in its present structure, reflects a ritual of rededication of the sanctuary in Jerusalem.[1] This is an attractive theory, though the visionary form in itself does not presuppose a ritual background. On the other hand, the oracle makes most sense when placed in a ritual setting. Three principal ritual moments appear in the oracle, each marked by an imperative:

> Listen! Listen! (2:6; MT 10)
> Sing and rejoice! (2:10; MT 14)
> Be silent! (2:13; MT 17)[2]

In the first part of the poem (2:6-9), the faithful are urgently summoned to flee from Babylon to Zion, and YHWH promises that the nations which plundered them will become plunder for them. However, in the third part (2:11-13), a happier promise is made: "Many nations will join themselves to YHWH" in the day of restoration. Both these statements sound like liturgical formulas; they reinforce the prophet's exhortation to restore the religious community of Zion. This theme dominates the remainder of the book, and the theme of the judgment of the nations does not appear again.

BUILDING THE CITY OF GOD

Before building a city, the ancient founders needed to answer some important questions. Should the city be walled? If so, how large should it be? Who would be allowed to live in it? Who would govern it? What laws would be followed?

Zechariah gave the following answers to these questions: The new Jerusalem would have no walls at all; therefore, there would be no need to lay out the city's boundaries (2:1-5; MT 2:5-9). A multitude of residents, from all nations, would live in open neighborhoods (2:11; MT 2:15). They would have two leaders—one cultic and one civil (3:1-10; 4:11-14; 6:9-14). And the laws would be those of the ancient covenant with YHWH (5:1-4; 7:8-10).

This program is not altogether startling. Any exilic Jew who remembered the old Jerusalem could have proposed most of it. But two features are quite unexpected: the absence of city walls and the coequality of the leaders. The old Jerusalem had walls, and it was ruled by a monarch. So Zechariah's proposal was genuinely new.

The picture of coequal rulers is not quite uniform in the book. In 6:12-13 the civil leader, in the person of Zerubbabel ("The Branch"), has precedence over the priest, who stands beside the other's throne. This superior status for Zerubbabel, descendant of the Davidides, may be implied also in 4:7-10, although it is not actually asserted there. Some scholars consider the monarchically flavored allusions to be secondary insertions, intended by the redactor as a corrective to Zechariah's original proposal. Be that as it may, the status assigned to the priestly leader in the book is an elevated one, and certainly approaches parity with the civil leader. This is no simple projection of the old Davidic kingship. The traditional royal ideology has been severely tempered here, if not displaced, by a new idea of shared governance.

Were Zechariah and other liked-minded Jews influenced by earlier prophetic criticisms of the Davidic kings, or was his view of the civil office merely what was demanded by Judea's status under Persian rule? We would like to know the ethical grounds of the proposal, but the book does not mention them, so we must be content to note that the messianism of the book is pale and tentative. Most significant is the proposal of a form of leadership which claims divine sanction but is limited in scope. We wish we had more from this writer.

Zechariah 1–8 reaches a climax in the oracle of 8:1-8, fashioned in traditional prophetic style, using the formula, "Thus says the LORD." The oracle contains five brief parts, each highlighted by this formula. The result is an emphatic proclamation on five themes:

YHWH is burning with zeal for Zion!
YHWH is coming back to dwell in Zion.
The streets of Jerusalem will be filled with young and old alike.
This will be a miracle beyond human comprehension.
Once more the gathered exiles will become YHWH's people,
and YHWH will be their God.

There is nothing new or remarkable here in relation to other prophetic writings. Yet the oracle speaks with force and conviction, and summarizes the message of the book. This is a strange book, but it is compelling in its own way.

ZECHARIAH 9–14

We enter a different world in the second part of the book of Zechariah, in both its historical setting and its concepts. The situation that confronted Zechariah (and Haggai) in the late sixth century no longer prevailed at the time of this writing, and the cause that preoccupied Zechariah was not this author's concern. It is probable that several authors were involved, actually, for these chapters are not unified but disparate and disjointed. I like Otto Eissfeldt's view of these materials—that Zechariah 9–11, Zechariah 12–14, and Malachi constitute three groups of diverse, anonymous texts, written during the late fourth century and added to the book of Zechariah. The three together form an appendix to the book of the Twelve Prophets. Malachi is more unifed than Zechariah 9–14 and about 150 years earlier. It reflects the situation in Judah in the Persian period, prior to the reforms of Nehemiah and Ezra, while Zechariah 9–14 reflects Jewish interests in the early Hellenistic period.[3]

Zechariah 9–14 is a hodgepodge of nationalistic and eschatological prophecies. It is a useful record of political sentiments in a certain period of Jewish history, but its value is largely historical, not theological. Apart from the famous prophecy of a king riding on a donkey (9:9-10), these chapters have played only a minor role in Christian teaching.

The messianic prophecy just mentioned, whose place in Christian tradition was fixed forever by the writers of the Gospels of Matthew (21:5) and John (12:15), is vivid in its simplicity. It reasserts the claim of the Davidic kings to sovereignty over all Palestine by divine right, a claim celebrated in the royal psalms (Pss 2, 18, 20, 21, 72, 89, 110, 144) and the Deuteronomic History (e.g., 2 Sam 7:1-17). But ironically, considering the use made of this text in Matthew and John, the claim was repudiated by Jesus himself. All that survives of this prophecy in Christian consciousness is the image of the humble messiah riding on a donkey, and the proclamation of universal peace (Zech 9:10). The military victories depicted by the prophet have been relegated to the realm of apocalyptic eschatology.

The idea of the abolition of warfare in the age of the ideal king resembles ideas expressed in the messianic texts of Isaiah 9:1-6 and 11:1-9. Isaiah 11 is eloquent in its description of the moral qualities of the ideal ruler. By contrast, the prophecy here is much more brief, and it omits any mention of the moral dimensions of messianic rule. Zechariah 9 is merely an expression of hope for the restoration of the Israelite kingship.

The enigmatic allusion to someone "pierced" in Zechariah 12:10 has been interpreted christologically since the time of the New Testament (cf. John 19:37 and Rev 1:7). However, nothing is said in Zechariah about the identity of this person, unless it is YHWH, the speaker, as the Hebrew text seems to suggest. If it is not YHWH, then the pierced one seems to have no significance except as an object of mourning. There is no hint of soteriological meaning in his experience, or in the ritual of mourning performed on his behalf. So the only link to the story of Jesus appears to be the piercing.

The Hebrew writer lists various groups of the mourning congregation, in an intriguing but mysterious arrangement: the house of David (royalty?), the house of Nathan (prophets?), the house of Levi (priests?), the house of Shimei (?), and the remaining families. Each group is subdivided into men and women. This is an elaborate arrangement, but no explanation is given.

The writers had severe grievances against certain leaders (the "shepherds," 11:4-17; 13:7-9), certain prophets (13:2-6), and of course, "the idols" (13:2). The grounds of the grievances are unclear in the first two cases: The shepherds harmed people, but how they did so is not explained; the prophets performed bizarre acts, including gashing themselves, but what they prophesied is not reported. Therefore, it is uncertain whether the writers found fault with what these prophets said or were opposed to prophecy on other grounds. This text shows an opposite attitude to the one expressed in Joel 3, in which the writer imagined a day of such splendid intimacy between YHWH and the community that everyone there would enjoy prophetic experience. In Zechariah 13, the writer hopes for a day when prophetic experience will be prohibited on pain of death. Either the two writers had radically different opinions of prophecy or they understood prophecy in radically different ways. In any case, Zechariah 13 tells us too little to form a reasoned judgment about the author's view.

Chapter 14 paints a curious picture of the day of YHWH. Although there are parallels to other such pictures in the Hebrew Bible, this picture as a whole is distinctive. One parallel is the heavy hostility toward foreign nations. One strange, unexplained feature is the promise that all the cooking pots in the entire city of Jerusalem will be sacred to YHWH! Does this mean that the dichotomy between sacred and profane will be broken down?

There is no mistaking the moral seriousness of Zechariah 9–14. Obviously, the writers understood themselves as champions of traditional Yahwism and defenders of the faith. But the case they present is so cryptic and fragmentary, and our knowledge of its setting so inadequate, we cannot explicate their religious ideas. Some commentators have made quite a lot out of these texts, but not convincingly.

MALACHI

This anonymous group of texts concludes the prophetic division of the Hebrew Bible. The name *Malaki*, "my messenger," is probably a title rather than a name, but either way, nothing is known about the author. Eissfeldt's judgment that it forms part of a threefold appendix to the book of the Twelve Prophets, together with Zechariah 9–11 and Zechariah 12–14, is an apt characterization of the material.[4] Eissfeldt and many others date it in the period after the restoration of the Judean cultus (515), but before the reforms of Nehemiah (ca. 445) and Ezra (428 or later). The dominant mood of the book is dismay over the moral laxity of the Judean community. To many commentators, this suggests a date in the prereform period. But reforms can be short-lived. For our purposes, it is enough to place the book in the period of the Second Temple.

LOVE AND HATRED

The book begins on what at first seems an auspicious note: "I have loved you," says YHWH. But this love is qualified in a peculiar way: YHWH's love for Israel ("Jacob") is manifested in his hatred for Edom ("Esau"). The statement, "They may build, but I will tear down!" appears to be a further example of the attitude William Stinespring dubbed "damn Edom."[5] The writer of Malachi took comfort in the thought of the perpetual desolation of Edom; he assured his readers that after seeing Edom's desolation, people even beyond the borders of Israel would know that YHWH was great (1:5). This may have been mere religious nationalism. On the other hand, it is conceivable that by the time of this writing, "Edom" had become a symbol for "wickedness" and no longer denoted simply the nation of Edom. If so, this passage could be construed as an affirmation of the righteousness of God. But even so, the writer's way of putting it sounds xenophobic.

GOD AS "FATHER"

One of the most appealing features of the book of Malachi for Christian readers has been its references to God as father (1:6; 2:10). This metaphor, which was central to traditional Christian piety, seldom occurs in the Hebrew Bible, so the texts that use it, cited here in the translation of the NJB, receive much attention:

> The son honours his father, the slave stands in awe of his master. But if I am indeed father, where is the honour due to me? And if I am indeed master, where is the awe due to me? says Yahweh Sabaoth to you priests who despise my name. (1:6)

> Is there not one Father of us all? Did not one god create us? Why, then, do we break faith with one another, profaning the covenant of our ancestors? (2:10)

The NJB and the NRSV use inclusive language for human beings whenever the meaning of the Hebrew text permits. Thus both versions say *ancestors* in 2:10, where other versions say *fathers*. The Hebrew word is the usual one used to refer to fathers in the masculine sense, but in the absence of a neutral alternative, it is also the word used to refer to ancestors in general. The NJB and NRSV translations are therefore legitimate here.

But these versions follow quite a different policy in dealing with references to God. They translate all the masculine Hebrew words for God into masculine English words. This is the practice common to all the standard versions of the Bible published so far. However, it is a moot question in the churches today whether to follow this practice, and it will probably continue to be moot for some time to come. I argued in connection with Hosea 11 that the image of God evoked there was the image of a parent, not necessarily of a father. But in that case, the image was only implied; the word for *father* was not used. In the two passages in Malachi, the word *father* is used, so here the question is how to translate the actual Hebrew word, not how to interpret what is merely implied. Accurate translation is important if the Bible is not to be misrepresented. At the same time, it is desirable to avoid sexism whenever possible. Sometimes these two principles collide, and users of the Bible will disagree over which is more important.

CRITICISM OF PRIESTS AND HUSBANDS

It seems clear that the writer of Malachi wanted to reform Judean worship, for ritual concerns dominate the book. He considered the priests particularly culpable for the profanations he saw, though much of his indictment is too vague for us to know what these profanations were. The only concrete charge he makes is that blemished animals are being accepted as offerings (1:6-14). In 2:1-9 he condemns the priests because their false teaching causes people to fall from the right path, but he doesn't say what their teaching was. We may guess from the context that it was ritual teaching, but that actually says little.

In 2:10-16 he accuses some of the men of Judah of profaning YHWH's sanctuary by "marrying the daughter of a foreign god" (vs 11), and of being treacherous to the wives of their youth (vss 14-15). The first charge seems to mean that they were marrying women who worshiped a foreign god; the second may mean that they were divorcing their first wives. This at least is the usual interpretation. The text is very difficult. The Hebrew text of verse 16 says, "If he hates, you should divorce, says YHWH the God of Israel, and he covers his clothing with violence, says YHWH of hosts." Some ancient rabbis thought this was an injunction to divorce a hated wife, and the Massoretes too must have thought so when they vocalized the text as they did.

Most English versions emend the consonantal Hebrew text: "For I hate divorce, says the LORD, the God of Israel, and covering one's garment with violence, says the LORD of hosts" (NRSV). The CBAT translation requires a smaller emendation (the addition of "and" in the first clause) and is therefore preferable to the other English versions:

> "For one who hates and divorces,"
> Says the LORD God of Israel,
> "Covers his clothing with violence,"
> Says the LORD of hosts.

The treachery of which the writer accuses the men may have been divorcing their first wives after marrying second wives. However, divorce in such cases would not have been required, since men were permitted more than one wife in Israel, nor would divorce, as such, have been a violation of the law. But verse 14 suggests that the writer considered the men's behavior a breach of covenant. Therefore their treachery may have been something other than divorce. One possibility is that the men were denying their first wives' marriage rights after marriage to a second wife. This would have been a breach of their marriage covenant.

Exodus 21:7-11 prohibits a man from denying marriage rights (food, clothing, and intercourse) to a concubine he dislikes, after he has married a second woman; it adds that if he refuses to honor the first wife's rights, he must "let her go out"—that is, leave his household. This means not merely divorce, but emancipation, since the woman in this case had not been free.

This situation is somewhat different from the one in Malachi, yet it is conceivable that the writer of Malachi was applying a similar principle. The consonantal text can be translated without any emendation: "If he hates, let him divorce . . . though he covers his clothing with violence." This would represent an acknowledgment of the principle contained in Exodus 21:11, but at the same time express the writer's own disapproval of divorce.

This pericope is filled with obscurities. There is no satisfactory explanation of verses 12, 13, or 15, where the meaning of many individual words is clouded, and the meaning of sentences themselves is all but opaque; it is impossible to know what the writer was condemning. Christian commentators have seized upon verse 16 as the only explicit repudiation of divorce in the Old Testament, and therefore the only statement that anticipates the New Testament teaching on divorce. However, there is no clear support for this conclusion in the text. On the other hand, it is clear—and it is the only thing clear in the whole passage—that the writer believed Judean husbands should not be treacherous to the wives of their youth (vs 15). Surely that conviction was beyond dispute.

THE JUSTICE OF GOD

Most of the remainder of the prophet's message has to do, in one way or another, with the theme of God's justice. Some people in Judah doubted God's justice because it seemed that every evildoer was favored by God (2:17). This must have meant that the skeptics did not see the evidence of retributive justice and therefore denied there was any justice at all. The prophet responded by prophesying the vindication of God's justice at some time in the future (3:1-4; 4:1-3). Thus, while the people had become disillusioned by experience and given up their doctrine, the prophet held on to the doctrine and found a way to justify it. Elsewhere, he merely dismissed the skeptics as godless, without any further comment (3:13-15).

The writer believed God would eventually punish sorcerers, adulterers, and perjurers, as well as those who oppressed wage-earners, widows, fatherless children, and resident aliens (3:5); this was in full accord with traditional covenantal teaching. Further, he affirmed God's unchanging readiness to accept repentant sinners (3:6-12), and this too was good covenantal theology. If penitent people would pay their cultic tithes, he said, then God would bring them ample rainfall and rid them of locusts. Also, in the day of judgment, the faithful ones would be God's special possession (3:16-18); they would tread down the wicked, who would be burned to ashes in the fire of divine judgment. So Malachi urged the people to remember the law of Moses (3:4) and wait for the return of the prophet Elijah, herald of the terrible day of YHWH (4:5).

Elijah's coming would have a decisive effect upon children and parents, turning their minds against one another. Most modern versions say "toward one another," making this a prophecy of generational reconcilation. But in this case, the Hebrew preposition (*'al*) more likely means *against*, making this the same kind of prophecy as the one in Mark 13:12: "Brother will deliver up brother to death, and a father his child, and children will rise against parents and have them put to death." There is little else that is conciliatory in Malachi. The dominant tone is retributive, especially in the prophecy of the day of YHWH. The last word of Malachi (4:1-3) is a message of rigorous justice, relentlessly applied, and this is consistent with the substance and mood of the entire book.

THE SCROLL OF THE TWELVE PROPHETS

These twelve books are grouped together in all the ancient canons, probably because they fit on a single scroll of standard length. They are arranged more or less chronologically, insofar as their dates are discernible, although the order was not completely fixed in ancient times. I can find no theological significance in the canonical ordering of the twelve, nor any indication of a unified redaction of the group as a whole. So much variety appears in the redaction of the individual books that one is forced to conclude that each was redacted separately. For example, the redaction of Amos consists of the addition of a short end-note on the restoration of the Davidic kingship (9:8*b*-15), and possibly the insertion of the Tyre, Edom, and Judah oracles (1:9-12; 2:4-5); the redaction of Micah and Zechariah involves the end-to-end placement of substantial blocks of material of disparate origin (Mic 1–3; 4–5; 6–7; Zech 1–8; 9–14); and the redaction of Hosea takes the form of numerous minor internal revisions. There is no common method or aim visible. In short, the message of the scroll of the Twelve Prophets consists of twelve separate messages. It cannot be compared with the overall redaction of the book of Isaiah, which, in spite of the great diversity of perspective manifest in the major components, manages to give the book a certain unity, albeit of a rather general sort.

This exposition of the individual books is at an end, and the final chapter will summarize the major elements in the prophetic witness of faith in God.

SELECT BIBLIOGRAPHY

Achtemeier, Elizabeth. *Nahum-Malachi.* Interpretation. Atlanta: John Knox Press, 1986.

Meyers, Carol L., and Eric C. Meyers. *Haggai, Zechariah 1–8.* Anchor Bible. Garden City, N.Y.: Doubleday, 1987.

Petersen, David L. *Haggai and Zechariah 1–8.* Philadelphia: Westminster Press, 1984.

Smith, Ralph L. *Micah-Malachi.* Word Biblical Commentary. Waco, Tex.: Word Books, 1984.

NOTES

1. "The Ritual Background of Zechariah's Temple Song," *CBQ* 40 (1978): 167-90.
2. Petersen's translation.
3. Otto Eissfeldt, *The Old Testament: An Introduction* (New York: Harper & Row, 1965), pp. 434-43.
4. Ibid., p. 441.
5. In chap. 13, see the discussion of Obadiah and the essay of Bruce Cresson cited in note 4.

CHAPTER SIXTEEN

The God of the Prophets

In this last chapter, I will attempt to summarize some of the prominent elements in the prophetic witness of faith in God. A summary of this sort cannot substitute for the exposition of the individual writings, since it cannot do justice to the wide variety of perspectives and ideas exhibited in these books. It can serve only as a kind of recapitulation of the salient theological themes of the prophetic corpus viewed as a whole. A good place to begin is with the prophetic assertion that God makes Godself known to human beings in the midst of their engagement with society and the world.

> The LORD took me from following the flock, and the LORD said to me, "Go, prophesy to my people Israel." (Amos 7:15)

To the prophets themselves, knowing God meant knowing God's call to prophesy. The conviction of receiving a direct, personal call from the living God was the foundation of prophetic activity. The calls of Amos, Hosea, Isaiah, Jeremiah, Ezekiel, the Servant of YHWH, and the unnamed prophet of Isaiah 61 are mentioned in the texts, and it is reasonable to assume that other prophets experienced similar calls. Although some similarities exist in the forms of the prophetic calls, the result no doubt of an established tradition, the individual differences, both in the calls and in the prophets themselves, stand out. Anyone might be called, regardless of profession, age, sex, or family. The psychological features of the experience, as expressed in visual or auditory terms, were quite individual, and so were the cognitive contents. No two calls were exactly alike, nor were the resulting commissions; each was appropriate to its historical context and reflected the distinctive insights and language of the individual prophet. In most cases the account of the call contains a summary of the prophet's message. This does not necessarily mean that the prophet knew from the beginning exactly what he would say, since all the accounts are retrospective. Yet it would be a mistake to deny the possibility of a prophet's grasping his whole message at the outset. This would have been particularly likely for prophets whose oracles were few, but it would not have been impossible for others.

It is not certain that a powerful visionary experience was necessary in every instance to validate a prophet's commission in the eyes of the public, but such an experience surely contributed to this validation. More important, the memory of the experience seems to have sustained the prophets in completing their commissions.

The prophets' deeply moving experience of the presence of God did not turn them inward to a private or mystical piety, but outward to public proclamation. The experience invested their perception of human events and relationships with moral urgency and religious ultimacy. It entailed a reordering of values, but entirely within the realm of ordinary human experience. There was nothing mythological or otherworldly in their interpretation of the experience; it was worldly in its context and worldly in its outcome. The God who met the prophets at the deepest point of their religious vocation was the God of all life. Meeting God in this way empowered the prophets toward renewed interaction with their fellows, in spite of opposition to their message; it did not lead them away from the community, but toward it. The realm of the holy, the place of meeting with God, was not a separate realm, but the realm of everyday life. The prophets' understanding of their vocation thus corresponded to their understanding of God.

Most of the prophets remained essentially anonymous. Although their names are mentioned, little or nothing is written about them as persons. A few external facts are reported about Amos, Hosea, Isaiah, and Ezekiel, but none about Micah, Zephaniah, Habakkuk, Nahum, Joel, Obadiah, Haggai, or Zechariah. Only Jeremiah is portrayed as a person. This general anonymity testifies to their selfless service of the word of YHWH, though it also reflects the interests of the traditioners and the lengthy process of literary redaction.

Fortunately, the traditioners saw fit to treat Jeremiah differently, and as a result his figure has become a paradigm of the servant of YHWH. The oracles of the prophets deal largely in social categories, and it requires considerable imagination on the part of the reader to translate what they said into the familiar categories of personal existence and faith, so the biblical portrait of Jeremiah is particularly welcome. Here the writers have given us an account of a personal journey of faith which parallels the experiences of countless others, whether or not they share the specific vocation of the prophet. Whether it is historically accurate is not crucially important; what is important is that it is an account of a personal journey. And it probably reflects the insights of more than one writer, but if so, it is all the more significant as a testament of faith.

> Thus says the LORD,
> I remember the devotion of your youth,

> your love as a bride,
> how you followed me in the wilderness,
> in a land not sown. (Jer 2:2)

The prophets' call experiences testify to an essential characteristic of human existence—that *persons can know God and discern God's will for their lives.* This point is not made as frequently as are the accusations of iniquity and threats of judgment, which dominate the prophetic oracles quantitatively, but it is a crucial theological point. The experiences of the prophets are distinctive in the sense that they issue in a specific prophetic commission, but they are not unique as encounters with God. The narrative traditions of the Bible are full of accounts of similar encounters, and in the psalms is evidence of the same sort of experience. The prophets had no special capacity for knowing God, nor did they claim to have any such capacity; the capacity they had was theirs simply because they were human beings. To be sure, the prophets perceived the implications of their faith with extraordinary clarity, and they expressed these implications with peculiar force. But their faith was common to many in Israel, and in principle, it was available to all.

The biblical writers did not phrase their assertions about knowing God as I have phrased them; they spoke about knowing God because God had made Godself known to them. The language of the writers, especially that of the prophets, is the language of revelation—it is not human discernment they attest to, but divine self-disclosure. Yet human discernment is the subjective accompaniment of God's self-disclosure, and though the prophets stress the latter, it seems to me that it is equally important, in trying to make sense of the prophetic witness in our time, that we stress the human possibility also.

Knowledge of God includes knowledge shared by the entire community of Israel, like that recalled in Jeremiah 2:2, quoted above. This knowledge provides the context for knowing God individually, the way the prophets did. The two kinds of knowledge—that transmitted by the religious tradition and that attained by personal insight and experience—combine to give genuine knowledge of God. But without the understanding communicated by the tradition, personal religious experience can be eccentric and self-serving, even self-deluding; and without the understanding gained through personal insight, traditional teaching can be merely formal, even dead. The creative interplay between traditional Yahwistic teaching and personal insight is exemplified in the work of the prophets.

The marriage metaphor in Jeremiah 2:2 that depicts the relationship of YHWH and Israel suggests mutual knowledge and devoted love as its essential qualities. The lasting, intimate bond is primary, and the particular demands of the relationship, although perennial, are made in response to the specific conditions and events of life in time. Metaphors suggestive of this enduring bond between God and Israel were employed as central features of Hosea's proclamation (Hos 1–3; 11), from whom Jeremiah may have borrowed them. Ezekiel, too, depicted the history of the relationship in similar images. Since it was the history of Israel's infidelity that Ezekiel chose to depict, his use of the language of love and marriage was entirely negative (Ezek 16; 23). Yet he made abundantly clear that the people of Israel could and should have devoted themselves to God; since God's grace toward Israel was evident, Israel was without excuse.

The point made by Jeremiah and Ezekiel was that Israel failed to respond in devotion to the manifest grace of God. That God's saving grace had been disclosed in the past—in the whole history of Israel—was not in question. In their dialogue with the people, this was assumed as the major premise of their indictment (e.g., Jer 2:4-6; 31:1-3; Ezek 20:1-13). And so it was for Amos (Amos 2:10; 3:1) and Isaiah (Isa 5:1-2). The anonymous oracle in Isaiah 63:7-9 is particularly eloquent:

> I will recount the gracious deeds of the LORD,
> the praiseworthy acts of the LORD,
> because of all that the LORD has done for us,
> and the great favor to the house of Israel
> that he has shown them according to his mercy,
> according to the abundance of his steadfast love.
> For he said, "Surely they are my people,
> children who will not deal falsely";
> and he became their savior
> in all their distress.
> It was no messenger or angel
> but his presence that saved them;
> in his love and in his pity he redeemed them;
> he lifted them up and carried them all the days of old.

However, it was precisely this conviction that was in question during the Babylonian exile, and which Second Isaiah addressed again and again. One of the major points at issue between Second Isaiah and his audience was whether there was any bond at all between God and Israel—whether they knew each other. Although Second Isaiah did not make much use of family metaphors in this connection—45:10-11 is the principal instance—he made much of the history of God's self-disclosure to Israel (e.g., 40:21; 41:8-10).

In the Bible, the encounter with God is never a formless emotional experience. It takes place in a communal setting and has communal consequences, as well as individual consequences. *Loving and serving God entail loving the neighbor as well,* although this is not the usual way it appears in the Hebrew Bible; the prophets speak most often of living and acting righteously or justly, or they list the concrete responsibilities of members of the religious community. The religious tradition which informs the prophetic witness is presented in its definitive form in the canonical Torah. Within this tradition, the memory of God's deliverance of Israel from slavery in Egypt is the paradigmatic example of God's determination to redeem the "people of the promise" from whatever might hinder the accomplishment of God's purpose for them.

> The people who survived the sword
>   found grace in the wilderness . . . .
> I have loved you with an everlasting love;
>   therefore I have continued my faithfulness to you.
> (Jer 31:1-2)

In addition to the text quoted here from Jeremiah, we may note Amos 2:10; 3:1; 9:7; Hosea 11:1; 12:9, 13; 13:4; Micah 6:4; 7:15; Isaiah 11:16; Ezekiel 20:5-6; Jeremiah 2:6; 7:22, 25; 11:4, 7; 16:14; 23:7; and Haggai 2:5.

The deliverance from Egypt was not the only tradition of God's redemption recalled by the prophets. God's relationship with Abraham and Jacob (Isa 41:8; 43:1; 48:12; 60:16; Ezek 33:24; Hos 12; Mic 7:20) and God's gift of the land to Israel (Amos 2:9-10; Hos 2:8, 15; Ezek 37:25) also figured in their understanding. The number of these explicit references to the past is not terribly large; however, we must remember that the prophets took these memories for granted in their dialogue with Israel. They did not dwell on God's gracious acts on Israel's behalf, but concentrated on the moral responsibility of Israel which these acts entailed.

The relationship between God and Israel which had been established in the past persisted in the present, because of course it was the very ground of Israel's being. The liturgical confession placed in the mouth of the people in Hosea 6:1-3 makes the point well: Life comes from knowing God, and God comes readily to God's people to be known by them. Here, "knowing" God means personal, existential knowledge—not merely intellectual knowledge. The prophet condemns the people's inconstancy in this instance but, in effect, affirms the validity of their assertion. It was their devotion (*hesed*), or "steadfast love" (RSV), that was in question, not their theology.

That same understanding of God's present accessibility is expressed in a variety of ways in the prophetic writings. Isaiah 65:1-2 is a good example:

> I was ready to be sought out by those who did not ask,
>   to be found by those who did not seek me.
> I said, "Here I am, here I am,"
>   to a nation that did not call on my name.
> I held out my hands all day long to a rebellious people.

We may refer also to other texts: Isaiah 1:18-20; 55:6-9; 57:15; Amos 5:4, 6, 14. To be sure, not many such texts are found among the preexilic writings, for those prophets were more concerned with reproaching Israel for apostasy and injustice, and warning of impending national destruction, than with the availability of God's grace. There was too much abuse of the means of grace in the

Israelite cultus for the preexilic prophets to want to speak of this dimension of the divine/human relationship. Ezekiel's image of the glory of YHWH leaving the temple for the duration of the age of exile (Ezek 10:18-19; 11:22-23) characterizes that whole phase of prophecy.

For those preexilic prophets who looked beyond the age of wrath, the time of God's saving accessibility was in the future. The fullest treatment of this theme is in Hosea (2:14-23; 3:1-5; 11:8-11; 14:1-8). In this example, the "wife," of course, is Israel:

> I will take you for my wife forever; I will take you for my wife in righteousness and in justice, in steadfast love, and in mercy. I will take you for my wife in faithfulness; and you shall know the LORD. (Hos 2:19-20)

In later materials, the prophecy of a future redemptive meeting with God becomes a prominent motif: Jeremiah 3:12-14; 29:10-14; 31:16-20, 31-34; Ezekiel 34:11-16, 25-31; 37:27; Micah 7:18-20; Joel 2:28-29; Isaiah 40:5; 43:8-13; 54:7-8, among others.

The text just quoted from Hosea 2 shows with particular clarity the inseparability in prophetic thought of redemption and obedience. *Israel is redeemed in order to serve God in righteousness and faith,* whether the redemption is one recalled in the past, experienced in the present, or promised in the future. This indissoluble link between God's grace and God's demand is so evident in all the prophetic books that it hardly requires illustration. From Isaiah to Malachi, the prophets remind Israel of the moral conditions of their existence as the people of YHWH. Israel's vocation is primarily one of special responsibility, rather than special privilege. To be sure, the gift of knowing God truly is a gift above all others, because by definition, it means possessing a valid understanding of the ultimate ground and end of life. So the possession of this knowledge, which is Israel's because of God's self-disclosure to them, is, in a sense, a special privilege.

However, such knowledge is available to everyone through Israel's witness of faith. It was Second Isaiah who explicated this point of prophetic theology, though it was implicit in that theology all along. But if knowing God truly was Israel's chief blessing, this did not carry with it any material advantage vis-à-vis other peoples. Despite the ancient traditions that depicted YHWH fighting for Israel against its enemies—traditions that in their canonical form are actually more nuanced than the chauvinistic convictions of the prophets' contemporaries—God was not Israel's simple ally in politics or warfare. Israel was subject to the same hazards of human conflict as everyone else. In fact, on the surface, the prophetic oracles of judgment seem to represent Israel as the most vulnerable of nations. However, this appearance is the result of the prophets' having addressed most of their oracles to Israel. Close analysis of their thought shows that they regarded Israel's destiny in international affairs to be subject to the same terms as those of other nations. It could not have been otherwise if there is only one God and one humanity.

Israel's service to God includes praise of God as well as righteous human relations. Although the prophets concentrated their attention on the latter, they did not eschew worship as an essential expression of faith and means of grace. Amos, Hosea, Isaiah, Jeremiah, and Ezekiel repudiated the empirical cultus of preexilic times as idolatrous and venal; but Hosea, Ezekiel, and Second Isaiah promised a renewal of proper worship in the age of restoration; and the writers of Third Isaiah, Haggai, Zechariah, and Malachi supported the postexilic temple establishment. Prophetic faith was not merely an ethical culture, but a thoroughly theistic faith. Active engagement with a living, transcendent God was the center of their existence and the core of their proclamation, and this engagement was nourished by ritual means of grace and celebrated in acts of praise. The influence of Israel's worship is reflected in various ways in the prophetic books, as I have shown. The calls of Isaiah (Isa 6) and Ezekiel (Ezek 1–3) especially reflect the forms and symbols of temple ritual, but there are other signs of positive influence as well—for example, the oracles of Amos that are constructed around a cultic hymn (Amos 4:13; 5:8; 9:5-6). Explicit affirmations of ritual worship are understandably few in preexilic texts, but in later prophecy this indispensable ingredient in Israel's life comes to the fore, as we would expect. Second Isaiah's invitation to "sing to YHWH a new song, his praise from the end of the earth" (Isa 42:10), is a fitting index of this side of Israel's service of God.

> [It is he] who brings princes to nought,
> and makes the rulers of the earth as nothing . . . .
> He gives power to the faint,
> and strengthens the powerless. (Isa 40:23, 29)

God exalts the humble and downtrodden and abases the proud and mighty. The abasement of proud oppressors, in Israel and elsewhere, is perhaps the most prominent theme in the prophetic tradition. If there is a "prophetic principle" in the Hebrew Bible, it surely involves the critique of the arrogant use of power, wealth, and privilege, to the disadvantage or harm of the weaker, poorer persons and groups. This is the overriding theme of the collections of oracles against foreign nations (Isa 13–23; Jer 46–52; Ezek 25–32), and of many oracles against Israel as well. God's exaltation of the humble is a relatively minor theme by comparison, largely because the prophets were not speaking to the humble but to the proud. When circumstances changed and the prophets' hearers were themselves humbled, as in the Babylonian exile, for example, the message changed accordingly. Then the theme of God's lifting the downtrodden was sounded vigorously. However, great stretches of Isaiah, Jeremiah, Ezekiel, and the book of the Twelve Prophets consist largely of oracles of divine punishment of the unjust and idolatrous proud ones of the earth.

The prophets announced the impending judgment against the enemies of God's righteousness with complete confidence in its certainty, attributing a greater moral coherence to history than most people are able to discern. Indeed, this characteristic of Hebrew prophecy makes it problematic in the minds of some interpreters.[1] There is no denying that at times it appears that a prophet has made a too simple correlation between the moral deserving of people and their historic rewards and punishments. As a universal rule of human experience, rigorously applied, the idea of divine retribution is empirically untrue; furthermore, it violates the biblical understanding of the grace of God and the freedom of God and human beings.

However, many writers of the prophetic books made ample allowance for grace and freedom, and did not attempt to apply a rigid doctrine of retribution to the course of history or to people's lives. We need only mention the interpretations of the careers of Jeremiah and the Servant of YHWH, presented in the books of Jeremiah and Isaiah, respectively, to make the point. Clearly, there is a vigorous debate within the pages of the prophetic canon on this central theological question. Moreover, the oracles of divine punishment for sin do not function in this canon as simple assertions of a general theory of retribution. Their function is more complex. Taken by themselves, their function is partly rhetorical and partly pedagogical; taken as components of larger literary complexes, it is more nuanced still. In this last setting, they serve as a necessary, but certainly not a sufficient, part of a sweeping interpretation of Israel's history, from the heyday of the monarchy to the beginnings of second-temple Judaism. And this story is only one part of the larger biblical story of YHWH and Israel, from the call of Abraham to the reform of Ezra. In this rich context, the possible theological implications of the prophetic oracles of judgment are many.

> They will not hurt or destroy
> on all my holy mountain;
> for the earth will be full of the knowledge of the LORD
> as the waters cover the sea. (Isa 11:9)

The ultimate goal of prophetic proclamation is the universal knowledge of God. It is also peace, blessing, and joy, but these are dependent upon the knowledge of God. "Then you [or they] shall know that I am YHWH"—the constant refrain of Ezekiel's message—would serve as well for the prophetic message generally. The prophets knew they could not produce the knowledge of God in Israel simply by proclaiming it. Much more was required. Yet the witness of faith of persons like the prophets was indispensable. Human experience, whether it be of the world or of the self, is subject to more than one interpretation. The prophets' interpretation had ardent rivals in ancient times and could not be taken for granted. They persisted in the assurance that it was their vocation to do so, and the conviction that the word they spoke would finally be received as the word of life.

SELECT BIBLIOGRAPHY

Bright, John. *Covenant and Promise: The Prophetic Understanding of the Future in Pre-Exilic Israel.* Philadelphia: Westminster Press, 1976.

Childs, Brevard S. *Old Testament Theology in a Canonical Context.* Philadelphia: Fortress Press, 1986.

Dentan, Robert C. *The Knowledge of God in Ancient Israel.* New York: Seabury Press, 1968.

Fretheim, Terence E. *The Suffering of God: An Old Testament Perspective.* Philadelphia: Fortress Press, 1984.

Gray, John. *The Biblical Doctrine of the Reign of God.* Edinburgh: T. & T. Clark, 1979.

Hanson, Paul D. *The People Called: The Growth of Community in the Bible.* San Francisco: Harper & Row, 1986.

Miller, Patrick D., Jr. *Sin and Judgment in the Prophets.* Society of Biblical Literature. Monograph Series 27. Chico, Calif.: Scholars Press, 1982.

Niebuhr, Reinhold. *The Nature and Destiny of Man.* New York: Charles Scribner's Sons, 1941.

Robinson, H. Wheeler. *Inspiration and Revelation in the Old Testament.* Oxford: Clarendon Press, 1946.

______. *Redemption and Revelation.* London: Nisbet & Co., 1942.

Zimmerli, Walther. *Old Testament Theology in Outline.* Atlanta: John Knox Press, 1978.

See also Select Bibliography, chapter 2.

NOTES

1. See discussion of this issue in Gerald T. Sheppard, "True and False Prophecy Within Scripture," *Canon, Theology, and Old Testament Interpretation*, ed. Gene M. Tucker et al. (Philadelphia: Fortress Press, 1988), pp. 262-82.